A Treasury of Biography

By Edgar Johnson

Fiction

UNWEAVE A RAINBOW: A SENTIMENTAL FANTASY

THE PRAYING MANTIS

Criticism

ONE MIGHTY TORRENT: THE DRAMA OF BIOGRAPHY

THE ANALYSIS OF SATIRE (in preparation)

A Treasury of Biography

By Edgar Johnson

New York
HOWELL, SOSKIN
Publishers

WOLSEY

THOMAS MORE

HAKLUYT

JOHN DONNE

BUNYAN

JOHN NORTH

GIBBON

JOHNSON

BOSWELL

FRANKLIN

SCOTT

THOREAU

DICKENS

MILL

RUSKIN

ADAMS

GOSSE

STRACHEY

STEFFENS

For
JARVIS KEILEY
and
MARGARET BREWSTER

FOREWORD

To DEFEND THE INCLUSIONS IN AN ANTHOLOGY IS AS USELESS AS TO
attack them. Everyone's taste is what it is; an honest editor can
only echo old Ben Jonson, although possibly a bit more politely:

By God, 'tis good; and if you like 't, you may! Of these selections, then, only one thing need be said. They involve no mere
kowtowing to prosy dullnesses of great name. No biography is
included here only because literary historians have devoted breath
to it. And no modern biography is here of which I did not feel
sure that it was not a shooting star whose fame would burn itself
away. Every biography represented is one I have found moving
or exciting, one that I have deeply admired.

There is a certain novelty of principle governing the individual
passages chosen. Most anthologies present a consecutive single
passage of whatever length the anthologist has decided he can
afford, a characteristic sample which he hopes will convey the
flavor of the whole. What has gone before and what the character's
later fate may have been the reader must either infer or learn from
other sources. Instead of this, I have chosen a number of significant
and dramatic moments from the whole life, bridging the gaps
when clarity demanded it by very brief summaries of intervening
events. Almost all of every narrative is in the biographer's own
words, exactly as he wrote them, and even my own interpolations
have often been woven of his own words. So that not only the
portrait of a human being during a single stage of his career is
here highlighted, but those experiences into which were concentrated the meaning of his life for him and for us: the entire con-
tour of his days.

Such an effort, I know, runs risks that are at least as great as
those of selecting a single chapter and letting it go at that. And

my selections are not offered as a tabloid substitute for really reading the great biographers, or in any spirit of boiling down the
essence of culture to pellet-size and suggesting that thereby the
reader digests all that is significant from the great banquet of
biography. No sample is ever more than a sample, and it can never
be the equivalent of a feast. But if I have done what I have tried
to do, these samples should more truly represent their wholes than
those chosen on other principles because they endeavor to reveal
the great pages from great biographies as parts of their wholes. If
some readers are led from this book to the desire for a more intimate acquaintance with Samuel Johnson in the pages of Boswell or with Lincoln Steffens in his great and fascinating *Autobiography*, that will be the crown of the editor's desire.

A word about mechanics. Omissions of no very considerable
length are indicated in the usual way by successive periods.
Longer gaps of entire pages are shown by a wider spacing between
paragraphs. Any words inserted by the editor for purposes of
clarity are enclosed within brackets. All connecting or summariz-
ing material by the editor is printed in italics, and when it includes phrases or clauses quoted from the biographer they are
enclosed within quotation marks and printed in the same type as
the body of the text.

The following publishers should be thanked for their permis-
sion to use copyright material:
Harcourt Brace and Company for *The Autobiography of Lin-
coln Steffens* and Lytton Strachey's *Cardinal Manning;*
Houghton Mifflin and Company for *The Education of Henry
Adams;*
Charles Scribners' Sons for Edmund Gosse's *Father and Son.*

The Contents

INTRODUCTION

WHY READ BIOGRAPHY? THE QUERY MIGHT, IN FACT, BE ENLARGED to ask, Why read? We all read for the most widely varied reasons. We read simply as an amusement, to pass the time, as we play cards or chat with an acquaintance, and sometimes later do not even retain the slightest memory of what we have read. Such reading is only a series of colored images tickling the mind. We read to evade boredom or grief, blurring a sorrow by losing ourselves in imagined realms or escaping the dullness of our own four walls by rioting in jeweled pleasure-domes or creeping through green jungles.

We read for factual information. We prize a stray glittering bit of knowledge as squirrels and magpies collect broken glass, bright beads, and ends of shining silk. But we may read for systematic knowledge too. Knowledge growing, tied together, and seen as a whole gives us an enjoyable sense of mental power. Knowledge used to satisfy our desires is physical power. Idle curiosity and monkeying around melt into directed enquiry, investigation, invention, discovery. Charles Darwin read Malthus's *Essay on Population* and wondered what would happen if you applied its ideas to animals instead of human society. It led him to *The Origin of Species*. Reading that begins as mere pointless time-passing may stimulate and feed such useful drives.

But reading may be even more deeply meaningful than as organized knowledge. Reading is a way of living. No matter how exciting the lives that we lead, none of us knows directly all the varieties of experience that life can provide. Few of us are mountain climbers, but in books we may scale the Matterhorn or Jungfrau or hug the wind-swept flanks of some icy peak in the Hima-

layas. We can swim the Hellespont with Leander, visit the celestial
court of Kubla Khan with Purchas or Marco Polo, tremble with
Dostoyevsky's Raskolnikov in the terrors of a murderer, suffer with
old Goriot the ingratitude and neglect of two snobbish daughters,
die in the gloomy darkness of Juliet's tomb. Through imaginative
sympathy we share thousands of lives, not merely doing deeds we
shall never do in fact, but entering into ardors, exultations,
agonies, swooping aloft and becoming living parts of man's un-
conquerable mind. We learn to know what other men are like by
living with many more than we shall ever live with in reality. In
the world of imagination we know their thoughts, feel the beating of their hearts. This is deeper than knowledge. It is understanding.

Biography shares all these potentialities with other materials of
reading. It may fill a libertine hour later dismissed from memory
to read of Byron's liaison with Marianna Segati or the weeping
Rousseau being taught the caresses of love by his "Mama," Madame de Warens. We may forget the routine of office or housekeeping by following the smiling figure of "Chinese" Gordon
advancing into battle with a light cane. We may lose our own
sorrows hovering over the couch of the dying Scott with the ripple
of the Tweed borne through the open window. We may glean
miscellaneous oddities like Johnson's collecting and drying of
orange peel. And the enjoyment of biography may lead us, as it
has done the present writer, to explore further and further into
its dramas of human character and reflect upon its principles,
may even bring financial rewards—as I hope it will, if enough
readers are attracted to this book!

These are not the greatest rewards, however, to either me or
the reader. Those lie deeper in experience; they inhere in an
enlarging and enrichment of living. No one drinks deeply enough
of that cup:

> *Life piled on life*
> *Were all too little—*

but biography offers an inner world of inexhaustible profundity.
There we find laughter and sorrow, struggles, victories, defeats,

lonely vigils and perils, glory, disgrace, hunger, longing, fulfill-
ment, and despair. There we find martyrs, statesmen, explorers,
regicides, tinkers, scholars, anarchists, printers, pirates, and poets.
There, deepest of all, we find the human heart, its secrets and its
loves and its tears. Wisdom is no more to be found buried in
books, of course, than won from ourselves in the struggle with
the world. But books—if we live not merely to read and escape
from living, but read as one of the enrichments of life—are among
the innumerable avenues by which wisdom may be gained.

II

Drama and fiction are no less vital for such ends than biography.
Biography has one virtue, though, that they do not share. It is
true. This is not to say that in some ways the truth of fiction may
not be of even deeper significance than the truth of fact. But
fictional truth is different from factual truth. On a simple and
almost naïve level the belief in factual truth is the appeal of the
True Confessions and True Romances. The way men have felt
about their actual fellow-men, the cravings they have had for
actual things—whether furs and sapphires or freedom of the
soul—their merriment over real joys and their tears in real despair, strike certain deeply vibrant chords in our emotions.

The actual truth means not more than the truth of the imagination. It is a different type of truth. Achilles and King Lear move
us in unexampled ways; do they move us more than Brutus, or
Shelley drowned, or Jesus? Why there is this special character of
feeling for what has really existed is hard to say. To analyze it may
be beyond our powers, fruitless to ask

What this strong music of the soul may be.

But men know it though they cannot describe it. They know it
when they hear Tom Paine declare, "Where liberty is not, there
is my country!" and they are stirred as by the sound of a trumpet.
They know it when the sad gaunt form of Lincoln brooding upon
the tragedy of the world moves their hearts to unavailing awe.

These are the reasons why truth is the one and greatest commandment of biography. They are why paltering with truth is

its unforgivable sin. So doing, a biographer violates the unspoken understanding between him and his reader, that everything set down is earnestly believed to be so, and tampers with one of the reader's primary motives in coming to him rather than to novelist or poet. Truth is the key virtue: an absolute candor, seeking neither to blacken nor to whitewash, but as clearly as may be, to understand.

This does not mean that biography is to be nothing but hard little nuggets of fact. Mere recitals of fact will not always unveil their inner meaning. Not what a man did, but why, may be more important for truth. We have to see the poor tortured heart of Rousseau as well as the sharp recriminations of Grimm and Diderot. And the why may have to be traced back through the years, through youth, through childhood, to infancy itself. It may enforce a search into the most tenuous and hidden chambers of the soul. The background of the social life and the times may be as needful as psychological analysis. So a dozen different lines of enquiry may converge before a single incident or characteristic can be shown in its true light.

But what *is* the "true light"? We do not know. What is a man's character, really? what is the heart of his mystery? It is a secret no one can ever be absolutely sure he knows. The truth about a man, for us, is what he seems to us to be when we have given full weight to every fact about him that we can learn, have wit. tingly distorted nothing, and have tried to see him as a whole. What he seems to us is the intersection between his personality and our own. Every biographer he can have will be a little different from the others and see him somewhat differently, just as each of us is a different person to his parents, his children, his enemies, and his friends. Human nature changes with the eyes that see it.

Truth for the biographer is thus a matter of interpretation and insight. A vulgar and superficial biographer commands only a cheap and superficial insight. The artist-biographer must have the psychological insight of the novelist and, at the same time, critical detachment. He must combine sympathy and understanding with judgment. He must be able to penetrate into the darkest

and most fetid swamps of the imagination and still find his way
back to the normal world. He must, on occasion, be able to call
upon the special knowledge of the psychiatrist, the sociologist,
or the historian, without becoming the partisan or victim of some
extraneous theory. He must not contort his tale into a parable to
convey a relentless moral.

It does not follow, of course, that the biographer is to find no
meaning in the life he recreates. Lives are not meaningless, but
their meanings are to be found, not imposed. A good biography
may be defined as the significant true story of an individual life.
It must be individual. No puppet will do, no figure-head of abstract or idealized qualities. We must have the living and life-like
human being, shaped to those deeds and colored with those quirks
that made him himself. It must be a story. Accident plays a part in
men's lives, but even accidents are not wholly chaotic: character
emerges in different ways from like circumstances. The work of
biographical art must find the chains of coherence that link into
unity the doings of blind chance.

And, most of all, there must be meaning. The reader cannot be
left asking, "So what?" The subject of the biography may be as
great as Michelangelo or Beethoven, or he may be as pitiful as
Chaplin's little man forever slapped and buffeted about and forever
setting off down the road again on his unending pilgrimage of
defeat. But we must see what his life has to say to us, and why it
was worth saying. Every great biography is a portrayal of life. In
it the individual, with his salt tears and his brief ecstasies, is more
than the thing he is. He is a revelation of men, and of the cruelty,
comedy, hideousness, beauty, wonder, and grandeur of the world.

III

"There is no wealth but life." That wealth lies in the richness,
the variety, the excitingness, and the charm of human personality.
It fills the mansions of biography with profuse vitality—"God's
plenty!" In the great company of men and women the reader will
meet in the pages that follow are illustrated all the interests and
activities of mankind: money, ambition, religion, truth-seeking,
happiness, love. He will find Gibbon's serene assurance that he is

rich, "since my income is superior to my expense, and my expense is equal to my wishes"; and will witness Scott's carelessness and ostentation, and its sad dénouement of toil and failing powers. He will see Cardinal Wolsey and Cardinal Manning fiercely clutching after power, and Henry Adams bitter at its eluding his grasp. Macaulay is revealed on a brisk and efficient climb to success, and Thomas More calmly bent upon preserving his spiritual integrity rather than upon retaining the Lord Chancellorship.

John Donne agonizes in the conflict between the good life and the world; Bunyan wrestles horribly with Satan; Samuel Johnson despairs over the judgment of a just God. Lincoln Steffens devotes a lifetime of search to understanding the forces that turn the wheels of modern society. Thoreau retires to the rigors of Walden Pond, refusing the luxurious seductions of the world. Love shows us Colonel Hutchinson pale as ashes with romantic devotion, and John Stuart Mill haloing with shimmering glory the memory of his wife; it throws a failing light over the ill-mated marriage of Jane and Thomas Carlyle and the misery of Dickens. And, last, there are the emotions of parents and children: Dickens's mother warm for sending the sobbing child back to the blacking factory, the Ruskins wrecking with too much solicitude the life of their dearly beloved son, the tenderness between More and his daughter Meg.

All the ages of life are here as well. The California earthquake tumbles baby Lennie Steffens out of his bed, smiling, as good as gold. Henry Adams awakes to the world at the age of three on a yellow kitchen floor. Little blue-eyed John Ruskin sits on a stool by his mother's billowing skirts and dreams of blue hills. Youth reveals us Franklin arriving in Philadelphia with two huge puffy rolls under his arms, the fiery Trelawny in Bombay thrashing a bullying naval lieutenant, the younger Gosse in an orchid-scented hothouse whimpering his need to have his father let his soul alone. In maturity we see Colonel Hutchinson evading the blandishments of the Lord Protector Cromwell, and Macaulay riding so triumphantly on the peak of fame that two lovely young women turn back from entering the zoo to gaze on the celebrity instead: "Is that Mr. Macaulay? Never mind the hippopotamus!"

With the approach of old age we find Johnson sitting over his tea at the Mitre, lovable and grubby, and bullying all his friends, Henry Adams turning a jaundiced eye to see all the evidence that mankind is a mistake and a failure, and Gibbon complacently entering upon "the period which, as the most agreeable of his long life, was selected by the judgment and experience of the sage Fontenelle." And finally death writes an end to them all—Wolsey dying of "an excoriation of the entrails," More serenely jesting before the falling of the headsman's axe, the flames rising around Ridley and Latimer, Johnson dying in his bed and calm at last before the approach of the terror that had shadowed all his life.

All these men and women, and the thousands more who crowd upon us out of the pages of biography, are more than merely the subjects of absorbing and moving stories. They are deep revelations of human nature as well. They show its height and its depths, its greatnesses and meanness, its inexhaustible profusion. Only less than life itself, biography is a mine of psychological lore waiting to be dug out by whoever will, to be smelted, assayed, gold of human understanding. But beyond even this, biography is a wonderful light upon the life of the past, a key to history.

IV

History is not easy to understand. Partly it is hard to understand because it is complicated and abstract; partly it is hard to understand because it is past, and we do not readily feel the intensity of struggles that were buried long ago. The historian inevitably generalizes. Subduing everything to an intellectual structure, he too often buries for us underneath its abstractions all the warm drama of men believing and fighting, men toiling and starving or idling and luxuriating. And we, in the tenuousness of our sympathies, too often fail to realize the humanity of men who have been swept away by the years. Our blindness finds their problems trivial and their beliefs empty of meaning.

"Queen Anne is dead," we say. But she is no more dead than Cleopatra who lives for us in Shakespeare's imperial drama shining and petulant and full of fire despite the ashes of centuries; or the armies of Napoleon reeling, sinking, and starving through the Rus-

sian winter in Tolstoy's *War and Peace*. And she comes to life in
Winston Churchill's monumental biography of the Duke of
Marlborough, happy in the "sunshine days" of her early reign,
devoted to her warm-hearted and sharp-tongued Sarah, and then
slowly alienated by the bullying of her indomitable friend.
Biography in truth can reconstitute the living flesh on these dead
bones of history.

The struggles of its abstract forces are always embodied in the
behavior and emotions of living men. Only when we glimpse the
colors of human lives will the great bleak abstractions round into
life and begin to move. The individual, private facts of life are
all parts of the stream of larger events. Even when their significance is quite unknown to the individual himself, they are
vital fragments of the great whole. They contain within themselves history in the concrete, its meanings made tangible, its
struggles brought near. And biography is the great storehouse of
this life of the past. As we explore its chambers, the dust that has
sifted down over the far-away is blown aside. The yellowed pages
that have been so shriveled and dry gradually open and take on
bright colorings like those hard little paper pellets that unfold in
water into flowers and trees and tiny castles.

They seem far enough away, where we begin, in this book, with
the glow and insolence of the Renaissance. But in an instant they
are life-size upon us. Wolsey billows in crimson damask, orgulous
and magnificent. Henry VIII, "lusty, disposed all to mirth and
pleasure," comes masked to the pageantry of Hampton Court; on
the leads of More's house he listens to his Chancellor discourse on
the motions of the stars. But his divorce was more than a sensual
itch for a black-eyed siren's beauty. Nationalism and the Protestant
Reformation joined hands and tore at the foundations of the
universal Catholic church. Wolsey's fall was followed by the suppression of the monasteries. Mary's efforts to turn back the tide
burned in the human torches of Smithfield, where we hear Protestantism cry out in the voice of Hugh Latimer: "We shall light
such a candle, by God's grace, in England, as I trust shall never
be put out."

That flame was one day to destroy the divine right of kings.

It flares against Charles I, that well-bred monarch so disastrously "resolved to be an absolute, uncontrollable sovereign . . . or none at all." Lucy Hutchinson, in her devoted memoir of her husband, Colonel John Hutchinson, shows us the progress of Charles's aggressions and betrayals culminating in the fall of the royal head, and through her eyes we see Cromwell usurping the dictatorship, and the chaotic interlude of the Rump Parliament.

Bunyan shows us the persecutions of the nonconformists under Charles II, and the obstinate iron of Puritan independence that refused to be melted from the backbones of humble Englishmen. North takes us into the green of college cloisters; Gibbon and Johnson into the sanity and balance of Georgian England. But they show us new forces stirring as well. Johnson thunders in vain against "levellers" and "patriots" asserting the faith of democracy and demanding political rights. The radical Wilkes is elected and re-elected in riotous meetings; Franklin, that new portent of the people, experiments with electricity and represents the colony of Pennsylvania against its proprietors; the Americans flame into revolt. Gibbon votes with the Crown but in private letters confesses the unwisdom of the government's course. In his old age he defies the dangers of travel across revolutionary France to comfort his friend Lord Sheffield in the loss of a wife.

The Napoleonic armies lunging across Europe are in the background of Trelawny's privateering under the French flag, and the incentive to Scott's furious galloping along the stretches of Portobello sands. Waterloo leaves dissatisfaction seething under the triumph of reaction. Mobs cry, "Burk Sir Walter!" when Scott comes out from voting against the Reform Bill of 1832; Carlyle reports the grim rejoicing with which crowds watched the Houses of Parliament burn to the ground; Macaulay warns the legislators of the land against defying the forces that had just dethroned the Bourbons in France. Dickens pours red-hot denunciation upon the horrors of industrial slums and Mill brands the existing system as "an evil worth any struggle to get rid of."

Thoreau, in America, revolts from a world where "things are in the saddle" and the masses of men, rich as well as poor, are spiritually enslaved. During the Civil War, Henry Adams sees the

British Government, indifferent to the principles that had abolished chattel slavery in the Empire, favoring the South and hoping to see it win—because the mills of Birmingham needed the
cotton grown by slaves. Skepticism eats away the old evangelical
faith in the heart of the boy Edmund Gosse, skepticism partly
pagan and partly born of the radical scientific questionings of
Lyell and Darwin. Skepticism darkens the world for Carlyle
and turns it into a dreadful machine, "a vast, gloomy, solitary
Golgotha and mill of death," from which he recoils into Old
Testament denunciation. Even Manning, shoring himself in an
old authoritarianism, had to deal with labor leaders and dockers'
strikes. Henry Adams, again, bleakly surveying the process in
America, saw the climax of empire approaching, "year after year,
as though Sulla were a President or McKinley a Consul." The
climax was 1914.

In the chorus of desperate criticism, disillusion, and revulsion
that sounds ever more loudly among our nineteenth century
biographers and rolls into the present, Lincoln Steffens strikes a
renewed tone of hope. And so we find ourselves with him in the
present once more. Steffens speaks for the enthusiasm and hope
of Shelley at the dawn of the nineteenth century, but speaks with
an optimism tempered by the empiricism of Mill, tentative, experimental. He urges, not belief in mere nebulous goodness, but in
seeing how that goodness may be put to work and made successful. Our darkness is deeper now even than when Steffens died in
1935. But courageous hearts and generous minds may still join
to rekindle the dawn of light.

Such is the world drama implicitly borne on these voices of
past lives. In this book it is woven of mingling threads from hardly
more than a few score of lives. The more we might weave into
the fabric the richer it would become and the more vividly the
great picture of the whole would compose itself. But even from
these few the vast curve of history emerges spirally into the present,
the latest manifestation of a tremendous pattern. From each of its
individuals, lines of force radiate and connect with others, and
enable us to chart events and their meanings. The people fuse
and mingle with the events of which they were a part, gaining

deeper significance from the rôles they played and endowing the abstract forces with their own vivid life.

For men do not lose their identities in this process; it is not like a mob scene in which the individuals shrink to dark anonymous dots. We, their readers and their fellow-men, continue to be simultaneously far and near. We watch the sweep and course and hue of societies and times. And we see the rise and fall of a bosom, see the emotion in an eye, hear the living tone of a voice. There is no single life. We have not lived unless our lives have mingled with the lives of other men. That mingling is but poverty-stricken if it is limited to physical contact. The mingling of hearts and imaginations goes far deeper.

GLITTERING FALL

THE LIFE OF WOLSEY IS BOTH A TRAGEDY OF FATE AND A PAGEANT
of Renaissance magnificence. Medievalism was withering away.
Its warrior barons, immured as in deep-sea caves within their
donjon keeps or scuttling forth to conflict in martial lobster shells,
were yielding before the power of great national states: Spain,
England, France. The vision of the City of God and a kingdom
not of this world slowly faded against the glitter of dominion. The
trade of the Orient and the gold of the New World stimulated rival
imperialisms in which Wolsey sought to poise England at the
fulcrum of power; new refinements of pomp flowered in Papal
Rome, the galleries of Hampton Court, the Field of the Cloth of
Gold. The rigors of the monastic ideal seemed cramped to ambitions glamored by a thousand pleasures. With this robust delight in the senses mingled the intellectual pride of Humanism,
making self-denial appear timid and dingy, flaunting a thousand
questions and skepticisms. The Church grew luxurious and corrupt, firing the moral indignation destined to bring on the Protestant Reformation of Luther and Calvin. For both good and
evil, men were breathing a new air of freedom and boundless confidence. Such is the world in which Wolsey's rise to power is followed by a tragic fall.

The shock of war and the tortuous convolutions of Wolsey's
diplomacy, however, and even the shimmer of rich stuffs, the
sparkle of jewels, and the brilliance of noble feasts with which
Cavendish fills his pages, are only incidental to his theme. That
theme is the theme of classic tragedy. It sounds a note growing
ever more ominous as the great ecclesiastic glories in a power that

is ruthless, domineering, and vindictive. Pride, which the ancient
Greeks called by the name of *hubris,* is the Cardinal's tragic sin.
No less tragic is the efficient cause of his downfall, for it is precisely
that royal will regardless of right that Wolsey had fostered for his
own ends. The great statesman's own responsibility for his fate
gives it a dark and bitter justice that is an essential part of tragedy.

The uncompromising honesty with which Cavendish portrays
Wolsey's flaws of character is tremendously effective. We see his
memory long and grim with animosity against the unfortunate Sir
Amyas Paulet who had put him in stocks years ago; we see him
pandering to the King's desires, pulling strings to eliminate Warham, Archbishop of Canterbury, as his rival; we behold him
swollen with the revenues of a dozen benefices. He hustles the
clergy, dominates the Universities, orders about the nobility. He
is servile in his readiness to do the dirty work of Henry VIII's
divorce. (Roper, as the reader will see, in his *Life of Sir Thomas
More,* states that Wolsey even initiated this project in revenge for
the failure of Catherine's nephew, Charles V, to swing him the
promised votes that would have elected him Pope. Cavendish has
no hint of this, but his portrait is otherwise sharp enough.) He
sends Anne Boleyn from Court, bullies and roars at young Lord
Percy: the same noble who, seven years later, as Earl of Northumberland, tremblingly arrests him for high treason.

But Cavendish's pen is not dipped in the malign acid of Lytton
Strachey. He was gentleman usher to Wolsey; and with no blindness to Wolsey's faults Cavendish loved his master. His truth in
delineating those faults makes us trust his story of the conspiracy
that leads to Wolsey's ruin; his devotion to Wolsey in his misery,
and the devotion of those hosts of faithful servants who wept for
his fall, convince us that Wolsey's character had a more estimable
side. The pitifulness of that slow and inexorable disgrace and
the proud man's humility and grief and too-late piety call irresistibly upon our sympathies. Cavendish seems almost naïve,
but he is no simpleton, and I am not sure that his very simplicity
is not art. He does not palliate Wolsey's flaws, but he makes us
pity and forgive. Above all, he makes us believe.

He makes us believe also in the background and the other fig-

ures whom he flashes before us so brilliantly. He reveals the
resentment and jealousy of those proud hounds of race for the
upstart butcher's cur who lords it over them so scornfully. He
shows old Northumberland cringing before Wolsey's demand that
he bully his son into submission as Wolsey himself was later to
cringe with a fearful courtesy before the son. He darts a glance
at Anne Boleyn "smoking" with rage at the Cardinal's interference, and traces her later influence as a "continual serpentine
enemy." He is all humility and submission in his portrayal of the
royal tyrant, but how marvelous is his report of Henry's cynically
perjured speech before the ecclesiastical court! How he makes us
hear the ice cracking and breaking under Wolsey's feet with the
Duke of Suffolk daring at last to say injuriously, "It was never
merry in England whilst we had cardinals among us!" How he
etches Wolsey's unpopularity with the single detail of a thousand
boats "waffeting" up and down the Thames, rejoicing in the belief that he was being sent to the Tower!

These are among the things that make *The Life and Death of
Thomas Wolsey,* although the earliest of English biographies, one
of the greatest. It is great in vividness. It is great in rendering of
character. It is great in truth. And it is great in the evocation of
wonder and sympathy.

The Life and Death of Thomas Wolsey

GEORGE CAVENDISH

[Wolsey died in 1530. Cavendish's biography was composed not later than 1557, but it was not published, and even then in a garbled form, until 1641. It was first printed from the original manuscript in 1815.]

IN THE FIFTEENTH CENTURY THE CHURCH WAS ALMOST THE ONLY *means of advancement to plebeian talent. Wolsey, a poor man's son, showing precocious ability, was "the boy-bachelor" at Oxford by the age of fifteen and made a fellow of Magdalen College shortly thereafter. The Marquess of Dorset was presently so pleased with Wolsey's services as a tutor to his children that he gave the young scholar a benefice of which he had the presentation. Wolsey made speed to take possession.*

And being there for that intent, one Sir Amyas Paulet, knight, dwelling in the country thereabout, took an occasion of displeasure against him, upon what ground I know not: but, sir, by your leave, he was so bold to set the schoolmaster by the feet during his pleasure; the which was afterward neither forgotten nor forgiven; for when the schoolmaster mounted the dignity of Chancellor of England, he was not oblivious of the old displeasure ministered unto him by master Paulet, but sent for him, and after many sharp and heinous words, enjoined him to attend upon the council until he were by them dismissed, and not to depart without licence, upon an urgent pain and forfeiture: so that he continued within the Middle Temple, the space of five or six years or more; whose lodging there was in the gate-house next the street, which he re-

edified very sumptuously, garnishing the same, on the outside
thereof, with cardinals' hats and arms, badges and cognisaunces
of the cardinal, with divers other devices, in so glorious a sort,
that he thought thereby to appease his old unkind displeasure.

Who would have thought then, when Sir Amyas Paulet punished this poor scholar, that ever he should have attained to be
Chancellor of England, considering his baseness in every condition. These be wonderful works of God and fortune.

*Wolsey became chaplain to Sir John Nanfant, the Treasurer of
Calais, and thence was advanced to become the chaplain of Henry
VII himself. Sent on a weighty mission to the Holy Roman Emperor Maximilian in Flanders, he traveled so fast that he was returned in four days. This was such incredible speed that Henry
conceived he had not even started and began to rebuke him:*

"Sir," quoth he, "if it may stand with your highness' pleasure, I
have already been with the emperor, and dispatched your affairs,
I trust, to your grace's contentation."
And with that delivered unto the king the emperor's letters of
credence. The king, being in a great confuse and wonder of his
hasty speed with ready furniture of all his proceedings, dissembled
all his imagination and wonder in that matter, and demanded of
him, whether he encountered not his pursuivant, the which he
sent unto him, supposing him not to be scantly out of London,
with letters concerning a very necessary cause neglected in his
commission and instructions, the which the king coveted much
to be sped.
"Yes, forsooth, Sire," quoth he, "I encountered him yesterday
by the way: and, having understanding by your grace's letters of
your pleasure therein, have, notwithstanding, been so bold, upon
mine own discretion, perceiving that matter to be very necessary
in that behalf, to dispatch the same. And for as much as I have
exceeded your grace's commission, I most humbly require your
gracious remission and pardon."

The king of his mere motion and gracious consideration, gave
him at that time for his diligent and faithful service, the deanery

of Lincoln, which at that time was one of the worthiest spiritual promotions that he gave under the degree of a bishoprick. And thus from thenceforward he grew more and more into estimation and authority, and after was promoted by the king to be his almoner.

Henry VII died, and his son Henry VIII, "young, lusty, and courageous," came to a magnificent coronation.

Now let us return again unto the almoner, of whom I have taken upon me to write, whose head was full of subtle wit and policy. Perceiving a plain path to walk in towards promotion, he handled himself so politicly, that he found the means to be one of the king's council, and to grow in good estimation and favour with the king, to whom the king gave a house at Bridewell, in Fleet Street, sometime Sir Richard Empson's, where he kept house for his family, and he daily attended upon the king in the court, being in his especial grace and favour, having then great suit made unto him, as counsellors most commonly have that be in favour. His sentences and witty persuasions in the council chamber were always so pithy that they always, as occasion moved them, assigned him, for his filed tongue and ornate eloquence, to be their expositor unto the king's majesty in all their proceedings. In whom the king conceived such a loving fantasy, especially for that he was most earnest and readiest among all the council to advance the king's only will and pleasure, without any respect to the case.

The king, therefore, perceived him to be a meet instrument for the accomplishment of his devised will and pleasure, called him more near unto him, and esteemed him so highly that his estimation and favour put all other ancient counsellors out of their accustomed favour, that they were in before; insomuch as the king committed all his will and pleasure unto his disposition and order. Who wrought so all his matters, that all his endeavour was only to satisfy the king's mind, knowing right well, that it was the very vein and right course to bring him to high promotion.

The king was young and lusty, disposed all to mirth and pleasure, and to follow his desire and appetite, nothing minding to

travail in the busy affairs of this realm. The which the almoner
perceived very well, and took upon him therefore to disburden the
king of so weighty a charge and troublesome business . . . And
whereas the other ancient counsellors would, according to the
office of good counsellors, divers times persuade the king to have
sometime an intercourse in to the council, there to hear what was
done in weighty matters, the which pleased the king nothing at
all, for he loved nothing worse than to be constrained to do any
thing contrary to his royal will and pleasure; and that knew the
almoner very well, having a secret intelligence of the king's natural
inclination, and so fast as the other counsellors advised the king to
leave his pleasure, and to attend to the affairs of his realm, so
busily did the almoner persuade him to the contrary; which delighted him much, and caused him to have the greater affection
and love to the almoner.

Thus the almoner ruled all them that before ruled him; such
did his policy and wit bring to pass. Who was now in high favour,
but Master Almoner? Who had all the suit, but Master Almoner?
And who ruled all under the king, but Master Almoner? Thus
he proceeded still in favour; at last, in came presents, gifts, and
rewards so plentifully, that I dare say he lacked nothing that might
either please his fantasy or enrich his coffers; fortune smiled so
upon him; but to what end she brought him, ye shall hear after.

This almoner, climbing thus hastily up fortune's wheel, that no
man was of that estimation with the king as he was, for his wisdom
and other witty qualities. He had a special gift of natural eloquence, with a filed tongue to pronounce the same, that he was
able with the same to persuade and allure all men to his purpose.
Proceeding thus in fortune's blissfulness, it chanced that the wars
between the realms of England and France to be open, but upon
what occasion I know not, in so much as the king, being fully
persuaded and resolved in his most royal person to invade his
foreign enemies with a puissant army, to delay their hault brags
within their own territory: wherefor it was thought very necessary, that this royal enterprise should be speedily provided and
plentifully furnished in every degree, of things apt and convenient

for the same; the expedition whereof, the king's highness thought
no man's wit so meet, for policy and painful travail, as his well-
beloved almoner's was, to whom therefore he committed his whole
affiance and trust therein. And he being nothing scrupulous in
any thing that the king would command him to do, and although
it seemed to other very difficile, yet took he upon him the whole
charge and burden of all this business, and proceeded so therein,
that he brought all things to a good pass and purpose in a right
decent order, as of all manner of victuals, provisions, and other
necessaries, convenient for so noble a voyage and puissant army."

With the victories of the army Wolsey's favor grew. In a single
year he was made Bishop of Tournai, Bishop of Lincoln, and
finally Archbishop of York. Now only Warham, Archbishop of
Canterbury, stood in his way. Warham was not disposed to yield;
he gave the new archbishop a "check for his presumption." *Wolsey*
pulled strings. Wherefore he obtained first to be made Priest
Cardinal, and *Legatus de latere;* unto whom the Pope sent a Cardinal's hat, with certain bulls for his authority in that behalf. Yet
by the way of communication ye shall understand that the Pope
sent him this hat as a worthy jewel of his honour, dignity, and
authority, the which was conveyed hither in a varlet's budget, who
seemed to all men to be but a person of small estimation. Whereof
York being advertised, of the baseness of the messenger, and of
the people's opinion and rumour, thought it for his honour meet,
that so high a jewel should not be conveyed by so simple a messenger; wherefore he caused him to be stayed by the way, immediately after his arrival in England, where he was newly furnished
in all manner of apparel, with all kind of costly silks, which
seemed decent for such an high ambassador. And that done, he
was encountered upon Blackheath, and there received with a great
assembly of prelates, and lusty gallant gentlemen, and from thence
conducted and conveyed through London, with great triumph.
Then was great and speedy provision and preparation made in
Westminster Abbey for the confirmation of his high dignity; the
which was executed by all the bishops and abbots nigh or about
London, in rich mitres and copes, and other costly ornaments;

which was done in so solemn a wise as I have not seen the like unless it had been at the coronation of a mighty prince or king.

Still not sufficiently avenged of Canterbury's "taunts and checks," Wolsey found means presently to have Warham dismissed from the Lord Chancellorship, and himself took the Great Seal. Then had he two great crosses of silver, whereof one of them was for his Archbishoprick, and the other for his Legacy, borne always before him whithersoever he went or rode, by two of the most tallest and comeliest priests that he could get within all this realm. And to the increase of his gains he had also the bishoprick of Durham, and the Abbey of St. Albans *in commendam;* howbeit after, when Bishop Fox, of Winchester, died, he surrendered Durham into the king's hands, and in lieu thereof took the Bishoprick of Winchester.

Glorious now was his state. The incomes of Bath, Worcester, and Hereford added their floods to his revenues. Cavendish lists his house-servants, including "in his kitchen a Master Cook who went daily in damask satin, or velvet, with a chain of gold about his neck"; *the officers and singing men of his chapel; the innumerable functionaries attached to him in his dignity as Chancellor. All told, they came close to five hundred.* But to speak of the furniture of his chapel passeth my capacity to declare the number of the costly ornaments and rich jewels, that were occupied in the same continually. For I have seen there, in a procession, worn forty-four copes of one suit, very rich, besides the sumptuous crosses, candlesticks, and other necessary ornaments to the comely furniture of the same.

His gentlemen, being in number very many, clothed in livery coats of crimson velvet of the most purest colour that might be invented, with chains of gold about their necks; and all his yeomen and other mean officers were in coats of fine scarlet, guarded with black velvet a hand broad . . . And after mass he would return in his privy chamber again, and being advertised of the furniture of his chambers without, with noblemen and gentlemen, and other persons, would issue out into them, apparelled all in

red, in the habit of a cardinal; which was either of fine scarlet, or
else of crimson satin, taffety, damask, or caffa, the best that he
could get for money: and upon his head a round pillion, with a
neck of black velvet set to the same in the inner side; he had
also a tippet of fine sables about his neck; holding in his hand a
very fair orange, whereof the meat or substance within was taken
out, and filled up again with the part of a sponge, wherein was
vinegar, and other confections against the pestilent airs; to the
which he most commonly smelt unto, passing among the press, or
else when he was pestered with many suitors.

Thus in great honour, triumph, and glory, he reigned a long
season, ruling all things within this realm, appertaining unto the
king, by his wisdom, and also all other weighty matters of foreign
regions, with which the king of this realm had any occasion to
intermeddle. All ambassadors of foreign potentates were always
dispatched by his discretion, to whom they had always access for
their dispatch. His house was also always resorted and furnished
with noblemen, gentlemen, and other persons, with going and
coming in and out, feasting and banqueting all ambassadors divers
times, and other strangers right nobly.

And when it pleased the king's majesty, for his recreation, to
repair unto the cardinal's house, as he did divers times in the year,
at which time there wanted no preparations, or goodly furniture,
with viands of the finest sort that might be provided for money
or friendship. Such pleasures were then devised for the king's
comfort and consolation, as might be invented, or by man's wit
imagined. The banquets were set forth, with masks and mum-
meries, in so gorgeous a sort, and costly manner, that it was an
heaven to behold. There wanted no dames, or damsels, meet or
apt to dance with the maskers, or to garnish the place for a time,
with other goodly disports. Then was there all kind of music and
harmony set forth, with excellent voices both of men and children.

I have seen the king suddenly come in thither in a mask, with
a dozen of other maskers, all in garments like shepherds, made of
fine cloth of gold and fine crimson satin paned, and caps of the

same, with visors of good proportion of visonomy; their hairs, and
beards, either of fine gold wire, or else of silver, and some being
of black silk; having sixteen torch bearers, besides their drums,
and other persons attending upon them, with visors, and clothed
all in satin, of the same colours.

[The Cardinal tried to pick the king out from among the
maskers.] "Me seemeth the gentleman with the black beard
should be even he." And with that he arose out of his chair, and
offered the same to the gentleman in the black beard, with his
cap in his hand. The person to whom he offered then his chair
was Sir Edward Neville, a comely knight of a goodly personage,
that much more resembled the king's person in that mask, than any
other. The king, hearing and perceiving the cardinal so deceived in his estimation and choice, could not forbear laughing;
but plucked down his visor, and Master Neville's, and dashed out
with such a pleasant countenance and cheer, that all noble estates
there assembled, seeing the king to be there amongst them, rejoiced very much. . . . Then the king took his seat under the
cloth of estate, commanding no man to remove, but sit still, as
they did before. Then in came a new banquet before the king's
majesty, and to all the rest through the tables, wherein, I suppose,
was served two hundred dishes or above, of wondrous costly meats
and delices, subtilly devised. Thus passed they forth the whole
night with banqueting, dancing, and other triumphant devices,
to the great comfort of the king, and pleasant regard of the nobility there assembled.

Thus passed the cardinal his life and time, from day to day,
and year to year, in such great wealth, joy, and triumph, and glory,
having always on his side the king's especial favour; until Fortune, of whose favour no man is longer assured than she is disposed, began to wax something wroth with his prosperous estate,
thought she would devise a mean to abate his high port; wherefore she procured Venus, the insatiate goddess, to be her instrument. To work her purpose, she brought the king in love with
a gentlewoman, that, after she perceived and felt the king's good
will towards her, and how diligent he was both to please her, and

to grant all her requests, she wrought the cardinal much displeasure; as hereafter shall be more at large declared. This gentlewoman, the daughter of Sir Thomas Boleyn, being at that time but only a bachelor knight, the which after, for the love of his daughter, was promoted to higher dignities.

Insomuch, my Lord Percy, the son and heir of the Earl of Northumberland, who then attended upon the Lord Cardinal, and was also his servitor; and when it chanced the Lord Cardinal at any time to repair to the court, the Lord Percy would then resort for his pastime unto the queen's chamber, and there would fall in dalliance among the queen's maidens, being at the last more conversant with Mistress Anne Boleyn than with any other; so that there grew such a secret love between them that, at length, they were ensured together, intending to marry. The which thing came to the king's knowledge, who was then much offended. Wherefore he could hide no longer his secret affection, but revealed his secret intendment unto my Lord Cardinal in that behalf; and consulted with him to infringe the precontract between them: insomuch, that after my Lord Cardinal was departed from the court, and returned home to his place at Westminster, not forgetting the king's request and counsel, being in his gallery, called there before him the said Lord Percy unto his presence, and before us his servants of his chamber, saying thus unto him:

"I marvel not a little," quoth he, "of thy peevish folly, that thou wouldest tangle and ensure thyself with a foolish girl yonder in the court, I mean Anne Boleyn. Dost thou not consider the estate that God hath called thee unto in this world? For after the death of thy noble father, thou art most like to inherit and possess one of the most worthiest earldoms of this realm. . . . But now behold what ye have done through your wilfulness. Ye have not only offended your natural father, but also your most gracious sovereign lord, and matched yourself with one, such as neither the king, nor yet your father will be agreeable with the matter. And hereof I put you out of doubt, that I will send for your father, and at his coming, he shall either break this unadvised contract, or else disinherit thee for ever."

"Sir," quoth the Lord Percy, all weeping, "I knew nothing of the king's pleasure therein, for whose displeasure I am very sorry. I considered that I was of good years, and thought myself sufficient to provide me of a convenient wife, whereas my fancy served me best, not doubting but that my lord my father would have been right well persuaded. And though she be a simple maid, and having but a knight to her father, yet is she descended of right noble parentage."

"Lo, sirs," quoth the cardinal, "ye may see what conformity or wisdom is in this wilful boy's head. I thought that when thou heardest me declare the king's intended pleasure and travail herein, thou wouldest have relented and wholly submitted thyself, and all thy wilful and unadvised fact, to the king's royal will and prudent pleasure, to be fully disposed and ordered by his Grace's disposition, as his highness should seem good."

"Sir, so I would," quoth the Lord Percy, "but in this matter I have gone so far, before many so worthy witnesses, that I know not how to avoid myself nor to discharge my conscience."

Then was the Earl of Northumberland sent for in all haste, in the king's name, who, upon knowledge of the king's pleasure, made quick speed to the court.

"Son," quoth he, "thou hast always been a proud, presumptuous, disdainful, and a very unthrift waster, and even so hast thou now declared thyself. . . . But that his Grace of his mere wisdom doth consider the lightness of thy head, and wilful qualities of thy person, his displeasure and indignation were sufficient to cast me and all my posterity into utter subversion and desolation: but he being my especial and singular good lord and favourable prince, and my Lord Cardinal, my good lord, hath and doth clearly excuse me in thy lewd fact, and doth rather lament thy lightness than malign the same; and hath devised an order to be taken for thee; to whom both thou and I be more bound than we be able well to consider.

"I pray to God that this may be to thee a sufficient monition and warning to use thyself more wittier hereafter; for thus I assure thee, if thou dost not amend thy prodigality, thou wilt be the last earl of our house."

Percy weakened under all this pressure, and was forced into a marriage with a daughter of the Earl of Shrewsbury. Anne Boleyn "was commanded to avoid the court, and sent home again to her father for a season; whereat she smoked: for all this while she knew nothing of the king's intended purpose."

Howbeit, after she knew the king's pleasure, and the great love that he bare her in the bottom of his stomach, then began she to look very hault and stout, having all manner of jewels, or rich apparel, that might be gotten with money. It was therefore judged by-and-by through all the court of every man, that she being in such favour, might work masteries with the king, and obtain any suit of him for her friends.

This perceiving, the great lords of the council, bearing a secret grudge against the cardinal, because that they could not rule in the scene well for him as they would, who kept them low, and ruled them as well as other mean subjects, whereat they caught an occasion to invent a mean to bring him out of the king's high favour, and them into more authority of rule and civil governance. . . . And she having both a very good wit, and also an inward desire to be revenged of the cardinal, was as agreeable to their requests as they were themselves.

Conspiring together "to take the cardinal in a brake," *they caused him to be sent as England's Ambassador Plenipotentiary to Francis I, hoping in his absence to undermine his influence. Wolsey bludgeoned the French court into submission to England's demands and returned, seemingly in more triumph than ever. He had concluded, he told them,* "such an amity and friendship as never was heard of in this realm in our time before," "a perpetual peace," *and Henry to* "receive yearly his tribute . . . for the Duchy of Normandy, with all other costs he had sustained in the wars." *His success was celebrated by a solemn mass at St. Paul's. Great banquets were given, with course after course wrought into sculptural ingenuity.*

There were castles with images in the same; Paul's church and steeple, in proportion for the quantity as well counterfeited as the painter should have painted it upon a cloth or wall. There were beasts, birds, fowls of divers kinds, and personages, most lively made and counterfeit in dishes; some fighting, as it were, with swords, some with guns and crossbows, some vaulting and leaping; some dancing with ladies, some in complete harness, justing with spears . . . But to describe the dishes, the subtleties, the many strange devices and order in the same, I do both lack wit in my gross old head, and cunning in my bowels to declare the wonderful and curious imaginations in the same invented and devised.

This done, then came in such a number of fair ladies and gentle-women that bare any bruit or fame of beauty in all this realm, in the most richest apparel, and devised in divers goodly fashions that all the cunningest tailors could devise to shape or cut, to set forth their beauty, gesture, and goodly proportion of their bodies: who seemed to all men more angelic than earthly, made of flesh and bone.

But hidden dangers were nearing Wolsey fast.

The long hid and secret love between the king and Mistress Anne Boleyn began to break out into every man's ears. The matter was then by the king disclosed to my Lord Cardinal; whose per-suasion to the contrary, made to the king upon his knees, could not effect: the king was so amorously affectionate, that will bare place, and high discretion banished for the time.

Henry demanded action. On Wolsey's motion the Universities debated whether the king's marriage to his brother's widow was legal. Finally under their seals they petitioned the Pope to estab-lish a court in England to try the cause. Wolsey and Cardinal Campeggio were appointed to preside.

Long was the desire, and greater was the hope on all sides, ex-pecting the coming of the legation and commission from Rome, yet at length it came. And after the arrival of the Legate Campeg-gio with this solemn commission in England, he being sore vexed with the gout, was constrained by force thereof to make a long journey or ever he came to London; who should have been most solemnly received at Blackheath, and so with great triumph con-veyed to London; but his glory was such, that he would in nowise be entertained with any such pomp or vainglory, who suddenly came by water in a wherry to his own house without Temple Bar, called then Bath Place, which was furnished for him with all manner of stuff and implements of my lord's provision; where he continued and lodged during his abode here in England.

Ye shall understand, as I said before, that there was a court erected in the Black Friars in London, where these two cardinals sat for judges.

The court being thus furnished and ordered, the judges commanded the crier to command silence; then was the judges' commission, which they had of the pope, published and read openly before all the audience there assembled. That done, the crier called the king, by the name of "King Harry of England come into the court, etc." With that the king answered and said. "Here, my lords!" Then he called also the queen, by the name of "Katherine Queen of England, come into the court, etc.;" who made no answer to the same, but rose up incontinent out of her chair, where as she sat, and because she could not come directly to the king for the distance which severed them, she took pain to go about unto the king, kneeling down at his feet in the sight of all the court and assembly, to whom she said in effect, in broken English, as followeth:

"Sir," quoth she, "I beseech you for all the loves that hath been between us, and for the love of God, let me have justice and right, take of me some pity and compassion, for I am a poor woman and a stranger born out of your dominion, I have here no assured friend, and much less indifferent counsel; I flee to you as to the head of justice within this realm. Alas! Sir, wherein have I offended you, or what occasion of displeasure have I designed against your will and pleasure? . . .

"This twenty years I have been your true wife or more, and by me ye have had divers children, although it hath pleased God to call them out of this world, which hath been no default in me.

"And when ye had me at the first, I take God to be my judge, I was a true maid without touch of man; and whether it be true or no, I put it to your conscience. If there be any just cause by the

law that ye can allege against me, either of dishonesty or any other
impediment to banish and put me from you, I am well content
to depart, to my great shame and dishonour; and if there be none,
then here I most lowly beseech you let me remain in my former
estate, and receive justice at your princely hands. . . . Therefore
I most humbly require you, in the way of charity, and for the
love of God, who is the just judge, to spare the extremity of this
new court, until I may be advertised what way and order my
friends in Spain will advise me to take. And if ye will not extend
to me so much indifferent favour, your pleasure then be fulfilled,
and to God I commit my case!"

And thus she departed out of that court, without any farther
answer at that time, or at any other, nor would never appear at any
other court after.

The king perceiving that she was departed in such sort, calling
to his Grace's memory all her lament words that she had pronounced before him and all the audience, said thus in effect:
"Forasmuch," quoth he, "as the queen is gone, I will, in her absence, declare unto you all my lords here presently assembled, she
hath been to me as true, as obedient, and as conformable a wife as
I could in my fantasy wish or desire. She hath all the virtuous
qualities that ought to be in a woman of her dignity, or in any
other of baser estate. Surely she is also a noble woman born, if
nothing were in her, but only her conditions will well declare the
same."

With that quoth my Lord Cardinal:

"Sir, I most humbly beseech your highness to declare me before
all this audience, whether I have been the chief inventor or first
mover of this matter unto your majesty; for I am greatly suspected
of all men herein."

"My Lord Cardinal," quoth the king, "I can well excuse you
herein. Marry indeed, ye have been rather against me in attempting or setting forth thereof. And to put you all out of doubt, I
will declare unto you the special cause that moved me hereunto;
it was a certain scrupulosity that pricked my conscience upon
divers words that were spoken at a certain time by the Bishop of
Bayonne . . . These words were so conceived within my scrupu-

lous conscience, that it bred a doubtful prick within my breast, which doubt pricked, vexed, and troubled so my mind, and so disquieted me, that I was in great doubt of God's indignation; which (as seemed me), appeared right well; much the rather for he hath not sent me any issue male; for all such issue male as I have received of the queen died incontinent after they were born; so that I doubt the punishment of God in that behalf. Thus being troubled in waves of a scrupulous conscience, and partly in despair of any issue male by her, it drave me at last to consider the estate of this realm, and the danger it stood in for lack of issue male to succeed me in this imperial dignity. I thought it good therefore in relief of the weighty burden of scrupulous conscience, and the quiet estate of this noble realm, to attempt the law therein, and whether I might take another wife in case that my first copulation with this gentlewoman were not lawful; which I intend not for any carnal concupiscence, nor for any displeasure or mislike of the queen's person or age, with whom I could be as well content to continue during my life, if our marriage may stand with God's law, as with any woman alive; in which point consisteth all this doubt that we go now about to try by the learned wisdom and judgment of you our prelates and pastors of this realm here assembled for that purpose; to whose conscience and judgment I have committed the charge according to the which, God willing, we will be right well contented to submit ourself, to obey the same for my part. Wherein after I once perceived my conscience wounded with the doubtful case herein, I moved first this matter in confession to you, my Lord of Lincoln, my ghostly father. And forasmuch as then yourself were in some doubt to give me counsel, moved me to ask farther counsel of all you my lords; wherein I moved you first my Lord of Canterbury, axing your license, forasmuch as you were our metropolitan, to put this matter in question; and so I did of all you my lords, to the which ye have all granted by writing under all your seals, the which I have here to be showed."

"That is truth if it please your highness," quoth the Bishop of Canterbury, "I doubt not but all my brethren here present will affirm the same."

"No, Sir, not I," quoth the Bishop of Rochester, "ye have not my consent thereto."

"No! ha' the!" quoth the king, "look here upon this, is not this your hand and seal?" and showed him the instrument with seals.

"No forsooth, Sire," quoth the Bishop of Rochester, "it is not my hand nor seal!"

To that, quoth the king to my Lord of Canterbury: "Sir, how say *ye*, is it not his hand and seal?"

"Yes, Sir," quoth he.

"That is not so," quoth the Bishop of Rochester, "for indeed you were in hand with me to have both my hand and seal, as other of my lords had already done; but then I said to you, that I would never consent to no such act, for it were much against my conscience; nor my hand and seal should never be seen at any such instrument, God willing, with much more matter touching the same communication between us."

"You say truth," quoth the Bishop of Canterbury, "such words ye said unto me; but at the last ye were fully persuaded that I should for you subscribe your name, and put-to a seal myself, and ye would allow the same."

"All which words and matter," quoth the Bishop of Rochester, "under your correction, my lord, and supportation of this noble audience, there is no thing more untrue."

"Well, well," quoth the king, "it shall make no matter; we will not stand with you in argument herein, for you are but one man."

And with that the court was adjourned until the next day of their session.

The case dragged on. One day the Bishop of Carlyle, being with the Cardinal in his barge, wiped his brow and complained of the heat.

" 'Yea, [said Wolsey] if ye had been as well chafed as I have been within this hour, ye would say it were very hot.' "

Thus went this strange case forward from court-day to court-day, until it came to judgment, so that every man expected the judgment to be given upon the next court-day. At which day the king came thither, and sat within a gallery against the door of

the same that looked unto the judges where they sat, whom he
might both see and hear speak, to hear what judgment they would
give in his suit; at which time all their proceedings were first
openly read in Latin. And that done, the king's learned counsel
at the bar called fast for judgment.

With that, quoth Cardinal Campeggio, "I will give no judgment herein until I have made relation unto the pope of all
our proceedings, whose counsel and commandment in this high
case I will observe. The case is too high and notable, known
through all the world, for us to give any hasty judgment, considering the highness of the persons and the doubtful allegations;
and also whose commissioners we be, under whose authority we
sit here. It were therefore reason, that we should make our chief
head a counsel in the same, before we proceed into judgment de-
finitive. I come not so far to please any man, for fear, meed, or
favour, be he king or any other potentate. I have no such respect
to the persons that I will offend my conscience. I will not for
favour or displeasure of any high estate or mighty prince do that
thing that should be against the law of God. I am an old man,
both sick and impotent, looking daily for death. What should
it then avail me to put my soul in the danger of God's displeasure,
to my utter damnation, for the favour of any prince or high estate
in this world?

"My coming and being here is only to see justice ministered
according to my conscience, as I thought thereby the matter either
good or bad. And forasmuch as I do understand, and having per-
ceivance by the allegations and negations in this matter laid for
both the parties, that the truth in this case is very doubtful to be
known, and also that the party defendant will make no answer
thereunto, but doth rather appeal from us, supposing that we be
not indifferent, considering the king's high dignity and authority
within this his own realm, which he hath over his own subjects;
and we being his subjects, and having our livings and dignities
in the same, she thinketh that we cannot minister true and indifferent justice for fear of his displeasure.

"Therefore, to avoid all these ambiguities and obscure doubts,
I intend not to damn my soul for no prince or potentate alive.

I will therefore, God willing, wade no farther in this matter, unless I have the just opinion and judgment, with the assent of the pope, and such other of his counsel as hath more experience and learning in such doubtful laws than I have. Wherefore I will adjourn this court for this time, according to the order of the court in Rome, from whence this court and jurisdiction is derived. And if we should go further than our commission doth warrant us, it were folly and vain, and much to our slander and blames; and might be for the same accounted breakers of the orders of the higher court from whence we have (as I said) our original authorities." With that the court was dissolved, and no more plea holden.

With that stept forth the Duke of Suffolk from the king, and by his commandment spake these words, with a stout and hault countenance, "It was never," quoth he, "merry in England, whilst we had cardinals among us:" which words were set forth both with such a vehement countenance, that all men marvelled what he intended; to whom no man made answer. Then the duke spake again in great despight.

To the which words my Lord Cardinal, perceiving his vehemency, soberly made answer and said, "Sir, of all men within this realm, ye have least cause to dispraise or be offended with cardinals; for if I, simple cardinal, had not been, you should have had at this present no head upon your shoulders, wherein you should have a tongue to make any such report in despight of us, who intended you no manner of displeasure; nor have we given you any occasion with such despight to be revenged with your hault words."

Suddenly a blow fell. Wolsey was deprived of the Great Seal, ordered from Court, and all his possessions seized. He made an inventory of everything:

And in his gallery there was set divers tables, whereupon a great number of rich stuff of silk, in whole pieces, of all colours, as velvet, satin, damask, caffa, taffeta, grograine, sarcenet, and of other not in my remembrance; also there lay a thousand pieces of fine holland cloth . . . Furthermore there was also all the walls of the gallery hanged with cloths of gold, and tissue of divers makings, and cloths of silver likewise on both the sides; and rich cloths of baudkin, of divers colours . . . In the gilt chambers was set out upon the tables nothing but all gilt plate; and a cupboard standing under a window, was garnished wholly with plate of clean gold, whereof some was set with pearl and rich stones.

And therewithal he made him ready to depart, with all his gentlemen and yeomen, which was no small number, and took his barge at his privy stairs, and so went by water unto Putney, where all his horses waited his coming. And at the taking of his barge there was no less than a thousand boats full of men and women of the city of London, waffeting up and down in Thames, expecting my lord's departing, supposing that he should have gone directly from thence to the Tower, whereat they rejoiced, and I dare be bold to say that the most part never received damage at his hands.

[The king sent Wolsey private encouragement by Sir Harry Norris] to be of good cheer, for he was as much in his highness's favour as ever he was . . . And in token thereof, he delivered him a ring of gold, with a rich stone, which ring he knew very well, for it was always the privy token between the king and him whensoever the king would have any special matter dispatched at his hands; and said furthermore, "that the king commanded him to be of good cheer, and take no thought, for he should not lack. And although the king hath dealt with you unkindly as ye suppose, he saith that it is for no displeasure that he beareth you, but only to satisfy more the minds of some (which he knoweth be not your friends), than for any indignation: and also ye know right well, that he is able to recompense you with twice as much as your goods amounteth unto; and all this he bade me that I should show you; therefore, Sir, take patience. And for my part, I trust to see you in better estate than ever ye were."

But when he heard Master Norris rehearse all the good and comfortable words of the king, he quickly lighted from off his mule, all alone, as though he had been the youngest person amongst us, and incontinent kneeled down in the dirt upon both his knees, holding up his hands for joy.

At Esher, hoping for reinstatement, he abode awhile "without beds, sheets, tablecloths, cups and dishes to eat our meat, or to lie in." *Here, on All-Hallows Day, in the Great Chamber, Cavendish came on Thomas Cromwell leaning in the window and praying, with tears brimming in his eyes.*

To whom I said, "Why, Master Cromwell, what meaneth all this your sorrow? Is my lord in any danger, for whom ye lament thus? or is it for any loss that ye have sustained by any misadventure?"

"Nay, nay," quoth he, "it is my unhappy adventure, which am like to lose all that I have travailed for all the days of my life, for doing of my master true and diligent service."

Wolsey's servants were summoned to hear him say farewell. And at the last my lord came thither, apparelled in a white rocket upon a violet gown of cloth like a bishop's, who went straight into the great window. Standing there a while, and his chaplains about him, beholding the number of his servants divided in two parts, he could not speak unto them for tenderness of his heart; the flood of tears that distilled from his eyes declared no less: the which perceived by his servants, caused the fountains of water to gush out of their faithful hearts down their cheeks, in such abundance as it would cause a cruel heart to lament.

Cromwell defeated an attainder of treason in Parliament, but a writ of premunire deprived Wolsey of all the income from his benefices. To the judges who pressed the charge Wolsey replied:

"The king's highness knoweth right well whether I have offended his majesty and his laws or no, in using of my prerogative legatine, for the which ye have me indicted, notwithstanding I have the king's license in my coffers, under his hand and broad seal, for exercising and using the authority thereof, in the largest wise, within his highness's dominions, the which remaineth now in the hands of my enemies. Therefore, because I will not stand in question or trial with the king in his own cause, I am content here of mine own frank will and mind, in your presence, to confess the offence in the indictment, and put me wholly in the mercy

and grace of the king, having no doubts in his godly disposition
and charitable conscience, whom I know hath an high discretion
to consider the truth, and my humble submission and obedience."

*His exultant foes still feared him too near the King. The Duke
of Norfolk warned Cromwell that Wolsey had better take himself
to York.*

"Sir," quoth he, "me thinketh that the cardinal your master
maketh no haste northward; show him, that if he go not away
shortly, I will, rather than he should tarry still, tear him with my
teeth. Therefore I would advise him to prepare him away as
shortly as he can, or else he shall be sent forward."

*Sick, now, but still humbly protesting, Wolsey removed from
Esher to Richmond, and then, in the beginning of Passion Week,
by slow stages, to Peterborough.* And upon Maundy Thursday he
made his Maundy in our Lady's Chapel, having fifty-nine poor
men, whose feet he then washed, wiped, and kissed.

*Here Cavendish told his master men wondered why he had
confessed and thrown himself on the King's mercy instead of asserting his innocence.*

Also they marvelled much that ye, being of so excellent a wit
and high discretion, would so simply confess yourself guilty in
the premunire, wherein ye might full well have stood in the trial
of your case. For they understood, by the report of some of the
king's counsel learned, that in your case well considered, ye had
great wrong; to the which I could make, as me thought, no sufficient answer, but said, "That I doubt not your so doing was
upon some greater consideration than my wit could understand."
"Is this," quoth he, "the opinion of wise men?"
"Yea, forsooth, my lord," quoth I, "and almost of all other men."
"Well, then," quoth he, "I see that their wisdoms perceive not
the ground of the matter that moved me so to do. For I considered, that my enemies had brought the matter so to pass against
me, and conveyed it so, that they made it the king's case, and
caused the king to take the matter into his own hands and quarrel,

and after that he had upon the occasion thereof seized all my goods and possessions into his domains, and then the quarrel to be his, rather than yield, or take a foil in the law, and thereby restore to me all my goods again, would sooner (by the procurement of my enemies and evil-willers) imagine my utter undoing and destruction; whereof the most ease therein had been for me perpetual imprisonment. . . . And also there was a continual serpentine enemy about the king that would, I am well assured, if I had been found stiff-necked, have called continually upon the king in his ear (I mean the night-crow) with such a vehemency that I should with the help of her assistance have obtained sooner the king's indignation than his lawful favour; and his favour once lost (which I trust at this present I have) would never have been by me recovered. Therefore I thought it better for me to keep still his loving favour, with loss of my goods and dignities, than to win my goods and substance with the loss of his love and princely favour, which is but only death; *Quia indignatio principis mors est.*"

Then about the feast of St. Michael next ensuing my lord took his journey towards Cawood Castle, the which is within seven miles of York; and passing thither he lay two nights and a day at St. Oswald's Abbey, where he himself confirmed children in the church, from eight of the clock in the morning until eleven of the clock at noon. And making a short dinner, resorted again to the church at one of the clock, and there began again to confirm more children until four of the clock, where he was at the last constrained for weariness to sit down in a chair, the number of the children was such. That done, he said his evensong, and then went to supper, and rested him there all that night. And the next morning he applied himself to depart towards Cawood; and or ever he departed, he confirmed almost an hundred children more . . .

The time drawing nigh of his stallation; sitting at dinner, upon the Friday next before Monday on the which he intended to be stalled at York, the Earl of Northumberland and Master Walshe, with a great company of gentlemen, as well of the earl's servants as of the country, which he had gathered together to accompany him in the king's name, not knowing to what purpose or what intent, came into the hall at Cawood, the officers sitting at dinner, and my lord not fully dined, but being at his fruits, nothing knowing of the earl's being in his hall. The first thing that the earl did, after he came into the castle, commanded the porter to deliver him the keys of the gates, who would in no wise deliver him the keys . . .

Of all these doings knew my lord nothing; for they stopped the stairs that went up into my lord's chamber where he sat, so that no man could pass up again that was come down. At the last one of my lord's servants chanced to look down into the hall at a loop that was upon the stairs, and returned to my lord, and showed him that my Lord of Northumberland was in the hall; whereat my lord marvelled, and would not believe him at the first; but commanded a gentleman, being his gentleman usher, to go down and bring him perfect word.

And as soon as my lord espied the earl, he put off his cap, and said to him, "My lord, ye be most heartily welcome"; and therewith they embraced each other. "Although, my lord," quoth he, "that I have often desired, and wished in my heart to see you in my house, yet if ye had loved me as I do you, ye would have sent me word before of your coming, to the intent that I might have received you according to your honour and mine. Notwithstanding ye shall have such cheer as I am able to make with you, with a right good will; trusting that ye will accept the same of me as of your very old and loving friend, hoping hereafter to see you often, when I shall be more able and better provided to receive you with better fare."

This said, he took the earl by the hand and led him into his bedchamber. And they being there all alone, save only I, that kept the door, according to my duty, being gentleman usher; these two lords standing at a window by the chimney, in my lord's bedchamber, the earl trembling said, with a very faint and soft voice, unto my lord, laying his hand upon his arm, "My lord, I arrest you of high treason."

The next day, being Sunday, my lord prepared himself to ride when he should be commanded; and after dinner, by that time that the earl had appointed all things in good order within the castle, it drew fast to night. There was assigned to attend upon him five of us, his own servants, and no more; that was to say, I, one chaplain, his barber, and two grooms of his chamber, and when he should go down the stairs out of the great chamber, my lord demanded for the rest of his servants; the earl answered, that they were not far; the which he had inclosed within the chapel, because they should not disquiet his departure.

"Sir, I pray you," quoth my lord, "let me see them or ever I depart, or else I will never go out of this house."

"Alack, my lord," quoth the earl, "they should trouble you; therefore I beseech you to content yourself."

"Well," quoth my lord, "then will I not depart out of this house, but I will see them, and take my leave of them in this chamber."

And his servants being inclosed in the chapel, having understanding of my lord's departing away, and that they should not see him before his departure, began to grudge, and to make such a rueful noise, that the commissioners doubted some tumult or inconvenience to arise by reason thereof, thought it good to let them pass out to my lord, and that done they came to him into the great chamber where he was, and there they kneeled down before him; among whom was not one dry eye, but pitifully lamented their master's fall and trouble. To whom my lord gave comfortable words and worthy praises for their diligent faithfulness and honest truth towards him, assuring them, that what chances soever should happen unto him, that he was a true man and a just to his sovereign lord. And thus with a lamentable manner, shaking each of them by the hands, was fain to depart, the night drew so fast upon them.

The King sent Sir William Kingston, Constable of the Tower, to take Wolsey in charge. Cavendish tried to mask the ominous meaning from his master. But Wolsey was not deceived:

"I perceive [he said] more than ye can imagine, or do know; experience of old hath taught me."

Master Kingston came towards him with much reverence; and at his approach he kneeled down and saluted him on the king's behalf; whom my lord, bareheaded, offered to take up, but he still kneeled. "Then," quoth my lord, "Master Kingston, I pray you stand up, and leave your kneeling unto a very wretch replete with misery, not worthy to be esteemed, but for a vile abject, utterly cast away, without desert; and therefore, good Master Kingston, stand up, or I will myself kneel down by you."

With that Master Kingston stood up, saying, with humble reverence, "Sir, the king's majesty hath him commended unto you."

"I thank his highness," quoth my lord, "I trust he be in health, and merry, the which I beseech God long continue."

"Yea, without doubt," quoth Master Kingston: "and so hath he commanded me first to say unto you, that you should assure yourself that he beareth you as much good will and favour as ever he did; and willeth you to be of good cheer."

" 'Master Kingston,' quoth my lord, 'I thank you for your good news: and, Sir, hereof assure yourself, that if I were as able and as lusty as I have been but of late, I would not fail to ride with you in post: but, Sir, I am diseased with a flux that maketh me very weak. But, Master Kingston, all these comfortable words which ye have spoken be but for a purpose to bring me in a fool's paradise: I know what is provided for me.' "

The next day he rode to Nottingham, and there lodged that night, more sicker, and the next day we rode to Leicester Abbey; and by the way he waxed so sick that he was divers times likely to have fallen from his mule; and being night or we came to the Abbey aforesaid, where at his coming in at the gates, the abbot of the place with all his convent met him with the light of many torches; whom they right honourably received with great reverence. To whom my lord said: "Father Abbot, I am come hither to leave my bones among you;" whom they brought on his mule to the stairs foot of his chamber, and there lighted, and Master Kingston then took him by the arm, and led him up the stairs; who told me afterwards that he never carried so heavy a burden in all his life. And as soon as he was in his chamber, he went incontinent to his bed, very sick. This was upon Saturday at night; and there he continued sicker and sicker.

Upon Monday in the morning, as I stood by his bedside, about eight of the clock, the windows being close shut, having wax lights burning upon the cupboard, I beheld him, as me seemed, drawing fast to his end. He perceived my shadow upon the wall by his bedside, asked who was there?

"Sir, I am here," quoth I. "How do you?" quoth he to me. "Very well, Sir," quoth I, "if I might see your Grace well."

"What is it of the clock?" said he to me.

"Forsooth, Sir," said I, "it is past eight of the clock in the morning."

"Eight of the clock?" quoth he, "that cannot be," rehearsing divers times, "eight of the clock, eight of the clock, nay, nay," quoth he at the last, "it cannot be eight of the clock: for by eight of the clock ye shall lose your master: for my time draweth near that I must depart out of this world."

Then was he in confession the space of an hour. And when he had ended his confession, Master Kingston bade him good-morrow, for it was about seven of the clock in the morning; and asked him how he did. "Sir," quoth he, "I tarry but the will and pleasure of God, to render unto him my simple soul into his divine hands."

"Not yet so, Sir," quoth Master Kingston; "with the grace of God, ye shall live, and do very well, if ye will be of good cheer."

"Master Kingston, my disease is such that I cannot live; I have had some experience in my disease, and thus it is: I have a flux with a continual fever; the nature whereof is this, that if there be no alteration with me of the same within eight days, then must either ensue excoriation of the entrails, or frenzy, or else present death; and the best thereof is death. And, as I suppose, this is the eighth day: and if ye see in me no alteration, then is there no remedy, although I may live a day or twain, but death, which is the best remedy of the three."

"Nay, Sir, in good faith," quoth Master Kingston, "ye be in such dolor and pensiveness, doubting that thing indeed ye need not to fear, which maketh you much worse than ye should be."

"Well, well, Master Kingston," quoth he, "I see the matter against me how it is framed; but if I had served God as diligently as I have done the king, he would not have given me over in my grey hairs. Howbeit this is the just reward that I must receive for my worldly diligence and pains that I have had to do him service . . .

"He is sure a prince of a royal courage, and hath a princely heart; and rather than he will either miss or want any part of his will or appetite, he will put the loss of one half of his realm in danger; for I assure you I have often kneeled before him in his privy chamber on my knees, the space of an hour or two, to persuade him from his will and appetite: but I could never bring to pass to dissuade him therefrom. Therefore, Master Kingston, if it chance hereafter you to be one of his privy council, as for your wisdom and other qualities ye be meet so to be, I warn you to be well advised and assured what matter ye put in his head, for ye shall never put it out again.

"Master Kingston, farewell. I can no more, but wish all things to have good success. My time draweth on fast. I may not tarry with you. And forget not, I pray you, what I have said and charged you withal: for when I am dead, ye shall peradventure remember my words much better." And even with these words he began to draw his speech at length, and his tongue to fail; his eyes being set in his head, whose sight failed him. Then we began to put him in remembrance of Christ's passion; and sent for the abbot of the place to anneal him, who came with all speed, and ministered unto him all the service to the same belonging; and caused also the guard to stand by, both to hear him talk before his death, and also to witness of the same; and incontinent the clock struck eight, at which time he gave up the ghost, and thus departed he this present life.

Here is the end and fall of pride and arrogancy of such men, exalted by fortune to honours and high dignities; for I assure you, in his time of authority and glory, he was the haultest man in all his proceedings that then lived, having more respect to the worldly honour of his person than he had to his spiritual profession; wherein should be all meekness, humility, and charity; the process whereof I leave to them that be learned and seen in the divine laws.

Who list to read and consider, with an indifferent eye, this history, may behold the wondrous mutability of vain honours, the brittle assurance of abundance, the uncertainty of dignities, the flattering of feigned friends, and the tickle trust to worldly princes. Whereof this lord cardinal hath felt both of the sweet and the sour in each degree; as fleeting from honours, losing of riches, deposed from dignities, forsaken of friends, and the inconstantness of princes' favour; of all which things he hath had in this world the full felicity, as long as Fortune smiled upon him: but when she began to frown, how soon was he deprived of all these dreaming joys and vain pleasures! The which in twenty years with great travail, study, and pains obtained, were in one year and less, with heaviness, care, and sorrow, lost and consumed. O madness! O foolish desire! O fond hope! O greedy desire of vain honours, dignities, and riches! O what inconstant trust and assurance is in rolling fortune! Wherefore the prophet said full well, *Thesaurisat, et ignorat, cui congregabit ea.* Who is certain to whom he shall leave his treasure and riches that he hath gathered together in this world? it may chance him to leave it unto such as he hath purposed; but the wise man saith, That another person, who peradventure he hated in his life, shall spend it out, and consume it.

SAINTLY CHANCELLOR

NEITHER IN MAGNITUDE NOR IN DIGNITY OF CONCEPTION IS ROPER'S *Life of Sir Thomas More* comparable with Cavendish. In length it is hardly more than a rather extended biographical essay. In conception it is lyrical and touching rather than tragic; it is like a pale water-color with passages of translucent charm. Roper revered his noble-spirited father-in-law, but there were many parts of his career with which Roper was no more than faintly acquainted and he can hardly be said to have understood him at all. Some of the charm, in fact, of Roper's portrait, is derived from an air of wistful simplicity, as of a man puzzled by things he does not altogether grasp but that he knows well are high and beautiful. This feeling pervades almost all the latter part of his story, with More looking forward serenely and even with a certain gaiety to the headman's axe.

Roper says nothing of More's *Utopia* and reveals little of the wise and brave-minded iconoclast who dreamed it. He never mentions More's friendship with Erasmus; he has none of Cavendish's Renaissance splendor, nothing of the luminous hopes of Humanism. His More seems more rooted in the Middle Ages than a man of the Renaissance. Perhaps Roper was too worshipful in the wrong way; one would hardly guess from him that More was brilliantly witty, full of quips and facetiousness. Seemingly More's solemn son-in-law understood the joker as little as he did the humanist and philosopher. And if he was blind to some aspects of More, others he painted too bright. More was not so courageous a Speaker of the House of Commons as Roper portrays him. For all his pleading of religious freedom in *Utopia* he dealt drastically enough with heresy for John Foxe to call him a "bitter persecutor of good men."

The merits of Roper's portrait lie in his rendering of a personality that is sweet and good and gay. He shows the man who refrained from asking the hand of the younger sister he wanted because he could not bear to give the elder sister pain, who hoped to meet his judges "merrily" in heaven, who wrote tenderly of his daughter's grieving farewell, "I never liked your manner better than when you kissed me last," who joked and comforted the officers charged with his execution. But beneath the serenity there is sometimes a faint note of melancholy too. More would not be so intransigent as to run upon martyrdom if it could decently be avoided. But should any devious wriggling be necessary, that he would not do. "I do nobody harm, I say none harm, I think none harm, but wish everybody good; and if this be not enough to keep a man alive, in good faith I long not to live."

The Life of Sir Thomas More, Knight

written by

WILLIAM ROPER ESQUIRE,

which married Margaret,

daughter of the said Thomas More

[More died in 1535. The *Life* seems to have been penned not long after, but it was not published till 1626.]

THIS SIR THOMAS MORE, AFTER HE HAD BEEN BROUGHT UP IN THE Latin tongue at St. Anthony's in London, was by his father's procurement received into the house of the right reverend, wise, and learned prelate Cardinal Morton; where, though he was young of years, yet would he at Christmas tide suddenly step in among the players, and never studying for the matter, make a part of his own there presently among them, which made the lookers-on more sport than all the players beside. In whose wit and towardness the Cardinal much delighting, would often say of him unto the nobles that divers times dined with him: "This child here waiting at the table, whoever shall live to see it, will prove a marvelous man."

The youngster studied Greek and Latin at Oxford, entered New Inn for the study of law, and from thence was admitted to Lincoln's Inn as a barrister. Deeply religious as well as learned, he lectured for a time on St Augustine's City of God, *and devoted*

himself to meditation and prayer at the Charterhouse, until he
was attracted by the three daughters of Mr Colt, a gentleman of
Essex.

And albeit his mind most served him to the second daughter, for
that he thought her the fairest and best favored, yet when he considered that it would be both great grief and some shame also to
the eldest to see her younger sister in marriage preferred before
her, he then of a certain pity framed his fancy toward her, and
soon after married her . . .

He aroused the animosity of Henry VII by opposing in Parlia-
ment a marriage-subsidy for that monarch's daughter—it was re-
ported to the King that his schemes had been defeated by "a
beardless boy." But in the new reign More gradually came into
favor, at last entering the Privy Council.

And so from time to time was he by the Prince advanced, con-
tinuing in his singular favor and trusty service twenty years and
above, a good part whereof used the King upon holidays, when
he had done his own devotions, to send for him into his travers,
and there sometime in matters of Astronomy, Geometry, Divinity,
and such other Faculties, and sometimes of his worldly affairs,
to sit and confer with him. And other whiles would he, in the
night, have him up into his leads, there for to consider with him
the diversities, courses, motions, and operations of the stars and
planets.

And because he was of a pleasant disposition, it pleased the
King and Queen, after the Council had supped, at the time of
their supper, for their pleasure, commonly to call for him to be
merry with them. Whom when he perceived so much in his talk
to delight, that he could not once in a month get leave to go home
to his wife and children (whose company he most desired) and
to be absent from the Court two days together, but that he should
be thither sent for again, he, much misliking this restraint upon
his liberty, began thereupon somewhat to dissemble his nature,
and so by little and little from his former accustomed mirth to
disuse himself, that he was of them from thenceforth at such
seasons no more so ordinarily sent for.

In 1523 More became Speaker of the House of Commons. A little later Wolsey tried to force through an unpopular subsidy by attending the deliberations of the House and demanding that individual members reply to his arguments. But by prearrangement all remained silent.

To whom, when none of them all would give so much as one word, being before agreed, as the custom was, by their Speaker to make answer: "Masters," quoth the Cardinal, "unless it be the manner of your House, as of likelihood it is, by the mouth of your Speaker, whom you have chosen for trusty and wise, as indeed he is, in such case to utter your minds, here is without doubt a marvelous obstinate silence."

And thereupon he required answer of Master Speaker, who first reverently upon his knees [excused] the silence of the House, abashed at the presence of so noble a personage, able to amaze the wisest and best learned in the realm, and . . . [proved] that for them to make answer was it neither expedient nor agreeable with the ancient liberty of the House . . . In conclusion [he] showed that though they had all with their voices trusted him, yet except every one of them could put into his one head all their general wits, he alone in so weighty a matter was unmeet to make his grace answer.

Whereupon the Cardinal, displeased with Sir Thomas More, that had not in this Parliament in all things satisfied his desire, suddenly arose and departed.

And after the Parliament ended, in his gallery at Whitehall in Westminster, uttered to him his griefs, saying, "Would to God you had been at Rome, Master More, when I made you Speaker."

"Your grace not offended, so would I too, my lord," quoth he.

. . . For the pleasure he took in his company, would his grace [the King] suddenly come home to his house at Chelsea, to be merry with him, whither on a time, unlooked for, he came to dinner with him; and after dinner, in a fair garden of his, walked with him by the space of an hour, holding his arm about his neck. [Roper rejoiced to More at this familiar favor, but More was less elated:] "Son Roper, I may tell thee I have no cause to be

proud thereof, for if my head could win him a castle in France"
—for then was there war between us—"it should not fail to go."

*To his family he would say that it was easy to go to heaven
when you saw virtue rewarded and vice punished,* "so that you are
carried up to heaven even by the chins." *But one must expect
tribulation:* "We may not look at our pleasure to go to heaven
in featherbeds."

*When Charles V treacherously supported Adrian of Utrecht
in the Papal election instead of Wolsey, the Cardinal* "waxed so
wood . . . that he studied to invent all ways of revengement of his
grief against the Emperor." *Catherine was Charles's aunt; Henry's*
"inconstant and mutable disposition" *could easily be withdrawn
from her and perhaps settled on one of the French King's sisters.
But Henry's infatuation with Anne Boleyn smote Wolsey with
profound dismay. So Roper interprets the course of events. Catherine's trial at Blackfriars drew on, and More foresaw the growth
of heresy:*

"I pray God that some of us, as high as we seem to sit upon the
mountains, treading heretics under our feet like ants, live not
the day that we gladly would wish to be at a league and composition with them, let them have their churches quietly to themselves,
so that they would be content to let us have ours quietly to ourselves."

*Wolsey fell from power, and More succeeded him as Chancellor.
His doors were open to all suitors; he was determined on open-
handed justice to all:* "Were it my father stood on the one side,
and the Devil on the tother, his cause being good, the Devil should
have right."

*It was a precarious tightrope that More was walking. The
witty companion of royalty, the humanist friend of Erasmus, was
also a faithful son of the Church. He would dress and behave as
other more worldly men, but* "secretly next his body he ware a
shirt of hair." *He would serve Henry in other matters, but not
in that of the divorce:* "falling down upon his knees," *he humbly
reminded his sovereign that he himself had* "taught his servant,
willing him first to look onto God, and after God to him." *Henry*

graciously yielded, but More knew he would not be safe for long. He begged, on grounds of ill-health, to be allowed to resign the Chancellorship. This loss of income forced him into stringent economies; and he began to prepare his family for worse:

"What a happy and blessed thing it was for the love of God to suffer loss of goods, imprisonment, loss of lands and life also." He would further say unto them that, "upon his faith, if he might perceive his wife and children would encourage him to die in a good cause, it should so comfort him that, for very joy thereof, it would make him merely run to death."

Thomas Cromwell brought him a message from the King.

"Master Cromwell," quoth he, "you are now entered into the service of a most noble, wise, and liberal prince. If you will follow my poor advice, you shall in your council-giving unto his grace ever tell him what he ought to do, but never what he is able to do. So shall you show yourself a true faithful servant, and a right worthy Councillor. For if a Lion knew his own strength, hard were it for any man to rule him."

At last Archbishop Cranmer pronounced Henry's marriage to Catherine void. More refused to attend the coronation of Anne Boleyn. To a group of bishops he explained himself in a witty parable of a virgin who had offended an emperor but who could not be put to death because there was a law against beheading virgins, until one of the emperor's councillors said: " 'Let her first be deflowered, and then after she may be devoured.' . . . Take good heed, my lords, that you keep your virginity still. For some there be that by procuring your lordships first at the coronation to be present . . . and Finally to write books to all the world in defense thereof, are desirous to deflower you . . . Now, my lords," quoth he, "it lieth not in my power but that they may devour me; but God being my good Lord, I will provide that they shall never deflower me."

Henry tried "by terrors and threats" to bring him to surrender; these were followed by accusations of bribery and taking gifts.

The day came, as More had foreseen, when he was attainted of treason. Returning home by boat, after being cross-examined, he was positively gay. Roper said:

"I trust, Sir, that all is well because you be so merry."

"It is so indeed, son Roper, I thank God . . . In good faith, I rejoiced that I had given the Devil a foul fall, and that with those Lords I had gone so far as without great shame I could never go back again."

Summoned to appear before the Lords [again], whereas he evermore used before, at his departure from his wife and children, whom he tenderly loved, to have them bring him to his boat, and there to kiss them all, and bid them farewell, Then would he suffer none of them forth of the gate to follow him, but pulled the wicket after him, and shut them all from him; and with a heavy heart, as by his countenance it appeared, with me and our four servants there took he his boat towards Lambeth. Wherein sitting still sadly a while, at the last he suddenly rounded me in the ear, and said: "Son Roper, I thank our Lord the field is won."

He was sent to the Tower, 17 April, 1534. To his daughter, visiting him there, he said:

"I believe, Meg, that they that have put me here, ween they have done me a high displeasure. But I assure thee, on my faith, my own good daughter, if it had not been for my wife and you that be my children, whom I account the chief part of my charge, I would not have failed long ere this to have closed myself in as strait a room, and straiter too."

When Sir Thomas More had continued a good while in the Tower, my Lady, his wife, obtained license to see him . . .

"What the good yere, Master More," quoth she, "I marvel that you, that have been always hitherto taken for so wise a man, will now so play the fool to lie here in this close, filthy prison, and thus be content to be shut up amongst mice and rats, when you might be abroad at your liberty, and with the favor and good will both of the King and his Council, if you would but do as all the Bishops and best learned of this realm have done. And seeing you have at Chelsea a right fair house, your library, your books, your gallery, your garden, your orchard, and all other necessaries so handsome about you, where you might in the company of me your wife, your children, and household be merry, I muse what of God's name you mean here still thus fondly to tarry."

After he had a while quietly heard her, with a cheerful countenance he said unto her:

"I pray thee, good Mistress Alice, tell me one thing."

"What is that?" quoth she.

"Is not this house," quoth he, "as nigh heaven as my own?"

To whom she, after her accustomed homely fashion, not liking such talk, answered, "Tille valle, tille valle!"

"How say you, Mistress Alice," quoth he, "is it not so?"

"Bone deus, bone deus, man, will this gear never be left?" quoth she.

Lord Rich tried to trap More by a sophistical argument into admitting the royal supremacy over the Church. Would More not take him for king upon an act of Parliament? "Would not you, then, Master More, [upon a similar act] take me for Pope?"

"Suppose the Parliament would make a law that God should not be God. Would you, then, Master Rich, say that God were not God?"

More defended himself against the indictment by an ingenious and typically legalistic argument. He had not "spoken maliciously" against the King's supremacy, he said; he had not "denied" it, he had merely refused to "affirm" it. And he had acted not maliciously, for he had tried to remain silent, not to foment dissension by publishing his sentiments. But condemnation, of course, had been predetermined. Sentence passed, he spoke serenely to his judges:

"Though your lordships have now here on earth been judges to my condemnation, we may yet hereafter in heaven merrily all meet together, to our everlasting salvation."

On his return from Westminster, he found his daughter Meg waiting for a glimpse of him by the Tower wharf.

She, hasting towards him, and, without consideration or care of herself, pressing in among the midst of the throng and company of the guards that with halberds and bills went round about him, hastily ran to him, and there openly, in the sight of them all, embraced him, took him about the neck, and kissed him; [and even after she had left him] suddenly turned back again, ran to him as before, took him about the neck, and divers times together most lovingly kissed him; and at last, with a full heavy heart, was fain to depart from him.

That night he wrote to her:
"Tomorrow long I to go to God; it were a day very meet and convenient for me . . . I never liked your manner towards me better than when you kissed me last."

"The King's pleasure is," [Sir Thomas Pope brought him word] "that at your execution you shall not use many words."

Pope . . . could not refrain from weeping. Which Sir Thomas More perceiving, comforted him in this wise: "Quiet yourself, good Master Pope, and be not discomforted; for I trust that we shall, once in heaven, see each other full merrily, where we shall be sure to live and love together, in joyful bliss eternally."

And so was he by Master Lieutenant brought out of the Tower, and from thence led to the place of execution. Where, going up the scaffold, which was so weak that it was ready to fall, he said merrily to Master Lieutenant: "I pray you, Master Lieutenant, see me safe up, and for my coming down let me shift for myself."

Then desired he all the people thereabout to pray for him, and to bear witness with him that he should now there suffer death in and for the faith of the Holy Catholic Church. Which done, he kneeled down, and after his prayers said, turned to the executioner, and with a cheerful countenance spake thus to him:

"Pluck up thy spirits, man, and be not afraid to do thine office; my neck is very short; take heed therefore thou strike not awry, for saving of thine honesty."

So passed Sir Thomas More out of this world to God, upon the very same day in which he himself had most desired.

ICE AND SAVAGES

ONE OF OUR COMPLACENT MODERN SUPERSTITIONS IS THE DARKNESS of the Dark Ages. Little children learn at school that all medieval Europe believed in sea-serpents and other horrible monsters coiling out beyond the mists of the demon-haunted Atlantic, believed in equatorial seas boiling with the heat and dreadful marine vegetation that would twine around a vessel and draw it down into the deep, believed that foolhardy mariners who sailed too far would fall off the flat edges of the world into the emptiness of a bottomless abyss. These beliefs did exist, but they were not shared by men of any learning. The *Geography* of Ptolemy, which was used in the schools of Europe for fourteen centuries, taught that the earth was a sphere. As early as the third century B.C. Aristarchus of Samos had claimed that it revolved around the sun; Copernicus, Kepler, and Galileo were to revive and prove ideas that educated Europe had never entirely forgotten.

Howling storms and cockleshell ships and the uncertainties of setting a course by blind guess were the real dangers and deterrents of navigation. The Portuguese edged their way cautiously down the coast of Africa; now and then a daring sailor made a dash out into the unknown like a chick fearful of getting lost before it fled back to the brood in a panicky return. The mariner's compass made it possible for the seafarer to steer boldly west and still beat his way home. Then the western water route to that Cathay of which Marco Polo had painted a glowing picture began to seem more and more feasible. The great age of exploration got under way in the fifteenth century, with the achievements of Prince

Henry the Navigator, of Columbus, the great "admiral of the ocean sea," and of Balboa and Magellan.

Seeking a northwest passage to India, in 1497 John Cabot discovered the mainland of North America for England. But the English did not really join the seamen of Genoa and Venice, of Portugal and Spain, in the great imperial game of exploration and discovery until the next century. Then came the exploits of Drake, Hawkins, Gilbert, Raleigh, Frobisher, Davys, Willoughby, and a host of others. Merchants, freebooters, soldiers, adventurers, explorers, pirates, and patriots all in one, they laid the foundations of England's enormous maritime Empire.

Their motives were varied. Greed of gold was one. Always the wealth of India, the Spice Islands, Cathay, allured imaginations. There were the Spaniards with the spoils of Mexico and Peru to be plundered, emeralds, topazes, and rubies to be seized, mines to be gutted, the silks of the East to be brought home. Patriotism was hardly less powerful. With the Pope carving up the New World between Portugal and Spain, it was important that England step in and grab her share. Love of adventure played a part: the excitement of battle with naked and painted savages, the dangers lurking in dark jungles, antres vast, wild beasts, cannibals, the blue towering masses of icebergs and the frozen wastes of Arctic seas.

Nor was the sense of wonder absent. Men were participating in the enlargement of the world; they dwelt in a universe whose physical boundaries and whose intellectual growth they were themselves constantly expanding. Its former constrained limits aroused amazement that they could have been borne: "A marvelous thing," George Best exclaims, "that man, who hath always abhorred so much thralldom and restraint, and so greedily desired liberty, could be contented so many thousand years, to be shut up in so narrow bounds." More's *Utopia* and Bacon's *New Atlantis* were inspired by the brave new worlds of the explorers to even larger wonders of thought and imagination beyond all previous knowledge.

Such are the enthusiasms Hakluyt feeds and voices. His *Principal Navigations, Voyages, and Discoveries of the English Nation,*

*made by sea or over land to the most remote and farthest distant
quarters of the earth at any time within the compass of these 1600
years* (such is its full generous title) collects all that Richard Hakluyt could gather together, from the legendary conquests of King
Arthur to the authentic narratives of Frobisher's search for the
northwest passage and Grenville's defense of the *Revenge*.

Best's accounts of the three voyages of Frobisher speak for themselves. The narrow passages north of Labrador through which
Frobisher made his way, and which he believed would be found
to extend to Cathay itself, still bear his name. The Northern Indians Best describes are neither as picturesque as those Columbus
found in Hispaniola nor as civilized as the Aztecs. The gold ore
he tells us they loaded on board proved not to repay the high expenses of the voyage. But the wild imaginative hopes, the cool
European habit of regarding natives as something between curiosi-
ties and cattle, the sharp pursuit of material gain, all are there.
And so are the wonder and excitement, the bravery, the devotion,
and the endurance.

The Second Voyage of Martin Frobisher

GEORGE BEST

[Best's narratives were first published in 1578. Hakluyt's first published work, *Divers Voyages Touching
the Discovery of America,* appeared in 1582. The
Principal Navigations made its appearance in 1589,
and an enlarged second edition in three volumes followed in 1598, 1599, and 1600.]

BEING FURNISHED WITH ONE TALL SHIP OF HER MAJESTY'S, NAMED
the *Aid,* of two hundred ton, and two other small barks, the one
named the *Gabriel,* the other the *Michael,* about thirty ton apiece,
being fitly appointed with men, munition, victuals, and all things
necessary for the voyage, the said Captain Frobisher, with the rest
of his company, came aboard his ships riding at Blackwall, intending (with God's help) to take the first wind and tide serving him,
the five and twentieth day of May, in the year of our Lord God, a
thousand five hundred seventy and seven.

On Monday morning the 27 of May, aboard the *Aid,* we received all the Communion, by the Minister of Gravesend, and prepared us, as good Christians towards God, and resolute men for all
fortunes: and towards night we departed to Tilbury Hope . . .
And sailing northward along the east coasts of England and Scotland, the seventh day of June, we arrived in Saint Magnus Sound
in Orkney Islands, called in Latin *Orcades,* and came to anchor on
the south side of the Bay.

Here our company going on land, the inhabitants of these

islands began to flee, as from the enemy, whereupon the Lieutenant willed every man to stay together, and went himself unto their houses to declare what we were and the cause of our coming thither, which being understood, after their poor manner they friendly entreated us, and brought us for our money such things as they had. And here our goldfinders found a mine of silver.

After we had provided us here of matter sufficient for our voyage, the 8 of June we set sail again, and passing through Saint Magnus Sound, having a merry wind by night, came clear and lost sight of all the land, and keeping our course west-northwest by the space of two days, the wind shifted upon us, so that we lay in traverse on the seas, with contrary, making good (as near as we could) our course to the westward, and sometimes to the northward, as the wind shifted . . . We traversed these seas by the space of 26 days, without sight of any land, and met with much drift wood and whole bodies of trees. We saw many monstrous fish, and strange fowl, which seemed to live only by the sea, being there so far distant from any land. At length God favored us with more prosperous winds, and after we had sailed four days with good wind in the poop, the 4th of July the *Michael* (being foremost ahead) shot off a piece of ordinance, and struck all her sails, supposing that they descried land, which by reason of the thick mists they could not make perfect: howbeit, as well our account, as also the great alteration of the water, which became more black and smooth, did plainly declare we were not far off the coast.

It is a marvelous thing to behold, of what great bigness and depth some islands of ice be here, some seventy or eighty fathoms under the water, besides that which is above, seeming islands more than half a mile in circuit. All these ice are in taste fresh, and seem to be bred in the sounds thereabouts, or in some land near the pole, and with the wind and tides are driven along the coasts. We found none of these islands of ice salt in taste, whereby appeareth they were not congealed of the ocean sea water, which is always salt, but of some standing or little moving lakes or great fresh waters near the shore, caused either by melted snow from the tops of mountains or by continual access of fresh rivers from the land, and intermingling with sea water, bearing yet the dominion (by the force of the extreme frost) may cause some part of salt water to freeze so with it, and so seem a little brackish, but otherwise the main sea freezeth not, and therefore there is no *mare glaciale* or frozen sea as the opinion hitherto hath been.

By the 18th of July they made the straits named after their leader. Here they had some parleying with natives, at first friendly, but presently, through a misunderstanding, breaking out into a conflict in which the savages chased the English to their boats "and hurt the general in the buttock with an arrow." *One of the savages was captured in the skirmish.*

This day also were divers storms and flaws, and by nine of the clock at night the storm was grown so great, and continued such until the morning, that it put our ships at sea in no small peril, for having mountains of floating ice on every side we went romer for one and luffed for another, some scraped us, and some happily escaped us, that the least of all of them were as dangerous to strike as any rock, and able to have split the strongest ship of the world.

Upon the two and twentieth of July we bare into the said sound, and came to anchor a reasonable breadth off the shore, where, thinking ourselves in good security, we were greatly endangered with a piece of drift ice, which the ebb brought forth of the sounds, and came thwart us ere we were aware.

Upon a small island within this sound, called Smith's Island (because he first set up his forge there), was found a mine of silver, but was not won out of the rocks without great labor. Here our goldfinders made assay of such ore as they found upon the Northerland, and found four sorts thereof to hold gold in good quantity. Upon another small island here was also found a great dead fish, which, as it should seem, had been embayed with ice, and was in proportion round like to a porpoise, being about twelve feet long, and in bigness answerable, having a horn of two yards long growing out of the snout or nostrils. This horn is wreathed and strait, like in fashion to a taper made of wax, and may be truly be thought to be the sea unicorn. This horn is to be seen and reserved as a jewel, by the Queen's majesty's commandment in her wardrobe of robes.

. . . In one of the small islands here, we found a tomb, wherein the bones of a dead man lay together, and our savage being with us and demanded by signs whether his countrymen had not slain this man and eat his flesh so from the bones, he made signs to the contrary, and that he was slain with wolves and wild beasts. Here also was found hid under stones good store of fish, and sundry other things of the inhabitants: as sleds, bridles, kettles of fish skins, knives of bone, and such other like. And our savage declared unto us the use of all those things. And taking in his hand one of those country bridles, he caught one of our dogs and hampered him handsomely therein, as we do our horses, and with a whip in his hand, he taught the dog to draw in a sled, as we do horses in a coach, setting himself thereupon like a guide: so that we might see they use dogs for that purpose as we do our horses. And we found since by experience that the lesser sort of dogs they feed fat and keep them as domestic cattle in their tents, for their eating, and the greater sort serve for the use of drawing their sleds.

. . . Upon the mainland over against the Countess's Island, we discovered and beheld to our great marvel the poor caves and houses of those country people which serve them (as it should seem) for their winter dwellings, and are made two fathom under ground, in compass round, like to an oven, being joined fast one by another, having holes like to a fox or coney burrow, to keep and come together. They undertrench these places with gutters, so that the water falling from the hills above them may slide away without their annoyance, and are seated commonly in the foot of a hill, to shield them better from the cold winds, having their door and entrance ever open towards the south.

From the ground upward they build with whales' bones, for lack of timber, which, bending one over another, are handsomely compacted in the top together, and are covered over with seals' skins, which instead of tiles fenceth them from the rain. In each house they have only one room, having the one half the floor raised with broad stones a foot higher than the other, whereon strewing moss, they make their nests to sleep in. They defile these dens most filthily with their beastly feeding, and dwell so long in a place (as we think) until their own sluttishness loathing them they are forced to seek a sweeter air and a new seat, and are (no doubt) a dispersed and wandering nation, as the Tartarians, and live in hordes and troops, without any certain abode, as may appear by sundry circumstances of our experience.

In the hope that some of their men who had been captured hereabouts on the previous voyage might still be preserved alive, Frobisher's company tried to seize some natives as hostages for exchange. A hot skirmish ensued.

[The natives], desperately returning upon our men, resisted them manfully in their landing, so long as their arrows and darts lasted; and after gathering up those arrows which our men shot at them, yea, and plucking our arrows out of their bodies, encountered fresh again, and maintained their cause until both weapons and life utterly failed them. And when they found they were mortally wounded, being ignorant what mercy meaneth, with deadly fury they cast themselves headlong from off the rocks into the sea, lest perhaps their enemies should receive glory or prey of their dead carcasses; for they supposed us to be like cannibals or eaters of man's flesh.

In this conflict one of our men was dangerously hurt in the belly with one of their arrows, and of them were slain five or six. The rest by flight escaped among the rocks, saving two women, whereof the one being old and ugly, our men thought she had been a devil or some which, and therefore let her go: the other being young, and cumbered with a sucking child at her back, hiding herself among the rocks, was espied by one of our men, who, supposing she had been a man, shot through the hair of her head and pierced through the child's arm, whereupon she cried out and was taken, and our surgeon, meaning to heal her child's arm, applied salves thereunto. But she, not acquainted with such kind of surgery, plucked those salves away, and by continually licking with her own tongue, not much unlike our dogs, healed up the child's arm.

Having now got a woman captive for the comfort of our man, we brought them both together, and every man with silence desired to behold the manner of their meeting and entertainment, the which was more worth the beholding than can well be expressed by writing. At their first encountering, they beheld each the other very wistly a good space, without speech or word uttered, with great change of color and countenance, as though it seemed the grief and disdain of their captivity had taken away the use of their tongues and utterance. The woman at the first very suddenly, as though she disdained or regarded not the man, turned away and began to sing, as though she minded another matter. But being again brought together, the man brake the silence first, and with stern and staid countenance began to tell a long solemn tale to the woman, whereunto she gave good hearing, and interrupted him nothing till he had finished, and afterwards being grown into more familiar acquaintance by speech, were turned together, so that (I think) the one would hardly have lived without the comfort of the other.

And, for so much as we could perceive, albeit they lived continually together, yet did they never use as man and wife, though the woman spared not to do all necessary things that appertained to a good housewife indifferently for them both, as in making clean their cabin, and every other thing that appertained to his ease: for when he was seasick she would make him clean, she would kill and flay the dogs for their eating and dress his meat. Only I think it worth noting the continency of them both; for the man would never shift himself, except he had first caused the woman to depart out of his cabin, and they both were most shamefast lest any of their privy parts should be discovered either of themselves or any other body.

Now had the general altered his determination for going any further into the straits at this time, for any further discovery of the passage, having taken a man and a woman of that country, which he thought sufficient for the use of language; and having also met with these people here which intercepted his men the last year (as the apparel and English furniture which was found in their

tents very well declared), he knew it was but labor lost to seek
them further off, when he had found them there at hand. And
considering also the short time he had in hand, he thought it best
to bend his whole endeavor for the getting of mine, and to leave
the passage further to be discovered hereafter. For his commission
directed him in this voyage only for the searching of the gold
ore, and to defer the further discovery of the passage until another time.

On Wednesday, the fourteenth of August, our general, with
two small boats, well appointed; for that he suspected the country people to lie lurking thereabout, went up a certain bay within
the Countess's Sound, to search for ore, and met again with the
country people, who so soon as they saw our men made great outcries and with a white flag made of bladders, sewed together with
the guts and sinews of beasts, wafted us amain unto them, but
showed not above three of their company. But when we came
near them, we might perceive a great multitude creeping behind
the rocks, which gave us good cause to suspect their traitorous
meaning: whereupon we made them signs that if they would lay
their weapons aside and come forth we would deal friendly with
them, though their intent was manifested unto us. But for all
the signs of friendship we could make them, they came still creeping towards us behind the rocks to get more advantage of us, as
though we had no eyes to see them, thinking belike that our
single wits could not discover so bare device and simple drifts of
theirs.

Their spokesman earnestly persuaded us, with many enticing
notices, to come, eat, and sleep ashore, with great arguments of
courtesy, and clapping his bare hands over his head in token of
peace and innocency, willed us to do the like. But the better to
allure our hungry stomachs, he brought us a trim bait of raw
flesh which, for fashion sake, with a boathook, we caught into our
boat: but when the cunning cater perceived his first cold morsel
could nothing sharpen our stomachs he cast about for a new train
of warm flesh to procure our appetites, wherefore he caused one
of his fellows in halting manner to come forth as a lame man from

behind the rocks, and the better to declare his kindness in carving, he hoisted him upon his shoulders, and bringing him hard to the water side where we were, left him there limping, an easy prey to be taken of us. His hope was that we would bite at this bait, and speedily leap ashore within their danger, whereby they might have apprehended some of us to ransom their friends home again, which before we had taken: but, I doubt, our flesh is so sweet meat for them that they will hardly part from so good morsels if we come once near their handling.

The gentlemen and soldiers had great will to encounter them ashore, but the general more careful by process of time to win them than wilfully at the first to spoil them, would in no wise admit that any man should put himself in hazard ashore, considering the matter he now intended was for the ore and not for the conquest. Notwithstanding, to prove this cripple's footmanship, he gave liberty for one to shoot: whereupon, the cripple having a parting blow, lightly recovered a rock, and went away a true and no feigned cripple, and hath learned his lesson for ever halting afore such cripples again. But his fellows which lay hid before, full quickly there appeared in their likeness, and maintained the skirmish with their slings, bows, and arrows very fiercely, and came as near as the water suffered them: and with as desperate mind as hath been seen in any men, without fear of shot or any thing, followed us all along the coast, but all their shot fell short of us, and are of little danger. They had belaid all the coast along for us, and being dispersed so, were not well to be numbered, but we might discern of them above one hundred persons, and had cause to suspect a greater number. And thus, without loss or hurt, we returned to our ships again.

Now, our work growing towards an end, and having only with five poor miners, and the help of a few gentlemen and soldiers, brought aboard almost two hundred ton of gold ore, in the space of twenty days, every man therewithal well comforted, determined lustily to work afresh for a bon voyage, to bring our labor to a speedy and happy end.

And upon Wednesday, at night, being the one and twentieth of August, we fully finished the whole work. And it was now good time to leave; for, as the men were well wearied, so their shoes and clothes were well worn, their baskets' bottoms torn out, their tools broken, and the ships reasonably well filled. Some with over-straining themselves received hurts not a little dangerous, some having their bellies broken, and other their legs made lame. And about this time the ice began to congeal and freeze about our ships' sides a night, which gave us a good argument of the sun's declining southward, and put us in mind to make more haste homeward.

The 24 of August, about three of the clock in the morning, having the wind large at west, we set sail again, and by nine of the clock at night we left the Queen's Forland astern us, and being clear of the Straits, we bare further into the main ocean, keeping our course more southerly, to bring ourselves the sooner under the latitude of our own climate.

The wind was very great at sea, so that we lay a hull all night, and had snow half a foot deep on the hatches . . .

The thirtieth of August, with the force of the wind, and a surge of the sea, the master of the *Gabriel* and the boatswain were stricken both overboard, and hardly was the boatswain recovered, having hold on a rope hanging overboard in the sea, and yet the bark was laced fore and aft with ropes a breast high within board.

The sixteenth of September, about eight of the clock in the morning sounding, we had sixty-five fathom osey sand, and thought ourselves thwart of Saint George's Channel a little within the banks. And bearing a small sail all night, we made many soundings, which were about forty fathoms, and so shallow that we could not well tell where we were.

The seventeenth of September we sounded, and had forty fathom, and were not far off the Land's End, branded sand with small worms and cockle-shells, and were shot between Scilly and Land's End, and being within the bay, we were not able to double the point with a south-and-by-east way, but were fain to make another board, the wind being at southwest-and-by-west, and yet could not double the point, to come clear of the Land's End to bear along the Channel: and the weather cleared up when we were hard aboard the shore, and we made the Land's End perfect, and so put up alongst Saint George's Channel: and the weather being very foul at sea, we coveted some harbor, because our steerage was broken, and so came to anchor in Padstowe Road in Cornwall.

About a month later they came to Bristol, where they found the Gabriel *already arrived.*

Here we heard good tidings also of the arrival of the other bark called the *Michael,* in the north parts, which was not a little joyful unto us, that it pleased God so to bring us to a safe meeting again, and lost in the voyage only one man, besides one that died at sea, which was sick before he came aboard, and was so desirous to follow this enterprise that he rather chose to die therein than not be one to attempt so notable a voyage.

FLAMES AT SMITHFIELD

EDWARD VI, THE SICKLY MALE HEIR OF HENRY VIII, DIED IN 1553 after a reign of only six years. Mary, Henry's daughter by Catherine of Aragon, came to the throne. Two years later Papal Supremacy was restored, the laws against heresy revived, and the Church of which Mary's father had declared himself head subjected to fiery persecution. Obstinate Protestants were sent to burning in droves.

Foxe's *Book of Martyrs* is a detailed chronicle of these trials and condemnations and burnings. Beginning with a cursory sketch of the persecutions of early Christians and the career of the Emperor Constantine, who made Christianity the official religion of the Roman Empire, it outlines the lives of reformers such as Wickliff, Huss, and the Lollards, and then focuses upon those sent to the stake under Mary Tudor. There are long and repetitious stretches dry with the slag and ashes of theological controversy, character is too often dimmed under a dust of undiscriminating piety, and the plan, a clumsy mingling of chronicle and biography, is tedious and cumbersome. But character comes in flashes, the bullying violence of Gardiner of Winchester, the milk-mildness and intellectual intricacy of Cranmer, the ringing courage of Latimer; and through the wandering narrative and holy rhetoric again and again drama rises to a glare of horror as the narratives speed toward their dreadful ends with smoke rising round the figures bound in chains. Then Foxe's dark dramas have the horrible fascination of the Elizabethan tragedy of blood, with its barbarous revenges and piles of slain.

Hardly less than Protestant edification, these facts probably account both for the immediate success of Foxe's work and the long popularity it enjoyed in many homes where the *Bible* and *Pilgrim's Progress* were its only companions. Foxe's account of Cranmer is the most subtle, psychologically revealing, and varied in dramatic texture. There are his involved arguments on Henry's divorce and Henry's jubilant, "That man has the sow by the right ear!" and his trial under Queen Mary, with the judges gagging his efforts to plead: "Short arguments, master doctor! short arguments!" and the cunning of his last minute affirmation of faith at the very stake, while consternated doctors yelp and bawl: "Stop the heretic's mouth!" But the extract here given, the deaths of Latimer and Ridley, is a nobler piece of prose, and rises to a more tragic evocation of horror.

The Acts and Monuments

Popularly Known As

The Book of Martyrs

JOHN FOXE

[The Acts and Monuments was published in 1563.]

UPON THE NORTH SIDE OF THE TOWN, IN THE DITCH OVER AGAINST Balliol College, the place of execution was appointed: and for fear of any tumult that might arise, to let the burning of them, the Lord Williams was commanded by the Queen's letters, to be there assistant, sufficiently appointed. And when everything was in readiness, the prisoners were brought forth.

Master Ridley had a fair black gown furred, and faced with foins, such as he was wont to wear being bishop, and a tippet of velvet furred likewise about his neck, a velvet nightcap upon his head, and a corner cap upon the same, going in a pair of slippers to the stake, between the mayor and an alderman.

After him came Master Latimer, in a poor Bristol frieze frock all worn, with his buttoned cap, and a kerchief on his head, a new long shroud hanging over his hose, down to the feet.

Master Ridley, looking back, espied Master Latimer coming after, unto whom he said, "Oh, be ye there!" "Yea," said Master Latimer, "have after as fast as I can follow." So at length they both came to the stake. Dr. Ridley, marvelous earnestly holding up both his hands, looked towards heaven. Then espying Master

Latimer, with a wondrous cheerful look he ran to him, embraced and kissed him; and comforted him, saying, "Be of good heart, brother, for God will either assuage the fury of the flame, or else strengthen us to abide it." With that went he to the stake, kneeled down by it, kissed it, and most effectuously prayed, and behind him Master Latimer kneeled, as earnestly calling upon God as he.

Then Dr Smith began his sermon to them upon this text of St Paul, "If I yield my body to the fire to be burnt, and have not charity, I shall gain nothing thereby." Wherein he alleged that the goodness of the cause and not the order of death, maketh the holiness of a person; which he confirmed by the example of Judas, and of a woman in Oxford that of late hanged herself. He ended with a very short exhortation to them to recant, and come home again to the church, and save their lives and souls.

Dr Ridley said to Master Latimer, "Will you begin to answer the sermon or shall I?" Master Latimer said, "Begin you first, I pray you." "I will," said Master Ridley.

Then, the wicked sermon being ended, Dr Ridley and Master Latimer kneeled down upon their knees towards my Lord Williams of Thame, unto whom Master Ridley said, "I beseech you, my lord, even for Christ's sake, that I may speak but two or three words." And whilst my lord bent his head to the mayor and vice-chancellor, to know whether he might give him leave to speak, the bailiffs and Dr Marshal, vice-chancellor, ran hastily unto him, and with their hands stopped his mouth, and said, "Master Ridley, if you will revoke your erroneous opinions, and recant the same, you shall have not only liberty so to do, but also the benefit of a subject: that is, your life."

"Not otherwise?" said Master Ridley.

"No," quoth Dr Marshal.

"Well," quoth Master Ridley, "so long as the breath is in my body, I will never deny my Lord Christ, and His known truth: God's will be done in me!"

Incontinently they were commanded to make them ready, which they with all meekness obeyed. Master Ridley took his gown and his tippet, and gave it to his brother-in-law, Master Shipside. Some other of his apparel that was little worth, he gave away; other the bailiffs took. He gave away besides, divers other small things to gentlemen standing by, pitifully weeping, as to Sir Henry Lea a new groat; and to divers of my Lord Williams's gentlemen some napkins, some nutmegs, and rases of ginger; his dial, and such other things as he had about him, to every one that stood next him. Some plucked the points off his hose. Happy was he that might get any rag of him.

Master Latimer very quietly suffered his keeper to pull off his hose, and his other array, which was very simple: being stripped into his shroud, he seemed as comely a person to them that were there present, as one should see: and whereas in his clothes he appeared a withered and crooked old man, he now stood bolt upright, as comely a father as one might lightly behold.

Master Ridley held up his hand and said, "O heavenly Father, I give unto thee most hearty thanks, for that Thou hast called me to be a professor of Thee, even unto death. I beseech Thee, Lord God, take mercy upon this realm of England, and deliver the same from all her enemies."

Then the smith took a chain of iron, and brought the same about both Dr. Ridley's and Master Latimer's middles: and, as he was knocking in a staple, Dr. Ridley took the chain in his hand, and shaked the same, and looking aside to the smith, said. "Good fellow, knock it in hard, for the flesh will have his course." Then his brother did bring him gunpowder in a bag, and would have tied the same about his neck. Master Ridley asked what it was. His brother said, "Gunpowder." "Then," said he, "I take it to be sent of God; therefore I will receive it as sent of Him. And have you any," said he, "for my brother"; meaning Master Latimer. "Yea sir, that I have," quoth his brother. "Then give it unto him," said he, "betime; lest ye come too late." So his brother went, and carried off the same gunpowder unto Master Latimer.

Then they brought a faggot, kindled with fire, and laid the same down at Dr Ridley's feet. To whom Master Latimer spake in this manner: "Be of good comfort, Master Ridley, and play the man. We shall this day light such a candle, by God's grace, in England, as I trust shall never be put out."

When Dr. Ridley saw the fire flaming up towards him, he cried with a wonderful loud voice, "Lord, Lord, receive my spirit." Master Latimer, crying as vehemently on the other side, "O Father of heaven, receive my soul!" received the flame as it were embracing of it. After that he had stroked his face with his hands, and as it were bathed them a little in the fire, he soon died (as it appeareth) with very little pain or none.

By reason of the evil making of the fire unto Master Ridley, because the wooden faggots were laid about the gorse, and over-high built, the fire burned first beneath, being kept down by the wood; which, when Master Ridley felt, he desired them for Christ's sake to let the fire come unto him. Which when his brother-in-law heard, but not well understood, intending to rid him out of his pain (for the which cause he gave attendance), as one in such sorrow not well advised what he did, he heaped faggots upon him, so that he clean covered him, which made the fire more vehement beneath, that it burned clean all his nether parts, before it once touched the upper; and that made him often desire them to let the flame come unto him, saying, "I cannot burn." Which indeed appeared well; for, after his legs were consumed he showed that side towards us clean, shirt and all untouched with flame. Yet in all this torment he forgot not to call unto God, having in his mouth, "Lord have mercy upon me," intermingling his cry, "Let the fire come unto me, I cannot burn."

In which pangs he labored till one of the standers-by with his bill pulled off the faggots above, and where he saw the fire flame up Master Ridley wrested himself unto that side. And when the flame touched the gunpowder, he was seen to stir no more.

It moved hundreds to tears, in beholding the horrible sight; for I think there was none that had not clean exiled all humanity and mercy, which would not have lamented to behold the fury of the fire so to rage upon their bodies. Signs there were of sorrow on every side. Some took it grievously to see their deaths, whose lives they held full dear: some pitied their persons, that thought their souls had no need thereof. Well! dead they are, and the reward of this world they have already. What reward remaineth for them in heaven, the day of the Lord's glory, when He cometh with His saints, shall declare.

TORTURED AMBITION

THE DEEPEST QUALITIES IN JOHN DONNE WERE HIS AMBITIONS, HIS sensual passions, and the fierce vacillations of his religious emotions. But these are only hinted at as undercurrents far beneath the serene stream of Walton's style through which we may only now and then perceive a streak suggesting more violent eddies than ever reach the unflurried surface. His worldly hopes are barely suggested, his youthful excesses no more than implied in a solitary phrase much later on. His struggles to discipline himself to resignation for his failure to attain the seat of power are presented only as doubts of his fitness for priesthood. His variations, from rejoicing in his salvation to fits of black despair, are portrayed only as the signs of a saintly piety.

Certainly Donne had piety, but it was not the saint who wrote those tortured dissections of sexual passion; who described love as "the tyrant Pike, our hearts the Fry," and furiously called love a spider that "can convert manna to gall." Nor was even the religious poet the serene and resigned spirit implied by the three poems Walton transcribes. There is more of Donne in "Batter my heart, three-person'd God" than in his *Hymn to God the Father;* infinitely more in

> *At the round earth's imagin'd corners, blow*
> *Your trumpets, Angels,*

with its agonized and trembling close.

The truth is that Walton was himself inclined to a devoutly reflective temper that colors his rendering of all his subjects. The clever diplomat Wotton and the unworldly Hooker, the courtly Herbert and the learned Dr Sanderson, are all subdued to a strangely marble sameness like memorial images in a college chapel. Walton does not lie: the Bishop of Chichester's "Honest Izaak" is justified. He only arranges, and thereby emphasizes the "more contemplative side of English life in the seventeenth century," to use Professor Saintsbury's words, that mingled with the explosive energies of the Renaissance and the drab rigors of Puritanism. Throughout all five of his biographies Walton's unobtrusive hand is forever molding and clipping what he will not conceal.

This requires art. And Walton has art: his arrangement is skilful, his style is translucent, his scenes are clear vignettes, his simplicity veils a subtle urbanity, with occasional exquisite touches of faint raillery. He conveys the feeling of being deeply at home with his subjects. Beneath his sympathy there is even a sly humor, sometimes making fun of his characters and sometimes of himself. Who could miss the hidden smile behind his comments on his own tendency to digression, or the quiet enjoyment with which he tells us of Hooker allowing his landlady to persuade him that he needed a wife and being surprised but not rebellious when she chose her own hardly attractive daughter?

If we bring to Walton's subtlety a matching subtlety of our own, much will be revealed beneath that pensive stillness of his. Then we may see the dark night of the soul out of which Donne carried himself and his listeners to heaven in holy raptures as he leaned over the pulpit of St. Paul's; the anguish that engendered his intricate poems and the terrible and magnificent sermons. The proud and bitter man lusted after the fleshpots all his life. God had favored him by denial; he had been blessed, and was a sinner to go on desiring; he would *not* be stubborn. But it was all useless.

The Life of Dr. John Donne,

Late Dean of St. Paul's Church, London

IZAAK WALTON

[The dates of Walton's *Lives* are: Donne, 1640; Wotton, 1651; Hooker, 1655; Herbert, 1670; Sanderson, 1678. The first four were collected in one volume in 1670.]

JOHN DONNE WAS BORN IN LONDON IN 1573, DESCENDED ON HIS *mother's side from the family of Sir Thomas More; and the family still retained Roman leaning, for Donne's tutors, who were secretly of that faith,* "were advised to instil into him particular principles of the Romish Church." *But he made no profession of faith, and so was enabled to enter Oxford in his eleventh year, where his abilities caused him to be hailed as another Pico della Mirandola. He avoided the test of taking an Oath by removing to Cambridge before taking a degree. No profession was open in England to an avowed Catholic; at about nineteen Donne began to study Divinity to determine where his heart should lie. Fortunately for his worldly prospects, his heart chose the Church of England:* "Truth had too much light about her," *writes Walton,* "to be hid from so sharp an inquirer; and he had too much ingenuity not to acknowledge that he had found her."

He was with the Earl of Essex's naval expeditions to Cadiz and the Azores in 1596 and 1597, and then spent several years in Italy and Spain.

Not long after his return into England, that exemplary Pattern of Gravity and Wisdom, the Lord Elsemore, then Keeper of the Great Seal, and Lord Chancellour of England, taking notice of his Learning, Languages, and other Abilities, and much affecting his Person and Behaviour, took him to be his chief Secretary; supposing and intending it to be an Introduction to some more weighty Employment in the State; for which, his Lordship did often protest, he thought him very fit.

Nor did his Lordship in this time of Master Donne's attendance upon him, account him to be so much his Servant, as to forget he was his Friend; and to testifie it, did alwayes use him with much courtesie, appointing him a place at his own Table, to which he esteemed his Company and Discourse to be a great Ornament.

He continued that employment for the space of five years, being daily useful, and not mercenary to his Friends. During which time he (I dare not say unhappily) fell into such a liking, as (with her approbation) increased into a love with a young Gentlewoman that lived in that Family, who was Niece to the Lady Elsemore, and Daughter to Sir George Moor, then Chancellor of the Garter and Lieutenant of the Tower.

Sir George had some intimation of it, and knowing prevention to be a great part of wisdom, did therefore remove her with much haste from that to his own house at Lothesley, in the County of Surrey; but too late, by reason of some faithful promises which were so interchangeably passed, as never to be violated by either party.

These promises were only known to themselves, and the friends of both parties used much diligence, and many arguments to kill or cool their affections to each other: but in vain; for love is a flattering mischief, that hath denied aged and wise men a foresight of those evils that too often prove to be the children of that blind father, a passion! that carries us to commit Errors with as much ease as whirlwinds remove feathers, and begets in us an unwearied industry to the attainment of what we desire. And such an Industry did, notwithstanding much watchfulness against it, bring them secretly together (I forbear to tell the manner how) and at last to a marriage too, without the allowance of those friends, whose approbation always was, and ever will be necessary, to make even a vertuous love become lawful.

And that the knowledge of their marriage might not fall, like an unexpected tempest, on those that were unwilling to have it so: and, that preapprehensions might make it the less enormous, when it was known: it was purposely whispered into the ears of many that it was so, yet by none that could affirm it. But, to put a period to the jealousies of Sir George (Doubt often begetting more restless thoughts than the certain knowledge of what we fear) the news was in favour to Mr. Donne, and with his allowance, made known to Sir George, by his honourable friend and neighbour Henry Earl of Northumberland: but it was to Sir George so immeasurably unwelcome, and, so transported him; that as though his passion of anger and inconsideration, might exceed theirs of love and errour, he presently engaged his Sister the Lady Elsemore, to join with him to procure her Lord to discharge Mr. Donne of the place he held under his Lordship.—This request was followed with violence; and though Sir George were remembered, that Errors might be overpunished, and desired therefore to forbear till second considerations might clear some scruples: yet, he became restless until his suit was granted, and the punishment executed. And though the Lord Chancellor did not at Mr. Donne's dismission, give him such a Commendation as the great Emperor Charles the Fifth, did of his Secretary Eraso, when he presented him to his Son and Successor Philip the Second, saying, That in his Eraso, he gave to him a greater gift then all his Estate, and all the Kingdoms which he then resigned to him: yet the Lord Chancellor said, "He parted with a Friend; and such a Secretary as was fitter to serve a King then a Subject."

Immediately after his dismission from his service, he sent a sad Letter to his Wife, to acquaint her with it: and, after the subscription of his name, writ,

John Donne, Anne Donne, Vn-done,

and God knows it proved too true.

For this bitter Physick of Mr. Donne's dismission was not strong enough to purge out all Sir George's choler; for, he was not satis-

fied till Mr. Donne and his sometime Compupil in Cambridge
that married him; namely, Samuel Brook (who was after Doctor
in Divinity, and Master of Trinity Colledge) and his brother Mr.
Christopher Brook, sometime Mr. Donne's Chamber-fellow in
Lincolns-Inn, who gave Mr. Donne his Wife, and witnessed the
marriage, were all committed, to three several prisons.

Mr. Donne was first enlarged, who neither gave rest to his
body or brain, nor to any friend in whom he might hope to have
an interest, until he had procured an enlargement for his two imprisoned friends.

He was now at liberty; but his days were still cloudy: and being
past these troubles, others did still multiply upon him; for his
wife was (to her extreme sorrow) detained from him; and though
with Jacob he endured not an hard service for her, yet he lost a
good one, and, was forced to make good his title, and to get
possession of her by a long and restless suit in Law; which proved
troublesome and sadly-chargeable to him, whose youth, and travel,
and needless bounty, had brought his estate into a narrow compass.

It is observed, and most truly, that silence and submission are
charming qualities, and work most upon passionate men; and it
proved so with Sir George; for these, and a general report of Mr.
Donne's merits, together with his winning behaviour (which
when it would entice, had a strange kind of elegant irresistible
art) these, and time had so dispassionated Sir George, that as the
world had approved his Daughter's choice, so he also could not
but see a more than ordinary merit in his new son: and this at
last melted him into so much remorse (for Love and Anger are
so like Agues, as to have hot and cold fits; and love in Parents,
though it may be quenched, yet is easily rekindled, and expires
not, till death denies mankind a natural heat) that he laboured
his Son's restauration to his place; using to that end, both his own
and his Sister's power to her Lord; but with no success; for his
Answer was, That though he was unfeignedly sorry for what he
had done, yet it was inconsistent with his place and credit, to
discharge and readmit servants at the request of passionate peti-
tioners.

Sir George's endeavour for Mr. Donne's readmission, was by all means to be kept secret (for men do more naturally reluct for errors, then submit to put on those blemishes that attend their visible acknowledgment.) But however it was not long before Sir George appeared to be so far reconciled, as to wish their happiness; and not to deny them his paternal blessing, but yet, refused to contribute any means that might conduce to their livelyhood.

Mr. Donne's estate was the greatest part spent in many and chargeable Travels, Books and dear-bought Experience: he out of all employment that might yield a support for himself and wife, who had been curiously and plentifully educated; both their natures generous, and accustomed to confer, and not to receive Courtesies: These and other considerations, but chiefly that his wife was to bear a part in his sufferings, surrounded him with many sad thoughts, and some apparent apprehensions of want.

Lord Ellesmere did nothing for him; everyone who might have advanced his career proved equally chary. Dr. Morton, Bishop of Durham, begged of him a private interview, in which he began significantly:

"Mr. Donne, I know your Education and Abilities; I know your expectation of a State-employment; and I know your fitness for it; and I know too, the many delays and contingencies that attend Court-promises; and let me tell you that, my love begot by our long friendship, and your merits, hath prompted me to such an inquisition after your present temporal estate, as makes me no stranger to your necessities; which I know to be such as your generous spirit could not bear, if it were not supported with a pious Patience: you know I have formerly persuaded you to wave your Court-hopes, and enter into holy Orders; which I now again persuade you to embrace. Remember, Mr. Donne, no man's Education or Parts make him too good for this employment, which is to be an Ambassadour for the God of glory, that God who by a vile death opened the gates of life to mankind. Make me no present answer; but remember your promise, and return to me the third day with your Resolution."

At the hearing of this, Mr. Donne's faint breath and perplext countenance gave a visible testimony of an inward conflict; but he performed his promise and departed without returning an answer till the third day, and then his answer was to this effect;

"My most worthy and most dear friend, since I saw you, I have been faithful to my promise, and have also meditated much of your great kindness, which hath been such as would exceed even my gratitude; but that it cannot do; and more I cannot return you; and I do that with an heart full of Humility and Thanks, though I may not accept of your offer; but, Sir, my refusal is not for that I think my self too good for that calling, for which Kings, if they think so, are not good enough: nor for that my Education and Learning, though not eminent, may not, being assisted with God's Grace and Humility, render me in some measure fit for it: but, I dare make so dear a friend as you are my Confessor; some irregularities of my life have been so visible to some men, that though I have, I thank God, made my peace with him by penitential resolutions against them, and by the assistance of his Grace banish'd them my affections; yet this, which God knows to be so, is not so visible to man, as to free me from their censures, and it may be that sacred calling from a dishonour."

Donne fell into deep depression. He wrote a friend:

"I have often suspected my self to be overtaken; which is, with an over earnest desire of the next life: and though I know it is not merely a weariness of this, because I had the same desire when I went with the tide, and enjoyed fairer hopes than I now do: yet, I doubt worldly troubles have increased it: 'tis now Spring, and all the pleasures of it displease me; every other tree blossoms, and I wither: I grow older and not better; my strength diminisheth and my load grows heavier; and yet, I would fain be or do something; but, that I cannot tell what, is no wonder in this time of my sadness; for, to chuse is to do; but, to be no part of any body, is as to be nothing; and so I am, and shall so judge my self, unless I could be so incorporated into a part of the world, as by business to contribute some sustentation to the whole. . . . Sir, I fear my present discontent does not proceed from a good root, that I am

so well content to be nothing, that is, dead. But, Sir, though my
fortune hath made me such, as that I am rather a Sickness or a
Disease of the world, than any part of it, and therefore neither love
it nor life; yet I would gladly live to become some such thing as
you should not repent loving me: Sir, your own Soul cannot be
more zealous for your good then I am, and, God, who loves that
zeal in me, will not suffer you to doubt it: you would pity me now,
if you saw me write, for my pain hath drawn my head so much
awry, and holds it so, that my eye cannot follow my pen. . . . Sir,
I profess to you truly, that my lothness to give over writing now,
seems to my self a sign that I shall write no more—

Your poor friend, and

God's poor patient

JOHN DONNE."

Sept. 7.

*He still waited, hoping for political preferment. The Earl of
Somerset once said to him,* "Stay in this garden till I go up to the
King and bring you word that you are Clerk of the Council."

But the King gave a positive denial to all requests . . . The
King descended to a persuasion, almost to a solicitation of him to
enter into Sacred Orders: which though he then denied not, yet
he deferred it for almost three years.

But God who is able to prevail, wrestled with him, as the Angel
did with Jacob, and marked him; mark'd him for his own; mark'd
him with a blessing; a blessing of obedience to the motions of
his blessed Spirit. And then, as he had formerly asked God with
Moses, Who am I? So now being inspired with an apprehension
of God's particular mercy to him, in the King's and other solicitations of him, he came to ask King David's thankful question, Lord,
who am I, that thou art so mindful of me? So mindful of me, as to
lead me for more then forty years through this wilderness of the
many temptations, and various turnings of a dangerous life: so
merciful to me, as to move the learned'st of Kings, to descend to
move me to serve at the Altar! so merciful to me, as at last, to
move my heart to embrace this holy motion: thy motions I will
and do imbrace: And, I now say with the blessed Virgin, Be it

with thy servant as seemeth best in thy sight: and so, blessed Jesus, I do take the cup of Salvation, and will call upon thy Name, and will preach thy Gospel.

Now the English Church had gain'd a second St. Austine, for, I think, none was so like him before his Conversion: none so like St. Ambrose after it: and if his youth had the infirmities of the one, his age had the excellencies of the other; the learning and holiness of both.

And now all his studies which had been occasionally diffused, were all concentred in Divinity. Now he had a new calling, new thoughts, and a new employment for his wit and eloquence: Now all his earthly affections were changed into divine love; and all the faculties of his own soul, were engaged in the Conversion of others: In preaching the glad tidings of Remission to repenting Sinners, and peace to each troubled soul. To these he applied himself with all care and diligence: and now, such a change was wrought in him, that he could say with David, *Oh how amiable are thy Tabernacles, O Lord God of Hosts!* Now he declared openly, that when he required a temporal, God gave him a spiritual blessing. And that, he was now gladder to be a door-keeper in the house of God, then he could be to enjoy the noblest of all temporal employments.

A Preacher in earnest; weeping sometimes for his Auditory, sometimes with them: always preaching to himself, like an Angel from a cloud, but in none; carrying some, as St. Paul was, to Heaven in holy raptures, and inticing others by a sacred Art and Courtship to amend their lives; here picturing a vice so as to make it ugly to those that practised it; and a vertue so, as to make it be beloved even by those that lov'd it not; and all this with a most particular grace and an unexpressible addition of comeliness . . .

That Summer, in the very same month in which he entred into sacred Orders, and was made the King's Chaplain, His Majesty then going his Progress, was entreated to receive an entertainment in the University of Cambridge. And Mr. Donne attending his Majesty at that time, his Majesty was pleased to recommend him to the University, to be made Doctor in Divinity; Doctor Harsnet (after Archbishop of York) was then Vice-Chancellor, who knowing him to be the Author of that learned Book the Pseudo-Martyr, required no other proof of his Abilities, but proposed it to the University, who presently assented, and exprest a gladness, that they had such an occasion to entitle him to be theirs . . .

Immediately after his return from Cambridge, his wife died; leaving him a man of a narrow unsettled estate, and (having buried five) the careful father of seven children then living, to whom he gave a voluntary assurance, never to bring them under the subjection of a step-mother; which promise he kept most faithfully, burying with his tears, all his earthly joys in his most dear and deserving wife's grave; and betook himself to a most retired and solitary life.

In this retiredness, which was often from the sight of his dearest friends, he became crucified to the world, and all those vanities, those imaginary pleasures that are daily acted on that restless stage; and they were as perfectly crucified to him. Nor is it hard to think (being passions may be both changed, and heightened by accidents) but that that abundant affection which once was betwixt him and her, who had long been the delight of his eyes, and the Companion of his youth; her, with whom he had divided so many pleasant sorrows, and contented fears, as Common-people are not capable of; not hard to think but that she, being now removed by death, a commeasurable grief took as full a possession of him as joy had done; and so indeed it did: for now his very soul was elemented of nothing but sadness; now, grief took so full a possession of his heart, as to leave no place for joy: If it did? It was a joy to be alone, where like a Pelican in the wilderness, he might bemoan himself without witness of restraint, and pour forth his passions like Job in the days of his affliction, Oh that I might have the desire of my heart! Oh that God would grant the thing that I long for! For then, as the grave is become her house, so I would hasten to make it mine also; that we two might there make our beds together in the dark. Thus as the Israelites sate mourning by the rivers of Babylon, when they remembred Sion; so he gave some ease to his oppressed heart by thus venting his sorrows: Thus he began the day, and ended the night; ended the restless night and began the weary day in Lamentations.

His marriage was the remarkable error of his life; an error which though he had a wit able and very apt to maintain Paradoxes, yet he was very far from justifying it: and though his wives Competent years, and other reasons might be justly urged to moderate severe Censures; yet he would occasionally condemn himself for it: and doubtless it had been attended with an heavy Repentance, if God had not blest them with so mutual and cordial affections, as in the midst of their sufferings made their bread of sorrow taste more pleasantly then the banquets of dull and low-spirited people.

The Recreations of his youth were Poetry, in which he was so happy, as if nature and all her varieties had been made only to exercise his sharp wit, and high fancy; and in those pieces which were facetiously Composed and carelesly scattered (most of them being written before the twentieth year of his age) it may appear by his choice Metaphors, that both Nature and all the Arts joyned to assist him with their utmost skill.

[But still his friends] that had often been a witness of his free and facetious discourse, asked him, "Why are you sad?" [He denied it, and insisted,] "I now plainly see it was His hand that prevented me from all temporal employment; and that it was His will I should never settle nor thrive till I entered into the ministry; in which I have now lived almost twenty years (I hope to His glory) "; [but again he would groan and admit] that he longed for the day of his dissolution, [or confess] "I were miserable if I might not die."

A Monument being resolved upon, Dr. Donne sent for a Carver to make for him in wood the figure of an Urn, giving him directions for the compass and height of it; and to bring with it a board of the just height of his body. These being got: then without delay a choice Painter was got to be in a readiness to draw his Picture, which was taken as followeth.——Several Charcoal-fires being first made in his large Study, he brought with him into that place his winding-sheet in his hand, and, having put off all his cloaths, had this sheet put on him, and so tyed with knots at his head and feet, and his hands so placed, as dead bodies are usually fitted to be shrowded and put into their Coffin, or grave.

Upon this Urn he thus stood with his eyes shut, and with so much of the sheet turned aside as might shew his lean, pale, and death-like face, which was purposely turned toward the East, from whence he expected the second coming of his and our Saviour Jesus. In this posture he was drawn at his just height; and when the Picture was fully finished, he caused it to be set by his bed-side, where it continued, and became his hourly object till his death.

In his last illness he lingered fifteen days expecting death. Only at the very end was he unable to speak.

Being speechless, and seeing heaven by that illumination by which he saw it; he did, as St. Stephen, look stedfastly into it, till he saw the Son of man, standing at the right hand of God his Father; and being satisfied with this blessed sight, as his soul ascended, and his last breath departed from him, he closed his own eyes; and then disposed his hands and body into such a posture as required not the least alteration by those that came to shroud him.

Thus variable, thus virtuous was the Life; thus excellent, thus exemplary was the Death of this memorable man.

He was by nature highly passionate, but more apt to reluct at the excesses of it. A great lover of the offices of humanity, and of so merciful a spirit, that he never beheld the miseries of Mankind without pity and relief.

He was earnest and unwearied in the search of knowledge; with which, his vigorous soul is now satisfied, and employed in a continual praise of that God that first breathed it into his active body; that body, which once was a Temple of the Holy Ghost, and is now become a small quantity of Christian dust:

But I shall see it reanimated.

I. W.

Feb. 15. 1639.

KING–KILLER

THE OBSTINATE ROYAL FOLLY OF CHARLES I SPLIT HIS REALM IN two. It was not really, however, as imaginative literature has so often represented it, a conflict of Cavalier and Roundhead, of courtly and romantic loyalists against gloomy Puritans moralizing rebellion and regicide. The desperate struggle divided families, the rival claims of interest or conscience pitting brother against brother. Lucy Hutchinson came of a family of Royalists, her father, Sir Allan Apsley, having been Lieutenant-Governor of the Tower; but her husband Colonel Hutchinson almost from the beginning declared himself on the side of the Parliament, and took a leading part in both military and legislative opposition to his King.

Mrs. Hutchinson's life of her husband is valuable not only as a vivid personal record but as a historical document. There is some loving exaggeration, no doubt, in her portrayal of Colonel Hutchinson, but how clearly he is painted, the red cloak in which he went to Ireton's funeral, his squabbles with the committee at Nottingham, his slightly over-ostentatious frankness, the finesse and bravery with which he defended himself under cross-examination, the bleakness of Sandown and his death in fever. His calm and serious cheerfulness and his cultivation in the arts show a side of Puritanism usually lost in the distortions of Restoration satire, and seldom revealed in popular history.

Mrs. Hutchinson is far from being the bigoted partisan and sour bluestocking her critics have sometimes called her. There is a very pleasing youthful romanticism in her earlier pages, and her judgments of both royalists and parliamentarians seem re-

markably fair. She does justice to Charles I as a husband, a man
of high personal character, and a cultivated gentleman; and her
portrayal of the Earl of Newcastle shows him as honest, liberal,
and magnanimous. Of Cromwell, whom she detests as a tyrant,
she nevertheless remarks, "to speak truth, he had much natural
greatness, and well became the place he had usurped." She is
a sharp critic of the character and squabbling of her own party: not
hesitating to brand a certain Sir John Gell "a foul adulterer" or
to describe the sufferings that came from "secret enemies and
refractory friends" in its own ranks. The drab dress and Old
Testament affectations of the more ostentatious Puritans she saw
very well to be only too often mere pretence and hypocrisy, the
badge of a faction, blackening the name of Puritanism with
zealotry and fanaticism.

She is a bit vain of her own talents and it may be that she represents Colonel Hutchinson as more invariably right than any
human being is apt to be. But mainly his character speaks for
itself; his behavior tells its own objective story. And her narrative
amply justifies her good opinion of herself. It is vivid, skillful
in construction and characterization, full of force and drama.
It is outstanding for clarity and balance of judgment. It is
saturated with the flavor and color of its time, sharply and
brilliantly conveyed.

Memoirs of the Life of Colonel Hutchinson

LUCY HUTCHINSON

[Colonel Hutchinson died in 1664. We do not know
when the Memoirs were composed. They were first
published in 1806.]

IT WAS ON THE 29TH DAY OF JANUARY, IN THE YEAR OF OUR LORD
1619–20, that in the Tower of London, the principal city of the
English Isle, I was, about four of the clock in the morning, brought
forth to behold the ensuing light. My father was Sir Allen Apsley,
lieutenant of the Tower of London; my mother, his third wife, was
Lucy, the youngest daughter of Sir John St. John, of Lidiard
Tregooze, in Wiltshire, by his second wife. My father had then
living a son and a daughter by his former wives, and by my mother
three sons, I being her eldest daughter. The land was then at peace
(it being towards the latter end of the reign of King James), if
that quietness may be called a peace, which was rather like the
calm and smooth surface of the sea, whose dark womb is already
impregnated with a horrid tempest.

My mother, while she was with child of me, dreamed that
she was walking in the garden with my father, and that a star
came down into her hand, with other circumstances, which,
though I have often heard, I minded not enough to remember perfectly; only my father told her, her dream signified she should
have a daughter of some extraordinary eminency; which thing,
like such vain prophecies, wrought as far as it could its own ac-

complishment: for my father and mother fancying me then beautiful, and more than ordinarily apprehensive, applied all their cares, and spared no cost to improve me in my education, which procured me the admiration of those that flattered my parents.

By the time I was four years old I read English perfectly, and having a great memory, I was carried to sermons; and while I was very young could remember and repeat them exactly, and being caressed, the love of praise tickled me, and made me attend more heedfully. When I was about seven years of age, I remember I had at one time eight tutors in several qualities, languages, music, dancing, writing, and needlework; but my genius was quite averse from all but my book, and that I was so eager of, that my mother thinking it prejudiced my health, would moderate me in it; yet this rather animated me than kept me back, and every moment I could steal from my play I would employ in any book I could find, when my own were locked up from me. After dinner and supper I still had an hour allowed me to play, and then I would steal into some hole or other to read. My father would have me learn Latin, and I was so apt that I outstripped my brothers who were at school, although my father's chaplain, that was my tutor, was a pitiful dull fellow. My brothers, who had a great deal of wit, had some emulation at the progress I made in my learning, which very well pleased my father; though my mother would have been contented if I had not so wholly addicted myself to that as to neglect my other qualities.

As for music and dancing, I profited very little in them, and would never practise my lute or harpsichords but when my masters were with me; and for my needle I absolutely hated it. Play among other children I despised, and when I was forced to entertain such as came to visit me, I tired them with more grave instructions than their mothers, and plucked all their babies to pieces, and kept the children in such awe, that they were glad when I entertained myself with elder company; to whom I was very acceptable, and living in the house with many persons that had a great deal of wit, and very profitable serious discourses being frequent at my father's table and in my mother's drawing-room, I was very attentive to all, and gathered up things that I would utter again, to great admiration of many that took my memory and imitation for wit.

It pleased God that, through the good instructions of my mother, and the sermons she carried me to, I was convinced that the knowledge of God was the most excellent study, and accordingly applied myself to it, and to practise as I was taught. I used to exhort my mother's maids much, and to turn their idle discourses to good subjects; but I thought, when I had done this on the Lord's day, and every day performed my due tasks of reading and praying, that then I was free to anything that was not sin; for I was not at that time convinced of the vanity of conversation which was not scandalously wicked. I thought it no sin to learn or hear witty songs and amorous sonnets or poems, and twenty things of that kind, wherein I was so apt that I became the confidant in all the loves that were managed among my mother's young women; and there was none of them but had many lovers, and some particular friends beloved above the rest.

John Hutchinson was the eldest surviving son of Sir Thomas Hutchinson of Owthorpe; his mother was a Byron of Newstead, the same family that later gave birth to Lord Byron. He grew up into a serious young man, scholarly and devout, with Puritan leanings; though he also "practised tennis, and played admirably well at it" [and] "improved to a great mastery on the viol." *He had already courteously reproved the flirtatious advances of ladies who were handsome, witty, wealthy, and* "set out with all the gaiety and vanity that vain women put on to set themselves off," *including one* "of such admirable tempting beauty . . . as would have thawed a rock of ice."

Putting off until the autumn an invitation to go into France, young Mr. Hutchinson spent the summer at the house of his music-master in Richmond.

In the same house with him there was a younger daughter of Sir Allen Apsley, late lieutenant of the Tower, tabled for the practice of her lute, staying till the return of her mother; who was gone into Wiltshire for the accomplishment of a treaty that had been made some progress in, about the marriage of her elder daughter with a gentleman of that country, out of which my lady herself came, and where her brothers, Sir John St. John and Sir Edward Hungerford, living in great honour and reputation, had invited her to visit them. This gentlewoman, that was left in the house with Mr. Hutchinson, was a very child, her elder sister being at that time scarcely passed it; but a child of such pleasantness and vivacity of spirit, and ingenuity in the quality she practised, that Mr. Hutchinson took pleasure in hearing her practise, and would fall in discourse with her.

She having the keys of her mother's house, some half a mile distant, would sometimes ask Mr. Hutchinson, when she went over, to walk along with her. One day when he was there, looking upon an odd by-shelf in her sister's closet, he found a few Latin books; asking whose they were, he was told they were her elder sister's; whereupon, inquiring more after her, he began first to be sorry she was gone, before he had seen her, and gone upon such an account that he was not likely to see her. Then he grew to love to hear mention of her, and the other gentlewomen who had been her companions used to talk much to him of her, telling him how reserved and studious she was, and other things which they esteemed no advantage. But it so much inflamed Mr. Hutchinson's desire of seeing her, that he began to wonder at himself, that his heart, which had ever entertained so much indifference for the most excellent of womankind, should have such strong impulses towards a stranger he never saw; and certainly it was of the Lord (though he perceived it not), who had ordained him, through so many various providences, to be yoked with her in whom he found so much satisfaction.

There scarcely passed any day but some accident or some discourse still kept alive his desire of seeing this gentlewoman; although the mention of her, for the most part, was inquiries whether she had yet accomplished the marriage that was in treaty. One day there was a great deal of company at Mr. Coleman's, the gentleman's house where he tabled, to hear the music; and a certain song was sung, which had been lately set, and gave occasion to some of the company to mention an answer to it, which was in the house, and upon some of their desires, read. A gentleman saying it was believed that a woman in the neighborhood had made it, it was presently inquired who; whereupon a gentleman, then present, who had made the first song, said, there were but two women that could be guilty of it, whereof one was a lady then among them, the other Mrs. Apsley. Mr. Hutchinson, fancying something of rationality in the sonnet beyond the customary reach of a she-wit, although, to speak truth, it signified very little, addressed himself to the gentleman, and told him he could scarcely believe it was a woman's; whereupon this gentleman, who was a man of good understanding and expression, and inspired with some passion for her himself, which made him regard all her perfections through a multiplying-glass, told Mr. Hutchinson, that though, for civility to the rest, he entitled another lady to the song, yet he was confident it was Mrs. Apsley's only, for she had sense above all the rest; and fell into such high praises of her, as might well have begotten those vehement desires of her acquaintance, which a strange sympathy in nature had before produced. Another gentleman, that sat by, seconded this commendation with such additions of praise as he would not have given if he had known her.

Mr. Hutchinson hearing all this, said to the first gentleman, "I cannot be at rest till this lady's return, that I may be acquainted with her." The gentleman replied, "Sir, you must not expect that, for she is of a humour she will not be acquainted with any of mankind; and however this song is stolen forth, she is the nicest creature in the world of suffering her perfections to be known; she shuns the converse of men as the plague; she only lives in the enjoyment of herself, and had not the humanity to communicate that happiness to any of our sex." "Well," said Mr. Hutchinson, "but I will be acquainted with her:" and indeed the information of this reserved humour pleased him more than all else he had heard, and filled him now with thoughts how he should attain the sight and knowledge of her.

While he was exercised in this, many days passed not, but a footboy of my lady her mother's came to young Mrs. Apsley as they were at dinner, bringing news that her mother and sister would in a few days return; and when they inquired of him, whether Mrs.

Apsley was married; having before been instructed to make them believe it, he smiled, and pulled out some bride laces, which were given at a wedding, in the house where she was, and gave them to the young gentlewoman and the gentleman's daughter of the house, and told them Mrs. Apsley bade him tell no news, but give them those tokens, and carried the matter so, that all the company believed she had been married. Mr. Hutchinson immediately turned pale as ashes, and felt a fainting to seize his spirits in that extraordinary manner, that, finding himself ready to sink at table, he was fain to pretend something had offended his stomach, and to retire from the table into the garden; where the gentleman of the house going with him, it was not necessary for him to feign sickness, for the distemper of his mind had infected his body with a cold sweat, and such a depression of spirit, that all the courage he could at present collect, was little enough to keep him alive.

Mr. Hutchinson chid himself for being so fantastic about an unknown person, but "it booted him not to be angry at himself, nor to set wisdom in her reproving chair, nor reason in her throne of council, the sick heart could not be chid nor advised into health." *The rumor proving untrue, they were presently acquainted, nor was* "his heart free to discern how little there was in her," *Lucy Hutchinson remarks,* "to answer so great an expectation."

I shall pass by all the little amorous relations, which, if I would take the pains to relate, would make a true history of a more handsome management of love than the best romances describe; but these are to be forgotten as the vanities of youth, not worthy of mention among the greater transactions of his life. There is this only to be recorded, that never was there a passion more ardent and less idolatrous; he loved her better than his life, with inexpressible tenderness and kindness, had a most high obliging esteem of her, yet still considered honour, religion, and duty above her, nor ever suffered the intrusion of such a dotage as should blind him from marking her imperfections; these he looked upon with such an indulgent eye as did not abate his love and esteem of her, while it augmented his care to blot out all those spots which might make her appear less worthy of that respect he paid her;

and thus indeed he soon made her more equal to him than he found her; for she was a very faithful mirror, reflecting truly, though but dimly, his own glories upon him, so long as he was present; but she, that was nothing before his inspection gave her a fair figure, when he was removed, was only filled with a dark mist, and never could again take in any delightful object, nor return any shining representation. The greatest excellency she had was the power of apprehending and the virtue of loving his; so as his shadow she waited on him everywhere, till he was taken into that region of light which admits of none, and then she vanished into nothing.

This lyric radiance was soon darkened:

. . . About the year 1639, the thunder was heard afar off rattling in the troubled air, and even the most obscure woods were penetrated with some flashes, the forerunners of the dreadful storm which the next year was more apparent. . . . King Charles was temperate, chaste, and serious; . . . men of learning and ingenuity in all arts were in esteem, and received encouragement from the King, [but he was proving] a worse encroacher upon the civil and spiritual liberties of his people by far than his father. He married a papist, a French lady, of a haughty spirit, and a great wit and beauty, to whom he became a most uxorious husband. By this means the court was replenished with papists, and many who hoped to advance themselves by the change, turned to that religion . . . [King Charles] was the most obstinate person in his self-will that ever was, and so bent upon being an absolute, uncontrollable sovereign, that he was resolved either to be such a king or none.

Strafford and Laud were powerful instruments of his tyranny. But the Long Parliament, convened in November, 1640, indicted both of high treason. They were convicted and sent to their deaths. Still the King would abide by no covenants. Open rebellion broke out. Defeated, he still connived secretly against his subjects, to betray his agreements. At last there seemed only one resort.

In January 1648, the court sat, the king was brought to his trial, and a charge drawn up against him for levying war against the parliament and people of England, for betraying the public trust reposed in him, and for being an implacable enemy to the commonwealth. But the king refused to plead, disowning the authority of the court, and after three several days persisting in contempt thereof, he was sentenced to suffer death. One thing was remarked in him by many of the court, that when the blood spilt in many of the battles where he was in his own person, and had caused it to be shed by his own command, was laid to his charge, he heard it with disdainful smiles, and looks and gestures which rather expressed sorrow that all the opposite party to him were not cut off, than that any were: and he stuck not to declare in words, that no man's blood spilt in this quarrel troubled him except one, meaning the Earl of Strafford. The gentlemen that were appointed his judges, and divers others, saw in him a disposition so bent on the ruin of all that opposed him, and of all the righteous and just things they had contended for, that it was upon the consciences of many of them, that if they did not execute justice upon him, God would require at their hands all the blood and desolation which should ensue by their suffering him to escape, when God had brought him into their hands.

He was sentenced to death, and beheaded at the block. The monarchy was superseded by a commonwealth.

But now had the poison of ambition so ulcerated Cromwell's heart, that the effects of it became more apparent than before; and while as yet Fairfax stood an empty name, he was moulding the army to his mind, weeding out the godly and upright-hearted men, both officers and soldiers, and filling up their rooms with rascally turn-coat cavaliers, and pitiful sottish beasts of his own alliance, and other such as would swallow all things, and make no questions for conscience' sake. Yet this he did not directly nor in tumult, but by such degrees that it was unperceived by all that were not of very penetrating eyes; and those that made the loudest outcries against him lifted up their voices with such apparent envy and malice that, in that mist, they rather hid than discovered his ambitious minings.

Among these, Colonel Rich and Commissary Staines and Watson had made a design even against his life, and the business was brought to the examination of the council of state. Before the hearing of it, Colonel Rich came to Colonel Hutchinson and implored his assistance with tears, affirming all the crimes of Cromwell, but not daring to justify his accusations, although the colonel advised him if they were true to stand boldly to it, if false to acknowledge his own iniquity. The latter course he took, and the council had resolved upon the just punishment of the men, when Cromwell, having only thus in a private council vindicated himself from their malice, and laid open what pitiful sneaking poor knaves they were, how ungrateful to him, and how treacherous and cowardly to themselves, became their advocate, and made it his suit that they might be no farther published or punished. This being permitted him, and they thus rendered contemptible to others, they became beasts and slaves to him, who knew how to serve himself by them without trusting them. This generosity, for indeed he carried himself with the greatest bravery that is imaginable herein, much advanced his glory, and cleared him in the eyes of superficial beholders; but others saw he creeped on, and could not stop him, while fortune itself seemed to prepare his way on sundry occasions.

All this while he carried to Mr. Hutchinson the most open face, and made the most obliging professions of friendship imaginable; but the colonel saw through him, and forbore not often to tell him what was suspected of his ambition, what dissimulations of his were remarked, and how dishonourable to the name of God and the profession of religion, and destructive to the most glorious cause, and dangerous in overthrowing all our triumphs, these things which were suspected of him, would be, if true. He would seem to receive these cautions and admonitions as the greatest demonstrations of integrity and friendship that could be made, and embrace the colonel in his arms, and make serious lying professions to him, and often inquire men's opinions concerning him, which the colonel never forbore to tell him plainly, although he knew he resented it not as he made show, yet it pleased him so to discharge his own thoughts.

When Cromwell came to London, there wanted not some little creatures of his, in the house, who had taken notice of all that had been said of him when he let the king slip by; how some stuck not in their fear and rage to call him traitor, and to threaten his head. These reports added spurs to his ambition, but his son-in-law, Ireton, deputy of Ireland, would not be wrought to serve him, but hearing of his machinations, determined to come over to England to endeavour to divert him from such destructive courses. But God cut him short by death, and whether his body or an empty coffin was brought into England, something in his name came to London, and was to be, by Cromwell's procurement, magnificently buried among the kings at Westminster. Colonel Hutchinson was, after his brother, one of the nearest kinsmen he had, but Cromwell, who of late studied to give him neglects, passed him by, and neither sent him mourning, nor particular invitation to the funeral, only the Speaker gave public notice in the house, that all the members were desired to attend it; and such was the flattery of many pitiful lords and other gentlemen, parasites, that they put themselves into deep mourning; but Colonel Hutchinson that day put on a scarlet cloak, very richly laced, such as he usually wore, and coming into the room where the members were, seeing some of the lords in mourning, he went to them to inquire the cause, who told him they had put it on to honour the general; and asked again, why he, that was a kinsman, was in such a different colour? He told them, that because the general had neglected sending to him, when he had sent to many who had no alliance, only to make up the train, he was resolved he would not flatter so much as to buy for himself, although he was a true mourner in his heart for his cousin, whom he had ever loved, and would therefore go and take his place among his mourners.

Ultimately Cromwell made himself tyrant under the title of Lord Protector. Colonel Hutchinson refused his solicitations to an office in the government, and retired to his house at Owthorpe, where he busied himself arranging his paintings, sculptures, and engravings, in improving his estate, enjoying music with his viol, "and entertaining tutors for the diversion and education of his children."

Cromwell and his army grew wanton with their power . . . His wife and children were setting up for principality, which suited no better with any of them than scarlet on the ape; only, to speak truth of himself, he had much natural greatness, and well became the place he had usurped.

But more and more he distrusted Colonel Hutchinson's honesty and freedom, and resolved at last to deprive him of his liberty.

Yet before his guards apprehended the colonel, death imprisoned himself, and confined all his vast ambition and all his cruel designs into the narrow compass of a grave.

Now was that glorious parliament come to a period, not more fatal to itself than to the three nations, whose sun of liberty then set, and all their glory gave place to the foulest mists that ever overspread a miserable people. A new parliament was to be chosen, and the county of Nottingham had yet such respect for Colonel Hutchinson, that they fixed their eyes on him to be their knight, but Mr. William Pierrepont having a great desire to bring in his son-in-law, the Lord Haughton, to be his fellow knight, the colonel would not come into the town until the election was passed; which if he had, he had been chosen without desiring it; for many people came, and when they saw he would not stand, returned and voted for none, among whom were fifty freeholders of the town of Newark.

Some time before the writs for the new elections came, the town of Nottingham, as almost all the rest of the island, began to grow mad, and to declare themselves so, in their desires of the king. The boys, set on by their fathers and masters, got drums and colours, and marched up and down the town, and trained themselves in a military posture, and offered many affronts to the soldiers of the army that were quartered there, which were two troops of Colonel Hacker's regiment. Insomuch that one night there were about forty of the soldiers hurt and wounded with stones,

upon the occasion of taking away the drums, when the youths were
gathering together to make bonfires to burn the Rump, as was
the custom in those mad days.

The colonel and Mr. Stanhope went up to the parliament,
which began on the 25th day of April, 1660; to whom the king
sending a declaration from Breda, which promised, or at least intimated, liberty of conscience, remission of all offences, enjoyment
of liberties and estates; they voted to send commissioners to invite
him. And almost all the gentry of all parties went, some to fetch
him over, some to meet him at the sea side, some to fetch him into
London, into which he entered on the 29th day of May, with a
universal joy and triumph, even to his own amazement; who, when
he saw all the nobility and gentry of the land flowing in to him,
asked where were his enemies. For he saw nothing but prostrates,
expressing all the love that could make a prince happy. Indeed
it was a wonder in that day to see the mutability of some, and
the hypocrisy of others, and the servile flattery of all. Monk, like
his better genius, conducted him, and was adored like one that
had brought all the glory and felicity of mankind home with this
prince.

The officers of the army had made themselves as fine as the
courtiers, and all hoped in this change to change their condition,
and disowned all things they before had advised. Every ballad
singer sang up and down the streets ribald rhymes, made in reproach of the late commonwealth, and of all those worthies that
therein endeavoured the people's freedom and happiness.

The presbyterians were now the white boys, and according to
their nature fell a thirsting, and then hunting after blood, urging
that God's blessing could not be upon the land, till justice had
cleansed it from the late king's blood. . . . Colonel Hutchinson,
who was not there at the beginning, came in, and was told what
they were about, and that it would be expected he should say
something. He was surprised with a thing he expected not, yet
neither then, nor in any like occasion, did he ever fail himself, but
told them, "That for his actings in those days, if he had erred, it was
the inexperience of his age, and the defect of his judgment, and

not the malice of his heart, which had ever prompted him to pursue the general advantage of his country more than his own; and if the sacrifice of him might conduce to the public peace and settlement, he should freely submit his life and fortunes to their disposal; that the vain expense of his age, and the great debts his public employments had run him into, as they were testimonies that neither avarice nor any other interest had carried him on, so they yielded him just cause to repent that he ever forsook his own blessed quiet, to embark in such a troubled sea, where he had made shipwreck of all things but a good conscience; and as to that particular action of the king, he desired them to believe he had that sense of it that befitted an Englishman, a Christian, and a gentleman."

The art and dexterity of this address temporarily effected his safety. The Act of Oblivion then seemed to free him from future danger. But the King was reported to have said that the Colonel "would do the same thing for him that he had done for his father." Efforts were made to intimidate him into betraying his late associates. Finally officers came to search the house for firearms and seize his person.

It was after sunset when they came, and they were at least two hours searching every corner and all about the house, and the colonel was not at that time very well in health, and not having been on horseback for six months before, had neither horses nor saddles at that time in the house; the coachman was also gone away, and the coachhorses turned out, and it was as bitter a stormy, pitchy, dark, black, rainy night as any that year; all which considered, the colonel desired that they would but stay for the morning light, that he might accommodate himself; but they would not, but forced him to go along with them then, his eldest son lending him a horse, and also voluntarily accompanying him to Newark, where, about four o'clock in the morning, he was brought into the Talbot, and put into a most vile room, and two soldiers kept guard upon him in that room.

A few days after, at nine o'clock at night, after his wife was gone from him, Cresset brought the colonel a warrant, to tell him that he must, the next morning tide, go down to Sandown Castle, in Kent; which he was not surprised at, it being the barbarous custom of that place to send away the prisoners, when they had no knowledge of, nor time to accommodate themselves for their journey . . .

When he came to the castle, he found it a lamentable old ruined place, almost a mile distant from the town, the rooms all out of repair, not weather proof, no kind of accommodation either for lodging or diet, or any conveniency of life. Before he came, there were not above half a dozen soldiers in it, and a poor lieutenant with his wife and children, and two or three cannoniers, and a few guns almost dismounted, upon rotten carriages; but at the colonel's coming thither, a company of foot besides were sent from Dover to help to guard the place, pitiful weak fellows, half-starved and eaten up with vermin, whom the governor of Dover cheated of half their pay, and the other half they spent in drink. These had no beds, but a nasty court of guard, where a sutler lived, within a partition made of boards, with his wife and family, and this was all the accommodation the colonel had for his victuals, which were bought at a dear rate in the town, and most horribly dressed at the sutler's. For beds he was forced to send to an inn in the town, and at a most unconscionable rate hire three, for himself, his man, and Captain Gregory; he had to get his chamber glazed, which was a thoroughfare room, having five doors in it, one of which opened upon a platform, that had nothing but the bleak air of the sea, whilst every tide washed the foot of the castle walls. This air made the chamber so unwholesome and damp, that even in the summer time the colonel's hat-case and trunks, and every-thing of leather, would be every day all covered over with mould,— wipe them as clean as you could one morning, by the next they would be mouldy again; and though the walls were four yards thick, yet it rained in through the cracks in them, and then one might sweep a peck of saltpetre off of them every day, which stood in a perpetual sweat upon them.

On the third of September, being Saturday, he had been walking by the sea-side, and coming home found himself aguish, with a kind of shivering and pain in his bones, and going to bed did sweat exceedingly: the next day he was a little better, and came down; but on the Monday, expecting another fit, which came upon him, he lay in bed all day, and rose again the next day, but went not down; and after that he slept no more till his last sleep came upon him, but continued in a feverish distemper, with violent sweatings, after which he used to rise out of his bed to refresh him, and when he was up used to read much in his Bible.

[Soon he] spoke no more, for convulsions wrought his mouth, yet did his sense remain perfect to his last breath; for when some named Mrs. Hutchinson, and said, "Alas, how will she be surprised!" he fetched a sigh, and within a little while departed; his countenance settling so amiably and cheerfully after death, that he looked after he was dead as he used to do when best pleased in life.

They made affidavit, which remains yet upon record, that the doctor said that the place had killed him, and, satisfied with this, they did not unlap the body.

From London he was brought down to Owthorpe, very seriously bewailed all the way he came along by all those who had been better acquainted with his worth than the strangers were among whom he died; and he was brought home with honour to his grave through the dominions of his murderers, who were ashamed of his glories, which all their tyrannies could not extinguish with his life.

upon himself

STRUGGLE WITH SATAN

THE RESTORATION WAS A COALITION BETWEEN THE COURT AND THE
merchants and country squires. The aristocracy would do the
ruling, but it was to rule in the interest of the mercantile and
rural middle classes. Puritanism was under a cloud. The fanaticism and bigotry that even Mrs. Hutchinson had deplored became
grotesque images for comic derision. A wave of licentiousness
swept over the world of rank and fashion. On the stage the witty
rake and the ridiculous, Bible-ranting, ledger-clutching tradesman
and cuckold grew into stock figures. Returned Cavaliers who had
felt the north wind in France jingled gold crowns in their pockets
again, and made them spin in tavern, gaming-house, theatre, and
ball. The solid middle class disapproved, but as long as it prospered in its counting-houses it ignored the vices of the Court.

But Puritanism had rooted itself deep in humbler soil. The
Ironsides of Cromwell's army, that had shattered Cavaliers before them, were drawn from the ranks of the peasantry, artisans,
laborers, small tradesmen. Among them nonconformity had
spread, and now, persecuted by the authorities and harried by
their own soul-searchings, they still assembled in their shabby
meeting-houses, still protested stubbornly the claims of a King
far different from the Merry Monarch Charles II. Such is the
background of Bunyan's autobiography. But it is background, not
immediate scene, for reasons that Bunyan himself leaves clear.

Grace Abounding is a spiritual autobiography. Of Bunyan's
parentage, education, outward career, he tells us almost nothing.
Here and there peeps out an act performed or a thing done to him:
playing cat as a boy, ringing church bells, becoming a preacher,

being slandered as a loose liver, being jailed for his religious views. But for Bunyan these were as nothing compared with the awful significance of the inward drama upon which he fixed his gaze. That drama was the drama of the search for truth. It was filled with agonies, temptations to betray, horrors and depressions and martyrdoms. If, in the end, truth upheld him, it was not his weakness that triumphed, but the might of God.

It is a narrow world that Bunyan reveals, but one of unfathomable depth. No one has given a deeper insight into the more tormented aspects of English Puritanism. For the humble Bedford tinker, the Devil is a real presence by his side, divine voices sound in his ears, the smoke and stench of hell's flames are horrible in his nostrils. Told in a voice of tense and terrible conviction, his story is a Dostoyevskyan drama of dread and damnation and repentance. The Biblical language is no unctuous rhetoric intoned by some squab cleric; it comes burning out of Bunyan's heart with an appalling sincerity. The world is darkness, the darkness of perdition, with no glimpse of the sunlit English scene, and there in a lurid hollow of light Bunyan struggles with the Devil for his soul.

We may not dismiss Bunyan as merely deranged. The man who wrote *The Pilgrim's Progress* is something more than that, and the religious possession that did indeed drive him *almost* insane has passed again and again through entire communities. Bunyan's is a penetrating record of its manifestations in a simple heart. There revealed in deep beyond deep we see fearful turmoils and monsters of the soul. This is only a part of the world that even Puritanism knows. It leaves out all the stir and bustle of everyday life; it leaves out the serenity of the Interpreter's House to which Bunyan later attained, and the fair vision of the Delectable Mountains, and the shining City of God. All that remains is the dark tension of a crisis, prolonged to endlessness, prolonged almost beyond all bearing.

Grace Abounding

To the Chief of Sinners

JOHN BUNYAN

[*Grace Abounding* was written in prison in 1666, and published the same year. Various additions were made at later times, including a *Continuation* in 1692.]

IN THIS MY RELATION OF THE MERCIFUL WORKING OF GOD UPON MY soul, it will not be amiss, if, in the first place, I do, in a few words, give you a hint of my pedigree, and manner of bringing up; that thereby the goodness and bounty of God towards me, may be the more advanced and magnified before the sons of men.

For my descent then, it was, as is well known by many, of a low and inconsiderable generation; my father's house being of that rank that is meanest and most despised of all the families in the land. Wherefore I have not here, as others, to boast of noble blood, or of a high-born state, according to the flesh; though, all things considered, I magnify the heavenly Majesty, for that by this door he brought me into this world, to partake of the grace and life that is in Christ by the gospel.

As a child of nine Bunyan was afflicted with thoughts of the day of judgment and trembled at the fearful torments of hell fire; but when these terrible dreams left him, he says, he loosed with all the more greediness the reins of his lusts, and became "the very ring-leader of all the youth that kept me company, into all manner of vice and ungodliness."

As I was in the midst of a game at cat, and having struck it one blow from the hole, just as I was about to strike it the second time, a voice did suddenly dart from heaven into my soul, which said, Wilt thou leave thy sins and go to heaven, or have thy sins and go to hell? At this I was put to an exceeding maze; wherefore, leaving my cat upon the ground, I looked up to heaven, and was, as if I had, with the eyes of my understanding, seen the Lord Jesus looking down upon me, as being very hotly displeased with me, and as if he did severely threaten me with some grievous punishment for these and other my ungodly practices. . . . Despair did so possess my soul, that I was persuaded I could never attain to other comfort than what I should get in sin; for heaven was gone already, so that on that I must not think; wherefore I found within me a great desire to take my fill of sin, still studying what sin was yet to be committed, that I might taste the sweetness of it; and I made as much haste as I could to fill my belly with its delicates, lest I should die before I had my desire; for that I feared greatly. In these things, I protest before God, I lie not, neither do I feign this sort of speech; these were really, strongly, and with all my heart, my desires; the good Lord, whose mercy is unsearchable, forgive me my transgressions.

Now, you must know, that before this I had taken much delight in ringing, but my conscience beginning to be tender, I thought such practice was but vain, and therefore forced myself to leave it, yet my mind hankered; wherefore I should go to the steeple house, and look on it, though I durst not ring. But I thought this did not become religion neither, yet I forced myself, and would look on still; but quickly after, I began to think, How, if one of the bells should fall? Then I chose to stand under a main beam, that lay overthwart the steeple, from the side to side, thinking there I might stand sure, but then I should think again, should the bell fall with a swing, it might first hit the wall, and then rebounding upon me, might kill me for all this beam. This made me stand in the steeple door; and now, thought I, I am safe enough; for, if a bell should then fall, I can slip out behind these thick walls, and so be preserved notwithstanding.

So, after this, I would yet go to see them ring, but would not go farther than the steeple door; but then it came into my head, How, if the steeple itself should fall? And this thought, it may fall for aught I know, when I stood and looked on, did continually so shake my mind, that I durst not stand at the steeple door any longer, but was forced to flee, for fear the steeple should fall upon my head.

. . . The tempter came in with his delusion, That there was no way for me to know I had faith, but by trying to work some miracle; urging those Scriptures that seem to look that way, for the enforcing and strengthening his temptation. Nay, one day as I was betwixt Elstow and Bedford, the temptation was hot upon me to try if I had faith, by doing of some miracle: which miracle at that time was this, I must say to the puddles that were in the horse pads, Be dry; and to the dry places, Be you the puddles. And truly, one time I was a-going to say so indeed; but just as I was about to speak, this thought came into my mind, But go under yonder hedge and pray first, that God would make you able. But when I had concluded to pray, this came hot upon me, That if I prayed, and came again and tried to do it, and yet did nothing notwithstanding, then be sure I had no faith, but was a castaway and lost. Nay, thought I, if it be so, I will never try yet, but will stay a little longer.

About this time, the state and happiness of these poor people at Bedford was thus, in a dream or vision, represented to me. I saw, as if they were set on the sunny side of some high mountain, there refreshing themselves with the pleasant beams of the sun, while I was shivering and shrinking in the cold, afflicted with frost, snow, and dark clouds. Methought, also, betwixt me and them, I saw a wall that did compass about this mountain; now, through this wall my soul did greatly desire to pass; concluding, that if I could, I would go even into the very midst of them, and there also comfort myself with the heat of their sun.

About this wall I thought myself, to go again and again, still prying as I went, to see if I could find some way or passage, by which I might enter therein; but none could I find for some time. At the last, I saw, as it were, a narrow gap, like a little doorway in the wall, through which I attempted to pass; but the passage being very strait and narrow, I made many efforts to get in, but all in vain, even until I was well-nigh quite beat out, by striving to get in; at last, with great striving, methought I at first did get in my head, and after that, by a sidling striving, my shoulders, and my whole body; then was I exceeding glad, and went and sat down in the midst of them, and so was comforted with the light and heat of their sun.

Now, this mountain and wall, etc., was thus made out to me—the mountain signified the church of the living God; the sun that shone thereon, the comfortable shining of his merciful face on them that were therein; the wall, I thought, was the Word, that did make separation between the Christians and the world; and the gap which was in this wall, I thought, was Jesus Christ, who is the way to God the Father (John xiv. 6, Matt. vii. 14). But forasmuch as the passage was wonderful narrow, even so narrow, that I could not, but with great difficulty, enter in thereat, it showed me that none could enter into life, but those that were in downright earnest, and unless also they left this wicked world behind them; for here was only room for body and soul, but not for body and soul, and sin.

I durst not take a pin or stick, though but so big as a straw, for my conscience now was sore, and would smart at every touch; I could not now tell how to speak my words, for fear I should misplace them. Oh, how gingerly did I then go in all I did or said! I found myself as on a miry bog that shook if I did but stir . . .

I heard one preach a sermon upon those words in the Song (iv. 1), "Behold, thou art fair, my love; behold, thou art fair."

So as I was a-going home, these words came again into my thoughts; and I well remember, as they came in, I said thus in my heart, What shall I get by thinking on these two words? This thought had no sooner passed through my heart, but the words began thus to kindle in my spirit, "Thou art my love, thou art my love," twenty times together; and still as they ran thus in my mind, they waxed stronger and warmer, and began to make me look up; but being as yet between hope and fear, I still replied in my heart, But is it true, but is it true? At which, that sentence fell in upon me, He "wist not that it was true which was done by the angel" (Acts xii. 9).

Then I began to give place to the word, which, with power, did over and over make this joyful sound within my soul, Thou art my love, thou art my love; and nothing shall separate thee from my love; and with that, Rom. viii. 39 came into my mind. Now was my heart filled full of comfort and hope, and now I could believe that my sins should be forgiven me; yea, I was now so taken with the love and mercy of God, that I remember I could not tell how to contain till I got home; I thought I could have spoken of his love, and of his mercy to me, even to the very crows that sat upon the ploughed lands before me, had they been capable to have understood me . . . I was much followed by this scripture, "Simon, Simon, behold, Satan hath desired to have you" (Luke xxii. 31). And sometimes it would sound so loud within me, yea, and as it were call so strongly after me, that once above all the rest, I turned my head over my shoulder, thinking verily that some man had, behind me, called to me; being at a great distance, methought he called so loud; it came, as I have thought since, to have stirred me up to prayer, and to watchfulness; it came to acquaint me that a cloud and a storm was coming down upon me, but I understood it not.

For about the space of a month after, a very great storm came down upon me, which handled me twenty times worse than all I had met with before; it came stealing upon me, now by one piece, then by another; first, all my comfort was taken from me, then darkness seized upon me, after which whole floods of blasphemies, both against God, Christ, and the Scriptures, were poured upon my spirit, to my great confusion and astonishment.

Now I thought, surely I am possessed of the devil; at other times again, I thought I should be bereft of my wits; for instead of lauding and magnifying God the Lord with others, if I have but heard him spoken of, presently some most horrible blasphemous thought or other would bolt out of my heart against him . . . I often, when these temptations have been with force upon me, did compare myself in the case of such a child, whom some gipsy hath by force took up under her apron, and is carrying from friend and country; kick sometimes I did, and also scream and cry; but yet I was as bound in the wings of the temptation, and the wind would carry me away . . .

In these days, when I have heard others talk of what was the sin against the Holy Ghost, then would the tempter so provoke me to desire to sin that sin, that I was as if I could not, must not, neither should be quiet until I had committed that; now, no sin would serve but that; if it were to be committed by speaking of such a word, then I have been as if my mouth would have spoken that word, whether I would or no; and in so strong a measure was this temptation upon me, that often I have been ready to clap my hand under my chin, to hold my mouth from opening; and to that end also I have had thoughts at other times, to leap with my head downward, into some muck-hill hole or other, to keep my mouth from speaking.

Now I blessed the condition of the dog and toad, and counted the estate of everything that God had made far better than this dreadful state of mine, and such as my companions was; yea, gladly would I have been in the condition of dog or horse, for I knew they had no soul to perish under the everlasting weights of hell for sin, as mine was like to do.

In prayer, also, I have been greatly troubled at this time; sometimes I have thought I should see the devil, nay, thought I have felt him, behind me, pull my clothes; he would be, also, continually at me in the time of prayer to have done; break off, make haste, you have prayed enough, and stay no longer, still drawing my mind away. Sometimes, also, he would cast in such wicked thoughts as these: that I must pray to him, or for him. I have thought sometimes of that—Fall down, or, "if thou wilt fall down and worship me" (Matt. iv. 9).

Also, when, because I have had wandering thoughts in the time of this duty, I have laboured to compose my mind and fix it upon God, then, with great force, hath the tempter laboured to distract me, and confound me, and to turn away my mind, by presenting to my heart and fancy the form of a bush, a bull, a besom, or the like, as if I should pray to those . . . I could neither eat my food, stoop for a pin, chop a stick, or cast mine eye to look on this or that, but still the temptation would come, Sell Christ for this, or sell Christ for that; sell him, sell him.

Sometimes it would run in my thoughts, not so little as a hundred times together, Sell him, sell him, sell him; against which I may say, for whole hours together, I have been forced to stand as continually leaning and forcing my spirit against it, lest haply, before I were aware, some wicked thought might arise in my heart that might consent thereto; and sometimes also the tempter would make me believe I had consented to it, then should I be as tortured upon a rack for whole days together.

This temptation did put me to such scares, lest I should at sometimes, I say, consent thereto, and be overcome therewith, that by the very force of my mind, in labouring to gainsay and resist this wickedness, my very body also would be put into action or motion by way of pushing or thrusting with my hands or elbows, still answering as fast as the destroyer said, Sell him; I will not, I will not, I will not, I will not; no, not for thousands, thousands, thousands of worlds. . . . But at last, after much striving, even until I was almost out of breath, I felt this thought pass through my heart, Let him go, if he will! and I thought also, that I felt my heart freely consent thereto. Oh, the diligence of Satan! Oh, the desperateness of man's heart!

Now was the battle won, and down fell I, as a bird that is shot from the top of a tree, into great guilt, and fearful despair.

Now I should find my mind to flee from God, as from the face of a dreadful judge; yet this was my torment, I could not escape his hand: "It is a fearful thing to fall into the hands of the living God" (Heb. x. 31). . . . This, I say, would come in upon my mind, when I was fleeing from the face of God; for I did flee from his face, that is, my mind and spirit fled before him; by reason of his highness, I could not endure; then would the text cry, "Return unto me"; it would cry aloud with a very great voice, "Return unto me, for I have redeemed thee." Indeed, this would make me make a little stop, and, as it were, look over my shoulder behind me, to see if I could discern that the God of grace did follow me with a pardon in his hand, but I could no sooner do that, but all would be clouded and darkened again by that sentence, "For you know how that afterward, when he would have inherited the blessing, he found no place of repentance, though he sought it carefully with tears." Wherefore I could not return, but fled, though at sometimes it cried, "Return, return," as if it did holloa after me.

Once as I was walking to and fro in a good man's shop, bemoaning of myself in my sad and doleful state, . . . suddenly there was, as if there had rushed in at the window, the noise of wind upon me, but very pleasant, and as if I heard a voice speaking, Didst ever refuse to be justified by the blood of Christ? And, withal my whole life and profession past was, in a moment, opened to me, wherein I was made to see that designedly I had not; so my heart answered groaningly, No. Then fell, with power, that word of God upon me, "See that ye refuse not him that speaketh" (Heb. xii. 25). This made a strange seizure upon my spirit; it brought light with it, and commanded a silence in my heart of all those tumultuous thoughts that before did use, like masterless hell-hounds, to roar and bellow, and make a hideous noise within me.

But verily, that sudden rushing wind was as if an angel had come upon me: . . . it commanded a great calm in my soul . . .

After he had been some five or six years awakened, some of "the saints" suggested to him that he had powers of exhortation, and begged him to become a preacher. Although abashed, as one himself "in chains to preach to them in chains," [and carrying] "that fire in my own conscience that I persuaded them to be aware of," he settled into public preaching. Doctors and priests railed against him, and Satan continued his assaults.

But when Satan perceived that his thus tempting and assaulting of me would not answer his design, to wit, to overthrow my ministry, and make it ineffectual, as to the ends thereof; then he tried another way, which was to stir up the minds of the ignorant and malicious, to load me with slanders and reproaches; now therefore I may say, that what the devil could devise, and his instruments invent, was whirled up and down the country against me, thinking, as I said, that by that means they should make my ministry to be abandoned.

It began therefore to be rumoured up and down among the people, that I was a witch, a jesuit, a highwayman, and the like.

To all which, I shall only say, God knows that I am innocent. But as for mine accusers, let them provide themselves to meet me before the tribunal of the Son of God, there to answer for all these things, with all the rest of their iniquities, unless God shall give them repentance for them, for the which I pray with all my heart.

But that which was reported with the boldest confidence, was, that I had my misses, my whores, my bastards, yea, two wives at once, and the like. Now these slanders, with the other, I glory in, because but slanders, foolish, or knavish lies, and falsehoods cast upon me by the devil and his seed; and should I not be dealt with thus wickedly by the world, I should want one sign of a saint, and a child of God. . . .

So then, what shall I say to those that have thus bespattered me? Shall I threaten them? Shall I chide them? Shall I flatter them? Shall I intreat them to hold their tongues? No, not I, were it not for that these things make them ripe for damnation, that are the authors and abettors, I would say unto them, Report it, because it will increase my glory.

Therefore I bind these lies and slanders to me as an ornament, it belongs to my Christian profession to be vilified, slandered, reproached and reviled . . .

THE CONCLUSION

Of all the temptations that ever I met with in my life, to question the being of God, and truth of his gospel, is the worst, and the worst to be borne; when this temptation comes, it takes away my girdle from me, and removeth the foundation from under me. Oh, I have often thought of that word, "Have your loins girt about with truth"; and of that, "When the foundations are destroyed, what can the righteous do?"

Sometimes, when, after sin committed, I have looked for sore chastisement from the hand of God, the very next that I have had from him hath been the discovery of his grace. Sometimes, when I have been comforted, I have called myself a fool for my so sinking under trouble. And then, again, when I have been cast down, I thought I was not wise to give such way to comfort. With such strength and weight have both these been upon me.

I have wondered much at this one thing, that though God doth visit my soul with never so blessed a discovery of himself, yet I have found again, that such hours have offended me afterwards. That I have been in my spirit so filled with darkness that I could not so much as once conceive what that God and that comfort was with which I had been refreshed . . .

Of all tears, they are the best that are made by the blood of Christ; and of all joy, that is the sweetest that is mixed with mourning over Christ. Oh! it is a goodly thing to be on our knees, with Christ in our arms, before God. I hope I know something of these things.

I find to this day seven abominations in my heart: (1) Inclinings to unbelief. (2) Suddenly to forget the love and mercy that Christ manifesteth. (3) A leaning to the works of the law. (4) Wanderings and coldness in prayer. (5) To forget to watch for that I pray for. (6) Apt to murmur because I have no more, and yet ready to abuse what I have. (7) I can do none of those things which God commands me, but my corruptions will thrust in themselves, "When I would do good, evil is present with me."

These things I continually see and feel, and am afflicted and oppressed with; yet the wisdom of God doth order them for my good. (1) They make me abhor myself. (2) They keep me from trusting my heart. (3) They convince me of the insufficiency of all inherent righteousness. (4) They show me the necessity of flying to Jesus. (5) They press me to pray unto God. (6) They show me the need I have to watch and be sober. (7) And provoke me to look to God, through Christ, to help me, and carry me through this world. Amen.

THE TIMOROUS SCHOLAR

ROGER NORTH IS THE LIVELIEST AND RACIEST OF BIOGRAPHERS. HIS high spirits are irrepressible, his zest for truth carried far beyond the bounds of dignity. The life of Dr. John North is the shortest of the three *Lives* he devoted to his brothers: Francis, Baron Guilford, Lord Keeper of the Seal under James II; Sir Dudley, a Turkey merchant; John, the youngest, the brilliant scholar, who became Master of Trinity at thirty-two.

Their motive was commemoration, and the affection that inspired them is obvious. "Their best brother," he often lovingly calls the Lord Keeper, and "our doctor," he proudly designates the scholar. But North allows no considerations of dignity or propriety to cloud the vividness of truth. "Nay, scars and blemishes, as well as beauties, ought to be expressed; otherwise it is but an outline filled with lilies and roses." "I fancy myself a picture-drawer," he boasts naïvely; and goes on to point out that while the leaves and branches of a tree are harder to draw than the trunk, if they were left out "it would make but a sorry picture of a tree." Life dwells in the trivia even more than in the grandiose outlines: if "the life-scraps come out very thin and meagre" biography dwindles to "a petit cycle of musty genealogy." And finally, "without the how and why, all history is jejune and unprofitable."

It would be hard to state the biographer's creed in fewer or more brisk words. North lives up to it. The brief glimpse of the Commonwealth from the loyalist point of view, as "a Babel of misshapen powers," is only one of the minor brightnesses in his absurd and entertaining portrait of the meticulous Doctor. We see the child, solemn with a docility that usually "argues imbecility of body and mind," his irrepressible brother remarks. We see the youthful Cambridge student cowering beneath the bedclothes in terror of beholding "an enorm spectre." No less exuberant is his picture of the mature and erudite scholar, pink-faced and yellow-polled, "his features scandalous," more like "a Madam *entravestie* than a bookworm," wavering among young noblemen like a Silenus on his Leon Errol legs. The scenes of his illness are right out of Molière: the terrific remedies of the medical faculty, the Doctor's docility in obeying them, the ruin to which they reduce him, "helmeted in caps upon caps," the tintinnabulation of tongs and curtain rings they insist on to keep him awake after his stroke, the "extreme surprise" of the physicians when he recovered without their remedies. Roger North is no respecter of persons.

But farce is not his only gift. His rendering of "the Doctor" shows serious devotion, too, and genuine pride in his scholarship. His character-drawing is distinguished for vivacity, convincingness, and penetration. If his chronology is sometimes a little confused, his sense of movement is nevertheless remarkable. His language is racy, flowing, vigorous, not only inventive but at times brilliantly slangy. No panegyrist, he is equally free from even a pinpoint of malice. These facts combine with his natural honesty and enquiringness to make his subjects delightfully human. Their sum total ranks him high among biographers.

The Life of the Honourable and Reverend Dr. John North

ROGER NORTH

[North's three brothers all died before the close of the seventeenth century, but North seems to have written the *Lives* during the earlier part of the next century. They were first published in 1744.]

DR. JOHN NORTH WAS THE FIFTH OF SEVEN SONS OF THE RIGHT Honourable Sir Dudley North, Knight of the Bath, Lord North, Baron of Kirtling, and Anne, one of the daughters and co-heirs of Sir Charles Mountagu, a younger brother of the Boughton family. He was born at London, September 4, 1645, and had divers brothers and sisters, elder and younger . . .

When he was very young, and also as he grew up, he was of a nice and tender constitution, not so vigorous and athletic as most of his brothers were. His temper was always reserved and studious; for which reason his noble parents destined him early for the church . . . If anything so early seemed amiss in him, it was a non-natural gravity, which, in youths, is seldom a good sign; for it argues imbecility of body and mind, or both; but his lay wholly in the former, for his mental capacity was vigorous, as none more.

His scholastic education was altogether at St. Edmund's Bury, in Suffolk, under Dr. Stephens, then master of an eminent school there. It was a piece of good fortune to be no forwarder; for his residence there fell in the dregs of time, when, after the martyrdom of King Charles I, a Babel of misshapen powers tormented the

people of England, until the happy restoration of King Charles II
to the crown, and the nation to their laws: a fit time for a monastic
retirement! The master was pedant enough, and noted for high
flights in poetry and criticism, and what we now call jingling, not
a little derived from the last age. All which qualities were not
amiss in his employment. The worst of him was, what his corpu-
lence declared, the being a wet epicure, the common vice of
bookish professions. We pass by his partialities (which were indeed scandalous, and pernicious to many of his scholars) because
they happened to turn in favor of our doctor; for his master was
exceedingly fond and proud of him.

One happiness was, that he was a noted Cavalier, then the title
of the king's friends, in opposition to the rebels, who, from a
precise cut they affected, were styled Roundheads. In the worst
of these times, the master, in his family, used the forms of loyalty
and orthodoxy; but, being reputed little better than a malignant,*
he was forced to use outwardly an occasional conformity, by observing the church duties, and days of super-hypocritical fastings
and seekings, wherewith the people, in those days, were tormented;
though now worn out of almost all credibility; and he walked to
the church after his brigade of boys, there to endure the inflictions
of divers holders-forth, tiring themselves and everybody else: and
by these means he made a shift to hold his school.

After the happy Restoration, and while our doctor was yet
at school, the master took occasion to publish his cavaliership by
all the ways he could contrive; and one was putting all the boarders,
who were of the chief families in the country, into red cloaks, because cavaliers about the court usually wore such; and scarlet
was commonly called the king's colour.

*"Our doctor" rapidly became an accomplished scholar, and, in
1661, was "planted" in Jesus College, Cambridge, where he "became settled in a severe course of studies" directed toward church
preferment.*

* The name the Roundheads applied to Royalists: and a fine example of
invidious labeling.

The doctor's greatest, or rather only, infirmity was a natural timidity, owing to a feeble constitution of body, inclining to the effeminate. This, under some circumstances, and without a mind as vigorous and strong as his body was weak, might have oppressed him. He was always sensible of this weakness, and, during the whole course of his life, laboured to conquer it, and, as to outward appearance, prevailed; and what was insuperable lay dormant within. One would have expected that a youth at the university, no freshman, nor mean scholar, should have got the better of being afraid in the dark; but it was not so with him, for when he was in bed alone, he durst not trust his countenance above the clothes. For some time he lay with his tutor, who once, coming home, found the scholar in bed with only his crown visible. The tutor, indiscreetly enough, pulled him by the hair; whereupon the scholar sunk down, and the tutor followed, and at last, with a great outcry, the scholar sprang up, expecting to see an enorm spectre.

Another time, which was after he was a fellow of the college, in a moon-shine night, he saw one standing in a white sheet. He surveyed it with all his optics, and was confirmed it was a spirit (as they call it), and resolved with himself, if he could, to find out what it came for. He got out of his bed, and being still of the same opinion, went nearer and nearer, till he might touch it; and then, reaching out his hand, he perceived it was only his towel, hung against the wall, with the moon shining full upon it; and then he went to bed and slept well.

In 1666 he was made a fellow of Jesus College, and began "to lay the foundations of a competent library": "he used to say that a man could not be a scholar at second hand," *but only from studying original authors rather than from quotations or accounts in other books.* "He had a very researching spirit"; "Greek became almost vernacular to him"; *he took pains to master Hebrew; he improved his English style by reading* "the best penned English books"; *he kept his accounts in Latin.*

The doctor had no favourite diversion, or manual exercise, to rest his mind a little, which he held bent with continual thinking. His parents, who were much addicted to music, recommended that to him for a diversion, and particularly the noble organ, as the fullest, and not only a complete solitary concert, but most proper for an ecclesiastic. . . . He was sensible the advice was very good, and accordingly got a small organ into his chamber at Jesus College, and suffered himself to be taught a lesson or two, which he practised over when he had a mind to be unbent; but he made no manner of advance, and one accident put him out of all manner of conceit of it. His under neighbor was a morose and importunate master of arts; and one night the doctor could not sleep; and thought to fit himself for it by playing upon his organ. The bellows knocking upon the floor, and the hum of the pipes, made a strange din at midnight, and the gentleman below, that never heard it so before, could not tell what to make of it; but at length he found it out to be his neighbor's organ. And thereupon, to retaliate this night's work, got out of his bed, and, with his two couple of bowls, went to bowls by himself. This made a much louder noise than the organ, and the doctor was as much at a loss to know what that meant, but, suspecting how the case stood, he left off, and scarce ever touched his organ again.

The doctor had found out one petit entertainment in his study besides books; and that was keeping of great house spiders in wide-mouthed glasses, such as men keep tobacco in. When he had them safe in hold, he supplied them with crumbs of bread, which they ate rather than starve: but their regale was flies, which he sometimes caught and put to them. When their imprisonment appeared inevitable, they fell to their trade of making webs, and made large expansions and more private recesses. It pleased him to observe the animals manage their interest in the great work of taking their prey. If it was a small fly given them, no more ceremony but take and eat him; but if a great master fleshfly, then to work, twenty courses round him, and perhaps not come near him, for he had claws sharp as a cat's; and, after divers starts to and fro, a web was with a hind leg dexterously clapped over two or three of his legs. After all his claws were in that manner secured, then, at a running pull, a broad web was brought over him, which bound him hand and foot; and, by being fixed to the spider's tail, the fly was carried off into one of his inmost recesses, there to be feasted upon at leisure.

Spiders, like other creatures of prey, eat one another, and, for their continual design of eating, are paid by a continual dread of being eaten. Two old spiders will not be kept in one glass, unless accidentally known to each other, or, it may be, male and female; but to work they go, coursing about till one hath got the better of the other, and then falls to, and heartily feeds upon him. They breed numerously; and the young ones, after the example of their fathers, use the same trade. The danger, as well as fear, is common to all. There is little regard to relation or families; and for that reason, like pikes in a pond, none ever takes a prey, but he turns suddenly round, lest another should take him. When the young are hatched, and can run about, they lie still, waiting for advantages over the rest, and care not rashly to expose themselves. If they are disturbed, and some made to run, the whole nation is alarmed, and many a life falls in the disorder before the wars cease; and then each, that survives, makes merry with his booty. Thus their numbers are reduced to a very few, who find means of retreating into castles of their own making.

They cast their skins at certain periods; and the manner of doing it is remarkable. They hang themselves to the ceiling of their webs, with their body downwards, and, holding themselves fast by all their legs brought together, remain striving and pulling each leg, till it comes out of the hose, and their body is free from its case; and then they turn and run away, leaving their old coat in their place; as we often see them hanging in cobwebs. The signal to them of this change coming on, is a dry parting of the skin upon their backs; whereupon they fall to work as was described. The doctor used to divert us with describing the course of life which his poor prisoners led.

He was always jocose and free in his ordinary conversation; and that made him very popular with the airy folks, as young gentlemen; and even with the fair sex; for he was a comely person, and withal very decently behaved, and respectful, which set off his wit; and with that he always made them an agreeable diversion . . . Next to those, he affected to refresh himself with the society of the young noblemen and fellow-commoners; and he used to say that he found more of candor and sincerity in them than in the graver sort. And for the like reason he inclined to those of the ancienter families, though he owned that the better parts were found with the latter. Sorting himself with these, he took great delight to oppose their raw wits with enigmatic questions, and often out of the classics. I have seen him merry as a school-boy with a knot of them, like the younglings about old Silenus, in deep consult about reconciling that passage in Ovid—"Sine pondere habentia pondus." . . . And I might mention some ladies with whom he pretended to be innocently merry and free; and indeed more so (often) than welcome; as when he touched the pre-eminencies of their sex. As, for instance, saying that of all the beasts of the field God Almighty thought woman the fittest companion for man.

But whatever was the cause, he had no relish at all for the conversation of his fellow collegiates; and they, I presume, had as little for his. He might not conform to their measures, or methods of living; or there being a seeming inequality betwixt them, by his place in the university, and advantages with respect to preferment; and his consorting rather with the young gentlemen than the grave, and, as he thought, perhaps, empty seniors of the college, and affecting a select company of the learneder sort in other colleges: all these ingredients turned sour, and jealousies, suspicions, and reflections, with morose countenances, bred out of them; so that he desired, if possible, without his great inconvenience, to remove himself to some other college, where, as he proposed, he might pass his time more agreeably.

The doctor was no great traveller; but sometimes he affected to go abroad, and, if he had his choice, always on horseback; for he fancied that exercise good for his health, and particularly in the case of gravel, with which he was troubled. Between Cambridge and his father's house, and to and fro from London, were the chief of his journeys. If his post was in the coach, he chose to change with a horseman. Once, after riding a very long journey, he came into the room of the inn where the company was, and threw himself down upon the bed. "Now," he said, "I have the pleasure of being very weary." . . .

Once, at the instance of his mother, he made a visit to the Lady Hatton, her sister, at Kerby in Northamptonshire. He found his aunt there forsaken by her husband the old Lord Hatton . . . The good old lady gave her nephew as good entertainment as she could; that is, took him into hugger mugger in her closet, where she usually had some good pie, or plum cake, which her neighbors, in compassion, sent her in; for the housekeeping was very mean, and she had not the command of anything.

The fame of his erudition brought him the Professorship of Greek at twenty-seven. His only publication, to be sure, was a small volume of selections from Plato, with commentaries; but he plunged deep into philology, metaphysics, and logic, and made himself a master of the new philosophy of Descartes. He planned enormous works: one against the Socinians, another against republics as "the worst of tyrannies under a mask of liberty," a critical history of philosophy showing the borrowings of the moderns from the ancients, a confutation of the pernicious doctrines of Hobbes. But he was never satisfied with his work; meticulous were his agonizings in composition. Bringing nothing to completion, he demanded, in his last illness, that all his notes be burned, and sent them "in lumps, as innocent martyrs, to the fire." Only one small notebook chanced to survive; and even in it, dreading lest it might fall into a strangers' hand, the doctor had written: "I beshrew his heart, that gathers my opinion from anything he finds wrote here."

He was always exceedingly thoughtful, and full of notions. He could not rest from working upon his designs, and, at the same time, so diffident of the event, that, between impulse and despair, he was like Mahomet in his tomb, or, as they say, Erasmus hung. Despair had the greatest influence; and it sat so hard upon his spirits that he desired rather to be utterly forgot, than that any memorial of his dealing in literature should remain to show that such a one as he existed, which should not be proof against the teeth of the next ages. After he had the government of himself he would not endure that a picture should be made of him, though he was much courted and invited by Sir Peter Lely to it. And, what was very odd, he would not leave the print in his bed, where he had lain, remain undefaced.

As to his person and constitution, excepting only the agreeable air of his countenance and florid head of flaxen hair, I have little to produce that may be commended. His temperature of body, and his austere course of life, were ill matched, and his complexion agreed with neither; for his face was always tinted with a fresh color, and his looks vegete and sanguine, and, as some used to jest, his features were scandalous, as showing rather a Madam *en-travestie* than a bookworn. But his flesh was strangely flaccid and soft, his going weak and shuffling, often crossing his legs as if he were tipsy; his sleep seldom, or never, easy, but interrupted with unquiet and painful dreams, the reposes he had were short and by snatches; his active spirit had rarely any perfect settlement or rest.

The distempers which most afflicted, or rather frighted him, were gravel and rheums. The former held him in sad expectations most part of his life, and the other were most urgent towards his latter end; and, in truth, were the occasion of his death, as will be shown afterwards. His worst indisposition lay in his mind, that is, an unhappy tendency to believe that, in all incidents and emergencies, the worst that in possibility might happen, would fall to his share; and accordingly, his mind always lighted upon extremes. He never had a fit of the stone in his life, but voided plenty of red gravel, which he was told was a symptom that no stone gathered. But that weighed little with him, for every morning he speculated his urine, and, as the use of splenetic folks is, called witnesses to see what quantities of gravel he voided.

In 1677, at the age of thirty-two, he became Master of Trinity. To his conscientious sense of inadequacy, the cares of college government were disastrous; his morbid rectitude made administration a gnawing round of anxieties. He was officiously rigid and strict in the enforcement of rules.

Youth will always mistake manhood to consist wholly in disorderly living, and that order and discipline belong only to boys.
And, to show how much men they are, they behave themselves,
as some did to him, contumaciously, and many of them contrived
to affront him. I have heard it said, but not credibly, that one
night, as he was walking in the cloister, some lads, merrymaking
in an opposite chamber, and fancying he came there to spy what
was doing, came down and used him ill; but I never heard him
speak of it, as he did of most things that concerned him; nor did
he make any inquiry about it, as he would have done, to dis-
courage such affronts; therefore I do not believe the story to be
true. This I was a witness of. One winter night, whilst we sat in
his dining-room by the fire, the chimney being opposite to the
windows (looking into the great quadrangle), a stone was sent
from the court, through the window, into the room, and fell but
a little short of the company. He seemed to take but little notice.
We guessed him to be inwardly vexed; and soon after the discourse
fell upon the subject of people's kicking against their superiors in
government, who preserved them as children are preserved by
parents; and then he had a scroll of instances out of Greek history
to the same purpose, concluding that no conscientious magistrate
can be popular; but, in lieu of that, he must arm himself with
equanimity.

*He was equally unpopular with his equals. The two preceding
Masters, more addicted to books than to business, had allowed the
eight seniors to determine affairs, and this had established an expectation in their minds that the Master would merely ratify their
opinions.*

But our doctor did not understand this method of proceeding,
and consulted his own reason, and would be guided by that, and
that only, whatever the rest thought; . . . and nothing, but reasoning, and convincing his judgment, would induce him to comply.
This behavior seemed a little new to them, who had been used so
much to dictate as scarce to endure contradiction; and they used
all means, civil and uncivil, to reduce their master under the like
reglement as the former . . . Once at a meeting, the seniors had

agreed upon a business; but the master did not think fit to join with them to establish it. They most importunately urged; as if their unanimous accord were enough to satisfy him . . . At last one of them said, "Master, since you will not agree, we must rise and break up the meeting." "Nay," said the master, "that you shall not do, for I myself will rise and be gone first." And, accordingly, he rose and went into his chamber, leaving them in a sort of consternation; for they knew that, without their master, they could do nothing at all.

It was very remarkable that nothing of any evil, which the doctor at any time in his life feared, ever came upon him; but somewhat else, and of which he had no imagination or dream, and indeed the worst, I think, that could befall human kind; that is, to be paralytic and epileptic . . . The distemper came upon him by these steps, first, a cold, then an unusual quantity of rheum discharged at his throat . . . A circulatory course (as they called it) of physic was prescribed, enough to have purged a strong man from off his legs; [and] after this career performed, the prescription was to take amber, as tobacco, in pipes, and to have certain astringent powders, in quills, blown into his mouth . . .

It is certain that, by these methods of physic, smoke, and powder, the doctor was reduced to extreme weakness, and, finding no amendment, ventured to come up to his friends in London. They knew nothing of his having been ill; for, in his letters, he complained of nothing but a cold he had got. They were amazed to see him come helmeted in caps upon caps, and meagre as one newly crept out of a fever. His regimen was no less changed than his habit and countenance. He must stir little abroad, and, for the world, not after sunset, though it was July (which was the only time of his friends' refreshment abroad), for fear of increasing his rheums. He must drink nothing small, nor much of anything. Grapes and peaches, being full of humidity, were poison; but nuts, and dry bread toasted, without stint, and all the while, at fit periods, the pipes and powders came; and one or another must blow for him. His friends had no notion of this latter medicament, nor, as I guess, his physicians; otherwise they had not prescribed, nor we suffered the continuance of it. After the doctor's death, I told the case to Dr. Lower, the prime physician of his time, and he said that he would undertake, by the smoke of amber only, to put the strongest man in the world into convulsion fits.

The Doctor's friends persuaded him to relax his rigors, and he made a partial recovery. But when he returned to Cambridge he resumed the regimen. The consequences soon declared themselves.

The master and seniors thought fit to revive an antiquated discipline, according to the statutes, of admonishing disorderly scholars, in order (without amendment) to expulsion; and in the morning the doctor came from the meeting (where probably he had been a little roiled) to perform his duty upon two scholars then brought to be admonished. And it was observed that he admonished them with more than usual earnestness and acrimony in his speech; for the lads were much to blame, and behaved themselves contumaciously. When the body is weak, passion is usually strong, and divers things occurred to stir it up in him, which probably touched the trigger, and, while he was speaking, down he dropped.

After the ordinary tormenting operations were over, he recovered a little sense, but was excessively drowsy; and it was judged that, unless that symptom could be conquered, he must drop from them. Whereupon, by direction, followed a perpetual noise and clangor, of one sort or other, to keep him awake. There was concert of tongs, firegrate, wainscot drum, and dancing of curtains and curtain rings, such as would have made a sound man mad. It was presumed that, if he fell asleep, he would never wake more; so his instruments were plied until his good mother (who was immediately sent for) came to take care of him . . . The good lady had no longer patience, but set up her maternal authority, and told them flat and plain that her son should have rest, and that quietly, for full two hours, and she would answer the consequences . . .

After this she opened the curtains, and called in the physicians, and the rest that had a mind to be there, and showed them how easy and quietly he lay, and breathing as nature required. His countenance had a good color, and his face was composed, which, before, was distorted in divers manners, with his eyes staring like one of the Furies. "Now, doctors," said she, "what think ye?" "But, madam," said one, "will he wake?" "You shall see," said she, and gently jogging him by the arm as he lay, he awoke, and, opening his eyes, knew several there, and spoke to them. The physicians were exceedingly surprised; for they expected great difficulty in waking him, and had been consulting methods of how to do it.

He kept his bed for some considerable time before he ventured to rise; and then was able, only with the help of a friend and crutch, to crawl a little about the room. His mouth and face were drawn up on the lame side, and his left arm and leg altogether enervous; and neither did him much service as long as he lived . . .

After he could lie awake and think, I guessed he had some reflection that he had been over severe with himself by too much hard study and abstemiousness, which, possibly, had brought that disease over him; and then fancied he must cure himself by a course clean contrary; and accordingly he thought that now he must be merry and jolly. Pursuant to this (conjectured) model, the company, that assisted about his bed to entertain him, must find merry tales to tell, and if a little smutty, the mirth paid for it. The lighter sort of books, and frivolous comedies, were read to him, and he heard them with notable attention, and, at the quaint passages, was unusually affected, and often laughed, but (as his visage was then distorted) most deformly.

His friends were mortified and embarrassed by his impeded utterance and unseemly hilarity; to them he seemed like "a high-flying fowl with one wing cut," *who tries to soar* "but always comes, with a side turn, down to the ground." *Instead of his former lofty flights, he was reduced to* "low concerns, and reptile conceits that scarce rose from the ground." *He who had once been so austere now* "used the strongest sherry, glass after glass, which, formerly, he would have thought more than a cup too much."

About three or four years after his first illness he made his last retirement from Cambridge, and seemed to bid all his friends adieu; and there he passed the sorry remainder of his life . . . He took most to silence, and, however seldom, yet, when he did speak, it was much to the purpose, and often very pathetic, and, perhaps, being offended, resentingly sarcastic . . . His weakness of body continually increased, and his fits came on quicker. His chief ease was the couch, where he usually lay expecting fits and wishing for death, the only means to free a limpid soul, as his certainly was, from that dungeon of flesh, in which he lay stuck fast as in a mire. At length, in one of his fits as was supposed, without discovery of any pain, about April 1683, he went out, rather than died. He lies interred in the ante-chapel, as he directed in his lifetime, and, as was noted, nothing significative but J. N. upon a small stone over him. He was desirous, if he could not leave somewhat behind him worthy to be remembered, of which (as I have shown) he never was satisfied, not to be remembered at all.

ROMAN PROFILE

GIBBON TELLS US IN HIS OPENING PAGES THAT HE INTENDS TO review the simple events "of a private and literary life" in a style "simple and familiar." But he saw himself primarily as the author of *The Decline and Fall of the Roman Empire*. He conceived that it was his eminent literary achievement that entitled the public to a legitimate curiosity about him. "He had written a magnificent history," says Augustine Birrell: "It remained to write the history of the historian." History is eminently the right word. It was hardly possible for Gibbon to regard his subject as of inferior moment to the Roman Empire, and he brought to the composition of his *Autobiography* the same weighty dignity he bestowed upon the panorama of a civilization crumbling into ruins.

"Truth, naked, unblushing truth," Gibbon held to be the first virtue of history, and added with elaborate modesty that it must be "the sole recommendation" of his own life-story. His muse is no shameless hussy, but neither is she squeamish. Gibbon has no fear, when he comes to his Oxford days, of referring to "the taverns and bagnios of Covent Garden," or of naming that tutor who "well remembered that he had a salary to receive and only forgot that he had a duty to perform." A kind of propriety Gibbon is restrained by, but it is displayed neither in a tactful avoidance of offense to others nor in a whitewashing of his own character. It is concerned instead with what is too personal or vulgar to dilate upon: his monetary affairs, or those illnesses of his childhood whose sickroom odor must not offend the reader's fastidious nostrils.

And, so doing, Gibbon edits himself a very little. He reflects faithfully his innocent vanity, certain traces of oddity, and a touch of mannered ostentation, but his elegant mirror chills a bit the warmth and tenderness of the man. It hardly does justice to the affection he felt for the aunt who nursed his childhood or the affection he inspired in his stepmother, who even as a very old lady adored her stepson. And from its pages one would hardly guess him capable, in old age and failing health, of braving the dangers of Revolutionary France to join his friend Lord Shef-field, whose wife had just died, and who might be somewhat com-forted, Gibbon felt, by his presence. But these are probably among those personal feelings that Gibbon judged to belong to one's friends rather than to the public.

It is, in fact, the public image of a public figure that Gibbon gives us, much more than the private man, although that strange and even faintly wistful person is never far in the background of his most pompously complacent pages. His reticence is in many ways characteristic of the eighteenth century. That age preferred that its earnestness and enthusiasm and depths of feeling should all wear the decent garb of civilized "reason." Gibbon reflects its worldliness, but also its sobriety and balance. His vision of him-self was clear and unclouded by enthusiasm. But his private char-acter, the naked man, was not the character of the great historian. The nature of the historian Gibbon rendered superbly, and in the process of painting that ingenious person gave us fascinating glimpses of the deeper man as well.

Autobiography of Edward Gibbon

[The form in which the *Autobiography* is usually printed is not Gibbon's final rendering of his story, but a skilful fusion of six partly finished attempts at it, put together after Gibbon's death by Lord Sheffield. This version was first published in 1796. Gibbon's original drafts were finally published in 1896 as *The Autobiographies of Edward Gibbon*.]

IN THE FIFTY-SECOND YEAR OF MY AGE, AFTER THE COMPLETION of an arduous and successful work, I now propose to employ some moments of my leisure in reviewing the simple transactions of a private and literary life. Truth, naked, unblushing truth, the first virtue of more serious history, must be the sole recommendation of this personal narrative. The style shall be simple and familiar: but the style is the image of character; and the habits of correct writing may produce, without labour or design, the appearance of art and study. My own amusement is my motive, and will be my reward.

I was born at Putney, in the county of Surrey, the 27th of April, O. S. in the year one thousand seven hundred and thirty-seven; the first child of the marriage of Edward Gibbon, Esq., and of Judith Porten. My lot might have been that of a slave, a savage, or a peasant; nor can I reflect without pleasure on the bounty of Nature, which cast my birth in a free and civilized country, in an age of science and philosophy, in a family of honourable rank, and decently endowed with the gifts of fortune. From my birth I have enjoyed the right of primogeniture; but I was succeeded by five brothers and one sister, all of whom were snatched away in their infancy. My five brothers, whose names may be found in the parish register of Putney, I shall not pretend to lament: but from my childhood to the present hour I have deeply and sincerely regretted my sister, whose life was somewhat prolonged, and whom I remember to have been an amiable infant. The relation of a brother and a sister, especially if they do not marry, appears to me of a very singular nature. It is a familiar and tender friendship with a female, much about our own age; an affection perhaps softened by the secret influence of sex, but pure from any mixture of sensual desire, the sole species of Platonic love that can be indulged with truth, and without danger.

The death of a new-born child before that of its parents may seem an unnatural, but it is strictly a probable event: since of any given number the greater part are extinguished before their ninth year, before they possess the faculties of the mind or body. Without accusing the profuse waste or imperfect workmanship of Nature, I shall only observe, that this unfavourable chance was multiplied against my infant existence. So feeble was my constitution, so precarious my life, that, in the baptism of my brothers, my father's prudence successively repeated my Christian name of Edward, that, in case of the departure of the eldest son, this patronymic appellation might be still perpetuated in the family.

—— *Uno avulso non deficit alter.*

To preserve and to rear so frail a being, the most tender assiduity was scarcely sufficient; and my mother's attention was somewhat diverted by her frequent pregnancies, by an exclusive passion for her husband, and by the dissipation of the world, in which his taste and authority obliged her to mingle. But the maternal office was supplied by my aunt, Mrs. Catherine Porten; at whose name I feel a tear of gratitude trickling down my cheek. A life of celibacy transferred her vacant affection to her sister's first child: my weakness excited her pity; her attachment was fortified by labour and success: and if there be any, as I trust there are some, who rejoice that I live, to that dear and excellent woman they must hold themselves indebted.

Many anxious and solitary days did she consume in the patient trial of every mode of relief and amusement. Many wakeful nights did she sit by my bedside in trembling expectation that each hour would be my last. Of the various and frequent disorders of my childhood my own recollection is dark; nor do I wish to expatiate on so disgusting a topic. Suffice it to say, that while every practitioner, from Sloane and Ward to the Chevalier Taylor, was successively summoned to torture or relieve me, the care of my mind was too frequently neglected for that of my health: compassion always suggested an excuse for the indulgence of the master, or the idleness of the pupil; and the chain of my education was broken as often as I was recalled from the school of learning to the bed of sickness.

As soon as the use of speech had prepared my infant reason for the admission of knowledge, I was taught the arts of reading, writing, and arithmetic. So remote is the date, so vague is the memory of their origin in myself, that, were not the error corrected by analogy, I should be tempted to conceive them as innate. In my childhood I was praised for the readiness with which I could multiply and divide, by memory alone, two sums of several figures: such praise encouraged my growing talent; and had I persevered in this line of application, I might have acquired some fame in mathematical studies.

In my ninth year (January, 1746), in a lucid interval of comparative health, my father adopted the convenient and customary mode of English education; and I was sent to Kingston-upon-Thames, to a school of about seventy boys, which was kept by Dr. Wooddeson and his assistants. Every time I have since passed over Putney Common, I have always noticed the spot where my mother, as we drove along in the coach, admonished me that I was now going into the world, and must learn to think and act for myself. The expression may appear ludicrous; yet there is not, in the course of life, a more remarkable change than the removal of a child from the luxury and freedom of a wealthy house, to the frugal diet and strict subordination of a school; from the tenderness of parents and the obsequiousness of servants, to the rude familiarity of his equals, the insolent tyranny of his seniors,

and the rod, perhaps, of a cruel and capricious pedagogue. Such
hardships may steel the mind and body against the injuries of
fortune; but my timid reserve was astonished by the crowd and
tumult of the school; the want of strength and activity disqualified
me for the sports of the playfield; nor have I forgotten how often
in the year forty-six I was reviled and buffeted for the sins of my
Tory ancestors. By the common methods of discipline, at the expense of many tears and some blood, I purchased the knowledge
of the Latin syntax: and not long since I was possessed of the
dirty volumes of Phaedrus and Cornelius Nepos, which I painfully construed and darkly understood.

My studies were too frequently interrupted by sickness; and
after a real or nominal residence at Kingston school of near two
years, I was finally recalled (December, 1747) by my mother's
death, which was occasioned, in her thirty-eighth year, by the consequences of her last labour. I was too young to feel the importance of my loss; and the image of her person and conversation
is faintly imprinted in my memory. The affectionate heart of my
aunt, Catherine Porten, bewailed a sister and a friend; but my
poor father was inconsolable, and the transport of grief seemed to
threaten his life or his reason. I can never forget the scene of
our first interview, some weeks after the fatal event; the awful
silence, the room hung with black, the midday tapers, his sighs
and tears; his praises of my mother, a saint in heaven; his solemn
adjuration that I would cherish her memory and imitate her
virtues; and the fervour with which he kissed and blessed me as
the sole surviving pledge of their loves. The storm of passion
insensibly subsided into calmer melancholy. At a convivial meeting of his friends, Mr. Gibbon might affect or enjoy a gleam
of cheerfulness; but his plan of happiness was for ever destroyed:
and after the loss of his companion he was left alone in a world, of
which the business and pleasures were to him irksome or insipid.
After some unsuccessful trials he renounced the tumult of London
and the hospitality of Putney, and buried himself in the rural or
rather rustic solitude of Buriton; from which, during several years,
he seldom emerged.

As far back as I can remember, the house near Putney Bridge and churchyard, of my maternal grandfather, appears in the light of my proper and native home. It was there that I was allowed to spend the greatest part of my time, in sickness or in health, during my school vacations and my parents' residence in London, and finally after my mother's death. Three months after that event, in the spring of 1748, the commercial ruin of her father, Mr. James Porten, was accomplished and declared. As his effects were not sold, nor the house evacuated, till the Christmas following, I enjoyed during the whole year the society of my aunt, without much consciousness of her impending fate.

I feel a melancholy pleasure in repeating my obligations to that excellent woman, Mrs. Catherine Porten, the true mother of my mind as well as of my health. Her natural good sense was improved by the perusal of the best books in the English language; and if her reason was sometimes clouded by prejudice, her sentiments were never disguised by hypocrisy or affectation. Her indulgent tenderness, the frankness of her temper, and my innate rising curiosity, soon removed all distance between us; like friends of an equal age, we freely conversed on every topic, familiar or abstruse; and it was her delight and reward to observe the first shoots of my young ideas. Pain and languor were often soothed by the voice of instruction and amusement; and to her kind lessons I ascribe my early and invincible love of reading, which I would not exchange for the treasures of India.

Gibbon's childhood illnesses made him a reader: wide, but undisciplined and erratic. With his sixteenth year his disorders vanished, and his father entered him as a gentleman-commoner at Magdalen College. He arrived at Oxford, Gibbon tells us, "with a stock of erudition that might have puzzled a doctor, and a degree of ignorance of which a schoolboy would have been ashamed."

To the University of Oxford I acknowledge no obligation; and she will as cheerfully renounce me for a son, as I am willing to disclaim her for a mother. I spent fourteen months at Magdalen College; they proved the fourteen months the most idle and unprofitable of my whole life: the reader will pronounce between the school and the scholar: but I cannot affect to believe that nature had disqualified me for all literary pursuits. The specious and ready excuse of my tender age, imperfect preparation, and hasty departure, may doubtless be alleged; nor do I wish to defraud such excuses of their proper weight. Yet in my sixteenth year I was not devoid of capacity or application; even my childish reading had displayed an early though blind propensity for books; and the shallow flood might have been taught to flow in a deep channel and a clear stream. In the discipline of a well-constituted academy, under the guidance of skilful and vigilant professors, I should gradually have risen from translations to originals, from the Latin to the Greek classics, from dead languages to living science: my hours would have been occupied by useful and agreeable studies, the wanderings of fancy would have been restrained, and I should have escaped the temptations of idleness, which finally precipitated my departure from Oxford.

Perhaps in a separate annotation I may coolly examine the fabulous and real antiquities of our sister universities, a question which has kindled such fierce and foolish disputes among their fanatic sons. In the meanwhile it will be acknowledged that these venerable bodies are sufficiently old to partake of all the prejudices and infirmities of age. The schools of Oxford and Cambridge were founded in a dark age of false and barbarous science; and they are still tainted with the vices of their origin. Their primitive discipline was adapted to the education of priests and monks; and the government still remains in the hands of the clergy, an order of men whose manners are remote from the present world, and whose eyes are dazzled by the light of philosophy. The legal incorporation of these societies by the charters of popes and kings had given them a monopoly of the public instruction; and the spirit of monopolists is narrow, lazy, and oppressive: their work is more costly and less productive than that of independent artists; and the new improvements so eagerly grasped by the competition of freedom, are admitted with slow and sullen reluctance in those proud corporations, above the fear of a rival, and below the confession of an error.

Our colleges are supposed to be schools of science, as well as of education; nor is it unreasonable to expect that a body of literary men, devoted to a life of celibacy, exempt from the care of their own subsistence, and amply provided with books, should devote their leisure to the prosecution of study, and that some effects of their studies should be manifested to the world. The shelves of their library groan under the weight of the Benedictine folios, of the editions of the fathers, and the collections of the middle ages, which have issued from the single abbey of St. Germain de Préz at Paris. A composition of genius must be the offspring of one mind; but such works of industry, as may be divided among many hands, and must be continued during many years, are the peculiar province of a laborious community. If I inquire into the manu-factures of the monks of Magdalen, if I extend the inquiry to the other colleges of Oxford and Cambridge, a silent blush, or a scornful frown, will be the only reply. The fellows or monks of my time were decent easy men, who supinely enjoyed the gifts of the founder; their days were filled by a series of uniform employ-ments; the chapel and the hall, the coffee-house and the common room, till they retired, weary and well satisfied, to a long slumber. From the toil of reading, or thinking, or writing, they had ab-solved their conscience; and the first shoots of learning and in-genuity withered on the ground, without yielding any fruits to the owners or the public.

Dr. Winchester well remembered that he had a salary to re-ceive, and only forgot that he had a duty to perform. Instead of guiding the studies, and watching over the behaviour of his disci-ple, I was never summoned to attend even the ceremony of a lec-ture; and, excepting one voluntary visit to his rooms, during the eight months of his titular office, the tutor and pupil lived in the same college as strangers to each other. The want of experience, of advice, and of occupation, soon betrayed me into some impro-prieties of conduct, ill-chosen company, late hours, and incon-siderate expense.

My growing debts might be secret; but my frequent absence was visible and scandalous: and a tour to Bath, a visit into Buckinghamshire, and four excursions to London in the same winter, were costly and dangerous frolics. They were, indeed, without a meaning, as without an excuse. The irksomeness of a cloistered life repeatedly tempted me to wander; but my chief pleasure was that of travelling; and I was too young and bashful to enjoy, like a manly Oxonian in town, the taverns and bagnios of Covent Garden. In all these excursions I eloped from Oxford; I returned to college; in a few days I eloped again, as if I had been an independent stranger in a hired lodging, without once hearing the voice of admonition, without once feeling the hand of control. Yet my time was lost, my expenses were multiplied, my behaviour abroad was unknown; folly as well as vice should have awakened the attention of my superiors, and my tender years would have justified a more than ordinary degree of restraint and discipline.

Completely neglected by the University, Gibbon was led by a fondness for religious controversy into a perusal of Bossuet, by whom "the ten-horned monster" *of Rome was easily* "transformed . . . into the milk-white hind, who must be loved as soon as she is seen." *With some bravado he announced his conversion to his father. In his first excitement the elder Gibbon let the cat out of the bag, and the youthful martyr was expelled from the University. His father sent him abroad to Lausanne,* "degraded to the dependence of a schoolboy," *placed under a Calvinist minister charged with reconverting him to Protestantism.*

That minister has described "the astonishment with which he gazed on Mr. Gibbon . . . a thin little figure, with a large head, disputing and urging, with the greatest ability, all the best arguments that had ever been used in favor of Popery." *But slowly he was weaned from the pernicious creed, and was at last able to announce his return to the true fold:* "I have at length good news to tell you. I am now good Protestant, and am extremely glad of it."

Meanwhile he had been repairing the gaps in his education by reading all the Latin classics and beginning Greek. He also read in modern literature. To one volume in particular he owed a valuable lesson. Pascal's Provincial Letters *taught him* "to manage the weapon of grave and temperate irony, even on subjects of ecclesiastical solemnity."

I hesitate, from the apprehension of ridicule, when I approach the delicate subject of my early love. By this word I do not mean the polite attention, the gallantry, without hope or design, which has originated in the spirit of chivalry, and is interwoven with the texture of French manners. I understand by this passion the union of desire, friendship, and tenderness, which is inflamed by a single female, which prefers her to the rest of her sex, and which seeks her possession as the supreme or the sole happiness of our being. I need not blush at recollecting the object of my choice; and though my love was disappointed of successs, I am rather proud that I was once capable of feeling such a pure and exalted sentiment. The personal attractions of Mademoiselle Susan Curchod were embellished by the virtues and talents of the mind. . . .

The report of such a prodigy awakened my curiosity; I saw and loved. I found her learned without pedantry, lively in conversation, pure in sentiment, and elegant in manners; and the first sudden emotion was fortified by the habits and knowledge of a more familiar acquaintance. . . . In a calm retirement the gay vanity of youth no longer fluttered in her bosom; she listened to the voice of truth and passion, and I might presume to hope that I had made some impression on a virtuous heart.

At Crassy and Lausanne I indulged my dream of felicity: but on my return to England, I soon discovered that my father would not hear of this strange alliance, and that without his consent I was myself destitute and helpless. After a painful struggle I yielded to my fate: I sighed as a lover, I obeyed as a son; my wound was insensibly healed by time, absence, and the habits of a new life. My cure was accelerated by a faithful report of the tranquillity and cheerfulness of the lady herself, and my love subsided in friendship and esteem.

The minister of Crassy soon afterwards died; his stipend died with him: his daughter retired to Geneva, where, by teaching young ladies, she earned a hard subsistence for herself and her mother; but in her lowest distress she maintained a spotless reputation, and a dignified behaviour. A rich banker of Paris, a citizen of Geneva, had the good fortune and good sense to discover and possess this inestimable treasure; and in the capital of taste and luxury she resisted the temptations of wealth, as she had sustained the hardships of indigence. The genius of her husband has exalted him to the most conspicuous station in Europe. In every change of prosperity and disgrace he has reclined on the bosom of a faithful friend; and Mademoiselle Curchod is now the wife of M. Necker, the minister, and perhaps the legislator, of the French monarchy.

At length, in the spring of the year 1758, my father signified his permission and his pleasure that I should immediately return home. We were then in the midst of a war: the resentment of the French at our taking their ships without a declaration had rendered that polite nation somewhat peevish and difficult. They denied a passage to English travellers, and the road through Germany was circuitous, toilsome, and, perhaps in the neighbourhood of the armies, exposed to some danger. In this perplexity, two Swiss officers of my acquaintance in the Dutch service, who were returning to their garrisons, offered to conduct me through France as one of their companions; nor did we sufficiently reflect that my borrowed name and regimentals might have been considered, in case of a discovery, in a very serious light.

The only person in England whom I was impatient to see was my aunt Porten, the affectionate guardian of my tender years. I hastened to her house in College Street, Westminster; and the evening was spent in the effusions of joy and confidence. It was not without some awe and apprehension that I approached the presence of my father. My infancy, to speak the truth, had been neglected at home; the severity of his look and language at our last parting still dwelt on my memory; nor could I form any notion of his character, or my probable reception. They were both more agreeable than I could expect. The domestic discipline of our ancestors has been relaxed by the philosophy and softness of the age; and if my father remembered that he had trembled before a stern parent, it was only to adopt with his own son an opposite mode of behaviour. He received me as a man and a friend; all constraint was banished at our first interview, and we ever afterwards continued on the same terms of easy and equal politeness. He applauded the success of my education; every word and action was expressive of the most cordial affection; and our lives would have passed without a cloud, if his economy had been equal to his fortune, or if his fortune had been equal to his desires.

During my absence he had married his second wife, Miss Dorothea Patton, who was introduced to me with the most unfavourable prejudice. I considered his second marriage as an act of displeasure, and I was disposed to hate the rival of my mother. But the injustice was in my own fancy, and the imaginary monster was an amiable and deserving woman. I could not be mistaken in the first view of her understanding, her knowledge, and the elegant spirit of her conversation: her polite welcome, and her assiduous care to study and gratify my wishes, announced at least that the surface would be smooth; and my suspicions of art and falsehood were gradually dispelled by the full discovery of her warm and exquisite sensibility. After some reserve on my side, our minds associated in confidence and friendship; and as Mrs. Gibbon had neither children nor the hopes of children, we more easily adopted the tender names and genuine characters of mother and of son.

My father's residence in Hampshire, where I have passed many light, and some heavy hours, was at Buriton, near Petersfield, one mile from the Portsmouth road, and at the easy distance of fifty-eight miles from London. An old mansion, in a state of decay, had been converted into the fashion and convenience of a modern house; and if strangers had nothing to see, the inhabitants had little to desire. The spot was not happily chosen, at the end of the village and the bottom of the hill: but the aspect of the adjacent grounds was various and cheerful; the downs commanded a noble prospect, and the long hanging woods in sight of the house could not perhaps have been improved by art or expense. . . . My father could never inspire me with his love and knowledge of farming. I never handled a gun, I seldom mounted a horse; and my philosophic walks were soon terminated by a shady bench, where I was long detained by the sedentary amusement of reading or meditation.

His studies were continued with assiduity. "I cannot forget the joy with which I exchanged a bank-note of twenty pounds for the twenty volumes of the *Memoirs of the Academy of Inscriptions;* nor would it have been easy, by any other expenditure of the same sum, to have procured so large and lasting a fund of rational amusement." *The scare of a French invasion in 1759 led Gibbon and his father to offer their names as volunteers in the Hampshire militia, a rash step from which they had expected nothing to come, but which turned out to involve them in two and a half years "of military servitude."*

The loss of so many busy and idle hours was not compensated by any elegant pleasure; and my temper was insensibly soured by the society of our rustic officers. In every state there exists, however, a balance of good and evil. The habits of a sedentary life were usefully broken by the duties of an active profession: in the healthful exercise of the field I hunted with a battalion, instead of a pack; and at that time I was ready, at any hour of the day or night, to fly from quarters to London, from London to quarters, on the slightest call of private or regimental business. But my principal obligation to the militia was the making me an Englishman, and a soldier. After my foreign education, with my reserved temper, I should long have continued a stranger to my native country, had I not been shaken in this various scene of new faces and new friends: had not experience forced me to feel the characters of our leading men, the state of parties, the forms of office, and the operation of our civil and military system. . . . The discipline and evolutions of a modern battalion gave me a clearer notion of the phalanx and the legion; and the captain of the Hampshire grenadiers (the reader may smile) has not been useless to the historian of the Roman empire.

The war over, he traveled in France, revisited his friends in Switzerland, and eventually made his way over the Alps to Rome.

My temper is not very susceptible of enthusiasm, and the enthusiasm which I do not feel I have ever scorned to affect. But, at the distance of twenty-five years, I can neither forget nor express the strong emotions which agitated my mind as I first approached and entered the eternal city. After a sleepless night, I trod, with a lofty step, the ruins of the Forum; each memorable spot where Romulus stood, or Tully spoke, or Caesar fell, was at once present to my eye; and several days of intoxication were lost or enjoyed before I could descend to a cool and minute investigation.

It was at Rome, on the 15th of October, 1764, as I sat musing amidst the ruins of the Capitol, while the barefooted friars were singing vespers in the Temple of Jupiter, that the idea of writing the decline and fall of the city first started to my mind. But my original plan was circumscribed to the decay of the city rather than of the empire: and, though my reading and reflections began to point towards that object, some years elapsed, and several avocations intervened, before I was seriously engaged in the execution of that laborious work.

His father died in 1770, and Gibbon came into a patrimony somewhat diminished by the elder's poor management.

I submitted to the order of nature; and my grief was soothed by the conscious satisfaction that I had discharged all the duties of filial piety. . . . The gratification of my desires (they were not immoderate) has been seldom disappointed by the want of money or credit; my pride was never insulted by the visit of an importunate tradesman; and my transient anxiety for the past or future has been dispelled by the studious or social occupation of the present hour. My conscience does not accuse me of any act of extravagance or injustice, and the remnant of my estate affords an ample and honourable provision for my declining age. I shall not expatiate on my economical affairs, which cannot be instructive or amusing to the reader. It is a rule of prudence, as well as of politeness, to reserve such confidence for the ear of a private friend, without exposing our situation to the envy or pity of strangers; for envy is productive of hatred, and pity borders too nearly on contempt. Yet I may believe, and even assert, that in circumstances more indigent or more wealthy, I should never have accomplished the task, or acquired the fame, of an historian; that my spirit would have been broken by poverty and contempt, and that my industry might have been relaxed in the labour and luxury of a superfluous fortune. . . .

It would most assuredly be in my power to amuse the reader with a gallery of portraits and a collection of anecdotes. But I have always condemned the practice of transforming a private memorial into a vehicle of satire or praise. By my own choice I passed in town the greatest part of the year; but whenever I was desirous of breathing the air of the country, I possessed an hospitable retreat at Sheffield Place in Sussex, in the family of my valuable friend Mr. Holroyd, whose character, under the name of Lord Sheffield, has since been more conspicuous to the public.

No sooner was I settled in my house and library, than I undertook the composition of the first volume of my History. At the outset all was dark and doubtful; even the title of the work, the true era of the Decline and Fall of the Empire, the limits of the introduction, the division of the chapters, and the order of the narrative; and I was often tempted to cast away the labour of seven years. The style of an author should be the image of his mind, but the choice and command of language is the fruit of exercise. Many experiments were made before I could hit the middle tone between a dull chronicle and a rhetorical declamation: three times did I compose the first chapter, and twice the second and third, before I was tolerably satisfied with their effect. In the remainder of the way I advanced with a more equal and easy pace; but the fifteenth and sixteenth chapters have been reduced by three successive revisals from a large volume to their present size; and they might still be compressed, without any loss of facts or sentiments. An opposite fault may be imputed to the concise and superficial narrative of the first reigns from Commodus to Alexander; a fault of which I have never heard, except from Mr. Hume in his last journey to London. Such an oracle might have been consulted and obeyed with rational devotion; but I was soon disgusted with the modest practice of reading the manuscript to my friends. Of such friends some will praise from politeness, and some will criticize from vanity. The author himself is the best judge of his own performance; no one has so deeply meditated on the subject; no one is so sincerely interested in the event.

At last the first volume of his History was ready for the press; it was corrected in proof; and issued in an edition of one thousand copies.

I am at a loss how to describe the success of the work, without betraying the vanity of the writer. The first impression was exhausted in a few days; a second and third edition were scarcely adequate to the demand; and the bookseller's property was twice invaded by the pirates of Dublin. My book was on every table, and almost on every toilette; the historian was crowned by the taste or fashion of the day; nor was the general voice disturbed by the barking of any profane critic. The favour of mankind is most freely bestowed on a new acquaintance of any original merit; and the mutual surprise of the public and their favourite is productive of those warm sensibilities, which at a second meeting can no longer be rekindled. If I listened to the music of praise, I was more seriously satisfied with the approbation of my judges. The candour of Dr. Robertson embraced his disciple. A letter from Mr. Hume overpaid the labour of ten years; but I have never presumed to accept a place in the triumvirate of British historians.

For nine years Gibbon lived in London as a Member of Parliament, man of fashion, and literary celebrity, but in 1783, after the fall of Lord North's ministry, he resolved to retire to Lausanne, where he hoped to spend the remainder of his life.

Since my establishment at Lausanne, more than seven years have elapsed; and if every day has not been equally soft and serene, not a day, not a moment, has occurred in which I have repented of my choice. . . .

My friends had been kindly apprehensive that I should not be able to exist in a Swiss town at the foot of the Alps, after having so long conversed with the first men of the first cities of the world. Such lofty connexions may attract the curious, and gratify the vain; but I am too modest, or too proud, to rate my own value by that of my associates; and whatsoever may be the fame of learning or genius, experience has shown me that the cheaper qualifications of politeness and good sense are of more useful currency in the commerce of life. By many, conversation is esteemed as a theatre or a school: but after the morning has been occupied by the labours of the library, I wish to unbend rather than to exercise my mind; and in the interval between tea and supper I am far from disdaining the innocent amusement of a game at cards.

I have presumed to mark the moment of conception: I shall now commemorate the hour of my final deliverance. It was on the day, or rather night, of the 27th of June, 1787, between the hours of eleven and twelve, that I wrote the last lines of the last page, in a summer-house in my garden. After laying down my pen, I took several turns in a *berceau*, or covered walk of acacias, which commands a prospect of the country, the lake, and the mountains. The air was temperate, the sky was serene, the silver orb of the moon was reflected from the waters, and all nature was silent. I will not dissemble the first emotions of joy on recovery of my freedom, and, perhaps, the establishment of my fame. But my pride was soon humbled, and a sober melancholy was spread over my mind, by the idea that I had taken an everlasting leave of an old and agreeable companion, and that whatsoever might be the future date of my History, the life of the historian must be short and precarious.

When I contemplate the common lot of mortality, I must acknowledge that I have drawn a high prize in the lottery of life. . . .

I am endowed with a cheerful temper, a moderate sensibility, and a natural disposition to repose rather than to activity: some mischievous appetites and habits have perhaps been corrected by philosophy or time. The love of study, a passion which derives fresh vigour from enjoyment, supplies each day, each hour, with a perpetual source of independent and rational pleasure; and I am not sensible of any decay of the mental faculties. The original soil has been highly improved by cultivation; but it may be questioned whether some flowers of fancy, some grateful errors, have not been eradicated with the weeds of prejudice. . . . Twenty happy years have been animated by the labour of my History, and its success has given me a name, a rank, a character, in the world, to which I should not otherwise have been entitled. The freedom of my writings has indeed provoked an implacable tribe; but, as I was safe from the stings, I was soon accustomed to the buzzing of the hornets: my nerves are not tremblingly alive, and my literary temper is so happily framed, that I am less sensible of pain than of pleasure . . .

This day may *possibly* be my last: but the laws of probability, so true in general, so fallacious in particular, still allow about fifteen years. I shall soon enter into the period which, as the most agreeable of his long life, was selected by the judgement and experience of the sage Fontenelle.

GRUB-STREET POET

FOR THE MODERN READER ONE OF THE STRONGEST ENJOYMENTS IN *The Lives of the Poets* is the sinewy quality of Johnson's mind. His judgments we read with interest sometimes because they are so penetrating and sometimes because they are Johnson's. For even Johnson's most violent pronouncements have a core of reason or, at the least, of mental power. *The Lives of the Poets* is, of course, not pure biography but a fusion of biography and literary criticism. The fifty-two narratives it contains were originally written, in fact, as introductions to a publisher's edition of the major English poets.

Johnson had always, however, been fascinated by the art of biography. Belligerently though he annihilated eccentricity in thought, in character it delighted him and he was insatiably curious about its manifestations. He seized avidly upon the trivial detail that could throw light upon personality; he loved anecdote. Mere surfaces never satisfied him. He was always turning human qualities inside out, looking for their inner meaning. And above all Johnson felt truth as a passion. "A story is a picture either of an individual or of human nature in general. If it is false, it is a picture of nothing." Biography, then, must, so far as we can make it so, be absolutely and unconditionally true. Now the truth about any human being can never be unadulterated praise. Therefore biography cannot be panegyric. No piety to the dead can justify the suppression of truth: "If we owe regard to the memory of the dead, there is yet more respect to be laid to knowledge, to virtue, and to truth."

These are the principles on which Johnson's work in biography is founded, insistence on truth, on vivid detail, on psychological insight. *The Life of Savage* is significant among the other lives because it demonstrates this uncompromising honesty in a striking form under circumstances that made honesty difficult.

Savage was not an amiable man, nor one of high character. But he had befriended Johnson when he was a starveling and black-browed young struggler in Grub Street, and loyalty ran deep in Johnson's character. In old age he told Boswell of another such, "He was a vicious man, but very kind to me. If you call a dog 'Hervey,' I shall love him." Johnson's essential honesty is nowhere tried more severely than here where a conflict between truth and loyalty is set. And from the test Johnson triumphantly rises.

Compassion is produced by the way Savage's hopes are disappointed, his schemes balked of success, his friends and protectors disgusted with him, justice distorted in his pursuit. But although Johnson extenuates Savage's vices by weighing and explaining them, he makes it clear that, for all his brilliance and specious charm, Savage was an ingrate and a dissipated scoundrel. Only the steadily deepening burden of misery creates a sympathy that depends on no shadow of falsification. Pity colors the style, but never impairs the rightness of the judgment.

There are readers who have felt that Johnson was less sympathetic to Milton's virtues than he was to Savage's vices. This is partly true, for there were few poets whose characters, religious principles, and political careers were more calculated to inflame Johnson's prejudices than Milton's. In part, then, his account of Milton turns into a lively belaboring of that dissenter and justifier of regicide—but it *is* lively, and on a careful reading will prove to have more justice than might at first appear on the surface.

And in the other fifty lives Johnson scores again and again. His flashes of description are brilliant in conveying character: Pope, who pretended that being satirized amused him, reading a lampoon upon him composed by Colley Cibber, "his features written with anguish"; Addison, in his fear of being thought "a promoter of insurrection," wandering nervously behind stage throughout the entire first night performance of his *Cato;* Prior silencing a too loudly appreciative Frenchman at the Paris opera by complaining of the tenor: "He sings so loud I can't hear you."

The critical parts are no less effective than the biographical. In both Johnson shows himself easily equal to the demands of his themes. He possesses, in fact, all the major qualifications of the good biographer. He was honest. With some effort he could control his prejudices. He had enormous grasps and powers of memory. His judgment was strong and clear. He had psychological insight and a flair for the revealing trait and episode. It is the combination of all these qualities that makes *The Lives of the Poets* so richly rewarding.

The Lives of the English Poets: Richard Savage

SAMUEL JOHNSON

[*The Life of Savage* was originally published in 1744, and only subsequently added to the other lives. These were published 1779–1781.]

THE HEROES OF LITERARY AS WELL AS CIVIL HISTORY HAVE BEEN VERY often no less remarkable for what they have suffered than for what they have achieved; and volumes have been written only to enumerate the miseries of the learned, and relate their unhappy lives and untimely deaths.

To these mournful narratives I am about to add the Life of Richard Savage, a man whose writings entitle him to an eminent rank in the classes of learning, and whose misfortunes claim a degree of compassion not always due to the unhappy, as they were often the consequences of the crimes of others rather than his own.

In the year 1697, Anne Countess of Macclesfield, having lived some time upon very uneasy terms with her husband, thought a public confession of adultery the most obvious and expeditious method of obtaining her liberty; and therefore declared that the child with which she was then great was begotten by the Earl Rivers. This, as may be imagined, made her husband no less desirous of a separation than herself, and he prosecuted his design in the most effectual manner; for he applied not to the ecclesiastical courts for a divorce, but to the parliament for an act by which his marriage might be dissolved, the nuptial contract annulled, and the children of his wife illegitimated.

While the Earl of Macclesfield was prosecuting this affair, his wife was, on the 10th of January, 1697–8, delivered of a son; and the Earl Rivers, by appearing to consider him as his own, left none any reason to doubt of the sincerity of her declaration; for he was his godfather and gave him his own name, which was by his direction inserted in the register of St. Andrew's parish in Holborn; but, unfortunately, left him to the care of his mother, whom, as she was now set free from her husband, he probably imagined likely to treat with great tenderness the child that had contributed to so pleasing an event. It is not indeed easy to discover what motives could be found to overbalance that natural affection of a parent, or what interest could be promoted by neglect or cruelty. The dread of shame or of poverty, by which some wretches have been incited to abandon or to murder their children, cannot be supposed to have affected a woman who had proclaimed her crimes and solicited reproach, and on whom the clemency of the legislature had undeservedly bestowed a fortune, which would have been very little diminished by the expenses which the care of her child could have brought upon her.

But, whatever were her motives, no sooner was her son born than she discovered a resolution of disowning him; and in a very short time removed him from her sight by committing him to the care of a poor woman, whom she directed to educate him as her own, and enjoined never to inform him of his true parents.

Such was the beginning of the life of Richard Savage. Born with a legal claim to honour and to affluence, he was in two months illegitimated by the parliament, and disowned by his mother, doomed to poverty and obscurity, and launched upon the ocean of life only that he might be swallowed by its quicksands or dashed upon its rocks.

His mother could not indeed infect others with the same cruelty. As it was impossible to avoid the inquiries which the curiosity or tenderness of her relations made after her child, she was obliged to give some account of the measures she had taken; and her mother, the Lady Mason, whether in approbation of her design or to prevent more criminal contrivances, engaged to transact with the nurse, to pay her for her care, and to superintend the education of the child.

He was, however, not yet wholly abandoned. The Lady Mason still continued her care and directed him to be placed at a small grammar-school near St. Alban's, where he was called by the name of his nurse, without the least intimation that he had a claim to any other.

Here he was initiated in literature, and passed through several of the classes, with what rapidity or with what applause cannot now be known. As he always spoke with respect of his master, it is probable that the mean rank in which he then appeared did not hinder his genius from being distinguished, or his industry from being rewarded; and if in so low a state he obtained distinction and rewards, it is not likely that they were gained but by genius and industry.

While he was thus cultivating his genius, his father, the Earl Rivers, was seized with a distemper which in a short time put an end to his life. He had frequently inquired after his son, and had always been amused with fallacious and evasive answers; but, being now in his own opinion on his death-bed, he thought it his duty to provide for him among his other natural children, and therefore demanded a positive account of him, with an importunity not to be diverted or denied. His mother, who could no longer refuse an answer, determined at least to give such as should cut him off for ever from that happiness which competence affords, and therefore declared that he was dead; which is perhaps the first instance of a lie invented by a mother to deprive her son of a provision which was designed him by another, and which she could not expect herself though he should lose it.

This was therefore an act of wickedness which could not be defeated, because it could not be suspected; the Earl did not imagine there could exist in a human form a mother that would ruin her son without enriching herself, and therefore bestowed upon some other person 6000l. which he had in his will bequeathed to Savage.

About this time his nurse, who had always treated him as her own son, died; and it was natural for him to take care of those effects which by her death were, as he imagined, become his own: he therefore went to her house, opened her boxes, and examined her papers, among which he found some letters written to her by the Lady Mason, which informed him of his birth, and the reasons for which it was concealed.

He was no longer satisfied with the employment which had been allotted him, but thought he had a right to share the affluence of his mother; and therefore, without scruple, applied to her as her son, and made use of every art to awaken her tenderness and attract her regard. But neither his letters nor the interposition of those friends which his merit or his distress procured him made any impression upon her mind. She still resolved to neglect, though she could no longer disown him.

It was to no purpose that he frequently solicited her to admit him to see her; she avoided him with the most vigilant precaution, and ordered him to be excluded from her house, by whomsoever he might be introduced, and what reason soever he might give for entering it.

Savage was at the same time so touched with the discovery of his real mother that it was his frequent practice to walk in the dark evenings for several hours before her door, in hopes of seeing her as she might come by accident to the window or cross her apartment with a candle in her hand.

But all his assiduity and tenderness were without effect, for he could neither soften her heart nor open her hand, and was reduced to the utmost miseries of want while he was endeavouring to awaken the affection of a mother. He was therefore obliged to seek some other means of support; and, having no profession, became by necessity an author.

He made unsuccessful attempts to write stage comedies, and gained the patronage of Sir Richard Steele. But Steele became estranged by a not unlikely accusation that Savage had ridiculed him. Once more friendless, Savage essayed a tragedy composed on scraps of paper picked up by accident and set down with pen and ink borrowed from some shop into which he would step. This gained him some notice, but misfortune still pursued. The rudeness of a companion started a coffee-house brawl in which a man was killed; and Savage was accused of inflicting the wound.

Sinclair had declared several times before his death that he received his wound from Savage; nor did Savage at his trial deny the fact, but endeavoured partly to extenuate it, by urging the suddenness of the whole action, and the impossibility of any ill design or premeditated malice; and partly to justify it by the necessity of self-defence, and the hazard of his own life, if he had lost that opportunity of giving the thrust: he observed that neither reason nor law obliged a man to wait for the blow which was threatened, and which, if he should suffer it, he might never be able to return; that it was always allowable to prevent an assault, and to preserve life by taking away that of the adversary by whom it was endangered . . .

This defence, which took up more than an hour, was heard by the multitude that thronged the court with the most attentive and respectful silence: those who thought he ought not to be acquitted, owned that applause could not be refused him; and those who before pitied his misfortunes, now reverenced his abilities.

The witnesses which appeared against him were proved to be persons of characters which did not entitle them to much credit; a common strumpet, a woman by whom strumpets were entertained, and a man by whom they were supported; and the character of Savage was by several persons of distinction asserted to be that of a modest, inoffensive man, not inclined to broils or to insolence, and who had, to that time, been only known for his misfortunes and his wit.

Had his audience been his judges, he had undoubtedly been acquitted; but Mr. Page, who was then upon the bench, treated him with his usual insolence and severity, and when he had summed up the evidence, endeavoured to exasperate the jury, as Mr. Savage used to relate it, with this eloquent harangue:

"Gentlemen of the jury, you are to consider that Mr. Savage is a very great man, a much greater man than you or I, gentlemen of the jury; that he wears very fine clothes, much finer clothes than you or I, gentlemen of the jury; that he has abundance of money in his pocket, much more money than you or I, gentlemen of the jury, but, gentlemen of the jury, is it not a very hard case, gentlemen of the jury, that Mr. Savage should therefore kill you or me, gentlemen of the jury?"

After this dispassionate summing-up, the jury convicted. But Queen Caroline, convinced of his innocence, was persuaded to intervene for his pardon. Lord Tyrconnel became his patron, allowing him a pension of £200 a year. His good fortune did not last long.

Lord Tyrconnel affirmed that it was the constant practice of Mr. Savage to enter a tavern with any company that proposed it, drink the most expensive wines with great profusion, and when the reckoning was demanded, to be without money: if, as it often happened, his company were willing to defray his part, the affair ended, without any ill consequences; but if they were refractory, and expected that the wine should be paid for by him that drank it, his method of composition was, to take them with him to his own apartment, assume the government of the house, and order the butler in an imperious manner to set the best wine in the cellar before his company, who often drank till they forgot the respect due to the house in which they were entertained, indulged themselves in the utmost extravagance of merriment, practised the most licentious frolics, and committed all the outrages of drunkenness.

Nor was this the only charge which Lord Tyrconnel brought against him. Having given him a collection of valuable books, stamped with his own arms, he had the mortification to see them in a short time exposed to sale upon the stalls, it being usual with Mr. Savage, when he wanted a small sum, to take his books to the pawnbroker.

Whoever was acquainted with Mr. Savage easily credited both these accusations; for having been obliged, from his first entrance into the world, to subsist upon expedients, affluence was not able to exalt him above them; and so much was he delighted with wine and conversation, and so long had he been accustomed to live by chance, that he would at any time go to the tavern without scruple, and trust for the reckoning to the liberality of his company, and frequently of company to whom he was very little known. This conduct indeed very seldom drew upon him those inconveniences that might be feared by any other person; for his conversation was so entertaining, and his address so pleasing, that few thought the pleasure which they received from him dearly purchased by paying for his wine. It was his peculiar happiness that he scarcely ever found a stranger whom he did not leave a friend; but it must likewise be added, that he had not often a friend long without obliging him to become a stranger.

He was banished from the table of Lord Tyrconnel, and turned again adrift upon the world, without prospect of finding quickly any other harbour. As prudence was not one of the virtues by which he was distinguished, he had made no provision against a misfortune like this. And though it is not to be imagined but that the separation must for some time have been preceded by coldness, peevishness, or neglect, though it was undoubtedly the consequence of accumulated provocations on both sides, yet everyone that knew Savage will readily believe that to him it was sudden as a stroke of thunder—that though he might have transiently suspected it, he had never suffered any thought so unpleasing to sink into his mind, but that he had driven it away by amusements, or dreams of future felicity and affluence, and had never taken any measures by which he might prevent a precipitation from plenty to indigence . . .

His condition did not appear to excite much compassion; for he had not always been careful to use the advantages he enjoyed with that moderation which ought to have been with more than usual caution preserved by him, who knew, if he had reflected, that he was only a dependant on the bounty of another, whom he could expect to support him no longer than he endeavoured to preserve his favour by complying with his inclinations, and whom he nevertheless set at defiance, and was continually irritating by negligence or encroachments . . .

His degradation, therefore, from the condition which he had enjoyed with such wanton thoughtlessness was considered by many as an occasion of triumph. Those who had before paid their court to him without success soon returned the contempt which they had suffered; and they who had received favours from him—for of such favours as he could bestow he was very liberal—did not always remember them. So much more certain are the effects of resentment than of gratitude: it is not only to many more pleasing to recollect those faults which place others below them than those virtues by which they are themselves comparatively depressed, but it is likewise more easy to neglect than to recompense; and though there are few who will practise a laborious virtue, there will never be wanting multitudes that will indulge in easy vice.

His later literary efforts met with indifferent success, but Savage did not blame himself. That was not his way.

By imputing none of his miseries to himself, he continued to act upon the same principles, and to follow the same path; was never made wiser by his sufferings, nor preserved by one misfortune from falling into another. He proceeded throughout his life to tread the same steps on the same circle; always applauding his past conduct, or at least forgetting it, to amuse himself with phantoms of happiness which were dancing before him; and willingly turned his eyes from the light of reason, when it would have discovered the illusion, and shown him, what he never wished to see, his real state.

He is even accused, after having lulled his imagination with those ideal opiates, of having tried the same experiment upon his conscience; and, having accustomed himself to impute all deviations from the right to foreign causes, it is certain that he was upon every occasion too easily reconciled to himself; and that he appeared very little to regret those practices which had impaired his reputation. The reigning error of his life was, that he mistook the love for the practice of virtue, and was indeed not so much a good man, as the friend of goodness.

Savage struck a mildly paying vein by writing an annual birth-day poem in honor of the Queen, for which he received £50 each

year. After each such donation he disappeared, to return as penni-
less as before. His life became a matter of chance; he ate when ac-
quaintances invited him to their tables, which was not often, be-
cause of the meanness of his dress.

He lodged as much by accident as he dined, and passed the
night sometimes in mean houses, which are set open at night to
any casual wanderers, sometimes in cellars, among the riot and
filth of the meanest and most profligate of the rabble; and sometimes, when he had not money to support even the expenses of
these receptacles, walked about the streets till he was weary, and
lay down in the summer upon a bulk, or in the winter, with his
associates in poverty, among the ashes of a glass-house . . .

Whoever was acquainted with him was certain to be solicited
for small sums, which the frequency of the request made in time
considerable, and he was therefore quickly shunned by those
who were become familiar enough to be trusted with his necessities . . .

It was observed, that he always asked favours of this kind without the least submission or apparent consciousness of dependence, and that he did not seem to look upon a compliance with
his request as an obligation that deserved any extraordinary
acknowledgments; but a refusal was resented by him as an affront,
or complained of as an injury; nor did he readily reconcile himself
to those who either denied to lend, or gave him afterwards any
intimation that they expected to be repaid.

He was sometimes so far compassionated by those who knew
both his merit and distresses that they received him into their
families, but they soon discovered him to be a very incommodious
inmate; for, being always accustomed to an irregular manner of
life, he could not confine himself to any stated hours, or pay any
regard to the rules of a family, but would prolong his conversation till midnight, without considering that business might require his friend's application in the morning; and, when he had
persuaded himself to retire to bed, was not, without equal difficulty, called up to dinner: it was therefore impossible to pay him
any distinction without the entire subversion of all economy, a

kind of establishment which, wherever he went, he always appeared ambitious to overthrow.

It must therefore be acknowledged, in justification of mankind, that it was not always by the negligence or coldness of his friends that Savage was distressed, but because it was in reality very difficult to preserve him long in a state of ease. To supply him with money was a hopeless attempt; for no sooner did he see himself master of a sum sufficient to set him free from care for a day than he became profuse and luxurious.

Shortly after the death of the Queen his pension was allowed to lapse, and he became utterly destitute. He sank lower and lower, until he was confined to Newgate for debt. Here he languished for eight months. One day he was seized with a pain in the back, and some days later became fevered.

The symptoms grew every day more formidable, but his condition did not enable him to procure any assistance. The last time that the keeper saw him was on July the 31st, 1743, when Savage, seeing him at his bedside, said with an uncommon earnestness, "I have something to say to you, Sir," but, after a pause, moved his hand in a melancholy manner, and finding himself unable to recollect what he was going to communicate, said, " 'Tis gone!" The keeper soon after left him, and the next morning he died. He was buried in the churchyard of St. Peter [at Bristol], at the expense of the keeper.

Such were the life and death of Richard Savage, a man equally distinguished by his virtues and vices, and at once remarkable for his weaknesses and abilities.

For his life, or for his writings, none, who candidly consider his fortune, will think an apology either necessary or difficult. If he was not always sufficiently instructed in his subject, his knowledge was at least greater than could have been attained by others in the same state. If his works were sometimes unfinished, accuracy cannot reasonably be exacted from a man oppressed with want, which he has no hope of relieving but by a speedy publication. The insolence and resentment of which he is accused were not easily to be avoided by a great mind, irritated by perpetual hardships, and constrained hourly to return the spurns of contempt, and repress the insolence of prosperity; and vanity surely may be readily pardoned in him to whom life afforded no other comforts than barren praises, and the consciousness of deserving them.

Those are no proper judges of his conduct who have slumbered away their time on the down of plenty; nor will any wise man easily presume to say, "Had I been in Savage's condition, I should have lived or written better than Savage."

GRAND CHAM

It is hard to deny that james boswell cuts a ludicrous and sometimes an even contemptible figure. His innumerable and preposterous love affairs—Zélide ("upon my soul, Temple, I must have her"), the Moffat woman ("can I do better than keep a dear infidel for my hours of Paphian bliss?"), Miss Bagnal ("a girl of excellent principles"; " 'Let me see such a woman,' cried I"), and the Signora, and La Belle Irlandaise, and an endless catalogue of others—he describes with no sense of incongruity in a series of letters to his friend Temple, a quiet Devonshire clergyman. He was a drunkard and a wastrel who made repeated and futile efforts to reform. He was inclined to bouts of maudlin self-pity and melancholy. With the years his state became worse. His health grew enfeebled, his wife died, his estates melted away, his drunkenness became confirmed, his humiliations mounted. For seven years of deepening poverty he toiled on, sustained by the most extraordinary confidence that his life of his great friend would make his reputation. It did.

And despite Boswell's absurdities and weaknesses, nothing should be more clear than the fact that his great biography was not the chance result of an inexplicable intimacy between a sage and a fool. Boswell was more than tolerated as a zany by Johnson, he was respected and loved—and Johnson did not bestow either of those emotions lightly. Nor was Johnson alone in these sentiments. Boswell was the friend of General Paoli; he succeeded in drawing both Rousseau and Voltaire into correspondence. He was what Johnson called a "clubbable man," and, save by Gibbon, whose dislike Boswell returned, was popular with all the Literary Club.

He was remarkably free from conventional opinion and mere dependence on authority. "You and I," Johnson commended him, "do not talk from books." He was no sycophant, but openly pursued an intimacy with Wilkes and Rousseau in spite of Johnson's violent disapproval of both those men, and he hesitated not to tell his overbearing friend that he was completely wrong about the American Revolution. He had a tremendous zest for life, ready to conceive and discuss anything, able even to embark on voyages of wild fantasy in which he sometimes left the sober Johnson indignantly behind.

And Boswell was intelligent, too, although he so often acted the clown. His seeming foolishness and lack of dignity are, in truth, products of his intelligence, his psychological curiosity, and his delight in social experiment. Any question that piqued his mind Boswell immediately set about finding the answer to, without worrying whether it made him look silly or not. "What would you do, sir, if you were shut up in a tower with a baby?" Whether Johnson flew into a tantrum at the absurd query or took it seriously would be equally interesting. What would Johnson do if things were engineered to make him meet Jack Wilkes, whom he had called "a retailer of sedition and obscenity"? The process became a kind of psychological bear-baiting, with curiosity rather than cruelty its object. The fear of ridicule disturbed Boswell no more than it does a modern psychologist playing with trick tunnels and holes in little boxes to experiment on the symptoms of hysteria in rats.

Boswell's *Life of Johnson* is the triumphant achievement of this intelligent curiosity. It is no more mere mosaic of anecdotes and quotations, but a clear, consistent, vivid, and penetrating portrait of a deeply revealing man. Its method and execution were, and Boswell knew that they were, consummate. "Mine is the best plan of biography that can be conceived," he exclaimed. He was going to let Johnson speak for himself; he was going to show him from a hundred angles, as he appeared to others; he was going not merely to relate the important events of his life, but interweave

what he privately wrote, and said, and thought. And this would
be no one-sided panegyric of Johnson, "but his Life; which, great
and good as he was, must not be supposed to be entirely perfect,"
but "must have shade as well as light." Boswell knew, of course,
that some of his details laid both himself and Johnson open to
"the petty exercise of ridicule, by men of superficial understanding, and ludicrous fancy." But only so could he achieve the speaking likeness he aimed at, and, most important of all, only so could
he be faithful to that absolute veracity that his revered friend had
always "recommended both by his precept and his example."

Never has a man in his very habit and daily appearance been
rendered more vividly. Boswell has portrayed a living man in
living words. The early days, it is true, when Johnson was a thin,
proud, hungry, and morose young booksellers' hack, are rather
sparsely handled. Boswell gets into his stride only after Johnson
had already become the figure he has made familiar to all of us:
the heavy-set old man with woollen stockings, wrinkled clothes,
and dusty wig, his rolling figure a strange combination of the
venerable and the grotesque. But that image Boswell has painted
so that we can never forget it. We see the Doctor and Bozzy rolling down Fleet Street together, exclaiming on its wonderful animation, or canvassing the exhilarating subject of gentlewomen in
liquor. We are with them at the Club, with Goldsmith sulking,
or Mr. Gibbon rapping his snuffbox, and the peremptory sage
shouting, "Clear your mind of cant, Sir!" And so, touch after
touch, he gives us his wonderful Flemish painting of the sad,
courageous, and lovable old bully drinking tea with his boon
companions in a comfortable haven.

But Boswell's story is more than merely vivid and moving. It
has depth. Johnson's wisdom and sanity were won by power of
mind from the assaults of a melancholy terrible almost to madness. His humor and courage were sustained in the face of a deep
consciousness of human frailty. Johnson's Toryism was no cranky
crotchet, but a philosophic Toryism based on a considered view
of human nature. The evil in men, he held, is kept in check by
such uncertain restraints that he was ready to accept various evils
in their institutions rather than risk overthrowing the habits of

discipline by a flighty-minded tinkering. Only when all the resources of the accumulated wisdom and tradition of civilization have been tried and found fruitless would he approve some cautious innovation. What institutions one lived under, he believed, mattered less than that they should be reasonably settled. All institutions were administered in a muddling way by fools and scoundrels, perfection were utopian to expect. The only real test of a good government was the degree of solicitude it displayed for the welfare of the poor, and the only tests of a good man were his concern for truth and justice and his love for other beings.

That there were in Johnson's opinion no good governments and few good men is a proof hardly less of his sanity than of the sadness of his heart. That he loved and forgave men despite their shortcomings, that he was warmhearted and generous and quick to forgive, are signs of the sweetness beneath the gruff bark. It is this combination of the massive strength, poise, and sanity of the Doctor's mind with the tenderness of his feelings that makes Johnson's life great and profound. His greatness could be felt, and conveyed to us in the greatest of biographies, only by a man himself great with the genius of sympathy and understanding.

The Life of Samuel Johnson

JAMES BOSWELL

[Johnson was born in 1709 and died in 1784. The *Life* was first published in 1791.]

SAMUEL JOHNSON WAS BORN IN LICHFIELD, IN STAFFORDSHIRE, ON the 18th of September, N.S. 1709 . . . His father was Michael Johnson, a native of Derbyshire, of obscure extraction, who settled in Lichfield as a bookseller and stationer. His mother was Sarah Ford, descended of an ancient race of substantial yeomanry in Warwickshire. They were well advanced in years when they married, and never had more than two children, both sons, Samuel, their first-born, . . . and Nathanael, who died in his twenty-fifth year.

One day, when the servant who used to be sent to school to conduct him home, had not come in time, he set out by himself, though he was then so near-sighted, that he was obliged to stoop down on his hands and knees to take a view of the kennel before he ventured to step over it. His school-mistress, afraid that he might miss his way, or fall into the kennel, or be run over by a cart, followed him at some distance. He happened to turn about and perceive her. Feeling her careful attention as an insult to his manliness, he ran back to her in a rage, and beat her, as well as his strength would permit.

Of the power of his memory, for which he was all his life eminent to a degree almost incredible, the following early instance was told me . . . When he was a child in petticoats, and had learnt to read, Mrs. Johnson one morning put the common prayer-book into his hands, pointed to the collect for the day, and said, "Sam, you must get this by heart." She went up stairs, leaving him to study it: but by the time she had reached the second floor, she heard him following her. "What's the matter?" said she. "I can say it," he replied; and repeated it distinctly, though he could not have read it more than twice. . . .

Young Johnson had the misfortune to be much afflicted with the scrophula, or king's-evil, which disfigured a countenance naturally well formed, and hurt his visual nerves so much, that he did not see at all with one of his eyes, though its appearance was little different from that of the other. There is amongst his prayers, one inscribed "When my EYE was restored to its use," which ascertains a defect that many of his friends knew he had, though I never perceived it. I supposed him to be only near-sighted; and indeed I must observe, that in no other respect could I discern any defect in his vision; on the contrary, the force of his attention and perceptive quickness made him see and distinguish all manner of objects, whether of nature or of art, with a nicety that is rarely to be found. . . . And the ladies with whom he was acquainted agree, that no man was more nicely and minutely critical in the elegance of female dress. . . . It has been said that he contracted this grievous malady from his nurse. His mother, yielding to the superstitious notion, which, it is wonderful to think prevailed so long in this country, as to the virtue of the regal touch, . . . carried him to London, where he was actually touched by Queen Anne . . . Johnson used to talk of this very frankly . . . Being asked if he could remember Queen Anne,—"He had (he said) a confused, but somehow a sort of solemn recollection of a lady in diamonds, and a long black hood." This touch, however, was without any effect.

He began to learn Latin with Mr. Hawkins, usher, or undermaster of Lichfield school, "a man (said he) very skilful in his little way." . . . Mr. Langton one day asked him how he had acquired so accurate a knowledge of Latin, in which, I believe, he was exceeded by no man of his time; he said, "My master whipt me very well. Without that, Sir, I should have done nothing." . . . Johnson, upon all occasions, expressed his approbation of enforcing instruction by means of the rod. "I would rather (said he) have the rod to be the general terrour to all, to make them learn, than tell a child, if you do thus, or thus, you will be more esteemed than your brothers or sisters. The rod produces an effect which terminates in itself. A child is afraid of being whipped, and gets his task, and there's an end on't; whereas, by exciting emulation and comparisons of superiority, you lay the foundation of lasting mischief; you make brothers and sisters hate each other." . . .

He never joined with the other boys in their ordinary diversions: his only amusement was in winter, when he took a pleasure in being drawn upon the ice by a boy barefooted, who pulled him along by a garter fixed around him; no very easy operation, as his size was remarkably large. His defective sight, indeed, prevented him from enjoying the common sports; and he once pleasantly remarked to me, "how wonderfully well he had contrived to be idle without them." . . .

Johnson was, at the age of fifteen, removed to the school of Stourbridge, in Worcestershire . . . He remained at Stourbridge little more than a year, and then he returned home, where he may be said to have loitered, for two years, . . . in what he thought idleness, and was scolded by his father for his want of steady application . . . Yet he read a great deal in a desultory manner . . .

He used to mention one curious instance of his casual reading when but a boy. Having imagined that his brother had hid some apples, behind a large folio upon an upper shelf in his father's shop, he climbed up to search for them. There were no apples; but the large folio proved to be Petrarch, whom he had seen mentioned as one of the restorers of learning. His curiosity having been thus excited, he sat down with avidity, and read a great part of the book. What he read during these two years; he told me, was not works of mere amusement, "not voyages and travels, but all literature, Sir, all ancient writers, all manly: though but little Greek, only some of Anacreon and Hesiod: but in this irregular manner (added he) I had looked into a great many books, which were not commonly known at the Universities, where they seldom read any books but what are put into their hands by their tutors;

so that when I came to Oxford, Dr. Adams, now master of Pembroke College, told me, I was the best qualified for the University that he had ever known come there."

That a man in Mr. Michael Johnson's circumstances should think of sending his son to the expensive University of Oxford, at his own charge, seems very improbable. The subject was too delicate to question Johnson upon; but I have been assured by Dr. Taylor, that the scheme never would have taken place, had not a gentleman of Shropshire, one of his school-fellows, spontaneously undertaken to support him at Oxford, in the character of his companion: though, in fact, he never received any assistance whatever from that gentleman.

He, however, went to Oxford, and was entered a Commoner of Pembroke College, on the 31st of October, 1728, being then in his nineteenth year.

Dr. Adams told me that Johnson, while he was at Pembroke College, "was caressed and loved by all about him, was a gay and frolicksome fellow, and passed there the happiest part of his life." But this is a striking proof of the fallacy of appearances, and how little any of us know of the real internal state even of those whom we see most frequently; for the truth is, that he was then depressed by poverty, and irritated by disease. When I mentioned to him this account as given me by Dr. Adams, he said, "Ah, Sir, I was mad and violent. It was bitterness which they mistook for frolick. I was miserably poor, and I thought to fight my way by my literature and my wit; so I disregarded all power and all authority." . . .

I do not find that he formed any close intimacies with his fellow-collegians. But Dr. Adams told me, that he contracted a love and regard for Pembroke College, which he retained to the last. . . . . . . He took a pleasure in boasting of the many eminent men who had been educated at Pembroke. . . . Being himself a poet, Johnson was peculiarly happy in mentioning how many of the sons of Pembroke were poets; adding, with a smile of sportive triumph, "Sir, we are a nest of singing birds."

But Johnson's poverty was extreme and his pride unbending. His debts increased, his father could no longer send him money

*from Lichfield. Johnson's feet came through his shoes, but when
an anonymous donor set a new pair at his door, in fierce anger he
threw them away. After three years he was obliged to withdraw
from the University. His father died. For a short time the young
man found hateful employment as usher in a school at Market-
Bosworth. Then, resigning the irksome post, he went to Birmingham. Here he met the lady he was to marry.*

In a man whom religious education has secured from licentious
indulgences, the passion of love, when once it has seized him, is
exceedingly strong; being unimpaired by dissipation, and totally
concentrated in one object. This was experienced by Johnson,
when he became the fervent admirer of Mrs. Porter, after her first
husband's death. Miss Porter told me, that when he was first introduced to her mother, his appearance was very forbidding: he
was then lean and lank, so that his immense structure of bones was
hideously striking to the eye, and the scars of the scrophula were
deeply visible. He also wore his hair, which was straight and stiff,
and separated behind: and he often had, seemingly, convulsive
starts and odd gesticulations, which tended to excite at once surprise and ridicule. Mrs. Porter was so much engaged by his conversation that she overlooked all these external disadvantages, and
said to her daughter, "this is the most sensible man that I ever
saw in my life."

Though Mrs. Porter was double the age of Johnson, and her
person and manner . . . were by no means pleasing to others, she
must have had a superiority of understanding and talents as she
certainly inspired him with an extraordinary passion; and she
having signified her willingness to accept of his hand, he went to
Lichfield to ask his mother's consent to the marriage; which he
could not but be conscious was a very imprudent scheme, both on
account of their disparity of years, and her want of fortune. But
Mrs. Johnson knew too well the ardour of her son's temper, and
was too tender a parent to oppose his inclinations.

I know not for what reason the marriage ceremony was not performed at Birmingham; but a resolution was taken that it should
be at Derby, for which place the bride and bridegroom set out on

horseback, I suppose in very good humour. But though Mr. Topham Beauclerk used archly to mention Johnson's having told him with much gravity, "Sir, it was a love marriage on both sides," I have had from my illustrious friend the following curious account of their journey to church upon the nuptial morn:—"Sir, she had read the old romances, and had got into her head the fantastical notion that a woman of spirit should use her lover like a dog. So, Sir, at first she told me that I rode too fast, and she could not keep up with me: and, when I rode a little slower, she passed me, and complained that I lagged behind. I was not to be made the slave of caprice; and I resolved to begin as I meant to end. I therefore pushed on briskly, till I was fairly out of her sight. The road lay between two hedges, so I was sure she could not miss it; and I contrived that she should soon come up with me. When she did, I observed her to be in tears."

This, it must be allowed, was a singular beginning of connubial felicity; but there is no doubt that Johnson, though he thus shewed a manly firmness, proved a most affectionate and indulgent husband to the last moment of Mrs. Johnson's life: and in his "Prayers and Meditations," we find very remarkable evidence that his regard and fondness for her never ceased, even after her death.

He now set up a private academy, for which purpose he hired a large house, well situated near his native city. In the Gentleman's Magazine for 1736, there is the following advertisement: "At Edial, near Lichfield, in Staffordshire, young gentlemen are boarded and taught the Latin and Greek Languages, by SAMUEL JOHNSON." But the only pupils that were put under his care were the celebrated David Garrick and his brother George, and a Mr. Offely, a young gentleman of good fortune who died early.

From Mr. Garrick's account he did not appear to have been profoundly reverenced by his pupils. His oddities of manner, and uncouth gesticulations, could not but be the subject of merriment to them; and in particular, the young rogues used to listen at the door of his bedchamber, and peep through the key-hole, that they might turn into ridicule his tumultuous and awkward fondness for Mrs. Johnson, whom he used to name by the familiar appellation of *Tetty* or *Tetsy*, which, like *Betty* or *Betsey*, is provincially used as a contraction for *Elizabeth,* her christian name, but which to us seems ludicrous, when applied to a woman of her age and appearance. Mr. Garrick described her to me as very fat, with a bosom of more than ordinary protuberance, with swelled cheeks, of a florid red, produced by thick painting, and increased by the liberal use of cordials; flaring and fantastick in her dress, and affected both in her speech and her general behaviour. I have seen Garrick exhibit her, by his exquisite talent of mimickry, so as to excite the heartiest burst of laughter; but he, probably, as is the case in all such representations, considerably aggravated the picture.

This school Johnson kept no more than a year and a half. Then he followed his pupil Garrick to London, hoping to make his fortune with his tragedy Irene. *He dined on a cut of meat, bread, and water for eightpence; it seems probable that like a friend he quoted in later years he paid visits on "clean-shirt day." Finally he obtained work on Sylvanus Cave's* Gentleman's Magazine, *filling out note-jottings of Parliamentary debates by clothing them in his own language, a feature that appeared under the title, "The Senate of Lilliput." His satiric poem* London *brought him some praise but small rewards. Alexander Pope tried to help him, and mentions his being afflicted by* "an infirmity of the convulsive kind" *that made him* "a sad spectacle."

The infirmity to which Mr. Pope alludes, appeared to me also, . . . to be of the convulsive kind, and . . . of the nature of that distemper called St. Vitus's dance . . .

Sir Joshua Reynolds, however, was of a different opinion, and favoured me with the following paper.

"Those motions or tricks of Dr. Johnson are improperly called convulsions. He could sit motionless, when he was told so to do, as well as any other man. My opinion is, that it proceeded from a habit which he had indulged himself in, of accompanying his thoughts with certain untoward actions, and those actions always appeared to me as if they were meant to reprobate some part of his past conduct. Whenever he was not engaged in conversation, such thoughts were sure to rush into his mind; and, for this reason, any company, any employment whatever, he preferred to being alone. The great business of his life (he said) was to escape from himself; this disposition he considered as the disease of his mind, which nothing cured but company."

[In 1744] he produced one work fully sufficient to maintain the high reputation which he had acquired. This was "THE LIFE OF RICHARD SAVAGE," a man, of whom it is difficult to speak impartially, without wondering that he was for some time the intimate companion of Johnson; for his character was marked by profligacy, insolence, and ingratitude: yet, as he undoubtedly had a warm and vigorous, though unregulated mind, had seen life in all its varieties, and been much in the company of the statesmen and wits of his time, he could communicate to Johnson an abundant supply of such materials as his philosophical curiosity most eagerly desired; and as Savage's misfortunes and misconduct had reduced him to the lowest state of wretchedness as a writer for bread, his visits to St. John's Gate naturally brought Johnson and him together.

It is melancholy to reflect that Johnson and Savage were sometimes in such extreme indigence, that they could not pay for a lodging; so that they have wandered together whole nights in the streets . . . One night in particular, when Savage and he walked round St. James's-Square for want of a lodging, they were not at all depressed by their situation; but in high spirits and brimful of patriotism, traversed the square for several hours, inveighed against the minister, and "resolved they would *stand by their country.*"

The year 1747 is distinguished as the epoch, when Johnson's arduous and important work, his DICTIONARY OF THE ENGLISH LANGUAGE, was announced to the world, by the publication of its Plan or PROSPECTUS.

How long this immense undertaking had been the object of his contemplation, I do not know. I once asked him by what means he had attained to that astonishing knowledge of our language, by which he was enabled to realise a design of such extent and accumulated difficulty. He told me, that "it was not the effect of

particular study; but that it had grown up in his mind insensibly."
I have been informed by Mr. James Dodsley, that several years
before this period, when Johnson was one day sitting in his
brother Robert's shop, he heard his brother suggest to him, that
a Dictionary of the English Language would be a work that would
be well received by the publick; that Johnson seemed at first to
catch at the proposition, but, after a pause, said, in his abrupt
decisive manner, "I believe I shall not undertake it." That he,
however, had bestowed much thought upon the subject, before he
published his "Plan," is evident from the enlarged, clear, and
accurate views which it exhibits . . .

The "Plan" was addressed to Philip Dormer, Earl of Chesterfield, then one of his Majesty's Principal Secretaries of State; a
nobleman who was very ambitious of literary distinction, and who,
upon being informed of the design, had expressed himself in terms
very favourable to its success. There is, perhaps, in every thing
of any consequence, a secret history which it would be amusing
to know, could we have it authentically communicated. Johnson
told me, "Sir, the way in which the plan of my Dictionary came
to be inscribed to Lord Chesterfield, was this: I had neglected to
write it by the time appointed. Dodsley suggested a desire to have
it addressed to Lord Chesterfield. I laid hold of this as a pretext
for delay, that it might be better done, and let Dodsley have his
desire. I said to my friend, Dr. Bathurst, 'Now if any good comes
of my addressing to Lord Chesterfield, it will be ascribed to deep
policy,' when, in fact, it was only a casual excuse for laziness." . . .

Dr. Adams found him one day busy at his Dictionary, when
the following dialogue ensued.—"ADAMS. This is a great work, Sir.
How are you to get all the etymologies? JOHNSON. Why, Sir, here
is a shelf with Junius, and Skinner, and others; and there is a
Welch gentleman who has published a collection of Welch
proverbs, who will help me with the Welch. ADAMS. But, Sir,
how can you do this in three years? JOHNSON. Sir, I have no doubt
that I can do it in three years. ADAMS. But the French Academy,
which consists of forty members, took forty years to compile their
Dictionary. JOHNSON. Sir, thus it is. This is the proportion. Let
me see; forty times forty is sixteen hundred. As three to sixteen

hundred, so is the proportion of an Englishman to a Frenchman."
With so much ease and pleasantry could he talk of that prodigious
labour which he had undertaken to execute.

In January, 1749, he published The Vanity of Human Wishes.
*Garrick had by now become manager of Drury Lane, and used his
influence to put on Johnson's* Irene. *His friendship carried it
through nine nights,* "so that the author had his three nights'
profit," *but the play was not popular.*

When asked how he felt upon the ill success of his tragedy, he
replied, "Like the Monument!" meaning that he continued firm
and unmoved as that column. And let it be remembered, as
an admonition to the genus irritabile of dramatick writers, that
this great man, instead of peevishly complaining of the bad taste
of the town, submitted to its decision without a murmur. He had,
indeed, upon all occasions a great deference for the general
opinion: "A man (said he) who writes a book, thinks himself
wiser or wittier than the rest of mankind; he supposes that he can
instruct or amuse them, and the publick to whom he appeals, must,
after all, be the judges of his pretensions."

On occasion of this play being brought upon the stage, Johnson had a fancy that as a dramatick author his dress should be more
gay than what he ordinarily wore; he therefore appeared behind
the scenes, and even in one of the side boxes, in a scarlet waistcoat,
with rich gold lace, and a gold-laced hat. . . . He for a considerable time used to frequent the Green-Room, and seemed to
take delight in dissipating his gloom, by mixing in the sprightly
chit-chat of the motley circle then to be found there. Mr. David
Hume related to me from Mr. Garrick, that Johnson at last denied
himself this amusement, from considerations of rigid virtue; saying, "I'll come no more behind your scenes, David; for the silk
stockings and white bosoms of your actresses excite my amorous
propensities."

In 1752 he was almost entirely occupied with his Dictionary.
The last paper of his Rambler was published March 2, this year;
after which, there was a cessation for some time of any exertion
of his talents as an essayist . . .

That there should be a suspension of his literary labours . . .
will not seem strange, when it is considered that soon after closing
his Rambler, he suffered the loss which there can be no doubt,
affected him with the deepest distress. For on the 17th of March,
O.S., his wife died. Why Sir John Hawkins should unwarrantably
take upon him even to *suppose* that Johnson's fondness for her was
dissembled (meaning simulated or assumed), and to assert, that
if it was not the case, "it was a lesson he had learned by rote," I
cannot conceive; unless it proceeded from a want of similar feelings in his own breast. . . .

The following very solemn and affecting prayer was found after
Dr. Johnson's decease, by his servant, Mr. Francis Barber . . .
I present it to the world as an undoubted proof of a circumstance
in the character of my illustrious friend, which, though some
whose hard minds I never shall envy, may attack as superstitious,
will I am sure endear him more to numbers of good men. I have
an additional, and that a personal motive for presenting it, because
it sanctions what I myself have always maintained and am fond
to indulge:

"April 26, 1752, being after 12
at Night of the 25th.

"O Lord! Governor of heaven and earth, in whose hands are
embodied and departed Spirits, if thou hast ordained the Souls
of the Dead to minister to the Living, and appointed my departed
Wife to have care of me, grant that I may enjoy the good effects
of her attention and ministration, whether exercised by appearance, impulses, dreams, or in any other manner agreeable to thy
Government. Forgive my presumption, enlighten my ignorance,
and however meaner agents are employed, grant me the blessed
influences of thy holy Spirit, through Jesus Christ our Lord.
Amen."

The circle of his friends . . . at this time was extensive and
various, far beyond what has been generally imagined. . . . When
Johnson lived in Castle-street, Cavendish-square, he used frequently to visit two ladies who lived opposite to him, Miss Cot-
terells, daughters of Admiral Cotterell. Reynolds used also to visit

there, and thus they met. . . . Sir Joshua, indeed, was lucky enough at their very first meeting to make a remark, which was so much above the commonplace style of conversation, that Johnson at once perceived that Reynolds had the habit of thinking for himself. The ladies were regretting the death of a friend, to whom they owed great obligations; upon which Reynolds observed, "You have however, the comfort of being relieved from a burthen of gratitude." They were shocked a little at this alleviating suggestion, as too selfish; but Johnson defended it in his clear and forcible manner, and was much pleased with the mind, the fair view of human nature, which it exhibited, like some of the reflections of Rochefoucauld. The consequence was, that he went home with Reynolds, and supped with him.

One night two of Johnson's younger friends, Topham Beauclerk and Bennet Langton, had supped at a tavern and sat drinking till three in the morning. It came into their heads "to go and knock up Johnson" and see if he would join the end of their party:

They rapped violently at the door of his chambers in the Temple, till at last he appeared in his shirt, with his little black wig on the top of his head, instead of a night-cap, and a poker in his hand, imagining, probably, that some ruffians were coming to attack him. When he discovered who they were, and was told their errand, he smiled, and with great good humour agreed to their proposal: "What, is it you, you dogs! I'll have a frisk with you." He was soon drest, and they sallied forth together into Covent-Garden, where the greengrocers and fruiterers were beginning to arrange their hampers, just come in from the country. Johnson made some attempts to help them; but the honest gardeners stared so at his figure and manner, and odd interference, that he soon saw his services were not relished. . . .

They did not stay long, but walked down to the Thames, took a boat, and rowed to Billingsgate. Beauclerk and Johnson were so well pleased with their amusement, that they resolved to persevere in dissipation for the rest of the day: but Langton deserted them, being engaged to breakfast with some young Ladies. Johnson scolded him for "leaving his social friends to go and sit with a set of wretched un-idea'd girls." Garrick being told of this ramble, said to him smartly, "I heard of your frolick t'other night. You'll be in the Chronicle." Upon which Johnson afterwards observed, "He durst not do such a thing. His wife would not let him!"

When the Dictionary was upon the eve of publication, Lord Chesterfield, who, it is said, had flattered himself with expectations that Johnson would dedicate the work to him, attempted, in a courtly manner, to soothe and insinuate himself with the Sage, conscious, as it should seem, of the cold indifference with which he had treated its learned authour; and further attempted to conciliate him, by writing two papers in *The World,* in recommendation of the work; and it must be confessed, that they contain some studied compliments, so finely turned, that if there had been no previous offence, it is probable that Johnson would have been highly delighted. Praise, in general, was pleasing to him; but by praise from a man of rank and elegant accomplishments, he was peculiarly gratified. . . .

This courtly device failed of its effect. Johnson, who thought that "all was false and hollow," despised the honeyed words, and was even indignant that Lord Chesterfield should, for a moment, imagine, that he could be the dupe of such an artifice. His expression to me concerning Lord Chesterfield, upon this occasion, was, "Sir, after making great professions, he had, for many years, taken no notice of me; but when my Dictionary was coming out, he fell a scribbling in *The World* about it. Upon which, I wrote him a letter expressed in civil terms, but such as might show him that I did not mind what he said or wrote, and that I had done with him."

This is that celebrated letter of which so much has been said, and about which curiosity has so long been excited, without being gratified:

"TO THE RIGHT HONOURABLE THE EARL OF CHESTERFIELD.
MY LORD,   February 7, 1755.
I HAVE been lately informed, by the proprietor of the World, that two papers, in which my Dictionary is recommended to the

publick, were written by your Lordship. To be so distinguished, is an honour, which, being very little accustomed to favours from the great, I know not well how to receive, or in what terms to acknowledge.

When, upon some slight encouragement, I first visited your Lordship, I was overpowered, like the rest of mankind, by the enchantment of your address, and could not forbear to wish that I might boast myself Le vainqueur du vainqueur de la terre;— that I might obtain that regard for which I saw the world contending; but I found my attendance so little encouraged, that neither pride nor modesty would suffer me to continue it. When I had once addressed your Lordship in publick, I had exhausted all the art of pleasing which a retired and uncourtly scholar can possess. I had done all that I could; and no man is well pleased to have his all neglected, be it ever so little.

Seven years, my Lord, have now past, since I waited in your outward rooms, or was repulsed from your door; during which time I have been pushing on my work through difficulties, of which it is useless to complain, and have brought it, at last, to the verge of publication, without one act of assistance, one word of encouragement, or one smile of favour. Such treatment I did not expect, for I never had a Patron before.

The shepherd in Virgil grew at last acquainted with Love, and found him a native of the rocks.

Is not a Patron, my Lord, one who looks with unconcern on a man struggling for life in the water, and, when he has reached ground, encumbers him with help? The notice which you have been pleased to take of my labours, had it been early, had been kind; but it has been delayed till I am indifferent, and cannot enjoy it; till I am solitary, and cannot impart it; till I am known, and do not want it.

I hope it is no very cynical asperity, not to confess obligations where no benefit has been received, or to be unwilling that the Publick should consider me as owing that to a Patron, which Providence has enabled me to do for myself.

Having carried on my work thus far with so little obligation to any favourer of learning, I shall not be disappointed though I should conclude it, if less be possible, with less; for I have been long wakened from that dream of hope, in which I once boasted myself with so much exultation,

> My Lord,
> Your Lordship's most humble
> Most obedient servant,
> SAM JOHNSON"

· · · ·

There is a curious minute circumstance which struck me, in comparing the various editions of Johnson's IMITATIONS OF JUVENAL. In the tenth Satire one of the couplets upon the vanity of wishes even for literary distinction stood thus:

> *Yet think what ills the scholar's life assail,*
> *Toil, envy, want, the* garret, *and the jail.*

But after experiencing the uneasiness which Lord Chesterfield's fallacious patronage made him feel, he dismissed the word *garret* from the sad group, and in all the subsequent editions the line stands,

> *Toil, envy, want, the* Patron, *and the jail.*

The Dictionary, with a Grammar and History of the English Language, being now at length published, in two volumes folio, the world contemplated with wonder so stupendous a work atchieved by one man, while other countries had thought such undertakings fit only for whole academies. . . .

A few of his definitions must be admitted to be erroneous. . . . A lady once asked him how he came to define Pastern the knee of a horse: instead of making an elaborate defence, as she expected, he at once answered:

"Ignorance, Madam, pure ignorance." . . .

His introducing his own opinions, and even prejudices, under general definitions of words, while at the same time the original meaning of the words is not explained, as his Tory, Whig, Pension, Oats, Excise, and a few more, cannot be fully defended, and must be placed to the account of capricious and humorous indulgence. . . .

Let it, however, be remembered, that this indulgence does not display itself only in sarcasm towards others, but sometimes in playful allusion to the notions commonly entertained of his own laborious task. Thus: "Grub-street, the name of a street in London, much inhabited by writers of small histories, dictionaries, and temporary poems; whence, any mean production is called Grub-street."—"Lexicographer, a writer of dictionaries, a harmless drudge."

In 1759, in the month of January, his mother died at the great age of ninety, an event which deeply affected him; not that "his mind had acquired no firmness by the contemplation of mortality"; but that his reverential affection for her was not abated by years, as indeed he retained all his tender feelings even to the latest period of his life. I have been told, that he regretted much his not having gone to visit his mother for several years previous to her death. But he was constantly engaged in literary labours which confined him to London; and though he had not the comfort of seeing his aged parent, he contributed to her support. . . .

"To Miss Porter, in Lichfield.

You will conceive my sorrow for the loss of my mother, of the best mother. If she were to live again, surely I should behave better to her. But she is happy, and what is past is nothing to her; and for me, since I cannot repair my faults to her, I hope repentance will efface them. . . . I have not power or composure to say much more. God bless you, and bless us all.

I am, dear Miss,
Your affectionate humble Servant,
Sam Johnson"

Jan. 23, 1759.

Soon after this event, he wrote his Rasselas, Prince of Abyssinia: . . . Mr. Strahan the printer told me, that Johnson wrote it, that with the profits he might defray the expence of his mother's funeral, and pay some little debts which she had left. He told Sir Joshua Reynolds, that he composed it in the evenings of one week, sent it to the press in portions as it was written, and had never since read it over. . . .

None of his writings has been so extensively diffused over Europe; for it has been translated into most, if not all, of the modern languages. This Tale, with all the charms of oriental imagery, and all the force and beauty of which the English language is capable, leads us through the most important scenes of human life, and shews us that this stage of our being is full of "vanity and vexation of spirit." . . . Voltaire's CANDIDE, written to refute the system of Optimism, which it has accomplished with brilliant success, is wonderfully similar in its plan and conduct to Johnson's RASSELAS; insomuch, that I have heard Johnson say, that if they had not been published so closely one after the other that there was not time for imitation, it would have been in vain to deny that the scheme of that which came latest was taken from the other.

The accession of George the Third to the throne of these king-doms, opened a new and brighter prospect to men of literary merit, who had been honoured with no mark of royal favour in the pre-ceding reign. His present Majesty's education in this country, as well as his taste and beneficence, prompted him to be the patron of science and the arts; and early this year Johnson having been represented to him as a very learned and good man, without any certain provision, his Majesty was pleased to grant him a pension of three hundred pounds a year. . . .

Lord Loughborough told me, that the pension was granted to Johnson solely as the reward of his literary merit, without any stipulation whatever, or even tacit understanding that he should write for administration. . . .

Sir Joshua Reynolds told me, that Johnson called on him after his Majesty's intention had been notified to him, and said he wished to consult his friends as to the propriety of his accepting this mark of the royal favour, after the definitions which he had given in his Dictionary of pension and pensioners. He said he should not have Sir Joshua's answer till next day, when he would call again, and desired he might think of it. Sir Joshua answered that he was clear to give his opinion then, that there could be no objection to his receiving from the King a reward for literary merit; and that certainly the definitions in his Dictionary were not applicable to him. . . .

[1763] is to me a memorable year; for in it I had the happiness to obtain the acquaintance of that extraordinary man whose memoirs I am now writing; an acquaintance which I shall ever esteem as one of the most fortunate circumstances in my life. Though then but two-and-twenty, I had for several years read his works with delight and instruction, and had the highest reverence for their authour, which had grown up in my fancy into a kind of mysterious veneration, by figuring to myself a state of solemn elevated abstraction, in which I supposed him to live in the immense metropolis of London. . . .

Mr. Thomas Davies the actor, who then kept a bookseller's shop in Russel-Street, Covent-Garden, told me that Johnson was very much his friend, and came frequently to his house, where he more than once invited me to meet him: but by some unlucky accident or other he was prevented from coming to us . . .

At last, on Monday the 16th of May, when I was sitting in Mr. Davies's back-parlour, after having drunk tea with him and Mrs. Davies, Johnson unexpectedly came into the shop; and Mr. Davies having perceived him through the glass-door in the room in which we were sitting, advancing towards us,—he announced his awful approach to me, somewhat in the manner of an actor in the part of Horatio, when he addresses Hamlet on the appearance of his father's ghost, "Look, my Lord, it comes." I found that I had a very perfect idea of Johnson's figure, from the portrait of him painted by Sir Joshua Reynolds soon after he had published his Dictionary, in the attitude of sitting in his easy chair in deep meditation . . .

Mr. Davies mentioned my name, and respectfully introduced me to him. I was much agitated; and recollecting his prejudice against the Scotch, of which I had heard much, I said to Davies, "Don't tell where I come from."—"From Scotland," cried Davies, roguishly. "Mr. Johnson, (said I) I do indeed come from Scotland, but I cannot help it." I am willing to flatter myself that I meant this as light pleasantry to soothe and conciliate him, and not as an humiliating abasement at the expence of my country. But however that might be, this speech was somewhat unlucky; for with that quickness of wit for which he was so remarkable, he seized the expression "come from Scotland," which I used in the sense of being of that country; and, as if I had said that I had come away from it, or left it, retorted, "That, Sir, I find, is what a very great many of your countrymen cannot help." This stroke stunned me a good deal; and when we had sat down, I felt myself not a little embarrassed, and apprehensive of what might come next. . . .

A few days afterwards I called on Davies, and asked him if he thought I might take the liberty of waiting on Mr. Johnson at his chambers in the Temple. He said I certainly might, and that Mr. Johnson would take it as a compliment. So on Tuesday the 24th of May, . . . I boldly repaired to Johnson. His chambers were on the first floor of No. 1, Inner-Temple-lane, and I entered them with an impression given me by the Reverend Dr. Blair, of Edinburgh, who had been introduced to him not long before, and described his having "found the Giant in his den"; an expression which, when I came to be pretty well acquainted with Johnson, I repeated to him, and he was diverted at this picturesque account of himself. . . .

He received me very courteously: but, it must be confessed, that his apartment, and furniture, and morning dress, were sufficiently uncouth. His brown suit of cloaths looked very rusty: he had on a little old shrivelled unpowdered wig, which was too small for his head; his shirt-neck and knees of his breeches were loose; his black worsted stockings ill drawn up; and he had a pair of unbuckled shoes by way of slippers. But all these slovenly particularities were forgotten the moment that he began to talk. Some gentlemen, whom I do not recollect, were sitting with him; and when they went away, I also rose; but he said to me, "Nay, don't go."—"Sir, (said I), I am afraid that I intrude upon you. It is benevolent to allow me to sit and hear you." He seemed pleased with this compliment, which I sincerely paid him, and answered, "Sir, I am obliged to any man who visits me."

As Dr. Oliver Goldsmith will frequently appear in this narrative, I shall endeavour to make my readers in some degree acquainted with his singular character. . . . No man had the art of displaying with more advantage as a writer, whatever literary acquisitions he made. "Nihil quod tetigit non ornavit." His mind resembled a fertile, but thin soil. There was a quick, but not a strong vegetation, of whatever chanced to be thrown upon it. No deep root could be struck. The oak of the forest did not grow there: but the elegant shrubbery and the fragrant parterre appeared in gay succession. It has been generally circulated and believed that he was a mere fool in conversation; but, in truth, this has been greatly exaggerated. He had, no doubt, a more than common share of that hurry of ideas which we often find in his countrymen, and which sometimes produces a laughable confusion in expressing them. He was very much what the French call *un étourdi,* and from vanity and an eager desire of being conspicuous wherever he was, he frequently talked carelessly without knowledge of the subject, or even without thought. His person was short, his countenance coarse and vulgar, his deportment that of a scholar awkwardly affecting the easy gentleman. Those who were in any way distinguished, excited envy in him to so ridiculous an excess, that the instances of it are hardly credible. When accompanying two beautiful young ladies with their mother on a tour in France, he was seriously angry that more attention was paid to them than to him; and once at the exhibition of the Fantoccini in London, when those who sat next him observed with what dexterity a puppet was made to toss a pike, he could not bear that it should have such praise, and exclaimed with some warmth, "Pshaw! I can do it better myself."

Rousseau's treatise on the inequality of mankind was at this time a fashionable topick. It gave rise to an observation . . . that the advantages of fortune and rank were nothing to a wise man, who ought to value only merit. JOHNSON. "If man were savage, living in the woods by himself, this might be true; but in civilised society we all depend upon each other, and our happiness is very much owing to the good opinion of mankind. Now,

Sir, in civilized society, external advantages make us more respected. A man with a good coat upon his back meets with a
better reception than he who has a bad one. . . . When I was
running about this town a very poor fellow, I was a great arguer
for the advantages of poverty; but I was, at the same time, very
sorry to be poor. Sir, all the arguments which are brought to represent poverty as no evil, shew it to be evidently a great evil.
You never find people labouring to convince you that you may
live very happily upon a plentiful fortune."

He again insisted on the duty of maintaining subordination of
rank. "Sir, I would no more deprive a nobleman of his respect,
than of his money. I consider myself as acting a part in the great
system of society, and I do to others as I would have them to do
to me. I would behave to a nobleman as I should expect he would
behave to me, were I a nobleman and he Sam. Johnson. Sir, there
is one Mrs. Macaulay in this town, a great republican. One day
when I was at her house, I put on a very grave countenance, and
said to her, 'Madam, I am now become a convert to your way
of thinking. I am convinced that all mankind are upon an equal
footing; and to give you an unquestionable proof, Madam, that
I am in earnest, here is a very sensible, civil, well-behaved fellow-
citizen, your footman; I desire that he may be allowed to sit down
and dine with us.' I thus, Sir, shewed her the absurdity of the
levelling doctrine. She has never liked me since. Sir, your levellers wish to level down as far as themselves; but they cannot bear
levelling up to themselves. They would all have some people under them; why not then have some people above them?"

On Tuesday, July 26, I found Mr. Johnson alone. . . . We
talked of the education of children; and I asked him what he
thought was best to teach them first. JOHNSON. "Sir, it is no matter
what you teach them first, any more than what leg you shall put
into your breeches first. Sir, you may stand disputing which is
best to put in first, but in the mean time your breech is bare. Sir,
while you are considering which of two things you should teach
your child first, another boy has learnt them both."

At supper this night he talked of good eating with uncommon satisfaction. "Some people (said he,) have a foolish way of not minding, or pretending not to mind, what they eat. For my part, I mind my belly very studiously, and very carefully; for I look upon it, that he who does not mind his belly, will hardly mind any thing else." . . . When at table, he was totally absorbed in the business of the moment; his looks seemed rivetted to his plate; nor would he, unless when in very high company, say one word, or even pay the least attention to what was said by others, till he had satisfied his appetite: which was so fierce, and indulged with such intenseness, that while in the act of eating, the veins of his forehead swelled, and generally a strong perspiration was visible. To those whose sensations were delicate, this could not but be disgusting; and it was doubtless not very suitable to the character of a philosopher, who should be distinguished by self-command. But it must be owned, that Johnson, though he could be rigidly abstemious, was not a temperate man either in eating or drinking. He could refrain, but he could not use moderately.

That the most minute singularities which belonged to him, and made very observable parts of his appearance and manner, may not be omitted, it is requisite to mention, that while talking or even musing as he sat in his chair, he commonly held his head to one side towards his right shoulder, and shook it in a tremulous manner, moving his body backwards and forwards, and rubbing his left knee in the same direction, with the palm of his hand. In the intervals of articulating he made various sounds with his mouth; sometimes as if ruminating, or what is called chewing the cud, sometimes giving a half whistle, sometimes making his tongue play backwards from the roof of his mouth, as if clucking like a hen, and sometimes protruding it against his upper gums in front, as if pronouncing quickly under his breath, too, too, too: all this accompanied sometimes with a thoughtful look, but more frequently with a smile. Generally when he had concluded a period, in the course of a dispute, by which time he was a good deal exhausted by violence and vociferation, he used to blow out his breath like a whale. This I suppose was a relief to his lungs;

and seemed in him to be a contemptuous mode of expression, as if he had made the arguments of his opponent fly like chaff before the wind.

This year [1765] was distinguished by his being introduced into the family of Mr. Thrale, one of the most eminent brewers in England, and member of Parliament for the borough of Southwark. . . . Mr. Thrale had married Miss Hester Lynch Salusbury, of good Welch extraction, a lady of lively talents, improved by education. . . . Johnson accepted of an invitation to dinner at Thrale's, and was so much pleased with his reception, both by Mr. and Mrs. Thrale, and they so much pleased with him, that his invitations to their house were more and more frequent, till at last he became one of the family, and an apartment was appropriated to him, both in their house at Southwark and in their villa at Streatham.

Johnson had a very sincere esteem for Mr. Thrale . . .

"I know no man, (said he,) who is more master of his wife and family than Thrale. If he but holds up a finger, he is obeyed. It is a great mistake to suppose that she is above him in literary attainments. She is more flippant; but he has ten times her learning: he is a regular scholar; but her learning is that of a schoolboy in one of the lower forms." My readers may naturally wish for some representation of the figures of this couple. Mr. Thrale was tall, well proportioned, and stately. As for Madam, or my Mistress, by which epithets Johnson used to mention Mrs. Thrale, she was short, plump, and brisk. She has herself given us a lively view of the idea which Johnson had of her person, on her appearing before him in a dark-coloured gown: "You little creatures should never wear those sort of clothes, however; they are unsuitable in every way. What! have not all insects gay colours!"

Johnson had been allowed the use of the splendid library in the Queen's house, and here, one morning in February, 1767, he met George III. Johnson was pleased by a long conversation in which the King displayed the most courteous civility toward his famous subject. Later, at Sir Joshua's, he described the whole episode to his friends.

During all the time in which Dr. Johnson was employed in relating . . . what had passed between the King and him, Dr.
Goldsmith remained unmoved upon a sopha at some distance,
affecting not to join in the least in the eager curiosity of the company. He assigned as a reason for his gloom and seeming inattention, that he apprehended Johnson had relinquished his
purpose of furnishing him with a Prologue to his play, with the
hopes of which he had been flattered; but it was strongly suspected
that he was fretting with chagrin and envy at the singular honour
Dr. Johnson had lately enjoyed. At length, the frankness, and
simplicity of his natural character prevailed. He sprung from
the sopha, advanced to Johnson, and in a kind of flutter, from
imagining himself in the situation which he had just been hearing
described, exclaimed, "Well, you acquitted yourself in this conversation better than I should have done; for I should have bowed
and stammered through the whole of it."

When we were alone, I introduced the subject of death, and
endeavoured to maintain that the fear of it might be got over. I
told him that David Hume said to me, he was no more uneasy to
think he should not be after his life, than that he had not been
before he began to exist. JOHNSON. "Sir, if he really thinks so, his
perceptions are disturbed; he is mad; if he does not think so, he
lies. He may tell you, he holds his finger in the flame of a candle,
without feeling pain; would you believe him? When he dies,
he at least gives up all he has." BOSWELL. "Foote, Sir, told me,
that when he was very ill he was not afraid to die." JOHNSON.
"It is not true, Sir. Hold a pistol to Foote's breast, or to Hume's
breast, and threaten to kill them, and you'll see how they behave."
BOSWELL. "But may we not fortify our minds for the approach of
death?"—Here I am sensible I was in the wrong, to bring before
his view what he ever looked upon with horrour; for although
when in a celestial frame of mind in his "Vanity of Human
Wishes," he has supposed death to be "kind Nature's signal for
retreat," from this state of being to "a happier seat," his thoughts
upon this awful change were in general full of dismal apprehensions. His mind resembled the vast amphitheatre, the Colisæum

at Rome. In the centre stood his judgement, which like a mighty gladiator, combated those apprehensions that, like the wild beasts of the Arena, were all around in cells, ready to be let out upon him. After a conflict, he drives them back into their dens; but not killing them, they were still assailing him. To my question, whether we might not fortify our minds for the approach of death, he answered, in a passion, "No, Sir, let it alone. It matters not how a man dies, but how he lives. The act of dying is not of importance, it lasts so short a time." He added, (with an earnest look,) "A man knows it must be so, and submits. It will do him no good to whine."

I attempted to continue the conversation. He was so provoked, that he said: "Give us no more of this;" and was thrown into such a state of agitation, that he expressed himself in a way that alarmed and distressed me: shewed an impatience that I should leave him, and when I was going away, called to me sternly, "Don't let us meet to-morrow."

I went home exceedingly uneasy. All the harsh observations which I had ever heard made upon his character, crowded into my mind; and I seemed to myself like the man who had put his head into the lion's mouth a great many times with perfect safety, but at last had it bit off.

Happening to meet Sir Adam Ferguson, I presented him to Dr. Johnson. Sir Adam expressed some apprehension that the Pantheon would encourage luxury. "Sir, (said Johnson,) I am a great friend to publick amusements; for they keep people from vice. You now (addressing himself to me,) would have been with a wench, had you not been here.—O! I forgot you were married."

Sir Adam suggested, that luxury corrupts a people, and destroys the spirit of liberty. JOHNSON. "Sir, that is all visionary. I would not give half a guinea to live under one form of government rather than another. It is of no moment to the happiness of an individual. Sir, the danger of the abuse of power is nothing to a private man. What Frenchman is prevented from passing his life as he pleases?" SIR ADAM. "But, Sir, in the British constitution it is surely of importance to keep up a spirit in the people, so as to preserve a balance against the crown." JOHNSON. "Sir, I perceive you are a vile Whig.—Why all this childish jealousy of the power of the crown? The crown has not power enough. When I say that all governments are alike, I consider that in no government power can be abused long. Mankind will not bear it. If a sovereign oppresses his people to a great degree, they will rise and cut off his head. There is a remedy in human nature against tyranny, that will keep us safe under every form of government."

The various views with which men travel in quest of new scenes, having been talked of, a learned gentleman who holds a considerable office in the law expatiated on the happiness of a savage life, and mentioned an instance of an office who had actually lived for some time in the wilds of America, of whom, when in that state, he quoted this reflection with an air of admiration, as if it had been deeply philosophical: "Here am I, free and unrestrained, amidst the rude magnificence of Nature, with this Indian woman by my side, and this gun, with which I can procure food when I want it: what more can be desired for human happiness?" . . . JOHNSON. "Do not allow yourself, Sir, to be imposed upon by such gross absurdity. It is sad stuff; it is brutish. If a bull could speak, he might as well exclaim,—Here am I with this cow and this grass; what being can enjoy better felicity?" . . .

On Tuesday, April 27 [1773], Mr. Beauclerk and I called on him in the morning. As we walked up Johnson's-Court, I said, "I have a veneration for this court;" and was glad to find that Beauclerk had the same reverential enthusiasm. We found him alone . . .

He said, "Goldsmith should not be for ever attempting to shine in conversation: he has not temper for it, he is so much mortified when he fails. Sir, a game of jokes is composed partly of skill, partly of chance, a man may be beat at times by one who has not the tenth part of his wit. Now Goldsmith's putting himself against another, is like a man laying a hundred to one who cannot spare the hundred. It is not worth a man's while. A man should not lay a hundred to one, unless he can easily spare it, though he has a hundred chances for him: he can get but a guinea, and he may lose a hundred. Goldsmith is in this state. When he contends, if he gets the better, it is a very little addition to a man of his literary reputation: if he does not get the better, he is miserably vexed." . . .

Goldsmith, however, was often very fortunate in his witty contests, even when he entered the lists with Johnson himself. Sir Joshua Reynolds was in company with them one day, when Goldsmith said, that he thought he could write a good fable, mentioned the simplicity which that kind of composition requires, and observed, that in most fables the animals introduced seldom talk in character. "For instance, (said he,) the fable of the little fishes, who saw birds fly over their heads, and envying them, petitioned Jupiter to be changed into birds. The skill (continued he,) consists in making them talk like little fishes." While he indulged himself in this fanciful reverie, he observed Johnson shaking his sides, and laughing. Upon which he smartly proceeded, "Why, Dr. Johnson, this is not so easy as you seem to think; for if you were to make little fishes talk, they would talk like WHALES." . . .

Upon another ocasion, when Goldsmith confessed himself to be of an envious disposition, I contended with Johnson that we ought not to be angry with him, he was so candid in owning it. "Nay, Sir, said Johnson, we must be angry that a man has such a super-abundance of an odious quality, that he cannot keep it within his own breast, but it boils over." In my opinion, however, Goldsmith had not more of it than other people have, but only talked of it freely.

I dined with Dr. Johnson at General Paoli's. . . . He maintained the dignity and propriety of male succession, in opposition to the opinion of one of our friends, who had that day employed Mr. Chambers to draw his will, devising his estate to his three sisters, in preference to a remote heir male. Johnson called them "three dowdies," and said, with as high a spirit as the boldest Baron in the most perfect days of the feudal system, "An ancient estate should always go to males. It is mighty foolish to let a stranger have it because he marries your daughter, and takes your name. As for an estate newly acquired by trade, you may give it, if you will, to the dog Towser, and let him keep his own name."

I have known him at times exceedingly diverted at what seemed to others a very small sport. He now laughed immoderately, without any reason that we could perceive, at our friend's making his will; call him the testator, and added, "I dare say he thinks he has done a mighty thing. He won't stay till he gets home to his seat in the country, to produce this wonderful deed: he'll call up the landlord of the first inn on the road; and, after a suitable preface upon mortality and the uncertainty of life, will tell him that he should not delay making his will; and here, Sir, will he say, is my will, which I have just made, with the assistance of one of the ablest lawyers in the kingdom; and he will read it to him, (laughing all the time). He believes he has made this will; but he did not make it: you, Chambers, made it for him. I trust you have had more conscience than to make him say, 'being of sound understanding;' ha, ha, ha! I hope he has left me a legacy. I'd have his will turned into verse, like a ballad."

In this playful manner did he run on, exulting in his own pleasantry . . . Mr. Chambers did not by any means relish this jocularity . . . and seemed impatient till he got rid of us. Johnson could not stop his merriment, but continued it all the way till he got without the Temple-gate. He then burst into such a fit of laughter, that he appeared to be almost in a convulsion; and, in order to support himself, laid hold of one of the posts at the side of the foot pavement, and sent forth peals so loud, that in the silence of the night his voice seemed to resound from Temple-bar to Fleet-ditch.

Macpherson's Ossian, *purporting to be translations from a Gaelic bard, had excited much controversy. Johnson denied that they had authenticity or merit; he remarked to Reynolds, "Sir, a man might write such stuff forever, if he would* abandon *his mind to it." Macpherson became incensed at Johnson's blunt accusation of forgery, and sent him a threatening letter which elicited a famous reply:*

"MR. JAMES MACPHERSON.

I RECEIVED your foolish and impudent letter. Any violence offered me I shall do my best to repel; and what I cannot do for myself, the law shall do for me. I hope I shall never be deterred from detecting what I think a cheat, by the menaces of a ruffian.

What would you have me retract? I thought your book an imposture; I think it an imposture still. For this opinion I have given my reasons to the publick, which I here dare you to refute. Your rage I defy. Your abilities, since your Homer, are not so formidable; and what I hear of your morals inclines me to pay regard not to what you shall say, but to what you shall prove. You may print this if you will.

SAM JOHNSON"

Dr. Barnard having once expressed to him an apprehension, that if he should visit Ireland he might treat the people of that country more unfavourably than he had done the Scotch, he answered, with strong pointed double-edged wit, "Sir, you have no reason to be afraid of me. The Irish are not in conspiracy to cheat the world by false representations of the merits of their countrymen. No, Sir; the Irish are a FAIR PEOPLE;—they never speak well of one another."

Dr. Johnson said to me in the morning, [22 March, 1776] "You will see, Sir, at Mr. Hector's, his sister, Mrs. Careless, a clergyman's widow. She was the first woman with whom I was in love. It dropt out of my head imperceptibly; but she and I shall always have a kindness for each other." He laughed at the notion that a man can never be really in love but once, and considered it as a mere romantick fancy. . . .

When he again talked of Mrs. Careless to-night, he seemed to have had his affection revived; for he said, "If I had married her, it might have been as happy for me." BOSWELL. "Pray, Sir, do you not suppose that there are fifty women in the world, with any one of whom a man may be as happy, as with any one woman in particular?" JOHNSON. "Ay, Sir, fifty thousand." BOSWELL. "Then, Sir, you are not of opinion with some who imagine that certain men and certain women are made for each other; and that they cannot be happy if they miss their counterparts." JOHNSON. "To be sure not, Sir. I believe marriages would in general be as happy, and often more so, if they were all made by the Lord

Chancellor, upon a due consideration of the characters and circumstances, without the parties having any choice in the matter."

I am now to record a very curious incident in Dr. Johnson's life, which fell under my own observation . . .

My desire of being acquainted with celebrated men of every description, had made me, much about the same time, obtain an introduction to Dr. Samuel Johnson and to John Wilkes, Esq. Two men more different could perhaps not be selected out of all mankind. They had even attacked one another with some asperity in their writings; yet I lived in habits of friendship with both. I could fully relish the excellence of each; for I have ever delighted in that intellectual chemistry, which can separate good qualities from evil in the same person . . .

I conceived an irresistible wish, if possible, to bring Dr. Johnson and Mr. Wilkes together. How to manage it, was a nice and difficult matter.

My worthy booksellers and friends, Messieurs Dilly in the Poultry, at whose hospitable and well-covered table I have seen a greater number of literary men, than at any other, except that of Sir Joshua Reynolds, had invited me to meet Mr. Wilkes and some more gentlemen, on Wednesday, May 15. "Pray (said I,) let us have Dr. Johnson."—"What with Mr. Wilkes? not for the world, (said Mr. Edward Dilly;) Dr. Johnson would never forgive me." —"Come, (said I,) if you'll let me negociate for you, I will be answerable that all shall go well." DILLY. "Nay, if you will take it upon you, I am sure I shall be very happy to see them both here."

Notwithstanding the high veneration which I entertained for Dr. Johnson, I was sensible that he was sometimes a little actuated by the spirit of contradiction, and by means of that I hoped I should gain my point. I was persuaded that if I had come upon him with a direct proposal, "Sir, will you dine in company with Jack Wilkes?" he would have flown into a passion, and would probably have answered, "Dine with Jack Wilkes, Sir! I'd as soon dine with Jack Ketch." I therefore, while we were sitting quietly by ourselves at his house in an evening, took occasion to open my plan thus:—"Mr. Dilly, Sir, sends his respectful compliments to you, and would be happy if you would do him the honour to dine with him on Wednesday next along with me, as I must soon go to Scotland." JOHNSON. "Sir, I am obliged to Mr. Dilly. I will wait upon him—" BOSWELL. "Provided, Sir, I suppose, that the company which he is to have, is agreeable to you." JOHNSON. "What do you mean, Sir? What do you take me for? Do you think I am so ignorant of the world, as to imagine that I am to prescribe to a gentleman what company he is to have at his table?" BOSWELL. "I beg your pardon, Sir, for wishing to prevent you from meeting people whom you might not like. Perhaps he may have some of what he calls his patriotick friends with him." JOHNSON. "Well, Sir, and what then? What care *I* for his patriotick friends? Poh!" BOSWELL. "I should not be surprized to find Jack Wilkes there." JOHNSON. "And if Jack Wilkes *should* be there, what is that to *me*, Sir? My dear friend, let us have no more of this. I am sorry to be angry with you; but really it is treating me strangely to talk to me as if I could not meet any company whatever, occasionally." BOSWELL. "Pray, forgive me, Sir: I meant well. But you shall meet whoever comes, for me." Thus I secured him, and told Dilly that he would find him very well pleased to be one of his guests on the day appointed.

Upon the much expected Wednesday, I called on him about an hour before dinner, as I often did when we were to dine out together, to see that he was ready in time, and to accompany him. I found him buffeting his books, as upon a former occasion, covered with dust, and making no preparation for going abroad. "How is this, Sir? (said I). Don't you recollect that you are to dine at Mr. Dilly's?" JOHNSON. "Sir, I did not think of going to Dilly's: it went out of my head. I have ordered dinner at home with Mrs. Williams." BOSWELL. "But, my dear Sir, you know you were engaged to Mr. Dilly, and I told him so. He will expect you, and will be much disappointed if you don't come." JOHNSON. "You must talk to Mrs. Williams about this."

Here was a sad dilemma. I feared that what I was so confident I had secured, would yet be frustrated. He had accustomed himself to shew Mrs. Williams such a degree of humane attention, as frequently imposed some restraint upon him; and I knew that if

she should be obstinate, he would not stir. I hastened down stairs
to the blind lady's room, and told her I was in great uneasiness, for
Dr. Johnson had engaged to me to dine this day at Mr. Dilly's,
but that he had told me he had forgotten his engagement, and
had ordered dinner at home. "Yes, Sir, (said she, pretty peevishly,)
Dr. Johnson is to dine at home."—"Madam, (said I,) his respect
for you is such, that I know he will not leave you, unless you
absolutely desire it. But as you have so much of his company,
I hope you will be good enough to forego it for a day: as Mr. Dilly
is a very worthy man, has frequently had agreeable parties at his
house for Dr. Johnson, and will be vexed if the Doctor neglects
him to-day. And then, Madam, be pleased to consider my situation; I carried the message, and I assured Mr. Dilly that Dr. Johnson was to come; and no doubt he has made a dinner, and invited
a company, and boasted of the honour he expected to have. I
shall be quite disgraced if the Doctor is not there." She gradually
softened to my solicitations, which were certainly as earnest as
most entreaties to ladies upon any occasion, and was graciously
pleased to empower me to tell Dr. Johnson, "That all things considered, she thought he should certainly go." I flew back to him,
still in dust, and careless of what should be the event, "indifferent
in his choice to go or stay;" but as soon as I had announced to him
Mrs. Williams's consent, he roared, "Frank, a clean shirt," and
was very soon drest. When I had him fairly seated in a hackney-
coach with me, I exulted as much as a fortune-hunter who has got
an heiress into a post-chaise with him to set out for Gretna-Green.

When we entered Mr. Dilly's drawing-room, he found himself
in the midst of a company he did not know. I kept myself snug
and silent, watching how he would conduct himself. I observed
him whispering to Mr. Dilly, "Who is that gentleman, sir?"—
"Mr. Arthur Lee."—JOHNSON. "Too, too, too," (under his breath,)
which was one of his habitual mutterings. Mr. Arthur Lee could
not but be very obnoxious to Johnson, for he was not only a
patriot, but an *American.* "And who is the gentleman in lace?"
—"Mr. Wilkes, Sir." This information confounded him still more;
he had some difficulty to restrain himself, and taking up a book,
sat down upon a window-seat and read, or at least kept his eye

upon it intently for some time, till he composed himself. His feelings, I dare say, were aukward enough. But he no doubt recollected his having rated me for supposing that he could be at all disconcerted by any company, and he, therefore, resolutely set himself to behave quite as an easy man of the world, who could adapt himself at once to the disposition and manners of those whom he might chance to meet.

The cheering sound of "Dinner is upon the table," dissolved his reverie, and we all sat down without any symptom of ill humour. There were present, beside Mr. Wilkes, and Mr. Arthur Lee, who was an old companion of mine when he studied physick at Edinburgh, Mr. (now Sir John) Miller, Dr. Lettsom, and Mr. Slater, the druggist. Mr. Wilkes placed himself next to Dr. Johnson, and behaved to him with so much attention and politeness, that he gained upon him insensibly. No man eat more heartily than Johnson, or loved better what was nice and delicate. Mr. Wilkes was very assiduous in helping him to some fine veal. "Pray give me leave, Sir;—It is better here—A little of the brown —Some fat, Sir—A little of the stuffing—Some gravy—Let me have the pleasure of giving you some butter—Allow me to recommend a squeeze of this orange;—or the lemon, perhaps, may have more zest."—"Sir, Sir, I am obliged to you, Sir," cried Johnson, bowing, and turning his head to him with a look for some time of "surly virtue," but, in short while, of complacency . . .

Mr. Arthur Lee mentioned some Scotch who had taken possession of a barren part of America, and wondered why they should choose it. JOHNSON. "Why, Sir, all barrenness is comparative. The Scotch would not know it to be barren." When I claimed a superiority for Scotland over England in one respect, that no man can be arrested there for a debt merely because another swears it against him; but there must first be the judgement of a court of law ascertaining its justice; and that a seizure of the person, before judgement is obtained, can take place only, if this creditor should swear that he is about to fly from the country, or, as it is technically expressed, is *in meditatione fugæ:* WILKES. "That, I should think, may be safely sworn of all the Scotch nation." JOHNSON. (To Mr. Wilkes) "You must know, Sir, I lately took my friend Boswell,

and shewed him genuine civilised life in an English provincial
town. I turned him loose at Lichfield, my native city, that he might
see for once real civility: for you know he lives among savages in
Scotland, and among rakes in London." WILKES. "Except when
he is with grave, sober, decent people, like you and me." JOHNSON.
(smiling) "And we ashamed of him." . . .

Mr. Burke gave me much credit for this successful negotiation;
and pleasantly said, "that there was nothing equal to it in the whole
history of the Corps Diplomatique."

I attended Dr. Johnson home, and had the satisfaction to hear
him tell Mrs. Williams how much he had been pleased with Mr.
Wilkes's company, and what an agreeable day he had passed.

I have no minute of any interview with Johnson till Thursday,
May 15th, [1783] when I find what follows: BOSWELL. "I wish
much to be in Parliament, Sir." JOHNSON. "Why, Sir, unless you
come resolved to support any administration, you would be the
worse for being in Parliament, because you would be obliged to
live more expensively."—BOSWELL. "Perhaps, Sir, I should be the
less happy for being in Parliament. I never would sell my vote,
and I should be vexed if things went wrong." JOHNSON. "That's
cant, Sir. It would not vex you more in the house than in the gallery: publick affairs vex no man." BOSWELL. "Have not they
vexed yourself a little, Sir? Have you not been vexed by all the
turbulence of this reign, and by that absurd vote of the House of
Commons, 'That the influence of the Crown has increased, is increasing, and ought to be diminished?'" JOHNSON. "Sir, I have
never slept an hour less, nor eat an ounce less meat. I would have
knocked the factious dogs on the head, to be sure; but I was not
vexed." BOSWELL. "I declare, Sir, upon my honour, I did imagine
I was vexed, and took a pride in it; but it *was*, perhaps, cant; for
I own I neither eat less, nor slept less." JOHNSON. "My dear friend,
clear your *mind* of cant. You may *talk* as other people do: you
may say to a man, 'Sir, I am your most humble servant.' You
are *not* his most humble servant. You may say, 'These are bad
times; it is a melancholy thing to be reserved at such times.'
You don't mind the times. You tell a man, 'I am sorry you had

such bad weather the last day of your journey, and were so much wet.' You don't care six-pence whether he is wet or dry. You may *talk* in this manner; it is a mode of talking in Society: but don't *think* foolishly."

Old age was at last beginning to enfeeble the gigantic frame that had been ravaged and scarred by disease. Sometimes he had to take opium to relieve his pains. In the summer of 1783 "he had a dreadful stroke of the palsy" *which temporarily deprived him of the powers of speech; his chest was congested with asthma and his legs swollen. The dependents his charity had maintained were dying, too. Levett and Mrs. Williams were already dead. Mrs. Desmoulins was so ill that she could be but little company, and the emptying house was lonely to him. He sought distraction in a jaunt to Staffordshire and Derbyshire, and a last pilgrimage to Lichfield.*

Soon after Johnson's return to the metropolis, both the asthma and dropsy became more violent and distressful. . . .

My readers are now, at last, to behold SAMUEL JOHNSON preparing himself for that doom, from which the most exalted powers afford no exemption to man. Death had always been to him an object of terrour; so that though by no means happy, he still clung to life with an eagerness at which many have wondered.

Johnson, with that native fortitude, which, amidst all his bodily distress and mental sufferings, never forsook him, asked Dr. Brocklesby, as a man in whom he had confidence, to tell him plainly whether he could recover. "Give me (said he) a direct answer." The Doctor having first asked him if he could bear the whole truth, which way soever it might lead, and being answered that he could, declared that, in his opinion, he could not recover without a miracle. "Then, (said Johnson,) I will take no more physick, not even my opiates: for I have prayed that I may render up my soul to GOD unclouded." In this resolution he persevered, and, at the same time, used only the weakest kinds of sustenance. . . .

Mr. Strahan has given me the agreeable assurance, that, after being in much agitation, Johnson became quite composed, and continued so till his death. . . .

THE LIFE OF SAMUEL JOHNSON

Having . . . made his will on the 8th and 9th of December, and settled all his worldly affairs, he languished till Monday, the 13th of that month, when he expired, about seven o'clock in the evening, with so little apparent pain that his attendants hardly perceived when his dissolution took place. . . .

"On Monday, the 13th of December [1784], the day on which he died, [the daughter of a friend] begged to be permitted to see the Doctor . . . The Doctor turned himself in the bed, and said, 'GOD bless you, my dear!' These were the last words he spoke.— His difficulty in breathing increased till about seven o'clock in the evening, when Mr. Barber and Mrs. Desmoulins, who were sitting in the room, observing that the noise he made in breathing had ceased, went to the bed, and found he was dead." . . .

A few days before his death, he had asked Sir John Hawkins, as one of his executors, where he should be buried; and on being answered, "Doubtless, in Westminster-Abbey," seemed to feel a satisfaction, very natural to a Poet; and indeed in my opinion very natural to every man of any imagination, who has no family sepulchre in which he can be laid with his fathers. Accordingly, upon Monday, December 20, his remains were deposited in that noble and renowned edifice; and over his grave was placed a large blue flag-stone, with this inscription:

> "SAMUEL JOHNSON, LL.D.
> *Obit* XIII *die Decembris,*
> *Anno Domini*
> M.DCC.LXXXIV.
> *Ætatis suæ* LXXV."

PRINTER–REBEL–PHILOSOPHER

WHEN FRANKLIN LANDED IN BRITTANY LATE IN THE YEAR 1776, THE French delightedly imagined the fur cap he had worn for warmth on the November voyage to be some strange insignia of homespun philosophy, part of the official garb of a Quaker sage. Franklin was not a Quaker nor was he a backwoods philosopher, having lived for thirty years among scientists, merchants, politicians, and men of fashion. But to the French he was a vision of both the dignity and the wisdom of natural man, and a promise of the shining future. Franklin blandly humored their enthusiastic illusion, and continued on ceremonial occasions, even in Paris, to wear the cap they had weighted with so much symbolism.

In fact both Franklin and his garb are significant. With them, in a way, the plain man has arrived in history. And he has arrived no longer as the satellite or the entertainer of the noble and the great, but standing on his own feet, commanding his own prestige. More emphatically than Johnson repulsing the patronage of the Earl of Chesterfield, Franklin in his whole career symbolizes a break with the past, symbolizes the upsurging energies of democracy. The son of the tallow-chandler talked, and not subserviently, with kings; the poor boy who had walked the streets of Philadelphia with a great puffy roll under each arm met aristocratic statesmen and beat them at their own game; the shrewd observer of ordinary things made an honored place for himself among the men of science.

The curve of the future is implicit in Franklin. The wave of empire was already surging westward over the Alleghanies, and although Franklin was no pioneer or frontiersman he saw the wild

fringes of civilized settlement beginning the long and bloody
martyrdom of the Indians, and warned Braddock of the dangers
that officer tasted before he ever reached Fort Duquesne.
Franklin epitomized the shrewd Yankee trader, not always too
scrupulous for a little chicanery with wooden nutmegs or worse,
the shopkeeper expanding into merchant, owner of clipper ships
sailing the Seven Seas, small craftsman swelling into manufacturer
and industralist. Franklin's interest in science fused a disinterested
but vivid snoopiness into the secrets of nature with the concern
for practical application that has dominated American science and
invention. Franklin's common-sense pursuit of truth is ancestor
to both the cracker-barrel philosophers and the unvarnished
candor of thinkers like Peirce and Dewey.

But no common man could thus have raised to genius the virtues
of the Common Man. Franklin was more than the embodiment of
a vulgar material attainment he has often been confused with,
more than the slavish follower of *Poor Richard's* cautious maxims.
He cannot be confined within any cheap formula, such as "from
soap-vat to fortune." He was not one of what Carl Van Doren
calls "the dry, prim people" who have tried to claim him "as a
treasure shut up in a savings bank to which they have the lawful
key." The frugality they praise him for he could never learn,
and he got his start in business by running himself in debt. Far
from practising a wool-mouthed prudence, he wittily talked back
to the statesmen he was dealing with and ridiculed them in satiric
fables; when over seventy he risked hanging as a rebel. He fell
into none of the snobbish affectations of crudity so dear to the
self-made man; he cultivated the graces and took an intelligent
interest in a good cuisine and vintage wines. He liked a delicate
naughtiness of language. He enjoyed flirtatious, and sometimes
more than flirtatious, contacts with feminine beauty and charm.
His curiosity was not limited to what was practically useful, but
ranged with an eager vitality everywhere. He was a man, not a
stick; a lover of living, not a penny-pincher and go-getter.

His *Autobiography* reflects almost all these facets of his attainment, although it does not do full justice to all of them. It ex-
tends hardly beyond his fiftieth year, and therefore includes no

picture of the worldwide stage of his tremendous fame. It mentions his experiments with electricity, but modestly refrains from
a more detailed recital we should willingly have had. But the
homely and yet urbane personality of Franklin suffuses every
page, steeping it in his characteristic mingling of pungent sanity
and benevolent cheerfulness. There is nothing like it among his
predecessors: certainly not in the religious agonizings of St.
Augustine or Bunyan, nor in the picaresque escapades of the
scapegrace Cellini, nor in the tumults and heart-searchings of
Rousseau's *Confessions*. Franklin's "was the first masterpiece of
autobiography by a self-made man," the first to tell such a career.

But Franklin was too great a man to write a mere success-story,
and too human a one to leave his humanity out. Through his account of the insolently argumentative boy, the credulous youth
imposed on by a Governor's promises, and the ambitious young
tradesman, we feel the wise and sometimes amused detachment of
the man approaching seventy. Only a superficial reader will fail
to see the flavor conveyed by the very adjectives in Franklin's account of "the bold and arduous project of arriving at moral perfection."—"I was surprised," he adds demurely, "to find myself so
much fuller of faults than I had imagined." The undertone of
humorous sedateness enables us to glimpse the tolerant sage
smiling at his own youthful priggishness, pomposity, and conceit.
But, still further beneath, we see with Franklin that there was
something morally admirable in that solemn effort too. Franklin
is one of the subtler as well as one of the least pretentious autobiographers. One of the sanest of the great, his balance is no
less marked than his personal tang and quiet humor.

Autobiography of Benjamin Franklin

[Most of the *Autobiography* was written in 1771; successive parts were added in 1784 and 1788. It was first published by Franklin's grandson, in an edited form, from an incomplete transcript in 1817, and first published from the original manuscript in 1868.]

THIS OBSCURE FAMILY OF OURS WAS EARLY IN THE REFORMATION, and continued Protestants through the reign of Queen Mary, when they were sometimes in danger of trouble on account of their zeal against popery. They had got an English Bible, and to conceal and secure it, it was fastened open with tapes under and within the cover of a joint-stool. When my great-great-grandfather read it to his family, he turned up the joint-stool upon his knees, turning over the leaves then under the tapes. One of the children stood at the door to give notice if he saw the apparitor coming, who was an officer of the spiritual court. In that case the stool was turned down again upon its feet, when the Bible remained concealed under it as before. This anecdote I had from my uncle Benjamin. The family continued all of the Church of England till about the end of Charles the Second's reign, when some of the ministers that had been outed for non-conformity holding conventicles in Northamptonshire, Benjamin and Josiah adhered to them, and so continued all their lives: the rest of the family remained with the Episcopal Church.

Josiah, my father, married young, and carried his wife with three children into New England, about 1682. The conventicles having been forbidden by law, and frequently disturbed, induced some considerable men of his acquaintance to remove to that country, and he was prevailed with to accompany them thither, where they expected to enjoy their mode of religion with freedom. By the same wife he had four children more born there, and by a second wife ten more, in all seventeen; of which I remember thirteen sitting at one time at his table, who all grew up to be men and women, and married; I was the youngest son, and the youngest child but two, and was born in Boston, New England.

I was put to the grammar-school at eight years of age, my father intending to devote me, as the tithe of his sons, to the service of the Church . . . I continued, however, at the grammar-school not quite one year, though in that time I had risen gradually from the middle of the class of that year to be the head of it, and farther was removed into the next class above it, in order to go with that into the third at the end of the year . . . At ten years old I was taken home to assist my father in his business, which was that of a tallow-chandler and sope-boiler; a business he was not bred to, but had assumed on his arrival in New England, and on finding his dying trade would not maintain his family, being in little request. Accordingly, I was employed in cutting wick for the candles, filling the dipping mold and the molds for cast candles, attending the shop, going of errands, etc.

I disliked the trade, and had a strong inclination for the sea, but my father declared against it; however, living near the water, I was much in and about it, learnt early to swim well, and to manage boats; and when in a boat or canoe with other boys, I was commonly allowed to govern, especially in any case of difficulty; and upon other occasions I was generally a leader among the boys, and sometimes led them into scrapes, of which I will mention one instance, as it shows an early projecting public spirit, tho' not then justly conducted.

There was a salt-marsh that bounded part of the mill-pond, on the edge of which, at high water, we used to stand to fish for minnows. By much trampling, we had made it a mere quagmire. My proposal was to build a wharff there fit for us to stand upon, and I showed my comrades a large heap of stones, which were intended for a new house near the marsh, and which would very well suit our purpose. Accordingly, in the evening, when the workmen were gone, I assembled a number of my play-fellows, and working

with them diligently like so many emmets, sometimes two or three
to a stone, we brought them all away and built our little wharff.
The next morning the workmen were surprised at missing the
stones, which were found in our wharff. Inquiry was made after
the removers; we were discovered and complained of; several of
us were corrected by our fathers; and, though I pleaded the usefulness of the work, mine convinced me that nothing was useful
which was not honest.

From a child I was fond of reading, and all the little money that
came into my hands was ever laid out in books. Pleased with the
Pilgrim's Progress, my first collection was of John Bunyan's work
in separate little volumes . . . This bookish inclination at length
determined my father to make me a printer, though he had already
one son (James) of that profession. In 1717 my brother James returned from England with a press and letters to set up his business
in Boston. I liked it much better than that of my father, but still
had a hankering for the sea. To prevent the apprehended effect of
such an inclination, my father was impatient to have me bound
to my brother. I stood out some time, but at last was persuaded,
and signed the indentures when I was yet but twelve years old.
I was to serve as an apprentice till I was twenty-one years of age,
only I was to be allowed journeyman's wages during the last year.
In a little time I made great proficiency in the business, and became a useful hand to my brother. I now had access to better
books. An acquaintance with the apprentices of booksellers enabled me sometimes to borrow a small one, which I was careful to
return soon and clean. Often I sat up in my room reading the
greatest part of the night, when the book was borrowed in the
evening and to be returned early in the morning, lest it should
be missed or wanted.

About this time I met with an odd volume of the *Spectator.* It
was the third. I had never before seen any of them. I bought it,
read it over and over, and was much delighted with it. I thought
the writing excellent, and wished, if possible, to imitate it. With
this view I took some of the papers, and, making short hints of
the sentiment in each sentence, laid them by a few days, and then,

without looking at the book, try'd to compleat the papers again, by
expressing each hinted sentiment at length, and as fully as it had
been expressed before, in any suitable words that should come to
hand. Then I compared my *Spectator* with the original, discovered some of my faults, and corrected them. But I found I
wanted a stock of words, or a readiness in recollecting and using
them, which I thought I should have acquired before that time if
I had gone on making verses; since the continual occasion for
words of the same import, but of different length, to suit the measure, or of different sound for the rhyme, would have laid me under a constant necessity of searching for variety, and also have
tended to fix that variety in my mind, and make me master of it.
Therefore I took some of the tales and turned them into verse;
and, after a time, when I had pretty well forgotten the prose,
turned them back again. I also sometimes jumbled my collections
of hints into confusion, and after some weeks endeavored to reduce them into the best order, before I began to form the full
sentences and compleat the paper. This was to teach me method in
the arrangement of thoughts. By comparing my work afterwards
with the original, I discovered many faults and amended them;
but I sometimes had the pleasure of fancying that, in certain particulars of small import, I had been lucky enough to improve the
method or the language, and this encouraged me to think I might
possibly in time come to be a tolerable English writer, of which
I was extreamly ambitious.

In 1720 Franklin's brother James began to print the New England Courant, *the second newspaper to be published in America.
A piece of political comment getting him into trouble with the
Assembly, he made his younger brother titular editor, cancelling
his old indentures of apprenticeship to make this seem plausible.
But the two had had angry disagreements, and young Benjamin
took advantage to skip off to New York. Fearing his plan might be
prevented if it were known, he made secret arrangements with the
captain of the sloop, pretending he* "had got a naughty girl with
child, whose friends would compel me to marry her." *Finding no
work in New York, he went on to Philadelphia.*

I was in my working dress, my best clothes being to come round by sea. I was dirty from my journey; my pockets were stuff'd out with shirts and stockings, and I knew no soul nor where to look for lodging. I was fatigued with travelling, rowing, and want of rest, I was very hungry; and my whole stock of cash consisted of a Dutch dollar, and about a shilling in copper. The latter I gave the people of the boat for my passage, who at first refus'd it, on account of my rowing; but I insisted on their taking it. A man being sometimes more generous when he has but a little money than when he has plenty, perhaps thro' fear of being thought to have but little.

Then I walked up the street, gazing about till near the market-house I met a boy with bread. I had made many a meal on bread, and, inquiring where he got it, I went immediately to the baker's he directed me to, in Second-street, and ask'd for bisket, intending such as we had in Boston; but they, it seems, were not made in Philadelphia. Then I asked for a three-penny loaf, and was told they had none such. So not considering or knowing the difference of money, and the greater cheapness nor the names of his bread, I bad him give me three-penny worth of any sort. He gave me, accordingly, three great puffy rolls. I was surpriz'd at the quantity, but took it, and, having no room in my pockets, walk'd off with a roll under each arm, and eating the other. Thus I went up Market-street as far as Fourth-street, passing by the door of Mr. Read, my future wife's father; when she, standing at the door, saw me, and thought I made, as I certainly did, a most awkward, ridiculous appearance. Then I turned and went down Chestnut-street and part of Walnut-street, eating my roll all the way, and, coming round, found myself again at Market-street wharf, near the boat I came in, to which I went for a draught of the river water; and, being filled with one of my rolls, gave the other two to a woman and her child that came down the river in the boat with us, and were waiting to go farther . . .

After dinner, my sleepiness return'd, and being shown to a bed, I lay down without undressing, and slept till six in the evening, was call'd to supper, went to bed again very early, and slept soundly till next morning. Then I made myself as tidy as I could, and went to Andrew Bradford the printer's. I found in the shop the old man his father, whom I had seen at New York, and who, travelling on horseback, had got to Philadelphia before me. He introduc'd me to his son, who receiv'd me civilly, gave me a breakfast, but told me he did not at present want a hand, being lately suppli'd with one; but there was another printer in town, lately set up, one Keimer, who, perhaps, might employ me; if not, I should be welcome to lodge at his house, and he would give me a little work to do now and then till fuller business should offer.

The old gentleman said he would go with me to the new printer; and when we found him, "Neighbor," says Bradford, "I have brought to see you a young man of your business; perhaps you may want such a one." He ask'd me a few questions, put a composing stick in my hand to see how I work'd, and then said he would employ me soon, though he had just then nothing for me to do; and, taking old Bradford, whom he had never seen before, to be one of the town's people that had a good will for him, enter'd into a conversation on his present undertaking and prospects; while Bradford, not discovering that he was the other printer's father, on Keimer's saying he expected soon to get the greatest part of the business into his own hands, drew him on by artful questions, and starting little doubts, to explain all his views, what interest he reli'd on, and in what manner he intended to proceed. I, who stood by and heard all, saw immediately that one of them was a crafty old sophister, and the other a mere novice. Bradford left me with Keimer, who was greatly surprised when I told him who the old man was.

Sir William Keith, the governor of the province, became interested in Franklin, and called at the printshop to invite him "to taste some excellent Madeira." "Keimer [says Franklin] stared like a pig poisoned." *Over the wine he proposed Franklin's setting up in the printing business for himself. Franklin was persuaded to return to his father to ask for aid. The flattered youth did not a little swaggering in new clothes before his brother's journeymen, and James Franklin was infuriated to vindictiveness. His father*

*felt it unsound to establish in business a boy still three years short
of manhood; he gently declined. Franklin started back to Philadelphia unsuccessful.*

*On the boat from Newport he almost yielded to the blandish-
ments of two attractive young women who later turned out to be
strumpets, but had the sense to let himself be warned. Governor
Keith offered to finance the printshop himself, and sent Franklin
off to England to choose the types. Not till he arrived, almost pen-
niless, did he learn that Keith was one of those people who seek
to make themselves liked by strewing promises they are unable to
fulfill. He had written no letter of credit; he had no credit. Certainly, Franklin is willing to admit, Keith meant no harm:* "But
what shall we think of a governor's playing such pitiful tricks, and
imposing so grossly on a poor ignorant boy!"

*Franklin got work at Palmer's, a famous London printing-house.
It was during this time that he tried unsuccessfully* ("another er-
ratum," *he calls it*) *to seduce the milliner-mistress of a friend.*

At my first admission into this printing-house I took to working
at press, imagining I felt a want of the bodily exercise I had been
us'd to in America, where presswork is mix'd with composing. I
drank only water; the other workmen, near fifty in number, were
great guzzlers of beer. On occasion, I carried up and down stairs
a large form of types in each hand, when others carried but one in
both hands. They wondered to see, from this and several instances,
that the Water-American, as they called me, was stronger than
themselves, who drank strong beer! We had an alehouse boy who
attended always in the house to supply the workmen. My companion at the press drank every day a pint before breakfast, a pint
at breakfast with his bread and cheese, a pint between breakfast and
dinner, a pint at dinner, a pint in the afternoon about six o'clock,
and another when he had done his day's work. I thought it a
detestable custom; but it was necessary, he suppos'd, to drink
strong beer, that he might be strong to labor.

*After about eighteen months in London he returned to Phila-
delphia, and was tempted by large wages to take the management
of Keimer's printing-house.*

I soon perceiv'd that the intention of engaging me at wages so much higher than he had been us'd to give, was, to have these raw, cheap hands form'd thro' me; and, as soon as I had instructed them, then they being all articled to him, he should be able to do without me. I went on, however, very cheerfully, put his printing-house in order, which had been in great confusion, and brought his hands by degrees to mind their business and to do it better . . .

But, however serviceable I might be, I found that my services became every day of less importance, as the other hands improv'd in the business; and, when Keimer paid my second quarter's wages, he let me know that he felt them too heavy, and thought I should make an abatement. He grew by degrees less civil, put on more of the master, frequently found fault, was captious, and seem'd ready for an outbreaking. I went on, nevertheless, with a good deal of patience, thinking that his encumber'd circumstances were partly the cause. At length a trifle snapt our connections; for, a great noise happening near the court-house, I put my head out of the window to see what was the matter. Keimer, being in the street, look'd up and saw me, call'd out to me in a loud voice and angry tone to mind my business, adding some reproachful words, that nettled me the more for their publicity, all the neighbors who were looking out on the same occasion being witnesses how I was treated. He came up immediately into the printing-house, continu'd the quarrel, high words pass'd on both sides, he gave me the quarter's warning we had stipulated, expressing a wish that he had not been oblig'd to so long a warning. I told him his wish was unnecessary, for I would leave him that instant; and so, taking my hat, walk'd out of doors, desiring Meredith, whom I saw below, to take care of some things I left, and bring them to my lodgings.

Franklin borrowed money and set up a rival printshop of his own.

I began now gradually to pay off the debt I was under for the printing-house. In order to secure my credit and character as a tradesman, I took care not only to be in reality industrious and frugal, but to avoid all appearances to the contrary. I drest plainly; I was seen at no places of idle diversion. I never went out a fish-ing or shooting; a book, indeed, sometimes debauch'd me from my work, but that was seldom, snug, and gave no scandal; and, to show that I was not above my business, I sometimes brought home the paper I purchas'd at the stores thro' the streets on a wheelbarrow. Thus being esteem'd an industrious, thriving young man, and paying duly for what I bought, the merchants who imported stationery solicited my custom; others proposed supplying me with books, and I went on swimmingly. In the mean time, Keimer's credit and business declining daily, he was at last forc'd to sell his printing-house to satisfy his creditors. He went to Barbadoes, and there lived some years in very poor circumstances.

Franklin now resolved to marry. The "hard-to-be-governed passion of youth hurried me frequently into intrigues with low women"; *and these lapses he determined must end. He had rather callously neglected Miss Read, with whom he had had a sort of engagement, during his London venture, but now they drew together again. They were married in 1730.*

They prospered; presently he was finding his sugar at breakfast "in a China bowl, with a spoon of silver!" *for which enormity his wife* "had no other excuse or apology to make, but that she thought *her* husband deserved a silver spoon and China bowl as well as any of his neighbors." "Mark how luxury will enter families," *Franklin says jokingly,* "and make a progress, in spite of principle."

It was about this time I conceiv'd the bold and arduous project of arriving at moral perfection. I wish'd to live without committing any fault at any time; I would conquer all that either natural inclination, custom, or company might lead me into. As I knew, or thought I knew, what was right and wrong, I did not see why I might not always do the one and avoid the other. But I soon found I had undertaken a task of more difficulty than I had imagined. While my care was employ'd in guarding against one fault, I was often surprised by another; habit took the advantage of inattention; inclination was sometimes too strong for reason. I concluded, at length, that the mere speculative conviction that it was our interest to be completely virtuous, was not sufficient to prevent our slipping; and that the contrary habits must be broken, and good ones acquired and established, before we can have any dependence on a steady, uniform rectitude of conduct. For this purpose I therefore contrived the following method.

In the various enumerations of the moral virtues I had met with in my reading, I found the catalogue more or less numerous, as different writers included more or fewer ideas under the same name. Temperance, for example, was by some confined to eating and drinking, while by others it was extended to mean the moderating every other pleasure, appetite, inclination, or passion, bodily or mental, even to our avarice and ambition. I propos'd to myself, for the sake of clearness, to use rather more names, with fewer ideas annex'd to each, than a few names with more ideas; and I included under thirteen names of virtues all that at that time occurr'd to me as necessary or desirable, and annexed to each a short precept, which fully express'd the extent I gave to its meaning.

These names of virtues, with their precepts, were:

1. TEMPERANCE.

Eat not to dullness; drink not to elevation.

2. SILENCE.

Speak not but what may benefit others or yourself; avoid trifling conversation.

3. ORDER.

Let all your things have their places; let each part of your business have its time.

4. RESOLUTION.

Resolve to perform what you ought; perform without fail what you resolve.

5. FRUGALITY.

Make no expense but to do good to others or yourself; *i.e.,* waste nothing.

6. INDUSTRY.

Lose no time; be always employ'd in something useful; cut off all unnecessary actions.

7. SINCERITY.

Use no hurtful deceit; think innocently and justly, and, if you speak, speak accordingly.

8. JUSTICE.

Wrong none by doing injuries, or omitting the benefits that are your duty.

9. MODERATION.

Avoid extreams; forbear resenting injuries so much as you think they deserve.

10. CLEANLINESS.

Tolerate no uncleanliness in body, cloaths, or habitation.

11. TRANQUILLITY.

Be not disturbed at trifles, or at accidents common or unavoidable.

12. CHASTITY.

Rarely use venery but for health or offspring, never to dulness, weakness, or the injury of your own or another's peace or reputation.

13. HUMILITY.

Imitate Jesus and Socrates.

I made a little book, in which I allotted a page for each of the virtues. I rul'd each page with red ink, so as to have seven columns, one for each day of the week, marking each column with a letter for the day. I cross'd these columns with thirteen red lines, marking the beginning of each line with the first letter of one of the virtues, on which line, and in its proper column, I might mark,

by a little black spot, every fault I found upon examination to have
been committed respecting that virtue upon that day.

I determined to give a week's strict attention to each of the
virtues successively. Thus, in the first week, my great guard was to
avoid every the least offence against Temperance, leaving the other
virtues to their ordinary chance, only marking every evening the
faults of the day. Thus, if in the first week I could keep my first
line, marked T, clear of spots, I suppos'd the habit of that virtue
so much strengthen'd, and its opposite weaken'd, that I might
venture extending my attention to include the next, and for the
following week keep both lines clear of spots. Proceeding thus to
the last, I could go thro' a course compleat in thirteen weeks, and
four courses in a year. And like him who, having a garden to
weed, does not attempt to eradicate all the bad herbs at once,
which would exceed his reach and his strength, but works on one
of the beds at a time, and, having accomplish'd the first, proceeds
to a second, so I should have, I hoped, the encouraging pleasure of
seeing on my pages the progress I made in virtue, by clearing successively my lines of their spots, till in the end, by a number of
courses, I should be happy in viewing a clean book, after a thirteen
weeks' daily examination.

My scheme of ORDER gave me the most trouble; and I found
that, tho' it might be practicable where a man's business was such
as to leave him the disposition of his time, that of a journeyman
printer, for instance, it was not possible to be exactly observed by
a master, who must mix with the world, and often receive people
of business at their own hours . . . This article, therefore, cost
me so much painful attention, and my faults in it vexed me so
much, and I made so little progress in amendment, and had such
frequent relapses, that I was almost ready to give up the attempt
and content myself with a faulty character in that respect, like the
man who, in buying an ax of a smith, my neighbour, desired to
have the whole of its surface as bright as the edge. The smith
consented to grind it bright for him if he would turn the wheel;
he turn'd, while the smith press'd the broad face of the ax hard
and heavily on the stone, which made the turning of it very

fatiguing. The man came every now and then from the wheel to see how the work went on, and at length would take his ax as it was, without farther grinding. "No," said the smith, "turn on, turn on; we shall have it bright by-and-by; as yet, it is only speckled." "Yes," says the man, "but I think I like a speckled ax best."

My list of virtues contain'd at first but twelve; but a Quaker friend having kindly informed me that I was generally thought proud; that my pride show'd itself frequently in conversation; that I was not content with being in the right when discussing any point, but was overbearing, and rather insolent, of which he convinc'd me by mentioning several instances; I determined endeavouring to cure myself, if I could, of this vice or folly among the rest, and I added Humility to my list, giving an extensive meaning to the word.

I cannot boast of much success in acquiring the reality of this virtue, but I had a good deal with regard to the appearance of it. I made it a rule to forbear all direct contradiction to the sentiments of others, and all positive assertion of my own. I even forbid myself, agreeably to the old laws of our Junto, the use of every word or expression in the language that imported a fix'd opinion, such as certainly, undoubtedly, etc., and I adopted, instead of them, I conceive, I apprehend, or I imagine a thing to be so or so; or it so appears to me at present. When another asserted something that I thought an error, I deny'd myself the pleasure of contradicting him abruptly, and of showing immediately some absurdity in his proposition; and in answering I began by observing that in certain cases or circumstances his opinion would be right, but in the present case there appear'd or seem'd to me some difference, etc. I soon found the advantage of this change in my manner; the conversations I engag'd in went on more pleasantly. The modest way in which I propos'd my opinions procur'd them a readier reception and less contradiction; I had less mortification when I was found to be in the wrong, and I more easily prevail'd with others to give up their mistakes and join with me when I happened to be in the right.

In reality, there is, perhaps, no one of our natural passions so hard to subdue as *pride*. Disguise it, struggle with it, beat it down, stifle it, mortify it as much as one pleases, it is still alive, and will every now and then peep out and show itself; you will see it, perhaps, often in this history; for even if I could conceive that I had compleatly overcome it, I should probably be proud of my humility.

Franklin's activities became ever more busy and crowded. In 1732 he began publishing Poor Richard's Almanack. *He learned French, then Italian and Spanish, and from them picked up Latin: a sequence he considered far easier than beginning in the usual way with Latin.* "It is true [he summarizes] that, if you can clamber and get to the top of a staircase without using the steps, you will more easily gain them in descending; but certainly, if you begin with the lowest, you will with more ease ascend to the top." *In 1736 he became Clerk of the General Assembly. He founded the first volunteer fire company; he invented the Franklin stove; he broached the proposals leading to founding the University of Pennsylvania; he was instrumental in establishing the first Philadelphia hospital. His mind steadily kept throwing out new ideas for improvement: publicly supported street-lighting, public cleaning of streets.* "Some may think these trifling matters," [he remarks; but] "Human felicity is produced not so much by great pieces of good fortune that seldom happen, as by little advantages that occur every day."

The outbreak of the French and Indian War found him purveying supplies for General Braddock's army.

This general was, I think, a brave man, and might probably have made a figure as a good officer in some European war. But he had too much self-confidence, too high an opinion of the validity of regular troops, and too mean a one of both Americans and Indians . . . In conversation with him one day, he was giving me some account of his intended progress.

"After taking Fort Duquesne," says he, "I am to proceed to Niagara; and, having taken that, to Frontenac, if the season will allow time; and I suppose it will, for Duquesne can hardly detain me above three or four days; and then I see nothing that can obstruct my march to Niagara."

"To be sure, sir, if you arrive well before Duquesne, with these fine troops, so well provided with artillery, that place not yet completely fortified, and as we hear with no very strong garrison, can probably make but a short resistance. The only danger I apprehend of obstruction to your march is from ambuscades of Indians, who, by constant practice, are dexterous in laying and executing them; and the slender line, near four miles long, which your army must make, may expose it to be attack'd by surprise in its flanks, and to be cut like a thread into several pieces, which, from their distance, can not come up in time to support each other."

He smil'd at my ignorance, and reply'd, "These savages may, indeed, be a formidable enemy to your raw American militia, but upon the king's regular and disciplin'd troops, sir, it is impossible they should make any impression." I was conscious of an impropriety in my disputing with a military man in matters of his profession, and said no more.

Captain Orme, who was one of the general's aids-de-camp, and, being grievously wounded, was brought off with him, and continu'd with him to his death, which happen'd in a few days, told me that he was totally silent all the first day, and at night only said, "Who would have thought it?" That he was silent again the following day, saying only at last, "We shall better know how to deal with them another time"; and dy'd in a few minutes after.

Franklin's scientific fame was already spreading. His electrical experiments were translated into French, Italian, German, and Latin: "I will not swell this narrative with an account of that capital experiment [*the one establishing the identity of lightning and electricity*], nor of the infinite pleasure I received in the success of a similar one I made soon after with a kite in Philadelphia, as both are to be found in the histories of electricity." *He was made a member of the Royal Society, and in 1753 presented with the Copley medal.*

Meanwhile the Province of Pennsylvania was having more and more friction with the proprietors. In 1757 Franklin was sent to England to negotiate the difficulties, and met with the Penns and their solicitor in London. "The conversation at first consisted of mutual declarations of disposition to reasonable accommodations, but I suppose each party had its own ideas of what should be meant by *reasonable.*" *After half a year of delays and fruitless meetings, the Penns tried to have Franklin replaced, complaining of informality and rudeness. These offenses consisted, Franklin says, of his failure to address them in a memorandum by* "their assumed titles of True and Absolute Proprietaries of the Province." *Finally a kind of accommodation was reached by Franklin contracting with Lord Mansfield that* "no injury would be done the proprietary estate" *by any taxes the Assembly imposed.*

*   *   *

With this episode Franklin's *Autobiography* breaks off. The rest belongs to history. As the tension between England and America deepened, Franklin became the agent for Georgia, New Jersey, Massachusetts. Smoothly and unanswerably he pushed the Ministry from one untenable position after another. His enormous prestige demanded that he be answered; his shrewd tactics left no answer but brute force. From discomfort and boredom their attitude toward Franklin hardened to rancor. They saw him forcing their hands; he saw the King behind their policy. At last the day came when Franklin knew that rebellion was inevitable. Tears coursed down his cheeks: America would win, but it would take ten years, and he would never live to see the end.

At home once more, he was a delegate to the Continental Congress. Seventy now, and the oldest of them all, he was, with Jefferson and the Adamses, earliest and firmest for independence. No time-serving old-man's-cautiousness for Franklin: he sharpened the words of Jefferson's Declaration to more uncompromising indictment, and is supposed to have signed it with a jesting "We must all hang together or we'll all hang separately." Appointed one of three commissioners to France, Franklin sailed late in October, 1776. "The indomitable old man, who was almost certain to be hanged for high treason if the *Reprisal* should be captured, noted the temperature of air and water every day, again studying the Gulf Stream."

In Paris he was surrounded by British spies, a fact that he calmly used by leaving open in his cabinet such information as he desired the British to get. The French were wild with enthusiasm for him. His image appeared in engravings, busts, prints, medallions for the lids of snuffboxes, miniatures to be set in rings; "his phiz," he wrote his daughter, was "as well known as that of the moon." At the Academy of Science clamors of applause forced him and Voltaire to embrace each other repeatedly: "The two aged actors upon this great theatre of philosophy and frivolity then embraced each other by hugging one another in their arms and kissing each other's cheeks, and then the tumult subsided." Turgot saluted him in epigram: "He snatched the lightning from the skies and the sceptre from tyrants (Eripuit coelo fulmen sceptrumque tyrannis). But Franklin protested that this gave him too much credit. The Revolution, he said, was "the work of many able and brave men, wherein it is sufficient honor for me if I am allowed a small share."

In his retreat at Passy Franklin worked hard but lived well. For breakfast he had bread and butter, honey, and coffee or chocolate; for dinner a joint, fowl or game, two sweets, two vegetables, pastry, hors d'œuvres, pickles, radishes, two fruits, two compôtes, cheese, biscuits, and bonbons. His cellar usually had something over a thousand bottles of wine: red and white Bordeaux, Burgundy, a little champagne, a good deal of sparkling white wine, vin ordinaire, a small amount of rum. He spent well over $12,000 a year.

Gout troubled him, and he was feeling the effects of old age. It was annoying to have to shift glasses for near and far; he invented bifocals. He flirted with Madame Brillon, who sat upon his knee and playfully accused him of inconstancy. Franklin replied that it was as plain as Euclid that whoever was constant to several persons was more constant than he who was constant only to one. To Madame Helvétius he pretended that in a visit to the Elysian Fields he had found her husband married to his own deceased wife, and decided indignantly to quit the shades and return to the sun: "Here I am. Let us avenge ourselves."

At last, in May, 1784, he received his release from Congress, and toward the end of July he sailed for home. He was seventy-eight, but his life was not yet over. Pennsylvania made him its President. He was a conciliatory influence at the Constitutional Convention. He became president of the first abolition society. He worked on the last part of his *Autobiography*, although by 1788 his stone was so bad that he needed opium to relieve the pain. But pain had little effect on his memory or wit, and none on his cheerfulness. His maladies grew worse. Told that he might recover and live many years, he placidly replied, "I hope not." At last he passed into a coma. Death came, 17 April, 1790, eighty-four years and three months after he was born.

CORSAIR

LESS DEEPLY SIGNIFICANTLY, IT MAY BE, THAN FRANKLIN, BUT certainly more melodramatic, Trelawny is also a symbol of a new age. While the Gothic novel was spawning its wild and moody heroes and Byron brooded over his tempestuous Laras and Conrads and Manfreds, life was molding Trelawny to a like pattern of Promethean defiance. The eighteenth century reign of convention and common sense had drawn to a darkly stormy close. There were new lights in the eastern sky and a new electric vibrance in the air. Nature and Art had not so much imitated each other as joined hands in framing these figures of ungovernable impulse and fiery revolt.

Trelawny's life is a huge sprawling saga, a romantic period piece in whose action and setting fantastically mingle the varied colorings of the age. There is a bleak childhood prologue; then three long and brilliantly kaleidoscopic acts shifting all over the globe from the Mauritius to Niagara, and ranging in theme from piratical violence to the tragic tableau of Shelley's funeral pyre flaming by the blue Spezzian bay; last, a sunset epilogue filled with wild hues slowly calming to level light.

The opening scenes might be the generic childhood of the Byronic heroes, with Trelawny's father a miserly Cornish squire who hates his son and tries to break his spirit, and Trelawny one of those boys who with ill treatment grow ever more sullen and ferociously rebellious. To get rid of him, Trelawny is packed off to sea. The first act that follows is reminiscent of both Marryat and Melville's green-fronded isles in the South Seas. The British navy was still the brutal bullying institution of Captain Bligh; in

Bombay we see Trelawny battering a Scotch lieutenant to unconsciousness and deserting to a French privateer. On board, with
his commander and hero De Ruyter, another Byronic figure, he
reads Shakespeare, Plutarch, Ossian, and Bernardin de Saint-
Pierre, perfect fare for a young romantic rebel; he battles and cap-
tures British frigates and pirate vessels all the way from Madagascar to the Isle of France; in an episode reminiscent of the lyric
passion of Haidée and Don Juan he takes an Arab bride. Still not
twenty when she dies, he returns to England.

Here the *Adventures of a Younger Son* come to their end. But
not Trelawny's life-adventures. The second act of his drama, his
friendship with Shelley, he later recorded in his *Recollections of
the Last Days of Shelley and Byron;* and these take him into the
third act as well, his participation in the Greek war for independence, where he joined the Greek guerrilla chieftain Odysseus.
With the naval victory of Navarino, which brought Grecian freedom from Turkish rule, his great days of adventure were over.
But even an epilogue, for Trelawny, was more packed with excitement than the whole drama of many men. He traveled in America,
fell in love with Fanny Kemble, swam the Niagara and was almost
swept over the Falls, struggling to shore disgusted that his escape
was due to luck rather than to his own exertions. He had married
a second wife and divorced her for infidelity, and been divorced
from a third, a Greek lady, by mutual agreement; at fifty he married for the fourth time and separated from this wife again at
sixty-eight. At seventy-six he was still enjoying sea-bathing.

Wild and undisciplined as Trelawny shows against his exotic
background of green frondage and coral sands and towering waves,
there is something noble, generous, and true-hearted about him
too. And of his romantic talent for vivid self-portrayal he is himself the most brilliant evidence.

Adventures of a Younger Son

EDWARD JOHN TRELAWNY

[Trelawny was born in 1792 and lived until 1881, an age of ninety-one. The *Adventures of a Younger Son* were first published anonymously in 1831, but the authorship was not concealed long.]

My BIRTH WAS UNPROPITIOUS. I CAME INTO THE WORLD, BRANDED and denounced as a vagrant; for I was a younger son of a family, so proud of their antiquity, that even gout and mortgaged estates were traced, many generations back, on the genealogical tree, as ancient heirlooms of aristocratic origin, and therefore reverenced. In such a house a younger son was like the cub of a felon-wolf in good King Edgar's days, when a price was set upon his head. There have been laws compelling parents to destroy their puny offspring; and a Spartan mother might have exclaimed with Othello, while extinguishing the life of her yet unconscious infant,

> *I that am cruel, am yet merciful,*
> *I would not have thee linger in thy pain;*

which was just and merciful, in comparison with the atrocious law of primogeniture. My grandfather was a general, and had little to give my father, his only son, but patronage in his profession. Nature, in some sort, made him amends by bestowing that which leads to fortune oftener than genius, virtue, or such discarded claimants—a handsome exterior set off by courtly manners. His youth was not distinguished by any marked peculiarity, running the course of the gallants of the day. Women, wine, the court, the camp, formed the theatre of his ambition, and there he was accounted to play his part well. . . .

At a ball, given by the county sheriff on his nomination, his daughter, an heiress, when desired by her father to give her hand, for the first dance, to the man of highest rank in the room, who happened to be the oldest, declared she would give it to the handsomest. She selected my father, and with him she danced . . . He married; found the lady's fortune a great deal less, and the lady a great deal worse than he had anticipated: went to town irritated and disappointed, with the consciousness of having merited his fate; sunk part of his fortune in idle parade to satisfy his wife; and, his affairs being embarrassed by the lady's extravagance, he was, at length, compelled to sell out of the army, and retire to economise in the country.

Malthus had not yet enlightened the world. Every succeeding year he reluctantly registered in the family Bible the birth of a living burthen. He cursed my mother's fertility, and the butcher's and baker's bills. He grew gloomy and desponding.

A bequest fell to him, and he seriously set about amassing money, which was henceforth the leading passion of his life. He became what is called a prudent man. If a poor relation applied to him, he talked of his duty to his wife and children; and when richest, complained most of his poverty, of extortion, and of the unconscionable price of everything.

Punishment and severity of all kinds were the only marks of paternal love that fell to my share, from my earliest remembrance.

My father had a fancy for a raven, that, with ragged wings, and a grave antique aspect, used to wander solitarily about the garden. He abhorred children; and whenever he saw any of us, he used to chase us out of his walks. I was then five years old. Had the raven pitched on any other spot than the one he selected—the fruit-garden—I certainly should never have disputed his right of possession. As it was, we had all, from the time we could walk, considered him and my father the two most powerful, awful, and tyrannical persons on earth. The raven was getting into years; he had a grey and grizzly look; he halted on one leg; his joints were stiff, his legs rough as the bark of a cork tree, and he was covered with large warts: his eyes had a bleared and sinister expression; and he passed most of his time idling in the sun under a south wall, against which grew the delicious plums of the garden. Many were the stratagems we used to lure him from this spot; the garbage, on which he gloated, was offered in vain. His moroseness and ferocity, and our difficulty in getting fruit, were insupportable. We tried to intimidate him with sticks, but were too weak to make the least impression on his weather-hardened carcase; and we got the worst of it. I used, when I could do so slily, to throw stones at him, but this had no effect. . . .

One day I had a little girl for my companion, whom I had enticed from the 'nursery to go with me to get some fruit clandestinely. We slunk out, and entered the garden unobserved. Just as we were congratulating ourselves under a cherry tree, up comes the accursed monster of a raven. It was no longer to be endured. He seized hold of the little girl's frock; she was too frightened to scream; I did not hesitate an instant. I told her not to be afraid, and threw myself upon him. He let her go, and attacked me with bill and talon. I got hold of him by the neck, and, heavily lifting him up, struck his body against the tree and the ground; but nothing seemed to hurt him. He was hard as a rock. Thus we struggled, I evidently the weaker party. The little girl, who was my favourite, said, "I'll go and call the gardener!"

I said, "No; he will tell my father; I will hang the old fellow" (meaning the raven, not my father) ; "give me your sash!"

She did so, and with great exertion I succeeded, though I was dreadfully mauled, in fastening one end round the old tyrant's neck; I then climbed the cherry tree, and, holding one end of the sash, I put it round a horizontal branch, when, jumping on the ground, I fairly succeeded in suspending my foe.

At this moment my brother came running towards me. When he saw the plight I was in, he was alarmed; but, on beholding our old enemy swinging in the air, he shouted for joy. Fastening the end of the sash, we commenced stoning him to death. After we were tired of that sport, and as he was, to all appearance, dead, we let him down. He fell on his side, when I seized hold of a raspberry-stake, to make sure of him by belabouring his head. To our utter amazement and consternation, he sprung up with a hoarse scream, and caught hold of me. Our first impulse was to run; but he withheld me, so I again fell on him, calling to my brother for assistance, and bidding him lay fast hold of the ribbon, and to climb the tree. I attempted to prevent his escape. His look was now most terrifying: one eye was hanging out of his head, the blood coming from his mouth, his wings flapping the earth in disorder, and with a ragged tail, which I had half plucked by pulling at him during his first execution. He made a horrible struggle for existence, and I was bleeding all over. Now, with the aid of my brother, and as the raven was exhausted by exertion and wounds, we succeeded in gibbeting him again; and then with sticks we cudgelled him to death, beating his head to pieces. Afterwards we tied a stone to him, and sunk him in a duck-pond. . . . It shows how long I could endure annoyance and oppression, and that when at last excited, I never tried half measures, but proceeded to extremities, without stop or pause. This was my grievous fault, and grievously have I repented it; for I have destroyed, where, in justice, I was justified, but where, in mercy, I ought only to have corrected; and thus the standers-by have considered that, which I only thought a fair retaliation, revenge.

In compliance with my father's notions respecting the inutility of early education, I was not sent to school till I was between nine and ten years old. I was then an unusually great, bony, awkward boy. Whilst my parents were in their daily discussion of the question as to the period in which the schooling of their sons was to commence, a trivial occurrence decided the question. I was perched on an apple tree, throwing the fruit down to my brother, when our father came on us suddenly. Every trifle put him in a passion. Commanding us to follow him, he walked rapidly on through the grounds, into the road, without entering the house. . . . Arriving at the farther extremity of the town, my father stopped, asked some questions inaudible to us, and stalked forward to a walled and dreary building. . . . In ten minutes, which seemed an eternity, entered a dapper little man, carrying his head high in the air, with large bright silver buckles in his shoes, a stock buckled tightly round his neck, spectacled, and powdered. There was a formal precision about him, most fearful to a boy. A hasty glance from his hawk's eye, first at our father, and then at us, gave him an insight into the affair. With repeated bows to our father, he requested him to take a chair, and pointed with his finger for us to do the same. There was an impatience and rapidity in everything he said; which indicated that he liked doing and not talking.

"Sir," said our parent, "I believe you are Mr. Sayers?"

"Yes, Sir."

"Have you any vacancies in your school?"

"Yes, Sir."

"Well, Sir, will you undertake the charge of these ungovernable vagabonds? I can do nothing with them. Why, Sir, this fellow" (meaning me) "does more mischief in my house than your sixty boys can possibly commit in yours."

At this the pedagogue, moving his spectacles towards the sharpened tip of his nose, peered over them, measuring me from head to foot; and clenching his hand, as if, in imagination, it already grasped the birch, gave an oblique nod, to intimate that he would subdue me. My inauguration proceeded—

"He is savage, incorrigible! Sir, he will come to the gallows, if you do not scourge the devil out of him. I have this morning detected him in an act of felony, for which he deserves a halter. My elder son, Sir, was instigated by him to be an accomplice; for naturally he is of a better disposition." With this, my father, after arranging what was indispensable, bowed to Mr. Sayers, and, without noticing us, withdrew.

Miserable as I was during my schooldays, the first was the bitterest. At supper, I remember, I was so choked with my feelings, that I could not swallow my dog-like food, arranged in scanty portions; and my first relief was when, in my beggarly pallet, the rushlights extinguished, and surrounded by the snoring of the wearied boys, to me a sound of comfort, I could give vent to my overcharged heart in tears. I sobbed aloud; but on any one's moving, as if awake, I held my breath till reassured. Thus I sobbed on, and was not heard; till the night was far advanced, and my pillow bathed in tears, when, outworn, I fell into a sleep, from which I was rudely shaken, unrefreshed, at seven in the morning. I then descended to the schoolroom. . . .

As my school-life was one scene of suffering, I am impelled to hasten it over as briefly as possible; more particularly as the abuses, of which I complain, are, if not altogether remedied, at least mitigated. I was flogged seldom more than once a day, or caned more than once an hour. After I had become inured to it, I was callous; and was considered by the master the most obdurate, violent, and incorrigible rascal that had ever fallen under his hands.

As my bodily strength increased, I became, out of school, the leader in all sports and mischief; but, in school, I was in the lowest class. I was determined not to apply to learning, and to defy punishment. Indeed I do not recollect that any of the boys acquired useful knowledge there. When satisfied with the ascendancy I had gained over my schoolfellows, I turned my whole thoughts to the possibility of revenging myself on the master. I first tried my hand on his under-strapper. Having formed a party of the most daring of my myrmidons, I planned and executed a castigation for our tutor. Once a week we were refreshed by long country walks; in the course of one of these the tutor sat down to rest himself; the boys, not acquainted with the plot, were busy gathering nuts; my chosen band loitered near, preparing rods; when I, backed by three of the strongest, fell suddenly upon our enemy. I got my hand round his dirty cravat, which I continued twisting; the others seized his arms and legs, and threw him on his back. A halloo brought six or seven more. He several times nearly succeeded in shaking us off; but I never resigned my hold, and when his struggles had driven away one boy, another took his place; till, completely overcome, he entreated us, as well as he could articulate, to have mercy, and not to strangle him. I gripped him the tighter, till the sweat dropped from his brow like rain from the eaves of a pigsty. We then gave him a sample of flogging he could never forget. . . . I was now desperate, and therefore without hope or fear. I received a message, by one of the servants, to go into the house. After some hesitation I went. I was confined in a bedroom by myself, and at supper-time bread and water was brought—spare diet certainly, but not much worse than the usual fare. I saw no one but the servant. Next day the same solitude—the same spare diet. At night a bit of candle was left to light me to bed; I know not what impelled me, I suppose the hope of release, not revenge—I set fire to the bed-curtains. The bed was in a bright flame, the smoke arose in clouds: without a thought of escape I viewed their progress with boyish delight; the wainscot and woodwork were beginning to burn, the fire crackling up the walls, while I could hardly breathe for smoke. The servant returned for the candle, and as the door opened the draught augmented the flame. I cried out, "Look here, George, I have lighted a fire myself, you said I should have none, though it was so cold." The man's shrieks gave the alarm. There was little furniture in this condemned hold, and the fire was extinguished. I was removed to another room, where a man sat up all night with me in custody; and I remember I exulted in the dread they all had of me. . . .

The next morning I was dispatched home under a guard.

Soon after this I was taken to Portsmouth, and shipped on board a line of battleship, the *Superb,* as passenger to join one of Nelson's squadron. She was commanded by Captain Keates; and thence we sailed to Plymouth to take on board Admiral Duckworth, who hoisted his flag, and detained the ship three days to get mutton and potatoes from Cornwall. By this delay we unfortuantely fell in with the Nelson fleet off Trafalgar, two days after his deathless victory.

Our captain's clerk, seeing I had a good store of books, with no place to put them in, thought they would be an ornament to his cabin, for he never read. He proposed to take care of them for me, offering me the use of his cabin, where I might read them. I gladly acquiesced in what I, simple fool that I then was, thought a most kind offer; and, for a few days, we got on very well together. One day I went for a book; he was angry about something or nothing, and had the impudence to say, "You may read here if you like; but I will not permit any books to be taken out of my cabin."

"Are they not mine?" I asked.

"Not now;" he replied.

"What!" I then asked, "do you intend to keep possession of my books?"

To this I received no other answer than, "Come—none of your insolence!"

Upon this, I said, "Give me my books; I will leave them here no longer, now I see your object." He dared me to touch them; I snatched one from the shelf; he struck me; I returned the blow . . .

He seized hold of me, and vociferating, "You young rascal, I will tame you!" gave me a blow with a ruler, which he broke over my head; then jammed me up against the bulk-head, so that I could not escape, and belaboured me without mercy. As long as my strength lasted, I opposed him. The lookers-on were encouraging me, and exclaiming shame on him. My head grew dizzy from blows; my mouth and nose were bleeding profusely; my body was subdued, but not my spirit. I asked not for mercy, but defied him; and on his attempting to kick me out of the cabin, I increased his fury by declaring I would not leave it till he had given me my books. We were thus contending, he to force me out and I to remain in, when he kicked me in the stomach, and I lay motionless; while he roared and sputtered, "Get out, you rascal! or I'll knock the life out of you!"

I felt I could no longer resist. I was in despair. The being beaten like a hound by a dastardly brute, and the insulting and triumphant language the fellow used, made me mad. My eye caught, by chance, something glittering close to me. The table was capsized, and a penknife within my grasp. The prospect of revenge renewed my strength. I seized it, and, repeating his words of knocking the life out of me, I added, as I held up the weapon, "Coward! look out for your own!"

I was then on one knee, struggling to get up. On seeing the knife, and my wild look haggard with passion, the mender of pens shrank back. After this, all I remember is, that I stabbed him in several places, and that he shut his eyes, held his hands up to his face, and screamed out in terror for mercy. Some one then called to me, with "Halloa! what are you at?"—I turned round and replied, "This cowardly ruffian was beating me to death, and I have killed him!"—I then threw down the knife, took up my book, and walked out of the cabin. . . .

Some hours after, the captain came to me and said, "Are you not ashamed of your conduct, Sir?"

I answered, "No!"

"What, Sir! is that the way to answer me? Get up, Sir, and take off your hat." I told him I was waiting for the irons. I, however, stood up.

"You will be hanged, Sir, for murder!"

I replied, "I had rather be hanged than kicked by your servants."

"Why, are you mad, Sir?"

"Yes! your ill-treatment has made me so. You, and your French lieutenant, are always punishing and abusing me without cause, and I will not submit to it. I came into the navy, an officer and a gentleman, and I am treated like a dog. Put me on shore! I will do no more duty; and I will allow neither you nor your domestics to abuse and beat me."

With that I advanced a step towards him, from what motive I know not. He seized me by the collar, and bade me sit down on the gun-carriage. "No!" I contended, "you told me never to sit down in your presence and I will not!"

"Will not!" said he, holding me tightly, and nearly strangling me with his grasp. I could not speak, but put my hand up to release myself; upon which, repeating the words, "You will not!" he gave me a violent blow in the face, and I, with another "No!" had the audacity to spit in his.

His flushed brow turned from deep scarlet to almost black in an instant. He could not articulate a word; but, dashing me from him with all his might, turned into his cabin, choking with rage. . . .

At sunset I was told I might go below; but I was never to show myself on deck. I never saw the gorbellied Scotch captain afterwards.

On the following voyage a bullying Scotch lieutenant excited Trelawny's ire; at Bombay he broke his sword on the fellow and then beat him into unconsciousness with a billiard cue.

He deserted, and sailed off with one De Ruyter, a French privateer of mysterious origin and a disposition mingling the cynical and the Quixotic. De Ruyter's "brow used to darken, his lip to quiver, and his eye to dilate" *at* "the barbarous policy, intolerance, and arrogance of the Anglo-Indian dictation in India." *It was an age, he said, of gold:* "Women, saints, and philosophers squabble now for nothing but loaves and fishes." "This merchant-company says they have an exclusive right (which is a general wrong) to the entire produce of this great empire. On what a grand scale is robbery now carried on!"

At Goa, returning from a secret conference with agents of the Rajah of Mysore, De Ruyter made a hairbreadth escape from the master of the port. They were pursued and almost captured by a British frigate, but after a sharp skirmish with some of its men, managed to slip away. They fought with Maratti pirates and captured their stronghold of St. Sebastian on Madagascar. It was here that a dying Arab consigned his daughter to Trelawny's care, and Trelawny discovered that in Arab custom this constituted a betrothal.

Having been now some days at sea, I thought of visiting my little female captive; not that I had neglected her hitherto, having given her my own, comparatively, comfortable cabin, and ordered the good old Rais to find out those of her father's tribe, or followers, on board. Besides, I sent him, privileged by his age and rank, to see her, talk to her, and assure her she should want nothing, and that all her wishes should be granted. He told me that three women, who had been with her in her father's ship, were already with her; that he had collected and given them what articles they wanted, and that in a few days she would be better. Indeed the old Rais, in respect of her father's having been, not only an Arab, but a sheikh, of a tribe in the Persian Gulf, near his own country, had anticipated all my wishes. He said, "I must do the same for her as for my own child; for we are all brothers."

De Ruyter, who heard our conversation, as he stood by, began to talk with the Rais, addressing him by the name of "Father"; for so he called him, the commander of his Arabs, and one who had been long with him. He consulted the Rais on every point connected with his men, and never opposed the fulfilment of their customs. On his secret expedition to the English ports, the entire command, in appearance, devolved on the old Arab, while De Ruyter took the character of a merchant, Parsee, Armenian, or American—they were all the same to him, as occasion served. "I have been telling this youngster of mine, Father," said he, "that the Arab girl is now lawfully his wife, in the most sacred manner, according to the customs of your country. Is it not so? Inform him."

The old Rais had heard all the particulars from the men present at the father's death, and said, "Most assuredly, malik; who can doubt it? Yet strange it sounded in my ears when I was told it. It is the first time, old as I am, that I ever heard of an Arab sheikh, whose generations are countless as the grains of sand on the great desert, giving his daughter, and mingling the blood of the ancestors of the human race with one of the infidels of a country, so newly discovered, that our fathers knew not of it, nor could her father have heard of its existence; a Yaoor!" . . .

I went on deck to keep the first watch. From Louis and turtle my thoughts reverted to my own little turtle-dove in her cage. Then, only looking on the sunny side of things, all was bright. I seemed to expand in bulk and stature. My thoughts ran nearly in the same channel with those of Alnaschar, the prattling barber's brother, the fabled glass merchant, of imaginative renown; for, like him, my fancy ran wild. I determined to be, at first, a kind and loving husband, then austerer and severe, or kind and cruel by turns. Certainly, though I thought of everything the most preposterous, not a single ray of light, useful or rational, shone on my midnight reveries. The gong sounded twelve; I was relieved from duty. The cares of married life not once disturbed my sleep. I wonder now I slept so soundly. . . .

After I had breakfasted, my thoughts again veered round to the right point of the compass—my virgin bride. I was schooled into

the proper guttural pronunciation of her name; no easy task, for
I was compelled to repeat the Z a hundred times, ere the old
duenna who tutored me was satisfied with its hissings aspiration.
Then she proceeded to impress on my memory ten thousand ceremonies and cautions to be used; I was not to touch the lady's veil,
or person, or garments, or talk too much, or ask questions, or stay
too long. . . .

The cabin door was opened by a little Malayan slave girl, from
the coast of Malabar, whom I had sent as my first gift, and I entered. The lady-mine was seated cross-legged on a low couch, so
shrouded and enveloped in yellow drapery, the mourning of her
country, that I could distinguish nothing of those wondrous
beauties the old Arab woman had talked of. On my entrance I
thought her one of those marble figures I had heard of in Egyptian
temples; but I found she was alive. Her feet were bare; she rose
and placed them in embroidered slippers, which lay on the deck
of the cabin; she took my hand, put it to her forehead, then to her
lips: I entreated her to be seated. She resumed her position, and
remained motionless, her arms drooping listlessly down; her little .
rosy feet nestled under her, like tiny birds under the mother's
wing. Her hair, the only part now visible, covered her like a jet-
black cloud. I had felt the pressure of her tremulous lips; and
imagination, or perhaps some faint outline which fancy had left
graved on my hand, pictured her mouth exquisitely soft and
small— (I loathe a large and hard one) ; and I think now, this silent
pressure wove the first link of that diamond chain which time nor
use could ever break or wear away. I seemed entranced. . . .

Taking from my hand a ring of gold, with an Arabic inscription,
and hooped with two circles of camel's hair, the same her expiring
father had placed on my finger, I held it towards her. The low and
suppressed moans she made on my entrance broke out into sobs,
so violent that I could see her loose vest agitated by the beating
of her heart. I was about to remove this object, which awakened
such painful remembrances, when she grasped it, pressed it to her
lips, and wept over it some time. The woman then said something to her; and, without the guidance of her eyes, she again put
forth her tapering little fingers, and replaced the ring.

Upon this I took a ring I had selected from De Ruyter's store of baubles; it was a deep ruby, of the shape and size of a wild grape, hooped and massy with virgin gold, and, by its size, seemed to have been worn by a fairy. Gently disengaging her hand from the drapery as it lay motionless by her side, I placed this ring on the forefinger of her right hand . . .

This interchange of rings was a definite acknowledgment of our union.

Zela told him he was "gentle, kind, beautiful as a zebra," *and love was ignited in his breast:* "Zela, from that day, was the star I was destined to worship." *Their first few months together were enjoyed on the picturesque volcanic Isle of Bourbon, odorous with* "citrons, raspberries, guavas, and wild mangoes," *flourishing with* "dusky-colored olive" *and* "dark-green fig-trees," *thickly embowered in* "wild vines, jessamine, and a multitude of deep scarlet-blossomed creepers."

There was a large plantation, with several small ones, divided by avenues of trees and paths between, and whitewashed wooden cottages, whence De Ruyter drew all his supplies, making it a point to produce every article he consumed in abundance.

"It would be more advantageous," said he, "in a worldly point of view, to cultivate that alone, in large quantities, which is best adapted to the peculiarity of the soil; and, by turning the overplus into specie, to purchase what necessaries or luxuries I might fancy. But, besides the satisfaction I feel in my plan, for what I lose in profit I gain in pleasure, health, and occupation, it enables me to ameliorate the hard fate of those suffering under a detestable system—which I abhor, but cannot remedy—I mean that of slavery. What I could, I have done. You will find no slave on my property. The bread you eat may not be the whitest or the lightest; but it is not stained by the blood and sweat of the galled and over-toiled captive, or leavened in execrations. Some score of slaves that I have redeemed, or found free, are my tenants. I have a tithe of their produce; I take it in kind. One is to supply me annually with corn, another with coffee, and so on to rice, sugar, spices, cotton, tobacco, wine, oil, spirit, and what else the ground will produce. What is superfluous I dispose of. Everything you eat and drink here is by free, not by forced labour; and I think we shall not relish our homely fare the less from knowing it is so. I am not one of those heavy-beamed moralists who preach, but hang astern from practice; fellows who scrutinise into the doctrine of a tailor before they venture into a pair of breeches of his making, without a thought of payment; I rather look at the goodness of their work, than at their godliness. I am better served by free people, working with all their hearts, than by the hands of heart-less slaves." . . .

My little orphan bride, thank Heaven! knew nothing of civilisation. Her shyness was that of the wood-pigeon, not the coquette's. She, poor simple thing, thought her husband alone should dwell in her thoughts; and imagined not that fashion had made that a crime in my country more heinous than adultery. The circumstances of our first meeting, our ship life, then our dwelling together in scenes formed for love, perfected in a few months what years would have perhaps been too short for in ordinary situations. . . . I taught her my language, and learnt more of hers— it was all she knew. Our breath mingled as I bent over her, our lips met, and our hearts beat together. She was an apt scholar, though her only punishment for idleness or neglect was the infliction of kisses, which were so long and ardent, that our lips seemed to grow together.

Violent adventures did not cease with marriage. Enraged at being cheated by a Parsee jeweler in Malaya, Trelawny assaulted him, and precipitated a riot that spread through the Bazaar. Near Borneo, they looted a Tartar junk painted with green and yellow dragons; Trelawny seized one of the crew by his long mustachios and sent a bullet through his open mouth. Almost shipwrecked in a simoon, drenched in icy water, Zela's labor pains came on prematurely, and she was delivered of a still-born child. Trelawny was almost slain by an ourang-outang and almost poisoned by a vengeful Javanese chieftain. Finally they arrived at Batavia, in Java.

In Europe there is or was a rage for golden-haired virgins; but here the mania was for golden complexions. At the same merchant's house where De Ruyter lodged, there lived a very rich widow, a native of the capital of Yug, which was situated on that part of the island still governed by its native princes. She was much admired at Batavia, and had, by the beauties of her person, attracted the beaux of the place, who revolved diurnally about her doors. She was nearly four feet and a half in stature, with a skin so brightly yellow that, when burnished with oil, it reflected the sun's rays like a gilded ball on a cupola, which her rich rotundity resembled. Her little jetty eyes sparkled in a face round and plump as an orange; her nose was minute as the bill of a humming-bird; her lips, both in substance and dimensions, betokened her African descent and the hairs on her globular head, if collected together, would hardly have amounted to the cherished number sprouting from my upper lip. Yet, such as I have described her, she was the beau-ideal of beauty at Java; and suitors from the four quarters of the island thronged to do her homage.

This globular object became infatuated with Trelawny.

Nothing doubting my rapturous assent, she, therefore, made a formal proposal in my behalf to De Ruyter, with the offer of an unconditional surrender of her charms, and large possessions of coffee-grounds, sugar, rice, and tobacco plantations, houses and tenements, slaves and personals, enough to put me on an equality with the most powerful princes in the province of Yug . . . The schooner was encumbered with bags of coffee, tobacco, and sugar-candy, besides daily and ample supplies of fresh and preserved fruits, flowers, and provisions, all enforced on my acceptance by the widow of Yug.

The widow of Yug was astounded at the intelligence of our going out of port for an indefinite period. Love overcoming her antipathy to the sea, she followed us in a row-boat, screaming, making signals, and scratching—thank Heaven, not me, but herself! Her melodramatic fury augmented to such a pitch, when she found I did not heave-to for her, that the devilish breeze she kicked up astern of us seemed to freshen the land-wind. With

my telescope I could observe her venting a portion of her wrath
on the slaves who rowed the boat, keeping time with the lusty
strokes of a bamboo on their naked backs . . .

I cannot tell why it was, but as we left the harbour of Batavia
and its begrimed water, the clear, pure, deep blue of the Indian
Ocean, which, since I had commanded the schooner, had always
filled my heart with delight, now, on the contrary, overwhelmed
me with sadness, that I could neither shake off nor repress. Doubt
and dread clouded my mind for the first time. Yet I was well in
health, and Zela (for I questioned her) was perfectly well; and
this was authenticated by the regularity of her pulse, the brightness
of her eye, her coral lip, and her breath sweeter than the odour
from May flowers on a spring morning. What then could it be?—
not the widow!—her love and her parting curses were forgotten
ere her boat was out of sight. Did her spirit cling to me like a
vampire? I remembered afterwards that, in her maledictions, she
had so threatened to haunt me if I abandoned her; and there were
rumours, which I laughed at, of her having dealt foully with
others.

*Bathing off Bombay, Zela was attacked and severely injured by
a shark. She made a slow recovery, but seemed to be getting well
when Trelawny was hastily summoned to her couch.*

She was writhing in extreme pain, and said that her stomach was
burning. I called to the mate on deck to make a signal to the grab
for the doctor, but she, unfortunately, was nearly out of sight
ahead, and it was almost a calm. Questioning Adoo as to the cause
of Zela's present state, she pointed to a jar on the table, and told
me that, her mistress not having eating anything for a long time,
she, with the other girl, had hunted in the storeroom for something
that would tempt her to eat. They found that jar of preserved
fruit; when her mistress, fond of sweetmeats, ate a great deal, and
gave some to the other little girl, who was seized with the same
pain after eating it. "Seeing my mistress liked it," said Adoo, "I
did but taste one of the fruit, and it has made me sick. I am sure
there is poison in that jar."

The word poison pierced my brain like a barbed arrow. Looking at the newly-opened jar, which had been closed with more than ordinary care by a resinous gum, I emptied out a portion of the fruit. They were a very fine sort of the wild green and yellow nutmegs, preserved in white sugar-candy. Had the small green snake, a native of Java, whose venom is the deadliest of all its tribe, erected its crest from out the jar, it would not so have shaken my nerves. For I remembered I had, at the widow's, eaten many preserved nutmegs from a jar, the counterpart of the one before me, and that they had made me sick . . . Now the frightful belief flashed on my mind, that the cunning strumpet, aided by the devil himself, had, as it were, stretched her arm across the Indian Ocean to ship the poisoned jar; for by no investigation could I ascertain how or when it came aboard.

While I stood pondering over the accursed fruit, half unconscious where I was, I thought I could hear the fiendish laugh of the widow mocking me. I thought I could see her, as she stood in the stern of the boat, threatening and cursing me as I left the harbour of Batavia, and began to repay her with loud and savage imprecations, till Zela, alarmed at my looks and gestures, believing me mad, forgot for a moment her own agony, took hold of my hand, pulled me on the bed, and soothed me with the softest accents, assuring me she was getting better. She bade me lay my head on her bosom, and she would rub it, for she saw the veins were distended on it. She said, almost playfully, "I can bear any pain but that of seeing you suffer. Your looks, my love, affright me. Take this fruit"—giving me a pomegranate—"which the poet Hafiz calls the pearl of fruits; and thus I imitate the example of the shell of the ocean, to fill with pearls the hand which wounds it."

The calmness with which she talked deceived me for a moment; but this effort of her mind almost destroyed her frail body: for then she talked wildly and incoherently, the subversion of her intellect foretelling the fatal issue that was at hand. Every muscle and nerve was writhing, as with a separate agony; her features were distorted; and in vain I tried every method I could think of to alleviate her pain. The poison was working on her vitals, and her mental derangement was a relief. . . .

One night she was startled . . . by a voice from the deck calling out that the Isle of France was in sight. She screamed out, "I am glad of it, very glad, dearest husband. Only, love, take me in your arms to carry me on shore; I am too weak to walk." Then throwing herself, with her last collected strength, in my arms, as I knelt by her low couch, she clasped me round the neck with her thin hands, and saying, "Now I am well and happy! I live in his heart!"—with her lips pressed to mine, she yielded up her mortality!

I had robed Zela in the richest costume of her country: her yellow vest was spangled with little rubies, and her chemise and flowing drawers, of sea-green Indian crape, were edged with gold; her outer garments were of the finest muslin of India; her slippers and the embroidered kerchiefs which bound up her hair, and concealed her bosom and the lower part of her face, were beaded and embossed with pearls. I preserved but one braid of her long, dark, silken hair, and, placing that in my breast, I kissed her eyelids, cheeks, and lips. . . . I walked through the surf to the shore. Its coolness strengthened me, and I was enabled to stagger on to the spot, where stood the funeral pile. I could recognize no other object. The figures that flitted about, and those who stopped to speak to me, looked like spectres gliding in a dance of death. A black iron furnace, like a coffin, was placed on the pile. After standing for some time entranced at its side, my senses, by some means, were sufficiently restored to make me aware of the necessity of going through what I had undertaken. I placed the body within the iron shell as delicately as a mother lays her sleeping child in its cradle. Then De Ruyter, the old Rais, and others withdrew me a short distance away, and held me there. Oils, spices, musk, camphor, and ambergris, I was afterwards told, were thrown in by baskets full. Dry bamboos and damped reeds thickly covered all; so that, when ignited, I could see nothing but a dark, impenetrable pyramid of smoke.

I tried to speak; then entreated by signs, for my throat was dry as death, that they would unhand me; but they held me fast, and my strength had totally fled.

De Ruyter agreed to take dispatches to Europe. At St. Malo, he urged Napoleon to destroy English power in the East, but the Emperor could not be made to understand that her commerce was both the source of England's power and her Achilles' heel. De Ruyter spoke fearlessly, Napoleon answered as man to man; he was "the only monarch that De Ruyter did not thoroughly despise, and him he hated for his selfish and insatiable ambition." *He had shaken the* "palsied old legitimate dotards from their mouldering, worm-eaten thrones": "Much good will ensue, but we owe him nothing, for he designed nothing but evil."

I am totally unable to write what I felt when the moment arrived which was to separate me from the man I loved better, a thousand times, than ever before one man could love another. The sun was setting, and the night must have been cold, for my limbs shook, and I could hardly support myself. . . . De Ruyter also was touched; his bronzed face was of a leaden hue; though I believe he talked calmly and distinctly, I could not afterwards remember a word he had said, but, "Farewell, my dear boy!"

Trelawny never saw him again. Off the Barbary coast an English frigate fell in with De Ruyter's vessel; a broadside of canister pierced him with a hundred balls. His body was wrapped in the French tricolor.

WIZARD OF THE NORTH

THE LIFE OF SIR WALTER SCOTT, BY HIS SON-IN-LAW JOHN GIBSON Lockhart, ranks second only to Boswell. In it, Andrew Lang wrote, "we have the full portrait of a man; the defects are blazoned by the intense light of genius and goodness," and if Boswell still emerges a little higher, that is because his hero is "a character more universally human, a wiser man, a greater humorist, his biography a more valuable possession than Sir Walter and Sir Walter's *Life*."

The accusation that Lockhart had been indiscreetly honest, given pain by his lack of reticence, rendered even his hero unheroic, Thomas Carlyle overwhelmed with brilliant derision. "How delicate, decent, is English biography, bless its mealy mouth!" he jeered. Nothing would do but that it must make its hero "a white, stainless, impersonal ghost hero!" But people brought into the circle of genius must expect to be revealed in the fierce light of its blaze: "They that will crowd about bonfires may sometimes very fairly get their beards singed; it is the price they pay for such illumination; natural twilight is safe and free to all."

If Lockhart failed in anything, Carlyle concluded, he failed only in that "Scott is altogether lovely to him, . . . that his very faults become beautiful, and that of his worth there is no measure." Here Carlyle somewhat exaggerated. Lockhart loved and admired Sir Walter; perhaps his affection blurred for him some of Scott's faults. But those "darker points" that he was aware of, "a stern sense of duty," he wrote, would induce him to draw "as freely as the others which were so predominant." And every subsequent biography, including that of Sir Herbert Grierson, has only underlined the essential justice of Lockhart's portrait. Sir Herbert corrects details; he shows that Lockhart softened Scott's irritability and that he did not know how much more Constable and his partner Cadell were to blame in the financial crash of 1825 than the unfortunate Ballantynes. But even these facts show that Scott was deliberately kept in ignorance of how desperate were his affairs so that anxiety should not dry up the profitable stream of fiction that flowed from him. They establish Scott's probity more stainless than ever.

Lockhart is too long, no doubt. The vast tract of eighty-four chapters originally published in seven volumes exhausts the reader's appetite, and overlabors the proof of points that have already been proved to the hilt. But the hues are as clear and transparent as if they had been rendered in water-color. Lockhart does not equal Boswell in reporting conversation, partly because Scott's excellence was not in repartee but in anecdote. Lockhart's method is to follow Scott into the outdoors, riding and hunting and walking and fording streams; he catches the nature of the man in action, in his laughter and his kindnesses, in his relations with other men. His story is more dramatic than Boswell's. There are grand contrasts of splendor and melancholy, and the darkness of the end is tragically connected with the careless profusion of Scott's prime. There is no greater pathos to be found in biography than the story Lockhart unrolls of that failing mind struggling on amid darkening hopes.

A neglected aspect of Lockhart is the picture he gives of the period. The Napoleonic Wars were over, and all England was riding a wave of luxuriousness and extravagant speculation. The booksellers were tied together by loans and agreements; and their capital, like every one else's, was intricately involved in South American mines, gas companies, and other precarious enterprises. The munificent advances Constable made on novels not only unwritten but even unconceived, and the baronial pile Scott was erecting at Abbotsford, were both built on the quaking ground of post-war inflation. A tightening of credit was bound to bring the whole flimsy structure in ruins to the ground. The crash came in

December, 1825, and Scott was only one of thousands to discover
that his opulence had been fairy gold.

Even more fundamentally does Scott embody the spirit of his
age, that romantic dualism that wavered between the problems of
an industrial revolution and dreams of the past. In the glowing
vision of himself as laird of Abbotsford and in the tang and excitement of being secretly involved in business Scott was slaking
the same impulses that made his novels breathless with Jacobite
conspiracies and hot with the siege of Torquilstone. He denounced
the bloated plutocracy fattening on the miseries of Manchester
slums and took refuge in the magic-lantern colors of a feudal past
and a kind imagined paternalism. But the enormous sales and
profits of his own books were made possible only by that same
finance-capitalism whose bitter fruits he saw with indignation.
Scott's character and career reflect the very essence of the early
nineteenth century and its basic conflicts. Of those conflicts Abbotsford is the symbol: its battlements new-built by bills of credit,
old suits of armor glittering among the jets of a recently invented
gas-lighting system—and its master killed by the effort to keep
it going.

The Life of Sir Walter Scott

.

JOHN GIBSON LOCKHART

[Scott died in 1832. The *Life* was originally published
in seven volumes, 1836–1838. Lockhart made an
abridgement for inclusion in an edition of Scott's
works in 1847. Both versions open with an autobiographical fragment by Scott.]

"EVERY SCOTTISHMAN," SCOTT BEGINS, "HAS A PEDIGREE." HIS GREAT-
grandfather, he goes on, was called Beardie *because of the great
beard he had sworn to leave uncut until the Stuart dynasty was
restored to the throne. His father was a Writer to the Signet. Scott
was born 15 August, 1771.*

*He became lame when he was eighteen months of age, and was
sent to his grandparents' farm at Sandy Knowe, to see what might
be done by country air and liberty. Here he was often left alone
on a knoll to watch the clouds and trees. Once he was forgotten
while a thunderstorm was coming on, and the aunt who ran to
fetch him* "found him lying on his back, clapping his hands at the
lightning, and crying out, 'Bonny! bonny!' at every flash." *The
child learned to talk much, and once the parish clergyman exclaimed in exasperation,* "One may as well speak in the mouth of a
cannon as where that child is."

At the age of four he was taken to his first play, As you Like It.
"I made, I believe, noise more than enough, and remember being
so much scandalized at the quarrel between Orlando and his
brother in the first scene, that I screamed out, 'A'n't they brothers?'
A few weeks' residence at home convinced me, who had till then

been an only child in the household of my grandfather, that a quarrel between brothers was a very natural event." [As a school-boy] "I glanced like a meteor from one end of the class to the other, and commonly disgusted my kind master as much by negligence and frivolity as I occasionally pleased him by flashes of intellect and talent."

But Spenser I could have ready for ever. Too young to trouble myself about the allegory, I considered all the knights and ladies and dragons and giants in their outward and exoteric sense, and God only knows how delighted I was to find myself in such society. As I had always a wonderful facility in retaining in my memory whatever verses pleased me, the quantity of Spenser's stanzas which I could repeat was really marvellous. But this memory of mine was a very fickle ally, and has through my whole life acted merely upon its own capricious motion, and might have enabled me to adopt old Beattie of Meikledale's answer, when com-plimented by a certain reverend divine on the strength of the same faculty:—"No, sir," answered the old Borderer, "I have no command of my memory. It only retains what hits my fancy, and probably, sir, if you were to preach to me for two hours, I would not be able when you finished to remember a word you had been saying." My memory was precisely of the same kind: it seldom failed to preserve most tenaciously a favourite passage of poetry, a play-house ditty, or, above all, a Border-raid ballad; but names, dates, and the other technicalities of history, escaped me in a most melan-choly degree.

If, however, it should ever fall to the lot of youth to peruse these pages—let such a reader remember, that it is with the deepest re-gret that I recollect in my manhood the opportunities of learning which I neglected in my youth; that through every part of my literary career I have felt pinched and hampered by my own ig-norance; and that I would at this moment give half the reputation I have had the good fortune to acquire, if by doing so I could rest the remaining part upon a sound foundation of learning and science . . . But all that was adventurous and romantic I devoured without much discrimination, and I really believe I have read as much nonsense of this class as any man now living.

Bishop Percy's Reliques of Ancient Poetry *inspired him with enthusiasm, and presently we find him as a young man "raiding" the countryside for border ballads and staying with Scottish farmers over night.*

"Eh me!" says Shortreed, "sic an endless fund o' humour and drollery as he then had wi' him! Never ten yards but we were either laughing or roaring and singing. Wherever we stopped, how brawlie he suited himsel' to everybody! He ay did as the lave did; never made himsel' the great man, or took ony airs in the company. I've seen him in a' moods in these jaunts, grave and gay, daft and serious, sober and drunk— (this, however, even in our wildest rambles, was but rare) but, drunk or sober, he was ay the gentleman. He looked excessively heavy and stupid when he was *fou,* but he was never out o' gude-humour."

He was disappointed in his first love and brooded over it for a time, but in 1797 he married Charlotte Carpenter, a lady of French descent. He was admitted to the bar, and his literary career began promisingly when his Minstrelsy of the Scottish Border *established him as a writer of erudition and charm. Outside term time in Edinburgh his days were active:*

He rose by five o'clock, lit his own fire when the season required one, and shaved and dressed with great deliberation—for he was a very martinet as to all but the mere coxcombries of the toilet, not abhorring effeminate dandyism itself so cordially as the slightest approach to personal sloveliness, or even those "bed-gown and slipper tricks," as he called them, in which literary men are so apt to indulge. Clad in his shooting-jacket, or whatever dress he meant to use till dinner time, he was seated at his desk by six o'clock, all his papers arranged before him in the most accurate order, and his books of reference marshalled around him on the floor, while at least one favourite dog lay watching his eye, just beyond the line of circumvallation. Thus, by the time the family assembled for breakfast between nine and ten, he had done enough (in his own language) "to break the neck of the day's work." After breakfast, a couple of hours more were given to his solitary tasks, and by noon he was, as he used to say, "his own man."

"Every day," says Mr. Skene, "we had some hours of coursing with the greyhounds, or riding at random over the hills, or of spearing salmon in the Tweed by sunlight: which last sport, moreover, we often renewed at night by the help of torches. This amusement of *burning the water,* as it is called, was not without some hazard, for the large salmon generally lie in the pools, the depths of which it is not easy to estimate with precision by torchlight,— so that not unfrequently, when the sportsman makes a determined thrust at a fish apparently within reach, his eye has grossly deceived him, and instead of the point of the weapon encountering the prey, he finds himself launched with corresponding vehemence heels over head into the pool, both spear and salmon gone, the torch thrown out by the concussion of the boat, and quenched in the stream, while the boat itself has of course receded to some distance. I remember the first time I accompanied our friend, he went right over the gunwale in this manner, and had I not accidentally been at his side, and made a successful grasp at the skirt of his jacket as he plunged overboard, he must at least have had an awkward dive for it. Such are the contingencies of burning the water. The pleasures consist in being penetrated with cold and wet, having your shins broken against the stones in the dark, and perhaps mastering one fish out of every twenty you take aim at."

"One of our earliest expeditions was to visit the wild scenery of the mountainous tract above Moffat, including the cascade of the Grey Mare's Tail, and the dark tarn called Loch Skene. In our ascent to the lake we got completely bewildered in the thick fog which generally envelopes the rugged features of that lonely region; and, as we were groping through the maze of bogs, the ground gave way, and down went horse and horsemen pell-mell into a slough of peaty mud and black water, out of which, entangled as we were with our plaids and floundering nags, it was no easy matter to get extricated. Indeed, unless we had prudently left our gallant steeds at a farm-house below, and borrowed hill-ponies for the occasion, the result might have been worse than laughable. As it was, we rose like the spirits of the bog, covered cap-à-pie with slime, to free themselves from which, our wily ponies took to rolling about on the heather, and we had nothing for it but following their example. At length, as we approached the gloomy loch, a huge eagle heaved himself from the margin and rose right over us, screaming his scorn of the intruders; and altogether it would be impossible to picture anything more desolately savage than the scene which opened, as if raised by enchantment on purpose to gratify the poet's eye; thick folds of fog rolling incessantly over the face of the inky waters, but rent asunder now in one direction, and then in another—so as to afford us a glimpse of some projecting rock or naked point of land, or island bearing a few scraggy stumps of pine—and then closing again in universal darkness upon the cheerless waste."

During the fears of French invasion in 1807 Scott's lameness was no obstacle to his joining a volunteer regiment of cavalry, and in intervals of drilling he could be seen spurring his powerful black steed to a furious gallop through the surging spray of Portobello sands.

He had now two boys and two girls; [1]—and he never had more. He was not one of those who take much delight in a mere infant; but no father ever devoted more time and tender care to his offspring than he did to each of his, as they reached the age when they could listen to him, and understand his talk. Like their playmates, Camp and the greyhounds, they had at all times free access to his study; he never considered their prattle as any disturbance; they went and came as pleased their fancy; he was always ready to answer their questions; and when they, unconscious how he was engaged, entreated him to lay down his pen and tell them a story, he would take them on his knee, repeat a ballad or a legend, kiss them, and set them down again to their marbles or ninepins, and resume his labour, as if refreshed by the interruption. From a

[1] Charlotte Sophia, born in October, 1799; Walter, October, 1801; Anne, February, 1803; Charles, December, 1805.

very early age he made them dine at table, and "to sit up to supper" was the great reward when they had been "very good bairns." In short, he considered it as the highest duty as well as the sweetest pleasure of a parent to be the companion of his children; he partook all their little joys and sorrows, and made his kind informal instructions to blend so easily and playfully with the current of their own sayings and doings, that so far from regarding him with any distant awe, it was never thought that any sport or diversion could go on in the right way, unless papa were of the party, or that the rainiest day could be dull, so he were at home.

As soon as his eldest girl could sit a pony, she was made the regular attendant of his mountain rides; and they all, as they attained sufficient strength, had the like advancement. He taught them to think nothing of tumbles, and habituated them to his own reckless delight in perilous fords and flooded streams; and they all imbibed in great perfection his passion for horses—as well, I may venture to add, as his deep reverence for the more important article of that Persian training. "Without courage," he said, "there cannot be truth; and without truth there can be no other virtue."

He had been made Clerk of the Court of Session, and was at the same time creating a name for himself in poetry. The Lay of the Last Minstrel *had been followed by* Marmion, *both enormously successful, but* The Lady of the Lake *surpassed all precedents.*

The whole country rang with the praises of the poet—crowds set off to view the scenery of Loch Katrine, till then comparatively unknown; and as the book came out just before the season for excursions, every house and inn in that neighbourhood was crammed with a constant succession of visitors. It is a well-ascertained fact, that from the date of the publication of the Lady of the Lake, the post-horse duty in Scotland rose in an extraordinary degree, and indeed it continued to do so regularly for a number of years, the author's succeeding works keeping up the enthusiasm for our scenery which he had thus originally created.

Of its success [Scott] speaks as follows in 1830:—"It was certainly so extraordinary as to induce me for the moment to conclude that I had at last fixed a nail in the proverbially inconstant wheel of Fortune. But, as the celebrated John Wilkes is said to have explained to King George the Third, that he himself was never a Wilkite, so I can with honest truth exculpate myself from having been at any time a partisan of my own poetry, even when it was in the highest fashion with the million."

James Ballantyne has preserved in his *Memorandum* an anecdote strikingly confirmative of the most remarkable statement in this page of Scott's confessions. "I remember," he says, "going into his library shortly after the publication of the Lady of the Lake, and finding Miss Scott (who was then a very young girl) there by herself. I asked her—'Well, Miss Sophia, how do you like the Lady of the Lake?' Her answer was given with perfect simplicity—'Oh, I have not read it: papa says there's nothing so bad for young people as reading bad poetry.'—But, in fact," (continues Ballantyne) —"he had often said to me that neither his own nor any modern popular style of composition was that from which he derived most pleasure. I asked him what it was. He answered— Johnson's; and that he had more pleasure in reading *London,* and *The Vanity of Human Wishes,* than any other poetical composition he could mention; and I think I never saw his countenance more indicative of high admiration than while reciting aloud from those productions."

Waverley, published anonymously in 1814, made even more of a furore that any of the poems had done. Meanwhile, Scott had already made the move to Abbotsford. He wrote:

"The neighbours have been much delighted with the procession of my furniture, in which old swords, bows, targets, and lances made a very conspicuous show. A family of turkeys were accommodated within the helmet of some preux chevalier of ancient Border fame; and the very cows, for aught I know, were bearing banners and muskets."

During these years Scott had also assumed his fatal silent partnership with the Ballantynes. James and John Ballantyne were both honest men, and they loved and revered their friend, but they had serious defects as businessmen. In a flurry of panic in 1813, Scott

was worried into crying, "For Heaven' sake, treat me as a man, not
as a milch cow." A sense of pressure was settling upon him, so that
even during violent attacks of cramps in 1817 he felt obliged to
grind out manuscript. "Ay, ay, Jemmie," *he said to James Ballan-*
tyne, " 'tis easy for you to bid me get on, but how the deuce can
I make Rob Roy's wife speak, with such a *curmurring* in my guts?"

But the flow of his imagination seemed endless and magical. In
hardly more than a year he wrote Ivanhoe, The Monastery, The
Abbot, *and* Kenilworth. *Why should the springs ever run dry?*
Stout, mock-majestic James Ballantyne gave a grandiose banquet
to celebrate the completion of each new novel.

The feast was, to use one of James's own favourite epithets,
gorgeous; an aldermanic display of turtle and venison, with the
suitable accompaniments of iced punch, potent ale, and generous
Madeira. When the cloth was drawn, the burly preses arose, with
all he could muster of the port of John Kemble, and spouted with
a sonorous voice the formula of Macbeth—

> *"Fill full!*
> *I drink to the general joy of the whole table!"*

This was followed by "The King, God bless him!" and second
came—"Gentlemen, there is another toast which never has been
nor shall be omitted in this house of mine—I give you the health
of Mr. Walter Scott with three times three!"—All honour having
been done to this health, and Scott having briefly thanked the
company with some expressions of warm affection to their host,
Mrs. Ballantyne retired;—the bottles passed round twice or thrice
in the usual way;—and then James rose once more, every vein on
his brow distended, his eyes solemnly fixed upon vacancy, to
propose, not as before in his stentorian key, but with " 'bated
breath," in the sort of whisper by which a stage conspirator thrills
the gallery—"Gentlemen, a bumper to the immortal Author of
Waverley!"—The uproar of cheering, in which Scott made a fashion
of joining, was succeeded by deep silence, and then Ballantyne
proceeded—

> *"In his Lord-Burleigh look, serene and serious,*
> *A something of imposing and mysterious"—*

to lament the obscurity in which his illustrious but too modest correspondent still chose to conceal himself from the plaudits of the world—to thank the company for the manner in which the nominis umbra had been received—and to assure them that the Author of *Waverley* would, when informed of the circumstance, feel highly delighted—"the proudest hour of his life," &c., &c. The cool demure fun of Scott's features during all this mummery was perfect; and Erskine's attempt at a gay nonchalance was still more ludicrously meritorious . . .

What a different affair was a dinner, although probably including many of the same guests, at the junior partner's! He in those days retained, I think, no private apartments attached to his auction-rooms in Hanover Street, over the door of which he still kept emblazoned "John Ballantyne and Company, Booksellers." At any rate, such of his entertainments as I ever saw Scott partake of, were given at his villa near to the Firth of Forth, by Trinity;— a retreat which the little man had invested with an air of dainty voluptuous finery, contrasting strikingly enough with the substantial citizen-like snugness of his elder brother's domestic appointments. His house was surrounded by gardens so contrived as to seem of considerable extent, having many a shady tuft, trellised alley, and mysterious alcove, interspersed among their bright parterres. His professional excursion to Paris and Brussels in quest of objects of vertu, had supplied both the temptation and the means to set forth the interior in a fashion that might have satisfied the most fastidious petite maîtresse of Norwood or St. Denis. John, too, was a married man: he had, however, erected for himself a private wing, the accesses to which, whether from the main building or the bosquet, were so narrow that it was physically impossible for the handsome and portly lady who bore his name to force her person through any one of them. His dinners were in all respects Parisian, for his wasted palate disdained such John Bull luxuries as were all in all with James. The piquant pasty of Strasburg or Perigord was never to seek; and even the pièce de résistance was probably a boar's head from Coblentz, or a turkey ready stuffed with truffles from the Palais Royal . . .

It was at one of those Trinity dinners this summer that I first

saw Constable. Being struck with his appearance, I asked Scott
who he was, and he told me—expressing some surprise that anybody should have lived a winter or two in Edinburgh without
knowing, by sight at least, a citizen whose name was so familiar to
the world. I happened to say that I had not been prepared to find
the great bookseller a man of such gentlemanlike and even distinguished bearing. Scott smiled, and answered—"Ay, Constable is
indeed a grand-looking chield. He puts me in mind of Fielding's
apology for Lady Booby—to wit, that Joseph Andrews had an air
which, to those who had not seen many noblemen, would give an
idea of nobility."

*Late in 1818 he was told the Prince Regent desired to confer on
him the rank of Baronet. After some hesitation, he accepted,
mainly influenced by the thought of advantage to his eldest son,
who was entering upon a military career. But he was also moved by
a certain innocent and naïve pride of birth.*

"After all, if one must speak for themselves, I have my quarters
and emblazonments, free of all stain but Border theft, and High
Treason, which I hope are gentlemanlike crimes; and I hope Sir
Walter Scott will not sound worse than Sir Humphry Davy, though
my merits are as much under his, in point of utility, as can well
be imagined. But a name is something, and mine is the better of
the two."

. . . On one of those flying visits to Abbotsford with which he
often indulged himself during a Saturday during term . . . there
appeared at breakfast John Ballantyne . . . and with him Mr.
Constable, his guest; . . . we all sallied out, before noon, on a
peraumbulation of his upland territories . . . At starting we were
joined by the constant henchman, Tom Purdie [whose] face shone
with rapture as he observed how severely the swag-bellied bookseller's activity was taxed. Scott exclaiming exultingly, though
perhaps for the tenth time, "This will be a glorious season for
our trees, Tom!"—"You may say that, Shirra," quoth Tom,—and
then lingering a moment for Constable,—"My certy," he added,
scratching his head, "and I think it will be a grand season for *our
buiks* too."

Messrs. Constable had such faith in the prospective fertility of his imagination, that they were by this time quite ready to sign bargains and grant bills for novels and romances to be produced hereafter, but of which the subjects and the names were alike unknown to them and to the man from whose pen they were to proceed. A forgotten satirist well says:—

> *"The active principle within*
> *Works on some brains the effect of gin";*

but in Sir Walter's case, every external influence combined to stir the flame, and swell the intoxication of restless exuberant energy.

"It would, I think, be extremely difficult to [Lockhart quotes a visitor to Abbotsford] give a just idea of his general conversation to any one who had not known him. Considering his great personal and literary popularity, and the wide circle of society in which he had lived, it is perhaps remarkable that so few of his sayings, real or imputed, are in circulation. But he did not affect sayings; the points and sententious turns, which are so easily caught up and transmitted, were not natural to him: though he occasionally expressed a thought very pithily and neatly. For example, he once described the Duke of Wellington's style of debating as 'slicing the argument into two or three parts, and helping himself to the best.'

"But the great charm of his 'table-talk' was in the sweetness and abandon with which it flowed,—always, however, guided by good sense and taste; the warm and unstudied eloquence with which he expressed rather sentiments than opinions; and the liveliness and force with which he narrated and described: and all that he spoke derived so much of its effect from indefinable felicities of manner, look, and tone—and sometimes from the choice of apparently insignificant words—that a moderately faithful transcript of his sentences would be but a faint image of his conversation.

"No one who has seen him can forget the surprising power of change which his countenance shewed when awakened from a state of composure. In 1823, his face, which was healthy and sanguine, and the hair about it, which had a strong reddish tinge, contrasted rather than harmonised with the sleek, silvery locks above; a contrast which might seem rather suited to a jovial and humorous, than to a pathetic expression. But his features were equally capable of both. The form and hue of his eyes (for the benefit of minute physiognomists it should be noted that the iris contained some small specks of brown) were wonderfully calculated for shewing great varieties of emotion. Their mournful aspect was extremely earnest and affecting; and when he told some dismal and mysterious story, they had a doubtful, melancholy, exploring look, which appealed irresistibly to the hearer's imagination.

"Occasionally, when he spoke of something very audacious or eccentric, they would dilate and light up with a tragi-comic, hare-brained expression, quite peculiar to himself; one might see in it a whole chapter of Cœur-de-lion and the Clerk of Copmanhurst. Never, perhaps, did a man go through all the gradations of laughter with such complete enjoyment, and a countenance so radiant. The first dawn of a humorous thought would shew itself sometimes, as he sat silent, by an involuntary lengthening of the upper lip, followed by a shy sidelong glance at his neighbours, indescribably whimsical, and seeming to ask from their looks whether the spark of drollery should be suppressed or allowed to blaze out. In the full tide of mirth he did indeed 'laugh the heart's laugh,' like Walpole, but it was not boisterous and overpowering, nor did it check the course of his words; he could go on telling or descanting, while his lungs did 'crow like chanticleer,' his syllables, in the struggle, growing more emphatic, his accent more strongly Scotch, and his voice plaintive with excess of merriment."

From a diary kept by Captain Basil Hall:

"Some one talked of the pains taken to provide the poor with receipts for making good dishes out of their ordinary messes. 'I dislike all such interference,' he said—'all your domiciliary, kind, impertinent visits;—they are all pretty much felt like insults, and do no manner of good: let people go on in their own way, in God's name. How would you like to have a nobleman coming to you to teach you how to dish up your beefsteak into a French kickshaw? Let the poor alone in their domestic habits: protect them, treat them kindly, trust them; but let them enjoy in quiet their dish of porridge, and their potatoes and herrings, or whatever it may be—for anysake don't torment them with your fashionable soups. And take care,' he added, 'not to give them anything gratis; except when they are under the gripe of immediate misery —what *they* think misery—consider it as a sin to do anything that can tend to make them lose the precious feeling of independence. For my part, I very very rarely give anything away. Now, for instance, this pile of branches which has been thinned out this morning is placed here for sale for the poor people's fires, and I am perfectly certain they are more grateful to me for selling it at the price I do (which, you may be sure, is no great matter), than if I were to give them ten times the quantity for nothing. Every shilling collected in this and other similar manners goes to a fund which pays the doctor for his attendance on them when they are sick; and this is my notion of charity.' "

The much-talked-of lady who began life as Miss Harriet Mellon, a comic actress in a provincial troupe, and died Duchess of St. Albans, was then making a tour in Scotland as Mrs. Coutts, the enormously wealthy widow of the first English banker of his time. No person of such consequence could, in those days, have thought a Scotch progress complete, unless it included a reception at Abbotsford; but Mrs. Coutts had been previously acquainted with Sir Walter . . .

It so happened that there were already in the house several ladies, Scotch and English, of high birth and rank, who felt by no means disposed to assist their host and hostess in making Mrs. Coutts's visit agreeable to her. I need not observe how effectually women of fashion can contrive to mortify, without doing or saying anything that shall expose them to the charge of actual incivility.

Sir Walter, during dinner, did everything in his power to counteract this influence of the evil eye, and something to over-awe it;—but the spirit of mischief had been fairly stirred, and it was easy to see that Mrs. Coutts followed these noble dames to the drawing-room in by no means that complacent mood which was customarily sustained, doubtless, by every blandishment of obsequious flattery, in this mistress of millions. He cut the gentlemen's sederunt short, and soon after joining the ladies, managed to withdraw the youngest, and gayest, and cleverest, who was also the highest in rank (the late Marchioness of Northampton), into his armorial-hall adjoining.

"I said to her" (he told me), "I want to speak a word with you about Mrs. Coutts;—we have known each other a good while, and I know you won't take anything I can say in ill part. It is, I hear, not uncommon among the fine ladies in London to be very well pleased to accept invitations, and even sometimes to hunt after them, to Mrs. Coutts's grand balls and fêtes, and then, if they meet her in any private circle, to practise on her the delicate manœuvre called *tipping the cold shoulder*. This you agree with me is shabby; but it is nothing new either to you or to me, that fine people will do shabbiness for which beggars might blush, if they once stoop so low as to poke for tickets.

"I am sure you would not for the world do such a thing; but you must permit me to take the great liberty of saying, that I think the style you have all received my guest Mrs. Coutts in, this evening, is, to a certain extent, a sin of the same order. You were all told a couple of days ago that I had accepted her visit, and that she would arrive to-day to stay three nights. Now if any of you had not been disposed to be of my party at the same time with her, there was plenty of time for you to have gone away before she came; and as none of you moved, and it was impossible to fancy that any of you would remain out of mere curiosity, I thought I had a perfect right to calculate on your having made up your minds to help me out with her."

Lady Northampton (who had been his ward) answered—"I thank you, Sir Walter;—you have done me the great honour to speak as if I had been your daughter, and depend upon it you shall be obeyed with heart and good will."

One by one, the other exclusives were seen engaged in a little tête-à-tête with her ladyship. Sir Walter was soon satisfied that things had been put into a right train; the Marchioness was requested to sing a particular song, because he thought it would please Mrs. Coutts. "Nothing could gratify her more than to please Mrs. Coutts." Mrs. Coutts's brow smoothed, and in the course of half an hour she was as happy and easy as ever she was in her life, rattling away at comical anecdotes of her early theatrical years, and joining in the chorus of Sir Adam's *Laird of Cockpen*. She stayed out her three days—saw, accompanied by all the circle, Melrose, Dryburgh, and Yarrow—and left Abbotsford delighted with her host, and, to all appearance, with his other guests.

Towards the end of September I returned to Scotland from a visit to London on some personal business. During that visit I had heard a great deal more than I understood about the commercial excitement of the time. There had been several years of extravagant speculation. Even persons who had extensive and flourishing businesses in their hands partook the general rage of infatuation. He whose own shop, counting-house, or warehouse, had been sufficient to raise him to a decent and safely-increasing opulence, and was more than sufficient to occupy all his attention, drank in the vain delusion that he was wasting his time and energy on things unworthy of a masculine ambition, and embarked the resources necessary for the purposes of his lawful calling in schemes worthy of the land-surveyors of El Dorado. It was whispered that *the trade* (so called, par excellence) had been bitten with this fever; and persons of any foresight who knew the infinitely curious links by which booksellers, and printers, and paper-makers (and therefore authors) are bound together, for good and for evil, already began to prophesy that, whenever the general crash, which must come ere long, should arrive, its effects would be felt far and wide among all classes connected with the productions of the press. When it was rumoured that this great bookseller, or printer, had become a principal holder of South American mining shares —that another was the leading director of a gas company—while a third house had risked about £100,000 in a cast upon the most capricious of all agricultural products, hops—it was no wonder that bankers should begin to calculate balances, and pause upon dis-

My residence had been removed to London before Sir Walter felt, or acknowledged, serious apprehensions: nor can I on this occasion quote his Diary so largely as would enable the reader to follow from day to day the fluctuations of hope, anxiety, and fear. I must limit myself to a few of what seem the most remarkable passages of that record. On the 18th of December he writes thus:—"If things go badly in London, the magic wand of the Unknown will be shivered in his grasp. He must then, faith, be termed the Too-well-known. . . . What a life mine has been!—half-educated, almost wholly neglected, or left to myself; stuffing my head with most nonsensical trash, and undervalued by most of my companions for a time; getting forward, and held a bold and a clever fellow, contrary to the opinion of all who thought me a mere dreamer; broken-hearted for two years; my heart handsomely pieced again—but the crack will remain till my dying day . . . I have the satisfaction to recollect that my prosperity has been of advantage to many, and to hope that some at least will forgive my transient wealth on account of the innocence of my intentions, and my real wish to do good to the poor. Sad hearts, too, at Darnick, and in the cottages at Abbotsford. I have half resolved never to see the place again. How could I tread my hall with such a diminished crest?—how live a poor indebted man where I was once the wealthy, the honoured? I was to have gone there on Saturday in joy and prosperity to receive my friends. My dogs will wait for me in vain. It is foolish—but the thoughts of parting from these dumb creatures have moved me more than any of the painful reflections I have put down. Poor things! I must get them kind masters!"

What, I think, affected him most of all, was a letter from Mr. Poole, his daughters' harp-master, offering £500,—"probably," says the Diary, "his all." From London, also, he received various kind communications. Among others, one tendering an instant advance of £30,000—a truly munificent message, conveyed through a distinguished channel, but the source of which was never revealed to him, nor to me until some years after his death, and even then under conditions of secrecy. To all his answer was the same. And within a few days he had reason to believe that the creditors would, as a body, assent to let things go in the course which he and his trustees suggested.

"Abbotsford, March 17.—A letter from Lockhart. My worst augury is verified;—the medical people think poor Johnnie is losing strength; he is gone with his mother to Brighton. The bitterness of this probably impending calamity is extreme. The child was almost too good for this world;—beautiful in features; and though spoiled by every one, having one of the sweetest tempers as well as the quickest intellect I ever saw; a sense of humour quite extraordinary in a child, and, owing to the general notice which was taken of him, a great deal more information than suited his years. The poor dear love had so often a slow fever, that when it pressed its little lips to mine, I always foreboded to my own heart what all I fear are now aware of."

"April 24.—Constable is sorely broken down.

> 'Poor fool and knave, I have one part in my heart
> That's sorry yet for thee.'

His conduct has not been what I deserved at his hand; but I believe that, walking blindfold himself, he misled me without malice prepense. It is best to think so at least, until the contrary be demonstrated. To nourish angry passions against a man whom I really liked would be to lay a blister on my own heart."

"Abbotsford, May 16.—She [Lady Scott] died at nine in the morning, after being very ill for two days—easy at last. I arrived here late last night. Anne is worn out, and has had hysterics, which returned on my arrival. Her broken accents were like those of a child—the language as well as the tones broken, but in the most gentle voice of submission. 'Poor mamma—never return again—gone for ever—a better place.' Then, when she came to herself, she spoke with sense, freedom, and strength of mind, till her weakness returned. It would have been inexpressibly moving to me as a stranger—what was it then to the father and the husband? For myself, I scarce know how I feel—sometimes as firm as the Bass Rock, sometimes as weak as the water that breaks on it. I am as alert at thinking and deciding as I ever was in my life. Yet, when

I contrast what this place now is, with what it has been not long since, I think my heart will break. Lonely, aged, deprived of my family—all but poor Anne; an improverished, an embarrassed man, deprived of the sharer of my thoughts and counsels, who could always talk down my sense of the calamitous apprehensions which break the heart that must bear them alone.—Even her foibles were of service to me, by giving me things to think of beyond my weary self-reflections."

"*May* 18.—Another day, and a bright one to the external world, again opens on us; the air soft, and the flowers smiling, and the leaves glittering. They cannot refresh her to whom mild weather was a natural enjoyment. Cerements of lead and of wood already hold her—cold earth must have her soon. But it is not my Charlotte—it is not the bride of my youth, the mother of my children, that will be laid among the ruins of Dryburgh, which we have so often visited in gaiety and pastime—No! no! . . .

"I remembered the last sight of her: she raised herself in bed, and tried to turn her eyes after me, and said, with a sort of smile, 'You all have such melancholy faces.' These were the last words I ever heard her utter, and I hurried away, for she did not seem quite conscious of what she said; when I returned, immediately departing, she was in a deep sleep. It is deeper now. This was but seven days since."

Formerly, however great the quantity of work he put through his hands, his evenings were almost always reserved for the light reading of an elbow-chair, or the enjoyment of his family and friends. Now he seemed to grudge every minute that was not spent at the desk. The little that he read of new books, or for mere amusement, was done by snatches in the course of his meals; and to walk, when he could walk at all, to the Parliament-House, and back again, through the Prince's Street Gardens, was his only exercise and his only relaxation. Every ailment, of whatever sort, ended in aggravating his lameness; and, perhaps, the severest test his philosophy encountered was the feeling of bodily helplessness that from week to week crept upon him. The winter, to make bad worse, was a very cold and stormy one. The growing sluggishness of his blood shewed itself in chilblains, not only on the feet but the fingers, and his handwriting becomes more and more cramped and confused.

The secret of the authorship of the Waverley Novels was widely known now, and was at last openly acknowledged at a banquet in February, 1827. Lord Meadowbrook was asked to propose a toast.

He knew that this was the first public dinner at which the object of the toast had appeared since his misfortunes, and taking him aside in the anteroom, asked him whether he would now consider it indelicate to hazard a distinct reference to the parentage of the Waverley Novels. Sir Walter smiled, and said, "Do just as you like—only don't say much about so old a story."—In the course of the evening the Judge rose accordingly, and said—

"I would beg leave to propose a toast—the health of one of the Patrons. The clouds have been dispelled—the darkness visible has been cleared away—and the Great Unknown—the minstrel of our native land—the mighty magician who has rolled back the current of time, and conjured up before our living senses the men and the manners of days which have long passed away, stands revealed to the eyes and hearts of his affectionate and admiring countrymen. We owe to him, as a people, a large and heavy debt of gratitude. He it is who has opened to foreigners the grand and characteristic beauties of our country;—it is to him that we owe that our gallant ancestors and illustrious patriots have obtained a fame no longer confined to the boundaries of a remote and comparatively obscure country—he it is who has conferred a new reputation on our national character, and bestowed on Scotland an imperishable name, were it only by her having given birth to himself. I propose the health of Sir Walter Scott."

But such triumphs were few. Illness grew upon him. Headaches and hemorrhages afflicted him. His friend Will Laidlaw watched him in distress.

He could not watch Scott from hour to hour—above all, he could not write to his dictation, without gradually, slowly, most reluctantly taking home to his bosom the conviction that the

mighty mind, which he had worshipped through more than thirty
years of intimacy, had lost something, and was daily losing something more, of its energy. The faculties were there, and each of
them was every now and then displaying itself in its full vigour;
but the sagacious judgment, the brilliant fancy, the unrivalled
memory, were all subject to occasional eclipse—

> *"Amid the strings his fingers stray'd,*
> *And an uncertain warbling made."*

Ever and anon he paused and looked around him, like one half-
waking from a dream, mocked with shadows. The sad bewilderment of his gaze shewed a momentary consciousness that, like
Samson in the lap of the Philistine, "his strength was passing from
him, and he was becoming weak like unto other men." Then
came the strong effort of aroused will—the cloud dispersed as
if before an irresistible current of purer air—all was bright
and serene as of old—and then it closed again in yet deeper darkness.

*The evils of the times distressed him. He had seen the misery of
poverty in Manchester: "God's justice is requiting," he exclaimed,
"and will yet further requite those who have blown up this country into a state of unsubstantial opulence at the expense of the
health and morals of the lower classes." But, a convinced Tory, he
distrusted democratic remedies, and his opposition to the Reform
Bill of 1832 led to his being hissed and hooted at a public meeting.*

He stood calmly till the storm subsided, and resumed; but the
friend, whose notes are before me, could not catch what he said,
until his voice rose with another illustration of the old style.

"My friends," he said, "I am old and failing, and you think me
full of very silly prejudices; but I have seen a good deal of public
men, and thought a good deal of public affairs in my day, and
I can't help suspecting that the manufacturers of this new constitution are like a parcel of schoolboys taking to pieces a watch
which used to go tolerably well for all practical purposes, in
the conceit that they can put it together again far better than
the old watchmaker. I fear they will fail when they come to the

reconstruction, and I should not, I confess, be much surprised if it were to turn out that their first step had been to break the main-spring."

Here he was again stopped by a Babel of contemptuous sounds, which seemed likely to render further attempts ineffectual. He, abruptly and unheard, proposed his Resolution, and then, turning to the riotous artisans, exclaimed— "I regard your gabble no more than the geese on the green." His countenance glowed with indignation, as he resumed his seat on the bench. But when, a few moments afterwards, the business being over, he rose to withdraw, every trace of passion was gone. He turned round at the door, and bowed to the assembly.

Two or three, not more, renewed their hissing; he bowed again, and took leave in the words of the doomed gladiator, which I hope none who had joined in these insults understood— "MORITURUS VOS SALUTO."

To assist them in amusing him in the hours which he spent out of his study, and especially that he might be tempted to make those hours more frequent, his daughters had invited his friend the authoress of *Marriage* to come out to Abbotsford; and her coming was serviceable. For she knew and loved him well, and she had seen enough of affliction akin to his to be well skilled in dealing with it. She could not be an hour in his company without observing what filled his children with more sorrow than all the rest of the case. He would begin a story as gaily as ever, and go on, in spite of the hesitation in his speech, to tell it with picturesque effect;—but before he reached the point, it would seem as if some internal spring had given way—he paused and gazed round him with the blank anxiety of look that a blind man has when he has dropped his staff. Unthinking friends sometimes pained him sadly by giving him the catchword abruptly. I noticed the delicacy of Miss Ferrier on such occasions. Her sight was bad, and she took care not to use her glasses when he was speaking; and she affected also to be troubled with deafness, and would say—"Well, I am getting as dull as a post—I have not heard a word since you said so and so": being sure to mention a circumstance behind that at which he had really halted. He then took up the thread with his habitual smile of courtesy—as if forgetting his case entirely in the consideration of the lady's infirmity.

On the 18th of May, I witnessed a scene which must dwell painfully on many memories besides mine. The rumours of brick-bat and bludgeon work at the hustings of this month were so prevalent, that Sir Walter's family, and not less zealously the Tory candidate (Henry Scott, heir of Harden, now Lord Polwarth), tried every means to dissuade him from attending the election for Roxburghshire. We thought overnight that we had succeeded, and, indeed, as the result of the vote was not at all doubtful, there could be no good reason for his appearing on this occasion. About seven in the morning, however, when I came down stairs intending to ride over to Jedburgh, I found he had countermanded my horse, ordered his chariot to the door, and was already impatient to be off for the scene of action.

We found the town in a most tempestuous state: in fact, it was almost wholly in the hands of a disciplined rabble, chiefly weavers from Hawick, who marched up and down with drums and banners, and then, after filling the Court-hall, lined the streets, grossly insulting every one who did not wear the reforming colours. Sir Walter's carriage, as it advanced towards the house of the Shortreed family, was pelted with stones; one or two fell into it, but none touched him. He breakfasted with the widow and children of his old friend, and then walked to the Hall between me and one of the young Shortreeds. He was saluted with groans and blasphemies all the way—and I blush to add that a woman spat upon him from a window; but this last contumely I think he did not observe . . .

The Diary contains this brief notice:—"*May* 18.—Went to Jedburgh greatly against the wishes of my daughters. The mob were exceedingly vociferous and brutal, as they usually are nowadays. The population gathered in formidable numbers—a thousand from Hawick also—sad blackguards. The day passed with much clamour and no mischief. Henry Scott was re-elected—for the last time, I suppose. Troja fuit. I left the borough in the midst

of abuse, and the gentle hint of Burk Sir Walter. Much obliged
to the brave lads of Jeddart."

It was about this time that we observed Sir Walter beginning to
entertain the notion that his debts were paid off. By degrees,
dwelling on this fancy, he believed in it fully and implicitly. It
was a gross delusion—but neither Cadell nor any one else had the
heart to disturb it by any formal statement of figures.

*In the hope that a trip abroad might restore his health the Brit-
ish government placed the frigate Barham at his disposal to convey
him to the Mediterranean. The splendors of Abbotsford were
briefly revived before his departure by a reunion at which Wordsworth was present. The poet wrote a sonnet on the approaching
voyage:*

> "A trouble, not of clouds, or weeping rain,
>   Nor of the setting sun's pathetic light
>   Engendered, hangs o'er Eildon's triple height:
> Spirits of power assembled there complain
> For kindred power departing from their sight;
> While Tweed, best pleased in chanting a blithe strain,
> Saddens his voice again, and yet again.
> Lift up your hearts, ye mourners! for the might
> Of the whole world's good wishes with him goes;
> Blessings and prayers, in nobler retinue
> Than sceptred King or laurelled Conqueror knows,
> Follow this wondrous potentate. Be true,
> Ye winds of Ocean, and the Midland Sea,
> Wafting your charge to soft Parthenope."

"London, October 2, 1831.—I have been very ill, and if not quite
unable to write, I have been unfit to do it. I have wrought, however, at two Waverley things, but not well. A total prostration of
bodily strength is my chief complaint. I cannot walk half a mile.
There is, besides, some mental confusion, with the extent of
which I am not, perhaps, fully acquainted. I am perhaps setting.
I am myself inclined to think so, and like a day that has been admired as a fine one, the light of it sets down amid mists and storms.
I neither regret nor fear the approach of death, if it is coming. I
would compound for a little pain instead of this heartless mud-
diness of mind."

*From Portsmouth, the Barham sailed down through the Bay of
Biscay, past Gibraltar, and on to a first pause at Malta. Scott rallied
for a time; staying at Naples, he made trips to Paestum, Baiae,
Misenum, and Averno. But his mind lingered much more in the
past and in the world of legend than on his surroundings.*

At Pompeii alone did his thoughts seem to be wholly commanded by the realities before him. There he had himself carried
from house to house, and examined everything leisurely; but said
little, except ever and anon in an audible whisper, "The city of
the dead—the city of the dead!"

He had wished to return by the route of the Tyrol and Germany, partly for the sake of the remarkable chapel and monuments of the old Austrian princes at Innsbruck, and the feudal
ruins upon the Rhine, but chiefly that he might have an interview
with Goethe at Weimar. That poet died on the 22nd of March,
and the news seemed to act upon Scott exactly as the illness of
Borthwickbrae had done in the August before. His impatience
redoubled: all his fine dreams of recovery seemed to vanish at
once— "Alas for Goethe!" he exclaimed: "but he at least died at
home—Let us to Abbotsford." . . .

During the time he was in Jermyn Street he was calm but never
collected, and in general either in absolute stupor or in a waking
dream. He never seemed to know where he was, but imagined
himself to be still in the steam-boat. The rattling of carriages, and
the noises of the street, sometimes disturbed this illusion—and
then he fancied himself at the polling-booth of Jedburgh, where
he had been insulted and stoned.

*He yearned to reach Abbotsford, and at last the journey from
London was begun. Waiting to be lifted into his carriage, he
seemed to have* "no distinct perception of where he was, or how he
came to be there."

His children were deeply affected, and Mrs. Lockhart trembled
from head to foot, and wept bitterly. Thus surrounded by those
nearest to him, he alone was unconscious of the cause or depth
of their grief, and while yet alive seemed to be carried to his
grave. . . .

At a very early hour on the morning of Wednesday the 11th, we again placed him in his carriage, and he lay in the same torpid state during the first two stages on the road to Tweedside. But as we descended the vale of the Gala he began to gaze about him, and by degrees it was obvious that he was recognising the features of that familiar landscape. Presently he murmured a name or two —"Gala Water, surely—Buckholm—Torwoodlee." As we rounded the hill at Ladhope, and the outline of the Eildons burst on him, he became greatly excited; and when, turning himself on the couch, his eye caught at length his own towers at the distance of a mile, he sprang up with a cry of delight. . . .

Mr. Laidlaw was waiting at the porch, and assisted us in lifting him into the dining-room, where his bed had been prepared. He sat bewildered for a few moments, and then resting his eye on Laidlaw, said—"Ha! Willie Laidlaw! O man, how often have I thought of you!" By this time his dogs had assembled about his chair—they began to fawn upon him and lick his hands, and he alternately sobbed and smiled over them, until sleep oppressed him. . . .

"I have seen much," he kept saying, "but nothing like my ain house—give me one turn more!"

On Monday he remained in bed, and seemed extremely feeble; but after breakfast on Tuesday the 17th he appeared revived some- what, and was again wheeled about on the turf. Presently he fell asleep in his chair, and after dozing for perhaps half an hour, started awake, and shaking the plaids we had put about him from off his shoulders, said—"This is sad idleness. I shall forget what I have been thinking of, if I don't set it down now. Take me into my own room, and fetch the keys of my desk." He repeated this so earnestly, that we could not refuse; his daughters went into his study, opened his writing-desk, and laid paper and pens in the usual order, and I then moved him through the hall and into the spot where he had always been accustomed to work. When the chair was placed at the desk, and he found himself in the old posi- tion, he smiled and thanked us, and said—"Now give me my pen, and leave me for a little to myself." Sophia put the pen into his

hand, and he endeavoured to close his fingers upon it, but they refused their office—it dropped on the paper. He sank back among
his pillows, silent tears rolling down his cheeks; but composing
himself by and by, motioned to me to wheel him out of doors
again. Laidlaw met us at the porch, and took his turn of the chair.
Sir Walter, after a little while, again dropped into slumber. When
he was awaking, Laidlaw said to me—"Sir Walter has had a little
repose."—"No, Willie," said he—"no repose for Sir Walter but
in the grave." . . .

After this he declined daily, but still there was great strength
to be wasted, and the process was long. He seemed, however, to
suffer no bodily pain; and his mind, though hopelessly obscured,
appeared, when there was any symptom of consciousness, to be
dwelling, with rare exceptions, on serious and solemn things; the
accent of the voice grave, sometimes awful, but never querulous,
and very seldom indicative of any angry or resentful thoughts.
Now and then he imagined himself to be administering justice as
Sheriff; and once or twice he seemed to be ordering Tom Purdie
about trees. A few times also, I am sorry to say, we could perceive that his fancy was at Jedburgh—and Burk Sir Walter escaped
him in a melancholy tone.

As I was dressing on the morning of Monday the 17th of September, Nicolson came into my room, and told me that his master
had awoke in a state of composure and consciousness, and wished
to see me immediately. I found him entirely himself, though in
the last extreme of feebleness. His eye was clear and calm—every
trace of the wild fire of delirium extinguished. "Lockhart," he
said, "I may have but a minute to speak to you. My dear, be a
good man—be virtuous—be religious—be a good man. Nothing
else will give you any comfort when you come to lie here."—
He paused, and I said—"Shall I send for Sophia and Anne?"—
"No," said he, "don't disturb them. Poor souls! I know they were
up all night—God bless you all."—With this he sunk into a very
tranquil sleep, and, indeed, he scarcely afterwards gave any sign
of consciousness, except for an instant on the arrival of his sons.

They, on learning that the scene was about to close, obtained
anew leave of absence from their posts, and both reached Abbots-

ford on the 19th. About half-past one p.m. on the 21st of September, Sir Walter breathed his last, in the presence of all his children. It was a beautiful day—so warm, that every window was wide open—and so perfectly still, that the sound of all others most delicious to his ear, the gentle ripple of the Tweed over its pebbles, was distinctly audible as we knelt around the bed, and his eldest son kissed and closed his eyes. No sculptor ever modelled a more majestic image of repose.

ANARCHIST

THOREAU, THE GENTLE POET AND LOVER OF NATURE, IS A FAMILIAR and somewhat sentimental figure. Not so familiar, but much more vital, is Thoreau, the anarchist and rebel. Thoreau's retirement to Walden Pond was not a timid retreat from the onslaughts of a brutal world. It was a criticism and an experiment. It was a criticism of the pushing commercial spirit, the enslavement to possessions, the dominion of material aims that was riding mankind. "Things are in the saddle," Emerson exclaimed: greed dulling the sun with factory smoke, bending men into question marks in counting-houses, burying them beneath a pyramid of gold. Meanwhile Thoreau was quietly saying to himself that he would not be owned by a mansion with crystal chandeliers or forced to pull a coach-and-four. To see whether his determination was practical he reduced his needs to a minimum. He would live by himself and by his own exertions, in the simplest way, so only that he had leisure to live in his mind and integrity to use it as he chose. With the two-years' experiment of Walden he proved his freedom from an intolerable burden of illusory needs.

He was not a solitary or a misanthrope. A neighboring farmer would turn up now and then for a social "crack." Friends trudged to the tiny cabin even through the winter snows, and made its walls "ring with boisterous mirth" in intervals of whittling "some shingles of thought well dried." If he is sometimes disdainful of other men, his scorn is less for them than for the ropes of sand they bind themselves in, the husks they mistake for nectar of the spirit. But he would not build his own life upon the exploitation of others, even though he thought his aims worthier than theirs. "If I devote myself to other thoughts and contemplations," he said, "I must first see, at least, that I do not pursue them sitting upon another man's shoulders. I must get off him first, so that he may pursue his own contemplations, too."

At its most intense, Thoreau's rebellion flamed into fiery anarchy. He would not yield his obedience to a government that demanded the return of fugitive slaves; he would not surrender a single penny in taxes to aid imperialist aggression against Mexico. He denied the right of any government, whether minority or majority, to make him a party to legalized plunder and murder. It might take him and break him, because it was physically strong. It could not make him its tool. But Thoreau's anarchy was no rigid, hard-and-fast system. He had no quarrel with government as such. The state might have his pennies for useful or harmless enterprises, like building roads, even for nonsense or extravagance. "He simply asked not to be made accessory to legalized crime."

There are times, even in the quiet serenity of *Walden,* where Thoreau's scorn rings out like a clarion; in the essay on *Civil Disobedience* it is a tocsin of revolt. But Thoreau was not one of your angry and humorless professional revolutionaries. His indignation could be strong for others; he didn't keep it on the boil for himself. When they jailed him for refusing on principle to pay his poll tax, he made no martyrdom out of it, but wrote, as John Macy remarks, "five drily humorous pages, about *My Prisons,* in which legal contrivances are made to look not merely oppressive but ridiculous . . . A man of humour, one might think, would be ashamed to appear on a street in Thoreau's town in blue uniform with a star on his breast, lest Thoreau emerge suddenly from the woods and contemplate the insignia of authority with a faintly acid smile." Nor is he incapable of turning that twinkle against himself and his own theories. When he was furnishing his hut, Thoreau tells us, a lady offered him a mat for his door. He refused: "It is best," he says demurely, "to avoid the beginnings of evil."

Here is the man in his own words. "This is how I lived," he tells us, "and this is what I lived for." He believed that building a splendid house is less important than building a good man to live in it. A great many gimcracks, he found, were unimportant when you really tried to build one.

Walden

HENRY DAVID THOREAU

[Thoreau was born in Concord, Massachusetts, in 1817, and died there in 1862. *Walden* was published in 1854.]

WHEN I WROTE THE FOLLOWING PAGES, OR RATHER THE BULK OF them, I lived alone, in the woods, a mile from any neighbor, in a house which I had built myself, on the shore of Walden Pond, in Concord, Massachusetts, and earned my living by the labor of my hands only. I lived there two years and two months. At present I am a sojourner in civilized life again.

I should not obtrude my affairs so much on the notice of my readers if very particular inquiries had not been made by my townsmen concerning my mode of life, which some would call impertinent, though they do not appear to me at all impertinent, but, considering the circumstances, very natural and pertinent. Some have asked what I got to eat; if I did not feel lonesome; if I was not afraid; and the like. Others have been curious to learn what portion of my income I devoted to charitable purposes; and some, who have large families, how many poor children I maintained. I will therefore ask those of my readers who feel no particular interest in me to pardon me if I undertake to answer some of these questions in this book. . . .

I have travelled a good deal in Concord; and everywhere, in shops, and offices, and fields, the inhabitants have appeared to me to be doing penance in a thousand remarkable ways. . . . I see young men, my townsmen, whose misfortune it is to have inherited

farms, houses, barns, cattle, and farming tools; for these are more
easily acquired than got rid of. Better if they had been born in
the open pasture and suckled by a wolf, that they might have seen
with clearer eyes what field they were called to labor in. Who
made them serfs of the soil? Why should they eat their sixty acres,
when man is condemned to eat only his peck of dirt? Why should
they begin digging their graves as soon as they are born? They
have got to live a man's life, pushing all these things before them,
and get on as well as they can. How many a poor immortal soul
have I met well-nigh crushed and smothered under its load, creeping down the road of life, pushing before it a barn seventy-five feet
by forty, its Augean stables never cleansed, and one hundred acres
of land, tillage, mowing, pasture, and wood-lot! The portionless,
who struggle with no such unnecessary inherited encumbrances,
find it labor enough to subdue and cultivate a few cubic feet of
flesh.

But men labor under a mistake. The better part of the man is
soon plowed into the soil for compost. By a seeming fate, commonly called necessity, they are employed, as it says in an old book,
laying up treasures which moth and rust will corrupt and thieves
break through and steal. It is a fool's life, as they will find when
they get to the end of it, if not before . . .

I have no doubt that some of you who read this book are unable
to pay for all the dinners which you have actually eaten, or for the
coats and shoes which are fast wearing or are already worn out,
and have come to this page to spend borrowed or stolen time,
robbing your creditors of an hour. It is very evident what mean
and sneaking lives many of you live, for my sight has been whetted
by experience; always on the limits, trying to get into business and
trying to get out of debt, a very ancient slough, called by the Latins
aes alienum, another's brass, for some of their coins were made of
brass; still living, and dying, and buried by this other's brass;
always promising to pay, promising to pay, to-morrow, and dying
to-day, insolvent; seeking to curry favor, to get custom, by how
many modes, only not state-prison offences; lying, flattering, voting, contracting yourselves into a nutshell of civility, or dilating
into an atmosphere of thin and vaporous generosity, that you may

persuade your neighbor to let you make his shoes, or his hat, or his coat, or his carriage, or import his groceries for him; making yourselves sick, that you may lay up something against a sick day, something to be tucked away in an old chest, or in a stocking behind the plastering, or, more safely, in the brick bank; no matter where, no matter how much or how little . . .

The mass of men lead lives of quiet desperation. What is called resignation is confirmed desperation. From the desperate city you go into the desperate country, and have to console yourself with the bravery of minks and muskrats. A stereotyped but unconscious despair is concealed even under what are called the games and amusements of mankind. There is no play in them, for this comes after work. But it is a characteristic of wisdom not to do desperate things. . . .

It is never too late to give up our prejudices. . . . What old people say you cannot do, you try and find that you can. . . .

I have lived some thirty years on this planet, and I have yet to hear the first syllable of valuable or even earnest advice from my seniors. . . .

One farmer says to me, "You cannot live on vegetable food solely, for it furnishes nothing to make bones with;" and so he religiously devotes a part of his day to supplying his system with the raw material of bones; walking all the while he talks behind his oxen, which, with vegetable-made bones, jerk him and his lumbering plow along in spite of every obstacle. Some things are really necessaries of life in some circles, the most helpless and diseased, which in others are luxuries merely, and in others still are entirely unknown. . . . Let us consider for a moment what most of the trouble and anxiety which I have referred to is about, and how much it is necessary that we be troubled, or at least careful. . . . By the words, necessaries of life, I mean whatever, of all that man obtains by his own exertions, has been from the first, or from long use has become, so important to human life that few, if any, whether from savageness, or poverty, or philosophy, ever attempt to do without it. . . . The necessaries of life for man in this climate may, accurately enough, be distributed under the several heads of Food, Shelter, Clothing, and Fuel; for not till we have secured these are we prepared to entertain the true problems of life with freedom and a prospect of success. . . .

At the present day, and in this country, as I find by my own experience, a few implements, a knife, an axe, a spade, a wheelbarrow, etc., and for the studious, lamplight, stationery, and access to a few books, rank next to necessaries, and can all be obtained at a trifling cost.

Near the end of March, 1845, I borrowed an axe and went down to the woods by Walden Pond, nearest to where I intended to build my house, and began to cut down some tall, arrowy white pines, still in their youth, for timber. It is difficult to begin without borrowing, but perhaps it is the most generous course thus to permit your fellow-men to have an interest in your enterprise. The owner of the axe, as he released his hold on it, said that it was the apple of his eye; but I returned it sharper than I received it. . . .

I hewed the main timbers six inches square, most of the studs on two sides only, and the rafters and floor timbers on one side, leaving the rest of the bark on, so that they were just as straight and much stronger than sawed ones. Each stick was carefully mortised or tenoned by its stump, for I had borrowed other tools by this time. My days in the woods were not very long ones; yet I usually carried my dinner of bread and butter, and read the newspaper in which it was wrapped, at noon, sitting amid the green pine boughs which I had cut off, and to my bread was imparted some of their fragrance, for my hands were covered with a thick coat of pitch. Before I had done I was more the friend than the foe of the pine tree, though I had cut down some of them, having become better acquainted with it. Sometimes a rambler in the wood was attracted by the sound of my axe, and we chatted pleasantly over the chips which I had made.

By the middle of April, for I made no haste in my work, but rather made the most of it, my house was framed and ready for the raising. I had already bought the shanty of James Collins, an Irishman who worked on the Fitchburg Railroad, for boards. . . . At six I passed him and his family on the road. One large bundle held their all,—bed, coffee-mill, looking-glass, hens,—all but the cat; she took to the woods and became a wild cat, and, as I learned afterward, trod in a trap set for woodchucks, and so became a dead cat at last.

I took down this dwelling the same morning, drawing the nails, and removed it to the pond-side by small cartloads, spreading the boards on the grass there to bleach and warp back again in the sun. . . .

I dug my cellar in the side of a hill sloping to the south, where a woodchuck had formerly dug his burrow, down through sumach and blackberry roots, and the lowest stain of vegetation, six feet square by seven deep, to a fine sand where potatoes would not freeze in any winter. The sides were left shelving, and not stoned; but the sun having never shone on them, the sand still keeps its place. It was but two hours' work. I took particular pleasure in this breaking of ground, for in almost all latitudes men dig into the earth for an equable temperature. Under the most splendid house in the city is still to be found the cellar where they store their roots as of old, and long after the superstructure has disappeared posterity remark its dent in the earth. The house is still but a sort of porch at the entrance of a burrow.

At length, in the beginning of May, with the help of some of my acquaintances, rather to improve so good an occasion for neighborliness than from any necessity, I set up the frame of my house . . . I began to occupy my house on the 4th of July, as soon as it was boarded and roofed, for the boards were carefully feather-edged and lapped, so that it was impervious to rain, but before boarding I laid the foundation of a chimney at one end, bringing two cartloads of stones up the hill from the pond in my arms. I built the chimney after my hoeing in the fall, before a fire became necessary for warmth, doing my cooking in the meanwhile out of doors on the ground, early in the morning: which mode I still think is in some respects more convenient and agreeable than the usual one.

Before winter I built a chimney, and shingled the sides of my house, which were already impervious to rain, with imperfect and sappy shingles made of the first slice of the log, whose edges I was obliged to straighten with a plane.

I have thus a tight shingled and plastered house, ten feet wide by fifteen long, and eight-feet posts, with a garret and a closet, a large window on each side, two trap-doors, one door at the end, and a brick fireplace opposite. The exact cost of my house, paying the usual price for such materials as I used, but not counting the work, all of which was done by myself, was as follows; and I give the details because very few are able to tell exactly what their houses cost, and fewer still, if any, the separate cost of the various materials which compose them:—

Boards	$8.03½,	mostly shanty boards.
Refuse shingles for roof and sides	4.00	
Laths	1.25	
Two second-hand windows with glass	2.43	
One thousand old brick . . .	4.00	
Two casks of lime	2.40	That was high.
Hair	0.31	More than I needed.
Mantle-tree iron	0.15	
Nails	3.90	
Hinges and screws	0.14	
Latch	0.10	
Chalk	0.01	
Transportation	1.40	{ I carried a good part on my back
In all	$28.12½	

These are all the materials excepting the timber, stones, and sand, which I claimed by squatter's right. I have also a small woodshed adjoining, made chiefly of stuff which was left after building the house.

I intend to build me a house which will surpass any on the main street in Concord in grandeur and luxury, as soon as it pleases me as much and will cost me no more than my present one.

I thus found that a student who wishes for a shelter can obtain one for a lifetime at an expense not greater than the rent which he now pays annually. If I seem to boast more than is becoming, my excuse is that I brag for humanity rather than for myself; and my shortcomings and inconsistencies do not affect the truth of my statement.

Before I finished my house, wishing to earn ten or twelve dollars by some honest and agreeable method, in order to meet my unusual expenses, I planted about two acres and a half of light and sandy soil near it chiefly with beans, but also a small part with potatoes, corn, peas, and turnips. The whole lot contains eleven acres, mostly growing up to pines and hickories, and was sold the preceding season for eight dollars and eight cents an acre. One farmer said that it was "good for nothing but to raise cheeping squirrels on." I put no manure whatever on this land, not being the owner, but merely a squatter, and not expecting to cultivate so much again, and I did not quite hoe it all once. I got out several cords of stumps in plowing, which supplied me with fuel for a long time, and left small circles of virgin mould, easily distinguishable through the summer by the greater luxuriance of the beans there. The dead and for the most part unmerchantable wood behind my house, and the driftwood from the pond, have supplied the remainder of my fuel. I was obliged to hire a team and a man for the plowing, though I held the plow myself. My farm outgoes for the first season were, for implements, seed, work, etc., $14.72½. The seed corn was given me. This never costs anything to speak of unless you plant more than enough. I got twelve bushels of beans, and eighteen bushels of potatoes, beside some peas and sweet corn. The yellow corn and turnips were too late to come to anything. My whole income from the farm was

$$
\begin{array}{lr}
 & \$23.44 \\
\text{Deducting the outgoes} \quad . \quad . \quad . & 14.72\frac{1}{2} \\
\hline
\text{There are left} \quad . \quad . \quad . \quad . \quad . & \$8.71\frac{1}{2},
\end{array}
$$

beside produce consumed and on hand at the time this estimate was made of the value of $4.50,—the amount on hand much more than balancing a little grass which I did not raise. All things considered, that is, considering the importance of a man's soul and of to-day, notwithstanding the short time occupied by my experiment, nay, partly even because of its transient character, I believe that that was doing better than any farmer in Concord did that year.

The next year I did better still, for I spaded up all the land which I required, about a third of an acre, and I learned from the experience of both years, not being in the least awed by many celebrated works on husbandry, Arthur Young among the rest, that if one would live simply and eat only the crop which he raised, and raise no more than he ate, and not exchange it for an insuf-ficient quantity of more luxurious and expensive things, he would need to cultivate only a few rods of ground, and that it would be cheaper to spade up that than to use oxen to plow it, and to select a fresh spot from time to time than to manure the old, and he could do all his necessary farm work as it were with his left hand at odd hours in the summer; and thus he would not be tied to an ox, or horse, or cow, or pig, as at present. . . .

I am wont to think that men are not so much the keepers of herds as herds are the keepers of men, the former are so much the freer. Men and oxen exchange work; but if we consider necessary work only, the oxen will be seen to have greatly the advantage, their farm is so much the larger. Man does some of his part of the exchange work in his six weeks of haying, and it is no boy's play. Certainly no nation that lived simply in all respects, that is, no nation of philosophers, would commit so great a blunder as to use the labor of animals. True, there never was and is not likely soon to be a nation of philosophers, nor am I certain it is desirable that there should be. However, *I* should never have broken a horse or bull and taken him to board for any work he might do for me, for fear I should become a horse-man or a herdsman merely; and if society seems to be the gainer by so doing, are we certain that what is one man's gain is not another's loss, and that the stable-boy has equal cause with his master to be satisfied? Granted that some public works would not have been constructed without this aid, and let man share the glory of such with the ox and horse; does it follow that he could not have accomplished works yet more worthy of himself in that case? When men begin to do, not merely

unnecessary or artistic, but luxurious and idle work, with their
assistance, it is inevitable that a few do all the exchange work with
the oxen, or, in other words, become the slaves of the strongest. . . .

By surveying, carpentry, and day-labor of various other kinds in
the village in the meanwhile, for I have as many trades as fingers,
I had earned $13.34. The expense of food for eight months,
namely, from July 4th to March 1st, the time when these estimates
were made, though I lived there more than two years,—not counting potatoes, a little green corn, and some peas, which I had raised,
nor considering the value of what was on hand at the last date,—
was

Rice	$1.73½	
Molasses	1.73	Cheapest form of the saccharine.
Rye meal	1.04¾	
Indian meal	0.99¾	Cheaper than rye.
Pork	0.22	
Flour	0.88	Costs more than Indian meal, both money and trouble.
Sugar	0.80	
Lard	0.65	
Apples	0.25	
Dried apple	0.22	
Sweet potatoes	0.10	
One pumpkin	0.06	
One watermelon	0.02	
Salt	0.03	

All experiments which failed.

Yes, I did eat $8.74, all told; but I should not thus unblushingly
publish my guilt, if I did not know that most of my readers were
equally guilty with myself, and that their deeds would look no
better in print. The next year I sometimes caught a mess of fish
for my dinner, and once I went so far as to slaughter a woodchuck
which ravaged my bean-field,—effect his transmigration, as a
Tartar would say,—and devour him, partly for experiment's sake;
but though it afforded me a momentary enjoyment, notwithstand-

ing a musky flavor, I saw that the longest use would not make that a good practice, however it might seem to have your woodchucks ready dressed by the village butcher.

Clothing and some incidental expenses within the same dates, though little can be inferred from this item, amounted to

$$\$8.40\tfrac{3}{4}$$

Oil and some household utensils .   2.00

So that all the pecuniary outgoes, excepting for washing and mending, which for the most part were done out of the house, and their bills have not yet been received,—and these are all and more than all the ways by which money necessarily goes out in this part of the world,—were

House	$28.12½
Farm one year	14.72½
Food eight months	8.74
Clothing, etc., eight months . .	8.40¾
Oil, etc., eight months	2.00
In all	$61.99¾

I address myself now to those of my readers who have a living to get. And to meet this I have for farm produce sold

	$23.44
Earned by day-labor	13.34
In all	$36.78,

which subtracted from the sum of the outgoes leaves a balance of $25.21¾ on the one side,—this being very nearly the means with which I started, and the measure of expenses to be incurred,—and on the other, beside the leisure and independence and health thus secured, a comfortable house for me as long as I choose to occupy it.

My furniture, part of which I made myself,—and the rest cost me nothing of which I have not rendered an account,—consisted of a bed, a table, a desk, three chairs, a looking-glass three inches in diameter, a pair of tongs and andirons, a kettle, a skillet, and a frying-pan, a dipper, a wash-bowl, two knives and forks, three plates, one cup, one spoon, a jug for oil, a jug for molasses, and a japanned lamp. None is so poor that he need sit on a pumpkin. That is shiftlessness. There is a plenty of such chairs as I like best in the village garrets to be had for taking them away. Furniture! Thank God, I can sit and I can stand without the aid of a furniture warehouse. . . .

I would observe, by the way, that it costs me nothing for curtains, for I have no gazers to shut out but the sun and moon, and I am willing that they should look in. The moon will not sour milk nor taint meat of mine, nor will the sun injure my furniture or fade my carpet; and if he is sometimes too warm a friend, I find it still better economy to retreat behind some curtain which nature has provided, than to add a single item to the details of housekeeping. A lady once offered me a mat, but as I had no room to spare within the house, nor time to spare within or without to shake it, I declined it, preferring to wipe my feet on the sod before my door. It is best to avoid the beginnings of evil.

For more than five years I maintained myself thus solely by the labor of my hands, and I found that, by working about six weeks in a year, I could meet all the expenses of living. The whole of my winters, as well as most of my summers, I had free and clear for study. . . .

In short, I am convinced, both by faith and experience, that to maintain one's self on this earth is not a hardship but a pastime, if we will live simply and wisely; as the pursuits of the simpler nations are still the sports of the more artificial. . . .

I went to the woods because I wished to live deliberately, to front only the essential facts of life, and see if I could not learn what it had to teach, and not, when I came to die, discover that I had not lived. I did not wish to live what was not life, living is so dear; nor did I wish to practise resignation, unless it was quite necessary. I wanted to live deep and suck out all the marrow of life, to live so sturdily and Spartan-like as to put to rout all that was not life, to cut a broad swath and shave close, to drive life into a corner, and reduce it to its lowest terms, and, if it proved to be mean, why then to get the whole and genuine meanness of it, and publish its meanness to the world; or if it were sublime, to know it by experience, and be able to give a true account of it in my next excursion. For most men, it appears to me, are in a strange uncertainty about it, whether it is of the devil or of God, and have somewhat hastily concluded that it is the chief end of man here to "glorify God and enjoy him forever."

Still we live meanly, like ants; though the fable tells us that we were long ago changed into men; like pygmies we fight with cranes; it is error upon error, and clout upon clout, and our best virtue has for its occasion a superfluous and evitable wretchedness. Our life is frittered away by detail. An honest man has hardly need to count more than his ten fingers, or in extreme cases he may add his ten toes, and lump the rest. Simplicity, simplicity, simplicity! I say, let your affairs be as two or three, and not a hundred or a thousand; instead of a million count half a dozen, and keep your accounts on your thumb-nail. In the midst of this chopping sea of civilized life, such are the clouds and storms and quicksands and thousand-and-one items to be allowed for, that a man has to live, if he would not founder and go to the bottom and not make his port at all, by dead reckoning, and he must be a great calculator indeed who succeeds. Simplify, simplify.

I left the woods for as good a reason as I went there. . . . I learned this, at least, by my experiment: that if one advances confidently in the direction of his dreams, and endeavors to live the life which he has imagined, he will meet with a success unexpected in common hours. He will put some things behind, will pass an invisible boundary; new, universal, and more liberal laws will begin to establish themselves around and within him; or the old laws be expanded, and interpreted in his favor in a more liberal sense, and he will live with the license of a higher order of beings. In proportion as he simplifies his life, the laws of the universe will appear less complex, and solitude will not be solitude, nor poverty poverty, nor weakness weakness. If you have built castles in the air, your work need not be lost; that is where they should be. Now put the foundations under them.

WHIG HISTORIAN

THE AGE THAT THOREAU HAD SCORNFULLY REJECTED, THE AGE whose industrial horrors had wrung the heart of Scott, found in Thomas Babington Macaulay its spokesman and apologist. He was a middle-class intellectual in a day when the middle class was dominant. A Whig, from the moment he entered politics he rode on the triumphant crest of liberalism and reform. With all the ardors of the battle he combined the refreshing certitude of being not only right but destined to succeed.

Like his age, he looked with complacency on its material progress, and exulted with the manufacturers of Manchester and Birmingham on the miles of steel rails that were covering England and the bolts of cotton that were pouring off its looms. He shared the insular conviction of other Englishmen that in the concert of nations God meant the voice of England to be paramount. No doubt entered his mind but that the backward portions of the world were the white man's burden. His judgments were dogmatic and sweeping, but he defended them with courage. Loud and impregnable on the surface, he concealed within himself a sentimental susceptibility that was the other face of Victorian hard-headedness and practicality.

His life was of a piece with the character of the age. Everyone knows the splendid public career marching from victory to victory unstained by a single shadow of failure, and crowned in harvest maturity with the honors of the man of letters and historian. "One of the happiest lives that it has ever fallen to the lot of a biographer to record," is Trevelyan's valediction. Indeed it had been like that of a fairy-tale Prince. The brambled wood had parted before his confident progress as if it were melting; the glass mountain to be scaled he had chugged up as if he were one of the newly invented locomotives with pistons pounding. There had never been a Princesse Lointaine, but Macaulay had not noticed. Never disappointed in his affections, brilliant, confident, acclaimed—what more could be asked? Perhaps it is hypercritical to find a flaw, to insinuate that Prince Charming, from long-continued triumph, became too self-assured, came to lack a certain delicacy and shading.

But looked at more sharply, the metallic surface sometimes seems an armor. There is a boyishness in Macaulay that overflows in noisy games of hide-and-seek with nephews and nieces, in the invention of extemporaneous ballads all of which he gravely attributed to an anonymity styled "the Judicious Poet," in all sorts of high jinks and jokes. But there is a sort of boyish pathos as well: his emotional life was completely and dependently centered upon his family, and was tremulous in its sensitivity. He could weep with a child's despair at the prospect of being parted from a beloved sister. His public life was earnest with the earnestness of a boy playing a game, all hammer blows, action, no nuance, a young prodigy pouring out a flood of vehement language, remorseless and undeviating. But all was tenderness within.

Trevelyan's biography follows the trail blazed by Boswell and Lockhart. "It takes two to give excellence to any man's *Life and Letters:* the author of the *Life* and the author of the *Letters . . .*" Macaulay's nephew, the son of his best-loved sister, contributes a clear, well-proportioned, and well-arranged narrative; its intimate and affectionate grasp of character is not clouded by idolatry. Macaulay, although not among the greatest of all letter-writers, is sparkling, vigorous, interesting, and clear. Between the two, they produce a triumph of the life-and-letters method.

The Life and Letters of Lord Macaulay

GEORGE OTTO TREVELYAN

[Macaulay died in 1859. The *Life* was first published
in two volumes in 1876.]

WHEN MRS. MACAULAY WAS NEAR HER CONFINEMENT, MRS. BABING-
ton, who belonged to the school of matrons who hold that the advantage of country air outweighs that of London doctors, invited
her sister-in-law to Rothley Temple; and there, in a room panelled
from ceiling to floor, like every corner of the ancient mansion,
with oak almost black from age,—looking eastward across the park,
and southward through an ivy-shaded window into a little garden,
—Lord Macaulay was born. It was on the 25th of October 1800,
the day of St. Crispin, the anniversay of Agincourt, (as he liked
to say,) that he opened his eyes on a world which he was destined
so thoroughly to learn and so intensely to enjoy.

His father was as pleased as a father could be; but fate seemed
determined that Zachary Macaulay should not be indulged in any
great share of personal happiness. The next morning the noise of
a spinning-jenny, at work in a cottage, startled his horse as he was
riding past. He was thrown, and both arms were broken; and he
spent in a sick-room the remainder of the only holiday worth the
name which, (as far as can be traced in the family records,) he
ever took during his married life. Owing to this accident the
young couple were detained at Rothley into the winter; and the
child was baptised in the private chapel which formed part of the
house, on the 26th November, 1800, by the names of Thomas

Babington:—the Rev. Aulay Macaulay, and Mr. and Mrs. Babington, acting as sponsors.

The two years which followed were passed in a house in Birchin Lane, where the Sierra Leone Company had its office. The only place where the child could be taken for exercise, and what might be called air, was Drapers' Gardens, which (already under sentence to be covered with bricks and mortar at an early date) lies behind Throgmorton Street, and within a hundred yards of the Stock Exchange. To this dismal yard containing as much gravel as grass, and frowned upon by a board of Rules and Regulations almost as large as itself, his mother used to convoy the nurse and the little boy through the crowds that towards noon swarmed along Cornhill and Threadneedle Street; and thither she would return after a due interval, to escort them back to Birchin Lane. So strong was the power of association upon Macaulay's mind that in after years Drapers' Garden was among his favourite haunts. Indeed, his habit of roaming for hours through and through the heart of the City, (a habit that never left him as long as he could roam at all,) was due in part to the recollections which caused him to regard that region as native ground.

Baby as he was when he quitted it, he retained some impression of his earliest home. He remembered standing up at the nursery window by his father's side, looking at a cloud of black smoke pouring out of a tall chimney. He asked if that was hell; an inquiry that was received with a grave displeasure which at the time he could not understand. The kindly father must have been pained, almost against his own will, at finding what feature of his creed it was that had embodied itself in so very material a shape before his little son's imagination. When in after days Mrs. Macaulay was questioned as to how soon she began to detect in the child a promise of the future, she used to say that his sensibilities and affections were remarkably developed at an age which to her hearers appeared next to incredible. He would cry for joy on seeing her after a few hours' absence, and, (till her husband put a stop to it,) her power of exciting his feelings was often made an exhibition to her friends. She did not regard this precocity as a proof of cleverness; but, like a foolish young mother, only thought that so tender a nature was marked for early death.

The next move which the family made was into as healthy an atmosphere, in every sense, as the most careful parent could wish to select. Mr. Macaulay took a house in the High Street of Clapham, in the part now called the Pavement, on the same side as the Plough inn, but some doors nearer to the Common. It was a roomy comfortable dwelling, with a very small garden behind, and in front a very small one indeed, which has entirely disappeared beneath a large shop thrown out towards the roadway by the present occupier, who bears the name of Heywood. Here the boy passed a quiet and most happy childhood.

From the time that he was three years old he read incessantly, for the most part lying on the rug before the fire, with his book on the ground, and a piece of bread and butter in his hand. A very clever woman, who then lived in the house as parlour-maid, told how he used to sit in his nankeen frock, perched on the table by her as she was cleaning the plate, and expounding to her out of a volume as big as himself. He did not care for toys, but was very fond of taking his walk, when he would hold forth to his companion, whether nurse or mother, telling interminable stories out of his own head, or repeating what he had been reading in language far above his years. His memory retained without effort the phraseology of the book which he had been last engaged on, and he talked, as the maid said, "quite printed words," which produced an effect that appeared formal, and often, no doubt, exceedingly droll. Mrs. Hannah More was fond of relating how she called at Mr. Macaulay's, and was met by a fair, pretty, slight child, with abundance of light hair, about four years of age, who came to the front door to receive her, and tell her that his parents were out, but that if she would be good enough to come in he would bring her a glass of old spirits: a proposition which greatly startled the good lady, who had never aspired beyond cowslip wine. When questioned as to what he knew about old spirits, he could only say that Robinson Crusoe often had some.

About this period his father took him on a visit to Lady Waldegrave at Strawberry Hill, and was much pleased to exhibit to his old friend the fair bright boy, dressed in a green coat with red collar and cuffs, a frill at the throat, and white trousers. After some time had been spent among the wonders of the Orford Collection, of which he ever after carried a catalogue in his head, a servant who was waiting upon the company in the gallery spilt some hot coffee over his legs. The hostess was all kindness and compassion, and when, after a while, she asked how he was feeling, the little fellow looked up in her face and replied: "Thank you, madam, the agony is abated."

But it must not be supposed that his quaint manners proceeded from affectation or conceit; for all testimony declares that a more simple and natural child never lived, or a more lively and merry one. He had at his command the resources of the Common; to this day the most unchanged spot within ten miles of St. Paul's, and which to all appearance will ere long hold that pleasant pre-eminence within ten leagues. That delightful wilderness of gorse bushes, and poplar groves, and gravel-pits, and ponds great and small, was to little Tom Macaulay a region of inexhaustible romance and mystery. He explored its recesses; he composed, and almost believed, its legends; he invented for its different features a nomenclature which has been faithfully preserved by two generations of children. A slight ridge, intersected by deep ditches, towards the west of the Common, the very existence of which no one above eight years old would notice, was dignified with the title of the Alps; while the elevated island, covered with shrubs, that gives a name to the Mount pond, was regarded with infinite awe as being the nearest approach within the circuit of his observation to a conception of the majesty of Sinai. Indeed, at this period his infant fancy was much exercised with the threats and terrors of the Law. He had a little plot of ground at the back of the house, marked out as his own by a row of oyster-shells, which a maid one day threw away as rubbish. He went straight to the drawing-room, where his mother was entertaining some visitors, walked into the circle and said very solemnly: "Cursed be Sally; for it is written, Cursed is he that removeth his neighbour's land-mark."

While still the merest child he was sent as a day-scholar to Mr. Greaves, a shrewd Yorkshireman with a turn for science, who had been originally brought to the neighbourhood in order to educate a number of African youths sent over to imbibe Western civilisation at the fountain-head. The poor fellows had found as much difficulty in keeping alive at Clapham as Englishmen experience at Sierra Leone; and, in the end, their tutor set up a school for boys of his own colour, and at one time had charge of almost the entire rising generation of the Common. Mrs. Macaulay explained to Tom that he must learn to study without the solace of bread and butter, to which he replied: "Yes, mama, industry shall be my bread and attention my butter." But, as a matter of fact, no one ever crept more unwillingly to school. Each several afternoon he made piteous entreaties to be excused returning after dinner, and was met by the unvarying formula: "No, Tom, if it rains cats and dogs, you shall go."

In October 1818 Macaulay went into residence at Trinity College, Cambridge. Mr. Henry Sykes Thornton, the eldest son of the member for Southwark, was his companion throughout his university career. The young men lived in the same lodgings, and began by reading with the same tutor: a plan which promised well, because, in addition to what was his own by right, each had the benefit of the period of instruction paid for by the other. But two hours were much the same as one to Macaulay, in whose eyes algebra and geometry were so much additional material for lively and interminable argument. Thornton reluctantly broke through the arrangement, and eventually stood highest among the Trinity wranglers of his year: an elevation which he could hardly have attained if he had pursued his studies in company with one who regarded every successive mathematical proposition as an open question.

Macaulay's intense enjoyment of all that was stirring and vivid around him undoubtedly hindered him in the race for university honours; though his success was sufficient to inspirit him at the time, and to give him abiding pleasure in the retrospect. He twice gained the Chancellor's medal for English verse, with poems admirably planned, and containing passages of real beauty, but which may not be republished in the teeth of the panegyric which, within ten years after they were written, he pronounced upon Sir

Roger Newdigate. Sir Roger had laid down the rule that no exercise sent in for the prize which he established at Oxford was to exceed fifty lines. This law, says Macaulay, seems to have more foundation in reason than is generally the case with a literary canon, "for the world, we believe, is pretty well agreed in thinking that the shorter a prize poem is, the better."

Trinity men find it difficult to understand how it was that he missed getting one of the three silver goblets given for the best English Declamations of the year. If there is one thing which all Macaulay's friends, and all his enemies, admit, it is that he could declaim English. His own version of the affair was that the Senior Dean, a relative of the victorious candidate, sent for him and said: "Mr. Macaulay, as you have not got the first cup, I do not suppose that you will care for either of the others." He was consoled, however, by the prize for Latin Declamation; and in 1821 he established his classical repute by winning a Craven University scholarship in company with his friend Malden, and Mr. George Long, who preceded Malden as Professor of Greek at University College, London.

Macaulay detested the labour of manufacturing Greek and Latin verse in cold blood as an exercise; and his Hexameters were never up to the best Etonian mark, nor his Iambics to the highest standard of Shrewsbury. He defined a scholar as one who reads Plato with his feet on the fender. When already well on in his third year he writes: "I never practised composition a single hour since I have been at Cambridge." "Soak your mind with Cicero," was his constant advice to students, at that time of life when writing Latin prose is the most lucrative of accomplishments. The advantage of this precept was proved in the Fellowship examination of the year 1824, when he obtained the honour which in his eyes was the most desirable that Cambridge had to give. The delight of the young man at finding himself one of the sixty masters of an ancient and splendid establishment; the pride with which he signed his first order for the college plate, and dined for the first time at the high table in his own right; the reflection that these privileges were the fruit, not of favour or inheritance, but of personal industry and ability,—were matters on which he loved to dwell long after the world had loaded him with its most envied prizes.

"At Holland House, the other day," writes his sister Margaret in September 1831, "Tom met Lady Lyndhurst for the first time. She said to him: 'Mr. Macaulay, you are so different to what I expected. I thought you were dark and thin, but you are fair, and really, Mr. Macaulay, you are fat.'" He at all times sat and stood straight, full, and square; and in this respect Woolner, in the fine statue at Cambridge, has missed what was undoubtedly the most marked fact in his personal appearance. He dressed badly, but not cheaply. His clothes, though ill put on, were good, and his wardrobe was always enormously overstocked. Later in life he indulged himself in an apparently inexhaustible succession of handsome embroidered waistcoats, which he used to regard with much complacency. He was unhandy to a degree quite unexampled in the experience of all who knew him. When in the open air he wore perfectly new dark kid gloves, into the fingers of which he never succeeded in inserting his own more than half way. After he had sailed for India there were found in his chambers between fifty and sixty strops, hacked into strips and splinters, and razors without beginning or end. About the same period he hurt his hand, and was reduced to send for a barber. After the operation, he asked what was to pay. "Oh, Sir," said the man, "whatever you usually give the person who shaves you." "In that case," said Macaulay, "I should give you a great gash on each cheek."

The fun that went on in Great Ormond Street was of a jovial, and sometimes uproarious, description. Even when the family was by itself, the school-room and the drawing-room were full of young people; and friends and cousins flocked in numbers to a resort where so much merriment was perpetually on foot. There were seasons during the school holidays when the house overflowed with noise and frolic from morning to night; and Macaulay, who at any period of his life could literally spend whole days in playing with children, was master of the innocent revels. Games of hide-and-seek, that lasted for hours, with shouting and the blowing of horns up and down the stairs and through every room, were varied by ballads, which, like the Scalds of old, he composed during the act of recitation, while the others struck in with the chorus. He had no notion whatever of music, but an infallible ear for rhythm. His knack of improvisation he at all times exercised freely. The verses which he thus produced, and which he invariably attributed to an anonymous author whom he styled "the Judicious Poet," were exclusively for home consumption. Some of these effusions illustrate a sentiment in his disposition which was among the most decided, and the most frequently and loudly expressed. Macaulay was only too easily bored, and those whom he considered fools he by no means suffered gladly. He once amused his sisters by pouring out whole Iliads of extempore doggrel upon the head of an unfortunate country squire of their acquaintance, who had a habit of detaining people by the button, and who was especially addicted to the society of the higher order of clergy.

> "His Grace Archbishop Manners Sutton
> Could not keep on a single button.
> As for Right Reverend John of Chester,
> His waistcoats open at the breast are.
> Our friend has filled a mighty trunk
> With trophies torn from Doctor Monk,
> And he has really tattered foully
> The vestments of Archbishop Howley.
> No button could I late discern on
> The garments of Archbishop Vernon,
> And never had his fingers mercy
> Upon the garb of Bishop Percy.
> The buttons fly from Bishop Ryder
> Like corks that spring from bottled cyder,—"

and so on, throughout the entire bench.

When he was no more than twenty-five his essay on Milton in the Edinburgh Review *made him famous. The following year he was called to the Bar, and soon after was a Commissioner of Bankruptcy, with an income of £900 a year. On the very eve of the great Reform Bill agitation he entered Parliament.*

Parliament adjourned over Christmas; and on the 1st of March
1831 Lord John Russell introduced the Reform Bill amidst
breathless silence, which was at length broken by peals of contemptuous laughter from the Opposition benches, as he read the
list of the hundred and ten boroughs which were condemned to
partial or entire disfranchisement. Sir Robert Inglis led the attack
upon a measure that he characterised as Revolution in the guise
of a statute. Next morning as Sir Robert was walking into town
over Westminster Bridge, he told his companion that up to the
previous night he had been very anxious, but that his fears were
now at an end, inasmuch as the shock caused by the extravagance
of the ministerial proposals would infallibly bring the country to
its senses. On the evening of that day Macaulay made the first of
his Reform speeches. When he sat down the Speaker sent for him,
and told him that in all his prolonged experience he had never
seen the House in such a state of excitement. Even at this distance
of time it is impossible to read aloud the last thirty sentences without an emotion which suggests to the mind what must have been
their effect when declaimed by one who felt every word that he
spoke, in the midst of an assembly agitated by hopes and apprehensions such as living men have never known, or have long forgotten.

From the peroration of Macaulay's speech:

"Now, therefore, while everything at home and abroad fore-
bodes ruin to those who persist in a hopeless struggle against
the spirit of the age, now, while the crash of the proudest throne
of the Continent is still resounding in our ears, now, while the roof
of a British palace affords an ignominious shelter to the exiled
heir of forty kings, now, while we see on every side ancient institutions subverted, and great societies dissolved, now, while the heart
of England is still sound, now, while old feelings and old associations retain a power and a charm which may too soon pass away,
now, in this your accepted time, now, in this your day of salvation,
take counsel, not of prejudice, not of party spirit, not of the ignominious pride of a fatal consistency, but of history, of reason, of
the ages which are past, of the signs of this most portentous time.
Pronounce in a manner worthy of the expectation with which

this great debate has been anticipated, and of the long remembrance which it will leave behind. Renew the youth of the State. Save property, divided against itself. Save the multitude, endangered by its own ungovernable passions. Save the aristocracy, endangered by its own unpopular power. Save the greatest, the fairest, and most highly civilised community that ever existed, from calamities which may in a few days sweep away all the rich heritage of so many ages of wisdom and glory. The danger is terrible. The time is short. If this bill should be rejected, I pray to God that none of those who concur in rejecting it may ever remember their votes with unavailing remorse, amidst the wreck of laws, the confusion of ranks, the spoliation of property, and the dissolution of social order."

The Bill passed, Macaulay's office was reformed out of existence, but presently he was one of the Commissioners of the Board of Control, which represented the Crown in its relations to the East India Company. Samuel Rogers asked him to the celebrated breakfasts; he was invited to Holland House and made it echo to floods of informative conversation. Meanwhile reorganization of the India service was being pressed. Macaulay was asked to become a member of the Supreme Council which would govern the Eastern Empire. He wrote his favorite sister Hannah:

"The advantages are very great. It is a post of the highest dignity and consideration. The salary is ten thousand pounds a year. I am assured by persons who know Calcutta intimately, and who have themselves mixed in the highest circles and held the highest offices at that Presidency, that I may live in splendour there for five thousand a year, and may save the rest of the salary with the accruing interest. I may therefore hope to return to England at only thirty-nine, in the full vigour of life, with a fortune of thirty thousand pounds. A larger fortune I never desired. . . .

"I have never made more than two hundred a year by my pen. I could not support myself in comfort on less than five hundred: and I shall in all probability have many others to support. The prospects of our family are, if possible, darker than ever. . . .

"If, as I expect, this offer shall be made to me, will you go with

me? I know what a sacrifice I ask of you. I know how many dear
and precious ties you must, for a time, sunder. I know that the
splendour of the Indian Court, and the gaieties of that brilliant
society of which you would be one of the leading personages,
have no temptation for you. I can bribe you only by telling you
that, if you will go with me, I will love you better than I love you
now, if I can."

*In February, 1834, they set sail. In India Macaulay labored
assiduously. He had spent the voyage out in mastering the principles of jurisprudence, which had bored him as an advocate but
fired his imagination now that he had to take on the responsibili-
ties of the law-maker. As President of the Committee on Public
Instruction he outlined an entire system of education, began
vigorously to create the machinery for bringing it into existence,
and threw himself into the tasks of administration. Most of the
Indian Penal Code was his personal work.*

"This Code," writes Macaulay, "should not be a mere digest of
existing usages and regulations, but should comprise all the reforms which the Commission may think desirable. It should be
framed on two great principles,—the principle of suppressing crime
with the smallest possible amount of suffering, and the principle
of ascertaining truth at the smallest possible cost of time and
money . . ."

The most readable of all Digests, its pages are alive with illus-
trations drawn from history, from literature, and from the habits
and occurrences of everyday life. The offence of fabricating evidence is exemplified by a case which may easily be recognised as
that of Lady Macbeth and the grooms; and the offence of voluntary
culpable homicide by an imaginary incident of a pit covered with
sticks and turf, which irresistibly recalls a reminiscence of Jack
the Giant-killer. . . . And, on the question whether the severity
of a hurt should be considered in apportioning the punishment,
we are reminded of "examples which are universally known.
Harley was laid up more than twenty days by the wound which he
received from Guiscard"; while "the scratch which Damien gave to
Louis the Fifteenth was so slight that it was followed by no feverish

symptoms." Such a sanguine estimate of the diffusion of knowledge with regard to the details of ancient crimes could proceed from no pen but that of the writer who endowed schoolboys with the erudition of professors, and the talker who, when he poured forth the stores of his memory, began each of his disquisitions with the phrase, "don't you remember?"

"Pocket editions of these Codes are published," [wrote Macaulay's eminent successor, Mr. Fitzjames Stephen], "which may be carried about as easily as a pocket Bible; and I doubt whether, even in Scotland, you would find many people who know their Bibles as Indian civilians know their Codes."

From one of Macaulay's letters:
"The Rajah was by no means the greatest fool whom I found at Mysore. I alighted at a bungalow appertaining to the British Residency. There I found an Englishman who, without any preface, accosted me thus: 'Pray, Mr. Macaulay, do not you think that Buonaparte was the Beast?' 'No, Sir, I cannot say that I do.' 'Sir, he was the Beast. I can prove it. I have found the number 666 in his name. Why, Sir, if he was not the Beast, who was?' This was a puzzling question, and I am not a little vain of my answer. 'Sir,' said I, 'the House of Commons is the Beast. There are 658 members of the House; and these, with their chief officers, —the three clerks, the Sergeant and his deputy, the Chaplain, the doorkeeper, and the librarian,—make 666.' 'Well, Sir, that is strange. But I can assure you that, if you write Napoleon Buonaparte in Arabic, leaving out only two letters, it will give 666.' 'And pray, Sir, what right have you to leave out two letters? And, as St. John was writing Greek, and to Greeks, is it not likely that he would use the Greek rather than the Arabic notation?' 'But, Sir,' said this learned divine, 'everybody knows that the Greek letters were never used to mark numbers.' I answered with the meekest look and voice possible: 'I do not think that everybody knows that. Indeed I have reason to believe that a different opinion,—erroneous no doubt,—is universally embraced by all the small minority who happen to know any Greek.' So ended the controversy. The man looked at me as if he thought me a very

wicked fellow; and, I dare say, has by this time discovered that, if you write my name in Tamul, leaving out T in Thomas, B in Babington, and M in Macaulay, it will give the number of this unfortunate Beast."

In 1838 he left India for home. He entered Parliament again as member for Edinburgh. During Lord Melbourne's government he held the Secretaryship at War. But the defeat of the government in 1841 gave him the leisure he had desired for resuming his literary career. His Lays of Ancient Rome *appeared in 1842.*

The sails of the little craft could dispense with an artificial breeze. Launched without any noise of trumpets, it went bravely down the wind of popular favour. Among the first to discern its merits was Macaulay's ancient adversary, Professor Wilson of Edinburgh, who greeted it in *Blackwood's Magazine* with a pæan of hearty, unqualified panegyric; which was uttered with all the more zest because the veteran gladiator of the press recognised an opportunity for depreciating, by comparison with Macaulay, the reigning verse-writers of the day.

"What! Poetry from Macaulay? Ay, and why not? The House hushes itself to hear him, even though Stanley is the cry? If he be not the first of critics, (spare our blushes,) who is! Name the Young Poet who could have written the Armada. The Young Poets all want fire; Macaulay is full of fire. The Young Poets are somewhat weakly; he is strong. The Young Poets are rather ignorant; his knowledge is great. The Young Poets mumble books; he devours them. The Young Poets dally with their subject: he strikes its heart. The Young Poets are still their own heroes; he sees but the chiefs he celebrates. The Young Poets weave dreams with shadows transitory as clouds without substance; he builds realities lasting as rocks. The Young Poets steal from all and sundry, and deny their thefts; he robs in the face of day. Whom? Homer."

The course which Macaulay pursued between the years 1841 and 1846 deserves to be studied as a model of the conduct which becomes a statesman in opposition. In following that course he had a rare advantage. The continuous and absorbing labours of his History filled his mind and occupied his leisure, and relieved him from the craving for occupation and excitement that lies at the root of half the errors to which politicians out of office are prone;—errors which the popular judgment most unfairly attributes to lack of patriotism, or excess of gall.

From a speech on the endowment of Maynooth College (a Catholic institution) in 1844:

"When I think of the spacious and stately mansions of the heads of houses, of the commodious chambers of the fellows and scholars, of the refectories, the combination rooms, the bowling greens, the stabling, of the state and luxury of the great feast days, of the piles of old plate on the tables, of the savoury steam of the kitchens, of the multitude of geese and capons which turn at once on the spits, of the oceans of excellent ale in the butteries; and when I remember from whom all this splendour and plenty is derived; when I remember what was the faith of Edward the Third and of Henry the Sixth, of Margaret of Anjou and Margaret of Richmond, of William of Wykeham and William of Waynefleet, of Archbishop Chicheley and Cardinal Wolsey; when I remember what we have taken from the Roman Catholics,—King's College, New College, Christ Church, my own Trinity; and when I look at the miserable Dotheboys Hall which we have given them in exchange, I feel, I must own, less proud than I could wish of being a Protestant and a Cambridge man."

From a speech on the Ten Hour Bill, limiting the hours of factory labor, in 1846:

"Man, man is the great instrument that produces wealth. The natural difference between Campania and Spitzbergen is trifling when compared with the difference between a country inhabited by men full of bodily and mental vigour, and a country inhabited by men sunk in bodily and mental decrepitude. Therefore it is that we are not poorer but richer, because we have, through many ages, rested from our labour one day in seven. That day is not lost. While industry is suspended, while the plough lies in the furrow, while the Exchange is silent, while no smoke ascends from the factory, a process is going on quite as important to the wealth of nations as any process which is performed on more busy days. Man, the machine of machines, the machine compared with which all the contrivances of the Watts and the Arkwrights are worthless, is repairing and winding up, so that he returns to his labours on the Monday with clearer intellect, with livelier spirits, with renewed corporal vigour. Never will I believe that what makes a population stronger, and healthier, and wiser, and better, can ultimately make it poorer. You try to frighten us by telling us that, in some German factories, the young work seventeen hours in the twenty-four; that they work so hard that among thousands there is not one who grows to such a stature that he can be admitted into the army; and you ask whether, if we pass this bill, we can possibly hold our own against such competition as this. Sir, I laugh at the thought of such competition. If ever we are forced to yield the foremost place among commercial nations, we shall yield it, not to a race of degenerate dwarfs, but to some people pre-eminently vigorous in body and mind."

Meanwhile he continued the monumental labors of his History.

"I am working intensely, and, I hope, not unsuccessfully. My third chapter, which is the most difficult part of my task, is done, and, I think, not ill done." Any one who will turn to the description of the town of Leeds, and will read the six paragraphs that precede it, and the three that follow it, may form a conception of the pains which those clear and flowing periods must have cost an author who expended on the pointing of a phrase as much conscientious research as would have provided some writers, who speak of Macaulay as showy and shallow, with at least half a dozen pages of ostentatious statistics. . . .

"I read," he says in December 1849, "a portion of my History to Hannah and Trevelyan with great effect. Hannah cried, and Trevelyan kept awake." . . .

"The state of my own mind is this: when I compare my book with what I imagine history ought to be, I feel dejected and ashamed; but when I compare it with some histories which have a high repute, I feel reassured."

He might have spared his fears. Within three days after its first appearance the fortune of the book was already secure. It was greeted by an ebullition of national pride and satisfaction which delighted Macaulay's friends, and reconciled him to most who remained of his old political adversaries. . . .

"My dear Macaulay," says Lord Jeffrey, "the mother that bore you, had she been yet alive, could scarcely have felt prouder or happier than I do at this outburst of your graver fame. I have long had a sort of parental interest in your glory; and it is now mingled with a feeling of deference to your intellectual superiority which can only consort, I take it, with the character of a female parent.". . .

At Dukinfield, near Manchester, a gentleman, who thought that there would be a certain selfishness in keeping so great a pleasure to himself, invited his poorer neighbours to attend every evening after their work was finished, and read the History aloud to them from beginning to end. At the close of the last meeting, one of the audience rose, and moved, in north-country fashion, a vote of thanks to Mr. Macaulay, "for having written a history which working men can understand." . . .

"*December* 4, 1848.—Stayed at home all the day, making corrections for the second edition. Shaw, the printer, came to tell me that they are wanted with speed, and that the first edition of 3,000 is nearly out. Then I read the eighth book of Thucydides. On the whole he is the first of historians.

"*December* 12, 1848.—Longman called. A new edition of 3,000 copies is preparing as fast as they can work. I have reason to be pleased. Of the *Lay of the Last Minstrel* two thousand two hundred and fifty copies were sold in the first year; of *Marmion* two thousand copies in the first month; of my book three thousand copies in ten days. Black says that there has been no such sale since the days of *Waverley.*"

"I have seen the hippopotamus, both asleep and awake; and I can assure you that, awake or asleep, he is the ugliest of the works of God. But you must hear of my triumphs. Thackeray swears that he was eye-witness and ear-witness of the proudest event of my life. Two damsels were just about to pass that doorway which we, on Monday, in vain attempted to enter, when I was pointed out to them. 'Mr. Macaulay!' cried the lovely pair. 'Is that Mr. Macaulay? Never mind the hippopotamus.' And having paid a shilling to see Behemoth, they left him in the very moment at which he was about to display himself to them, in order to see—but spare my modesty."

His health was wavering, but he continued, although not very actively, to represent Edinburgh in Parliament. The following extract from a newspaper gives some idea of the sensation on the rare occasions when he spoke:

"You were loitering along the Committee lobby upstairs, wondering which of the rooms you should take next, when, as you paused uncertain, you were bumped against by somebody. He begged your pardon, and rushed on;—a Member; a stout Member; a man you couldn't conceive in a run, and yet he's running like mad. You are still staring at him, when two more men trot past you, one on each side, and they are Members too. The door close to you, marked 'Members' Entrance,' is flung open, and five Members dash from it, and plunge furiously down the lobby. More doors open; more Members rush out; Members are tearing past you, from all points, but in one direction. Then wigs and gowns appear. Their owners tell you, with happy faces, that their committees have adjourned; and then come a third class, the gentlemen of the Press, hilarious. Why, what's the matter? Matter? Macaulay is up. . . . See the division; and yet, before Mr. Macaulay had spoken, you might have safely bet fifty to one that Lord Hotham would have carried his bill. After that speech the bill was not thrown out, but pitched out."

The third and fourth volumes of his History were ready late in 1855.

"*November* 23.—Longman came. All the twenty-five thousand copies are ordered. Monday, the 17th of December, is to be the day; but on the evening of the preceding Saturday those booksellers who take more than a thousand are to have their books. The stock lying at the bookbinders' is insured for ten thousand pounds. The whole weight is fifty-six tons. It seems that no such edition was ever published of any work of the same bulk. I earnestly hope that neither age nor riches will narrow my heart." . . .

"I shall not be satisfied," he wrote in 1841, "unless I produce something which shall for a few days supersede the last fashionable novel on the tables of young ladies." It may be said, for the credit of his countrymen no less than for his own, that the annual sale of his History has frequently since 1857 surpassed the sale of the fashionable novel of the current year. . . . Within a generation of its first appearance, upwards of a hundred and forty thousand copies of the History will have been printed and sold in the United Kingdom alone.

"*August* 28, 1857.—A great day in my life. . . . An offer of a peerage; the Queen's pleasure already taken. I was very much surprised. Perhaps no such offer was ever made without the slightest solicitation, direct or indirect, to a man of humble origin and moderate fortune, who had long quitted public life. I had no hesitation about accepting, with many respectful and grateful expressions; but God knows that the poor women at Delhi and Cawnpore are more in my thoughts than my coronet. It was necessary for me to choose a title offhand. I determined to be Baron Macaulay of Rothley. I was born there; I have lived much there; I am named from the family which long had the manor; my uncle was Rector there."

In his chambers in the Albany, and later at Holly Lodge, in Kensington, Macaulay constantly saw all his young nephews and nieces, and was in almost daily contact with his sister Hannah. Her marriage while they were in India had only added Trevelyan as a brother to his family. But in 1859 Trevelyan was offered the Governorship of Madras, "and Macaulay was fully convinced that, when he and his sister parted, they would part for ever."

The prospect of a separation from one with whom he had lived in close and uninterrupted companionship since his childhood and his own early manhood,—a prospect darkened by the thought that his last hour would surely come when she was thousands of miles away,—was a trial which weighed heavily on Macaulay's sinking health. . . .

In a letter to Mr. Ellis, written on the 24th of October 1859, Macaulay says: "I have been very well in body since we parted; but in mind I have suffered much, and the more because I have had to put a force upon myself in order to appear cheerful. It is at last settled that Hannah and Alice are to go to Madras in February. I cannot deny that it is right; and my duty is to avoid whatever can add to the pain which they suffer. But I am very unhappy. However, I read, and write, and contrive to forget my sorrow for whole hours. But it recurs, and will recur."

"*December* 19.—Still intense frost. I could hardly use my razor for the palpitation of the heart. I feel as if I were twenty years older since last Thursday;—as if I were dying of old age. I am perfectly ready, and shall never be readier. A month more of such days as I have been passing of late would make me impatient to get to my little narrow crib, like a weary factory child."

Late on the afternoon of the 28th, his nephew found him very depressed and miserable.

On hearing my report of his state, my mother resolved to spend the night at Holly Lodge. She had just left the drawing-room to make her preparations for the visit, (it being, I suppose, a little before seven in the evening,) when a servant arrived with an urgent summons. As we drove up to the porch of my uncle's house, the maids ran crying out into the darkness to meet us, and we knew that all was over. We found him in the library, seated in his easy chair, and dressed as usual; with his book on the table beside him, still open at the same page. He had told his butler that he should go to bed early, as he was very tired. The man proposed his lying on the sofa. He rose as if to move, sat down again, and ceased to breathe.

He died as he had always wished to die;—without pain; without any formal farewell; preceding to the grave all whom he loved; and leaving behind him a great and honourable name, and the memory of a life every action of which was as clear and transparent as one of his own sentences. It would be unbecoming in me to dwell upon the regretful astonishment with which the tidings of his death were received wherever the English language is read; and quite unnecessary to describe the enduring grief of those upon whom he had lavished his affection, and for whom life had been brightened by daily converse with his genius, and ennobled by familiarity with his lofty and upright example. "We have lost," (so my mother wrote,) "the light of our home, the most tender, loving, generous, unselfish, devoted of friends. What he was to me for fifty years how can I tell? What a world of love he poured out upon me and mine! The blank, the void he has left,—filling, as he did, so entirely both heart and intellect,— no one can understand. For who ever knew such a life as mine, passed as the cherished companion of such a man?"

THE INIMITABLE BOZ

CERTAINLY THE CAREER OF CHARLES DICKENS WAS NO LESS THAN THAT of Macaulay a spectacular success. And yet, through all the blare and glitter of adulation, we feel that Dickens had never really gotten what he wanted. His life had been full of high spirits. He had made a great name; he had grown wealthy; he had bought Gadshill Place, the mansion he used to dream of in his childhood, and made it even more luxurious. But none of these things really satisfied him. Ever a restless energy drove him insatiably; and again and again there went up from him a cry for a "vague unhappy loss or want of something," a sense "as of one happiness I have missed," "one friend and companion I have never made." Was it love that was wanting, as he believed?—the young sister of Catherine Hogarth, the sister he had failed to marry, and whose shade had stood dimly between them? Or did that emptiness grow out of something farther back, out of those early years of shabby indigence, out of his shame and grief over being a child drudge in the blacking-factory?

Dickens overcame those handicaps of his youth by exerting tremendous powers of will. Doing so, he became "hard and aggressive," and yet he craved with "the most eager craving for sympathy." "What it was that in society made him often uneasy, shrinking, and over-sensitive," Forster observes, "he knew; but all the danger he ran in bearing down and overmastering the feeling he did not know." His education had been erratic. The many things *he* knew that cultivated men did not know, did not relieve his embarrassment for the things they knew that he did not. He was not quite sure he was a gentleman. He was not quite confident of his own manners. His uncertainty made him hate aristocracy and sentimentalize the virtues of the poor. It made him now uneasy, and now flaunting with a bumptious vulgarity.

But it also gave him the insight into the lives of the vulgar and the sympathy with oppression that are among the laurels crowning his name. He flamed into indignation over the slums and workhouses of London, the horrors of the factory system, the pitiless and inhuman dogmas of orthodox political economy chanting that England's prosperity would be ruined if laborers received another penny for their bread. He heard the bitter cry of the children and observed the gin-drowned miseries of the proletariat. He exposed cruelties and abuses with an unsparing hand. "Every movement for practical reforms, to obtain more efficient sanitary legislation, to get better compulsory education practicable for the poor, and to better the condition of laboring people, he assisted earnestly to his last hour."

And to this noble indignation he added the gusto of a great, humorous, healthy Rabelaisian imagination. Sam Weller and Mr. Pickwick mingle their rollicking comedy with monstrous images of Fagin and Sikes, the oily Pecksniff is succeeded by the ferocious Hannibal Chollop, Micawber appears and reappears declaiming, Sairey Gamp retails the saga of her communions with Mrs. 'Arris. No writer reveals a livelier exuberance, hardly any other writer except Shakespeare has such power in creating human beings. The paradox and pathos of Dickens lie fearfully intertwined, the "sparkling, clear, and sunny utterance," and, "deeper than all," as Carlyle says, "if one has the eye to see deep enough, dark, fateful, silent elements, tragical to look upon, and hiding, amid dazzling radiances as of the sun, the elements of death itself."

The Life of Charles Dickens

JOHN FORSTER

[Dickens was born in 1812 and died in 1870. Forster's
Life was issued in three volumes, 1872–1874.]

HE HAS OFTEN TOLD ME THAT HE REMEMBERED THE SMALL FRONT
garden to the house at Portsea, from which he was taken away
when he was two years old, and where, watched by a nurse
through a low kitchen window almost level with the gravel walk,
he trotted about with something to eat, and his little elder sister
with him. He was carried from the garden one day to see the
soldiers exercise; and I perfectly recollect that, on our being at
Portsmouth together while he was writing *Nickleby*, he recognised
the exact shape of the military parade seen by him as a very infant,
on the same spot, a quarter of a century before . . .

He was a very little and a very sickly boy. He was subject to
attacks of violent spasms which disabled him for any active exertion. He was never a good little cricket-player; he was never a
first-rate hand at marbles, or peg-top, or prisoner's base; but he had
great pleasure in watching the other boys, officers' sons for the
most part, at these games, reading while they played; and he had
always the belief that this early sickness had brought to himself
one inestimable advantage, in the circumstances of his weak health
having strongly inclined him to reading. It will not appear, as my
narrative moves on, that he owed much to his parents, or was
other than in his first letter to Washington Irving he described
himself to have been, a "very small and not-over-particularly-taken-
care-of boy"; but he has frequently been heard to say that his first

desire for knowledge, and his earliest passion for reading, were awakened by his mother, from whom he learnt the rudiments, not only of English, but also, a little later, of Latin. She taught him regularly every day for a long time, and taught him, he was convinced, thoroughly well. I once put to him a question in connection with this to which he replied in almost exactly the words he placed five years later in the mouth of David Copperfield: "I faintly remember her teaching me the alphabet; and when I look upon the fat black letters in the primer, the puzzling novelty of their shapes, the easy good nature of O and S always seem to present themselves before me as they used to do." . . .

"My father had left a small collection of books in a little room upstairs to which I had access (for it adjoined my own), and which nobody else in our house ever troubled. From that blessed little room, Roderick Random, Peregrine Pickle, Humphrey Clinker, Tom Jones, The Vicar of Wakefield, Don Quixote, Gil Blas and Robinson Crusoe came out, a glorious host, to keep me company. They kept alive my fancy, and my hope of something beyond that place and time—they, and the *Arabian Nights,* and the *Tales of the Genii*—and did me no harm; for, whatever harm was in some of them, was not there for me; *I* knew nothing of it. It is astonishing to me now, how I found time, in the midst of my porings and blunderings over heavier themes, to read those books as I did. It is curious to me how I could ever have consoled myself under my small troubles (which were great troubles to me), by impersonating my favourite characters in them. . . . I have been Tom Jones (a child's Tom Jones, a harmless creature) for a week together. I have sustained my own idea of Roderick Random for a month at a stretch, I verily believe. I had a greedy relish for a few volumes of voyages and travels— I forget what, now—that were on those shelves; and for days and days I can remember to have gone about my region of our house, armed with the centre-piece out of an old set of boot-trees: the perfect realisation of Captain Somebody, of the Royal British Navy, in danger of being beset by savages, and resolved to sell his life at a great price. . . ."

The usual result followed. The child took to writing himself;

and became famous in his childish circle for having written a
tragedy called *Misnar, the Sultan of India,* founded (and very
literally founded, no doubt) on one of the *Tales of the Genii.*
Nor was this his only distinction. He told a story offhand so
well, and sang small comic songs so especially well, that he used
to be elevated on chairs and tables, both at home and abroad,
for more effective display of these talents; and when he first told
me of this, at one of the Twelfth-night parties on his eldest son's
birthday, he said he never recalled it that his own shrill little
voice of childhood did not again tingle in his ears, and he blushed
to think what a horrible little nuisance he must have been to many
unoffending grown-up people who were called upon to admire
him.

*He loved the marine parade at Chatham (his father was in the
navy pay-office) and the sight of* "the gay, bright regiments always
going and coming, the continual paradings and firings, the suc-
cessions of sham-sieges and sham-defenses, . . . and the ships floating out in the Medway, with their far visions of sea . . ." *But his
father became involved in money-troubles (they were connected
with something mysterious to a little boy's ears, called "the deed")
and the child had to take a long stage-coach from the bright port
to London.* "I consumed my sandwiches in solitude and dreariness, and it rained hard all the way."

Bayham Street was about the poorest part of the London sub-
urbs then, and the house was a mean small tenement, with a
wretched little back-garden abutting on a squalid court . . .
Many, many times has he spoken to me of . . . how he seemed
at once to fall into a solitary condition apart from all other boys
of his own age, and to sink into a neglected state at home . . .
"I degenerated into cleaning [my father's] boots of a morning
. . ." "I know that we got on very badly with the butcher and
baker; that very often we had not too much for dinner; and that
at last my father was arrested."

To help out, the child was found work in a blacking warehouse.

"It was a crazy, tumbledown old house, abutting of course on
the river, and literally overrun with rats. Its wainscotted rooms

and its rotten floors and staircase, and the old grey rats swarming
down in the cellars, and the sound of their squeaking and scuffling
coming up the stairs at all times, and the dirt and decay of the
place, rise up visibly before me, as if I were there again. The
counting-house was on the first floor, looking over the coal-barges
and the river. There was a recess in it, in which I was to sit and
work. My work was to cover the pots of paste-blacking: first with
a piece of oil-paper, and then with a piece of blue paper; to tie
them round with a string; and then to clip the paper close and
neat all round, until it looked as smart as a pot of ointment from
an apothecary's shop. When a certain number of grosses of pots
had attained this pitch of perfection, I was to paste on each a
printed label; and then go on again with more pots. Two or three
other boys were kept at similar duty downstairs on similar wages.
One of them came up, in a ragged apron and a paper cap, on the
first Monday morning, to show me the trick of using the string and
tying the knot. His name was Bob Fagin; and I took the liberty
of using his name, long afterwards, in *Oliver Twist* . . .

"No words can express the secret agony of my soul as I sunk
into this companionship; compared these everyday associates with
those of my happier childhood; and felt my early hopes of growing
up to be a learned and distinguished man crushed in my breast.
The deep remembrance of the sense I had of being utterly
neglected and hopeless; of the shame I felt in my position; of the
misery it was to my young heart to believe that, day by day, what
I had learned, and thought, and delighted in, and raised my fancy
and my emulation up by, was passing away from me, never to be
brought back any more; cannot be written. My whole nature was
so penetrated with the grief and humiliation of such considerations, that even now, famous and caressed and happy, I often forget in my dreams that I have a dear wife and children; even that I
am a man; and wander desolately back to that time of my life.

"My mother and my brothers and sisters (excepting Fanny in
the royal academy of music) were still encamped, with a young
servant-girl from Chatham Workhouse, in the two parlours in the
emptied house in Gower Street North. It was a long way to go and
return within the dinner-hour, and, usually, I either carried my

dinner with me, or went and bought it at some neighbouring shop. In the latter case, it was commonly a saveloy and a penny loaf; sometimes, a fourpenny plate of beef from a cook's shop; sometimes, a plate of bread and cheese, and a glass of beer, from a miserable old public-house over the way; the Swan, if I remember right, or the Swan and something else that I have forgotten. Once, I remember tucking my own bread (which I had brought from home in the morning) under my arm, wrapped up in a piece of paper like a book, and going into the best dining-room in Johnson's alamode beef-house in Clare Court, Drury Lane, and magnificently ordering a small plate of alamode beef to eat with it. What the waiter thought of such a strange little apparition, coming in all alone, I don't know; but I can see him now, staring at me as I ate my dinner, and bringing up the other waiter to look. I gave him a halfpenny, and I wish, now, that he hadn't taken it."

"I was so young and childish, and so little qualified—how could I be otherwise?—to undertake the whole charge of my own existence that, in going to Hungerford Stairs of a morning, I could not resist the stale pastry put out at half-price on trays at the confectioners' doors in Tottenham Court Road; and I often spent in that the money I should have kept for my dinner. Then I went without my dinner, or bought a roll, or a slice of pudding. There were two pudding shops between which I was divided, according to my finances. One was in a court close to St. Martin's Church (at the back of the church), which is now removed altogether. The pudding at that shop was made with currants, and was rather a special pudding, but was dear: two penn'orth not being larger than a penn'orth of more ordinary pudding. A good shop for the latter was in the Strand, somewhere near where the Lowther Arcade is now. It was a stout, hale pudding, heavy and flabby; with great raisins in it, stuck in whole, at great distances apart. It came up hot, at about noon every day; and many and many a day did I dine off it . . .

"I was such a little fellow, with my poor white hat, little jacket, and corduroy trowsers, that frequently, when I went into the bar of a strange public-house for a glass of ale or porter to wash down the saveloy and the loaf I had eaten in the street, they didn't like to give it me. I remember, one evening (I had been somewhere for my father, and was going back to the Borough over Westminster Bridge), that I went into a public-house in Parliament Street, which is still there though altered, at the corner of the short street leading into Cannon Row, and said to the landlord behind the bar, 'What is your very best—the VERY best—ale, a glass?' For, the occasion was a festive one, for some reason: I forget why. It may have been my birthday, or somebody else's. 'Twopence,' says he. 'Then,' says I, 'just draw me a glass of that, if you please, with a good head to it.' The landlord looked at me, in return, over the bar, from head to foot, with a strange smile on his face; and instead of drawing the beer, looked round the screen and said something to his wife, who came out from behind it, with her work in her hand, and joined him in surveying me. Here we stand, all three, before me now, in my study in Devonshire Terrace. The landlord, in his shirt-sleeves, leaning against the bar window-frame; his wife, looking over the little half-door; and I, in some confusion, looking up at them from outside the partition. They asked me a good many questions, as what my name was, how old I was, where I lived, how I was employed, etc. To all of which, that I might commit nobody, I invented appropriate answers. They served me with the ale, though I suspect it was not the strongest on the premises; and the landlord's wife, opening the little half-door and bending down, gave me a kiss that was half-admiring and half-compassionate, but all womanly and good, I am sure."

At last his misery was more than he could bear. He wept when he saw his father, now released from debtors' prison. "I do believe he had never thought . . . about it," Dickens wrote, years later, but now he began to feel "it was not quite right."

"My father said I should go back no more, and should go to school. I do not write resentfully or angrily: for I know how all these things have worked together to make me what I am: but I never afterwards forgot, I never shall forget, I never can forget, that my mother was warm for my being sent back."

There was a brief interval as a day scholar at a private school.
Then we find him as an office-lad in an attorney's office, trying to
teach himself a system of shorthand.

"The changes that were rung upon dots, which in such a position
meant such a thing, and in such another position something else
entirely different; the wonderful vagaries that were played by
circles; the unaccountable consequences that resulted from marks
like flies' legs; the tremendous effects of a curve in a wrong place,
not only troubled my waking hours, but reappeared before me in
my sleep. When I had groped my way, blindly, through these
difficulties, and had mastered the alphabet, there then appeared
a procession of new horrors, called arbitrary characters; the most
despotic characters I have ever known; who insisted, for instance,
that a thing like the beginning of a cobweb meant "expectation,"
and that a pen-and-ink sky-rocket stood for "disadvantageous."
When I had fixed these wretches in my mind, I found that they
had driven everything else out of it; then, beginning again, I forgot
them; while I was picking them up, I dropped the other fragments of the system; in short, it was almost heart-breaking."

At nineteen he was a Parliamentary reporter and contributing
sketches signed "Boz" to the Evening Chronicle. *In 1836 a new*
series was suggested. Dickens says, "I thought of Mr. Pickwick."
By the fifteenth number the demand had risen from four hundred
to forty thousand.

The young author was full of health and high spirits. He was
forever sending his friend Forster little notes proposing jaunts in
the country.

"What a brilliant morning for a country walk!" he would write,
with not another word in his dispatch. Or, "Is it possible that
you can't, oughtn't, shouldn't, mustn't, *won't* be tempted, this
gorgeous day!" Or, "I start precisely—precisely mind—at half-past
one. Come, come, *come,* and walk in the green lanes. You will
work the better for it all the week. COME! I shall expect you."
Or, "You don't feel disposed, do you, to muffle yourself up, and
start off with me for a good brisk walk, over Hampstead Heath?
I knows a good 'ous there where we can have a red-hot chop for

dinner, and a glass of good wine": which led to our first experience of Jack Straw's Castle, memorable for many happy meetings in coming years.

Meanwhile he was writing Oliver Twist, Nicholas Nickleby, The Old Curiosity Shop, *and* Barnaby Rudge. *Their amazing and unexpected success made him resentful of the terms on which they were brought out. He finally forced his publishers to a new financial arrangement. So fortified, Dickens and his wife (he had married Catherine Hogarth in 1836) set out for a tour of the Highlands.*

"There isn't a basin in the Highlands that will hold my face; not a drawer that will open after you have put your clothes in it; not a water-bottle capacious enough to wet your toothbrush . . . The weather is what they call "soft"—which means that the sky is a vast waterspout that never leaves off emptying itself . . ." His next letter [described] the Pass of Glencoe . . . "Glencoe itself is perfectly *terrible*. The pass is an awful place. It is shut in on each side by enormous rocks from which great torrents come rushing down . . . There are scores of glens, high up, which form such haunts as you might imagine yourself wandering in, in the very height and madness of a fever."

Soon, however, he was experiencing wilder adventures. It was proposed that he travel in America, and keep a notebook of his impressions. In January, 1842, he embarked on the Britannia.

"Four dozen plates were broken at dinner. One steward fell down the cabin stairs with a round of beef, and injured his foot severely. Another steward fell down after him, and cut his eye open. The baker's taken ill: so is the pastry-cook. A new man, sick to death, has been required to fill the place of the latter officer, and has been dragged out of bed and propped up in a little house upon deck, between two casks, and ordered (the captain standing over him) to make and roll out pie-crust; which he protests, with tears in his eyes, it is death to him in his bilious state to look at. Twelve dozen of bottled porter has got loose upon deck, and the bottles are rolling about distractedly, overhead.

Lord Mulgrave (a handsome fellow, by the by, to look at, and
nothing but a good 'un to go) laid a wager with twenty-five other
men last night, whose berths, like his, are in the fore-cabin which
can only be got at by crossing the deck, that he would reach his
cabin first. Watches were set by the captain's, and they sallied
forth, wrapped up in coats and storm caps. The sea broke over
the ship so violently, that they were five and twenty minutes holding on by the hand-rail at the starboard paddle-box, drenched to
the skin by every wave, and not daring to go on or come back,
lest they should be washed overboard. News! A dozen murders
in town wouldn't interest us half as much."

"On looking back through these sheets, I am astonished to find
how little I have told you, and how much I have, even now, in
store which shall be yours by word of mouth. The American
poor, the American factories, the institutions of all kinds—I have
a book, already. There is no man in this town, or in this State
of New England, who has not a blazing fire and a meat dinner
every day of his life. A flaming sword in the air would not attract
so much attention as a beggar in the streets. There are no charity
uniforms, no wearisome repetition of the same dull ugly dress, in
that blind school. All are attired after their own tastes, and every
boy and girl has his or her individuality as distinct and unimpaired
as you would find it in their own homes. At the theatres, all the
ladies sit in the fronts of the boxes. The gallery are as quiet as the
dress circle at dear Drury Lane. A man with seven heads would
be no sight at all, compared with one who couldn't read and
write."

"Now, the phase of character in the Americans which amuses
me most, was put before me in its most amusing shape by the
circumstances attending this affair. I had noticed it before, and
have since, but I cannot better illustrate it than by reference to
this theme. Of course I can do nothing but in some shape or
other it gets into the newspapers. All manner of lies get there,
and occasionally a truth so twisted and distorted that it has as
much resemblance to the real fact as Quilp's leg to Taglioni's. But
with this ball to come off, the newspapers were if possible un-

usually loquacious; and in their accounts of me, and my seeings, sayings, and doings on the Saturday night and Sunday before, they describe my manner, mode of speaking, dressing, and so forth. In doing this, they report that I am a very charming fellow (of course), and have a very free and easy way with me; 'which,' say they, 'at first amused a few fashionables'; but soon pleased them exceedingly. Another paper, coming after the ball, dwells upon its splendour and brilliancy; hugs itself and its readers upon all that Dickens saw; and winds up by gravely expressing its conviction, that Dickens was never in such society in England as he has seen in New York, and that its high and striking tone cannot fail to make an indelible impression on his mind! For the same reason I am always represented, whenever I appear in public, as being 'very pale'; 'apparently thunderstruck'; and utterly confounded by all I see. . . . You recognise the queer vanity which is at the root of all this? I have plenty of stories in connection with it to amuse you with when I return."

"In the ladies' car, there is no smoking of tobacco allowed. All gentlemen who have ladies with them, sit in this car; and it is usually very full. Before it, is the gentlemen's car; which is something narrower. As I had a window close to me yesterday which commanded this gentlemen's car, I looked at it pretty often, perforce. The flashes of saliva flew so perpetually and incessantly out of the windows all the way, that it looked as though they were ripping open feather-beds inside, and letting the wind dispose of the feathers. But this spitting is universal. In the courts of law, the judge has his spittoon on the bench, the counsel have theirs, the witness has his, the prisoner his, and the crier his. The jury are accommodated at the rate of three men to a spittoon (or spit-box as they call it here); and the spectators in the gallery are provided for, as so many men who in the course of nature expectorate without cessation. There are spit-boxes in every steamboat, bar-room, public dining-room, house of office, and place of general resort, no matter what it be. In the hospitals, the students are requested, by placard, to use the boxes provided for them, and not to spit upon the stairs. I have twice seen gentlemen, at evening parties in New York, turn aside when they were not engaged in conversation, and spit upon the drawing-room carpet. And in every bar-room and hotel passage the stone floor looks as if it were paved with open oysters—from the quantity of this kind of deposit which tessellates it all over. . . ."

"On the bridge at Richmond there is a notice against fast driving over it, as it is rotten and crazy: penalty—for whites, five dollars; for slaves, fifteen stripes. My heart is lightened as if a great load had been taken from it, when I think that we are turning our backs on this accursed and detested system. I really don't think I could have borne it any longer. It is all very well to say 'be silent on the subject.' They won't let you be silent. They *will* ask you what you think of it; and *will* expatiate on slavery as if it were one of the greatest blessings of mankind. 'It's not,' said a hard, bad-looking fellow to me the other day, 'it's not the interest of a man to use his slaves ill. It's damned nonsense that you hear in England.'—I told him quietly that it was not a man's interest to get drunk, or to steal, or to game, or to indulge in any other vice, but he did indulge in it for all that. That cruelty, and the abuse of irresponsible power, were two of the bad passions of human nature, with the gratification of which, considerations of interest or of ruin had nothing whatever to do; and that, while every candid man must admit that even a slave might be happy enough with a good master, all human beings knew that bad masters, cruel masters, and masters who disgraced the form they bore, were matters of experience and history, whose existence was as undisputed as that of slaves themselves."

"I'll tell you what the two obstacles to the passing of an international copyright law with England, are: firstly, the national love of 'doing' a man in any bargain or matter of business; secondly, the national vanity. Both these characteristics prevail to an extent which no stranger can possibly estimate. The Americans read him; the free, enlightened, independent Americans; and what more would he have? Here's reward enough for any man. The national vanity swallows up all other countries on the face of the earth, and leaves but this above the ocean.

"As to telling them they will have no literature of their own, the universal answer (out of Boston) is, 'We don't want one. Why should we pay for one when we can get it for nothing? Our people don't think of poetry, sir. Dollars, banks, and cotton are *our* books, sir.' And they certainly are in one sense; for a lower average of general information than exists in this country on all other topics it would be very hard to find. So much, at present, for international copyright."

Travel on the Continent enlarged the scene of his criticism. Poverty was even worse in France and Italy than in England. The lazzaroni were "mere squalid, abject, miserable animals or vermin to batten on; slouching, slinking, ugly, shabby, scavenging scarecrows!" *Amid this misery, speculation was high. On the Bourse there were constant crashes, disaster elbowing luxury:* "thoroughbred horses without end, and red velvet carriages . . . go by all day long; [speculators] all howling and haggard"; "Concierges and people like that perpetually blow their brains out . . ."

Dickens's immense vitality was beginning to give way under the pressure of his laborious writing and lecturing and traveling. He developed coughs and was stethoscoped, rubbings were ordered for his chest. Restlessness kept him forever moving.

"Why is it, that as with poor David [David Copperfield], a sense comes always crushing on me now, when I fall into low spirits, as of one happiness I have missed in life, and one friend and companion I have never made?" . . . "I find that the skeleton in my domestic closet is becoming a pretty big one."

It would be unjust and uncandid not to admit that these and other similar passages in the letters that extended over the years while he lived abroad, had served in some degree as a preparation for what came after his return to England in the following year. It came with a great shock nevertheless; because it told plainly what before had never been avowed, but only hinted at more or less obscurely. The opening reference is to the reply which had been made to a previous expression of his wish for some confidences as in the old time. I give only what is strictly necessary to account for what followed, and even this with deep reluctance.

"Your letter of yesterday was so kind and hearty, and sounded so gently the many chords we have touched together, that I cannot leave it unanswered, though I have not much (to any purpose) to say. My reference to 'confidences' was merely to the relief of saying a word of what has long been pent up in my mind. Poor Catherine and I are not made for each other, and there is no help for it. It is not only that she makes me uneasy and unhappy, but that I make her so too—and much more so. She is exactly what you know, in the way of being amiable and complying; but we are strangely ill-assorted for the bond there is between us. God knows she would have been a thousand times happier if she had married another kind of man, and that her avoidance of this destiny would have been at least equally good for us both. I am often cut to the heart by thinking what a pity it is, for her own sake, that I ever fell in her way; and if I were sick or disabled to-morrow, I know how sorry she would be, and how deeply grieved myself, to think how we had lost each other. But exactly the same incompatibility would arise, the moment I was well again; and nothing on earth could make her understand me, or suit us to each other. Her temperament will not go with mine. It mattered not so much when we had only ourselves to consider, but reasons have been growing since which make it all but hopeless that we should even try to struggle on. What is now befalling me I have seen steadily coming, ever since the days you remember when Mary was born; and I know too well that you cannot, and no one can, help me. Why I have even written I hardly know; but it is a miserable sort of comfort that you should be clearly aware how matters stand. The mere mention of the fact, without any complaint or blame of any sort, is a relief to my present state of spirits—and I can get this only from you, because I can speak of it to no one else."

During all these months many sorrowful misunderstandings had continued in his home, and the relief sought from the misery had but the effect of making desperate any hope of a better understanding. . . . "Quite dismiss from your mind any reference whatever to present circumstances at home. Nothing can put *them* right, until we are all dead and buried and risen. It is not, with me, a matter of will, or trial, or sufferance, or good humour, or making the best of it, or making the worst of it, any longer. It is all despairingly over. Have no lingering hope of, or for, me in this association. A dismal failure has to be borne, and there an end." . . . Thenceforward he and his wife lived apart. The eldest son went with his mother, Dickens at once giving effect to her expressed wish in this respect; and the other children remained with himself, their intercourse with Mrs. Dickens being left entirely to themselves.

Party divisions he cared for less and less as life moved on; but the decisive, peremptory, dogmatic style into which a habit of rapid remark on topics of the day will betray the most candid and considerate commentator, displayed its influence, perhaps not always consciously to himself, in the underlying tone of bitterness that runs through the books which followed *Copperfield*. The resentment against remediable wrongs is as praiseworthy in them as in the earlier tales; but the exposure of Chancery abuses, administrative incompetence, politico-economic shortcomings, and social flunkeyism, in *Bleak House, Little Dorrit, Hard Times,* and *Our Mutual Friend,* would not have been made less odious by the cheerier tone that had struck with much sharper effect at prison abuses, parish wrongs, Yorkshire schools, and hypocritical humbug, in *Pickwick, Oliver Twist, Nickleby,* and *Chuzzlewit*. It will be remembered of him always that he desired to set right what was wrong, that he held no abuse to be unimprovable, that he left none of the evils named exactly as he found them, and that to influences drawn from his writings were due not a few of the salutary changes which marked the age in which he lived; but anger does not improve satire, and it gave latterly, from the causes named, too aggressive a form to what, after all, was but a very wholesome hatred of the cant that everything English is perfect, and that to call a thing un-English is to doom it to abhorred extinction.

"I am hourly strengthened in my old belief," he wrote (3 February, 1855), "that our political aristocracy and our tuft-hunt-

ing are the death of England. In all this business I don't see a
gleam of hope. As to the popular spirit, it has come to be so
entirely separated from the Parliament and Government, and so
perfectly apathetic about them both, that I seriously think it a
most portentous sign." . . . What he said with too much bitterness, in his heart he believed; and had, alas! too much ground for
believing. "A country," he wrote (27 April, 1855), "which is discovered to be in this tremendous condition as to its war affairs;
with an enormous black cloud of poverty in every town which
is spreading and deepening every hour, and not one man in two
thousand knowing anything about, or even believing in, its existence; with a non-working aristocracy, and a silent parliament,
and everybody for himself and nobody for the rest; this is the
prospect, and I think it a very deplorable one." *

*Dickens's restlessness did not diminish. He began to be sub-
ject to attacks of faintness and often he was unable to sleep at night.
After having been in a terrible railway accident he had curious
feelings of soreness in his body. Nevertheless he insisted on under-*

---

* Dickens's radicalism stems from an early date. Even in 1841 he had been
writing angry rhymed squibs on Tory doctrines.

Thus ran his new version of "*The Fine Old English Gentleman*, to be said or
sung at all Conservative dinners":

"I'll sing you a new ballad, and I'll warrant it first-rate,
    Of the days of that old gentleman who had that old estate;
    When they spent the public money at a bountiful old rate
    On ev'ry mistress, pimp, and scamp, at ev'ry noble gate,
            In the fine old English Tory times;
            Soon may they come again!

The good old laws were garnished well with gibbets, whips, and chains,
    With fine old English penalties, and fine old English pains,
    With rebel heads and seas of blood once hot in rebel veins:
    For all these things were requisite to guard the rich old gains
            Of the fine old English Tory times;
            Soon may they come again!

                            •   •   •

The bright old day now dawns again; the cry runs through the land,
    In England there shall be—dear bread! In Ireland—sword and brand!
    And poverty, and ignorance, shall swell the rich and grand,
    So, rally round the rulers with the gentle iron hand,
            Of the fine old English Tory days;
            Hail to the coming time!"

taking a second American tour in 1867. People stood in lines eight hundred long to buy tickets for his readings:

"Members of family relieved each other in the queues; waiters flew across the streets and squares from the neighboring restaurant, to serve parties who were taking their breakfast in the open December air; while excited men offered five and ten dollars for the mere permission to exchange places with other persons standing nearer the head of the line!"

He got back to England, and almost immediately plunged into another series of readings there. With terrible exertion and gruesome effect he would read the scene of Sikes murdering Nancy. The readings came to an end at last. He returned to his home at Gadshill Place.

The few days at Gadshill had been given wholly to work on his novel. He had been easier in his foot and hand; and though he was suffering severely from the local hemorrhage before named, he made no complaint of illness. But there was observed in him a very unusual appearance of fatigue. "He seemed very weary." He was out with his dogs for the last time on Monday, 6 June, when he walked with his letters into Rochester. On Tuesday the 7th, after his daughter Mary had left on a visit to her sister Kate, not finding himself equal to much fatigue, he drove to Cobham Wood with his sister-in-law, there dismissed the carriage, and walked round the park and back. He returned in time to put up in his new conservatory some Chinese lanterns sent from London that afternoon; and the whole of the evening, he sat with Miss Hogarth in the dining-room that he might see their effect when lighted. More than once he then expressed his satisfaction at having finally abandoned all intention of exchanging Gadshill for London; and this he had done more impressively some days before. While he lived, he said, he should wish his name to be more and more associated with the place; and he had a notion that when he died he should like to lie in the little graveyard belonging to the Cathedral at the foot of the Castle wall.

On 8 June he passed all the day writing in the Chalet. He

came over for luncheon; and, much against his usual custom, returned to his desk. . . .

He was late in leaving the Chalet; but before dinner, which was ordered at six o'clock with the intention of walking afterwards in the lanes, he wrote some letters, among them one to his friend Mr. Charles Kent appointing to see him in London next day; and dinner was begun before Miss Hogarth saw, with alarm, a singular expression of trouble and pain in his face. "For an hour," he then told her, "he had been very ill"; but he wished dinner to go on. These were the only really coherent words uttered by him. They were followed by some, that fell from him disconnectedly, of quite other matters; of an approaching sale at a neighbour's house, of whether Macready's son was with his father at Cheltenham, and of his own intention to go immediately to London; but at these latter he had risen, and his sister-in-law's help alone prevented him from falling where he stood. Her effort then was to get him on the sofa, but after a slight struggle he sank heavily on his left side. "On the ground" were the last words he spoke. It was now a little over ten minutes past six o'clock. His two daughters came that night with Mr. F. Beard, who had also been telegraphed for, and whom they met at the station. His eldest son arrived early next morning, and was joined in the evening (too late) by his younger son from Cambridge. All possible medical aid had been summoned. . . . But human help was unavailing. There was effusion on the brain; and though stertorous breathing continued all night, and until ten minutes past six o'clock on the evening of Thursday, 9 June, there had never been a gleam of hope during the twenty-four hours. He had lived four months beyond his 58th year.

A REASONING MACHINE

JOHN STUART MILL WAS A CHILD OF THEORY. CHOSEN BY JAMES MILL and Jeremy Bentham to be their successor in the spreading of Philosophical Radicalism, he was also to be a flesh-and-blood proof of the omnipotence of education. His autobiography was written partly to record an unusual educational experiment which proved how much more might be taught, even in early childhood, than was commonly supposed, and partly to demonstrate that the mind which was the product of that education "was always pressing forward" in later years, "equally ready to learn and to unlearn either from its own thoughts or from those of others."

In a stable social order, education is more or less taken for granted. Men apply the principles or rules of thumb that served their fathers; if disaster results, it is easy to believe it the fault of the individual rather than of society or his education. But in periods of widespread change, education too is queried. Since Rousseau wrote *Émile* in 1762 men have grown more and more troubled over the problem of fitting the individual to the world he lives in and of remolding that world itself closer to the heart's desire.

The nineteenth century, with the roar of machines sounding in its ears and scrambling new classes greedy for privileges, creating thousands of new problems, resounded with debate over the subject. At Rugby, Thomas Arnold set himself to developing Christian English gentlemen, molding to the worship of athletics and good form the future statesmen of Britain's colonial imperialism. Carlyle blisteringly denounced the governing classes for not knowing how to govern. Matthew Arnold fastidiously recoiled from the philistine crassness of the rising manufacturing powers and their faith in machinery, and warned them that only culture, the study of perfection, could save them. How to attain an education was the Sphinx's query to all thoughtful men. The serious minds of the times were aware that they lived in a changing world in which only a radically changed technique of education could cope with the new problems.

Thoughtful autobiographers have echoed these preoccupations. In such modern autobiographies as those of Henry Adams and Lincoln Steffens, as in Mill, education becomes the dominant note, and the author's whole career comes to be regarded as a prolonged and continuous process of learning. This constitutes a vast gap between even such serious autobiographers as Gibbon and Franklin and those of more modern times. The eighteenth century writers learned from experience, yes; but to them what they *learned* and what they *were* were almost independent categories; youth and manhood brought them out of the chrysalis, and from then on they were what they were, in a clear and unchanging world.

But to John Stuart Mill the world itself changed as his understanding continued to develop throughout life. And that capacity for growth he believed he owed to his father's early training. It had not been perfect. Lack of varied exercise had left him physically clumsy. Lack of boyish companionship had impeded, although not destroyed, his power to adapt himself to social intercourse with others. James Mill's fear of emotional display had left an unfilled longing for warmth and sympathy, of which his son's crisis of despair in the early twenties was the warning and revenge. But Mill's feelings welled up of themselves, found their natural objects, and attained a balance. He had learned self-discipline and the habit of work. He had learned to think for himself. His growth took him far from doctrinaire Benthamism. He modified his father's psychology, became sensible of a range of emotional values to which his father was blind, deepened his philosophy of history far beyond the depth James Mill and Jeremy Bentham had sounded, and pierced with radical foresight into the social problems of the next century. Few nineteenth century minds were so constantly growing.

Mill's *Autobiography* is not an emotional document, but it is moving to the reader who can respond to the clear pursuit of truth. Mill makes no outcry about himself. He is logical and restrained, the emotion discernable mostly as a sort of underglow to the course of statement, save in occasional passages of sympathy or tribute. Carlyle, reading in his lonely old age, and remembering the man whom he had loved, was bitterly disappointed: "It is wholly the life of a logic-chopping engine, little more of human in it than if it had been done by a thing of mechanized iron. Autobiography of a steam-engine, you may sometimes read it . . . The thought of poor Mill altogether, and of his life and history in this poor muddy world, gives me real pain and sorrow."

But Carlyle was wrong. There is real feeling in Mill's *Autobiography:* nothing could be more unperceptive than to dismiss him as "a mere reasoning machine." His panegyrics to his wife are lyrical with the highest romantic devotion. The congealed grief of that youthful period of despair he makes starkly convincing. His judgments on moral issues are conveyed with a grave eloquence that is often moving. Emotion is muted and subdued to the major object of following his educational development. But it is neither feeble nor absent.

Autobiography of John Stuart Mill

[Mill was born in 1806 and died at Avignon in 1873. The *Autobiography* was published in the year of his death.]

IT SEEMS PROPER THAT I SHOULD PREFIX TO THE FOLLOWING BIO-graphical sketch, some mention of the reasons which have made me think it desirable that I should leave behind me such a memorial of so uneventful a life as mine. I do not for a moment imagine that any part of what I have to relate, can be interesting to the public as a narrative, or as being connected with myself. But I have thought that in an age in which education, and its improvement, are the subject of more, if not of profounder study than at any former period of English history, it may be useful that there should be some record of an education which was unusual and remarkable, and which, whatever else it may have done, has proved how much more than is conmmonly supposed may be taught, and well taught, in those early years which, in the common modes of what is called instruction, are little better than wasted.

It has also seemed to me that in an age of transition in opinions, there may be somewhat both of interest and of benefit in noting the successive phases of any mind which was always pressing forward, equally ready to learn and to unlearn either from its own thoughts or from those of others. But a motive which weighs more with me than either of these, is a desire to make acknowledgment of the debts which my intellectual and moral development owes to other persons; some of them of recognised eminence, others less known than they deserve to be, and the one to whom most of all is due, one whom the world had no opportunity of knowing. The reader whom these things do not interest, has only himself to blame if he reads farther, and I do not desire any other indulgence from him than that of bearing in mind, that for him these pages were not written.

I was born in London, on the 20th of May, 1806, and was the eldest son of James Mill, the author of the *History of British India*.

I have no remembrance of the time when I began to learn Greek, I have been told that it was when I was three years old. My earliest recollection on the subject, is that of committing to memory what my father termed vocables, being lists of common Greek words, with their signification in English, which he wrote out for me on cards. . . .

What he was himself willing to undergo for the sake of my instruction, may be judged from the fact, that I went through the whole process of preparing my Greek lessons in the same room and at the same table at which he was writing: and as in those days Greek and English lexicons were not, and I could make no more use of a Greek and Latin lexicon than could be made without having yet begun to learn Latin, I was forced to have recourse to him for the meaning of every word which I did not know. This incessant interruption, he, one of the most impatient of men, submitted to, and wrote under that interruption several volumes of his History and all else that he had to write during those years.

The only thing besides Greek, that I learnt as a lesson in this part of my childhood, was arithmetic: this also my father taught me: it was the task of the evenings, and I well remember its disagreeableness. But the lessons were only a part of the daily instruction I received. Much of it consisted in the books I read by myself, and my father's discourses to me, chiefly during our walks. From 1810 to the end of 1813 we were living in Newington Green, then an almost rustic neighbourhood. My father's health required considerable and constant exercise, and he walked habitually before breakfast, generally in the green lanes towards Hornsey. In these walks I always accompanied him, and with my earliest recollections of green fields and wild flowers, is mingled that of the account I gave him daily of what I had read the day before. To the best of my remembrance, this was a voluntary rather than a prescribed exercise. I made notes on slips of paper while reading, and from these in the morning walks, I told the story to him; for the books were chiefly histories, of which I read in this manner a great number: Robertson's histories, Hume, Gibbon; but my greatest delight, then and for long afterwards, was Watson's *Philip the Second and Third.* The heroic defence of the Knights of Malta against the Turks, and of the revolted Provinces of the Netherlands against Spain, excited in me an intense and lasting interest. . . . In these frequent talks about the books I read, he used, as opportunity offered, to give me explanations and ideas respecting civilization, government, morality, mental cultivation, which he required me afterwards to restate to him in my own words . . .

Of children's books, any more than of playthings, I had scarcely any, except an occasional gift from a relation or acquaintance: among those I had, *Robinson Crusoe* was pre-eminent, and continued to delight me though all my boyhood. It was no part, however, of my father's system to exclude books of amusement, though he allowed them very sparingly. Of such books he possessed at that time next to none, but he borrowed several for me; those which I remember are the *Arabian Nights,* Cazotte's *Arabian Tales, Don Quixote,* Miss Edgeworth's *Popular Tales,* and a book of some reputation in its day, Brooke's *Fool of Quality.*

In my eighth year I commenced learning Latin, in conjunction with a younger sister, to whom I taught it as I went on, and who afterwards repeated the lessons to my father: and from this time, other sisters and brothers being successively added as pupils, a considerable part of my day's work consisted of this preparatory teaching. It was a part which I greatly disliked; the more so, as I was held responsible for the lessons of my pupils, in almost as full a sense as for my own: I, however, derived from this discipline the great advantage, of learning more thoroughly and retaining more lastingly the things which I was set to teach: perhaps, too, the practice it afforded in explaining difficulties to others, may even at that age have been useful.

By his eleventh year, aided by his father's comment, he was able to read Mitford's Greece *and be on his guard* "against the Tory prejudices of this writer, and his perversions of facts for the white-washing of despots, and blackening of popular institutions." *He even compiled a history of Roman government himself, stressing* "the struggles between the patricians and plebeians," *vindicating* "the Agrarian Laws," *and upholding* "the Roman Democratic party."

He was allowed to read some poetry, but he took little pleasure in it, except for Campbell's Gertrude of Wyoming, *which he found* "the perfection of pathos." *Then, in his twelfth year, his father began the second stage of his education. He had been stored with a multitude of facts; now the time had come for criticism, generalizing, evaluation. He started the boy on Aristotle's* Organon, *the medieval schoolmen, and Hobbes.*

I know of nothing, in my education, to which I think myself more indebted for whatever capacity of thinking I have attained. The first intellectual operation in which I arrived at any proficiency, was dissecting a bad argument, and finding in what part the fallacy lay: and though whatever capacity of this sort I attained, was due to the fact that it was an intellectual exercise in which I was most perseveringly drilled by my father, yet it is also true that the school logic, and the mental habits acquired in studying it, were among the principal instruments of this drilling. I am persuaded that nothing, in modern education, tends so much, when properly used, to form exact thinkers, who attach a precise meaning to words and propositions, and are not imposed on by vague, loose, or ambiguous terms. The boasted influence of mathematical studies is nothing to it; for in mathematical processes, none of the real difficulties of correct ratiocination occur.

The boy made such progress that his father put Ricardo's Principles of Political Economy *in his hands.*

The path was a thorny one, even to him, and I am sure it was so to me, notwithstanding the strong interest I took in the subject. He was often, and much beyond reason, provoked by my failures in cases where success could not have been expected; but in the main his method was right, and it succeeded. I do not believe that any scientific teaching ever was more thorough, or better fitted for training the faculties, than the mode in which logic and political economy were taught to me by my father. Striving, even in an exaggerated degree, to call forth the activity of my faculties, by making me find out everything for myself, he gave his explanations not before, but after, I had felt the full force of the difficulties; and not only gave me an accurate knowledge of these two great subjects, as far as they were then understood, but made me a thinker on both. I thought for myself almost from the first, and occasionally thought differently from him, though for a long time only on minor points, and making his opinion the ultimate standard. At a later period I even occasionally convinced him, and altered his opinion on some points of detail: which I state to his honour, not my own. It at once exemplifies his perfect candour, and the real worth of his method of teaching. . . .

My father never permitted anything which I learnt to degenerate into a mere exercise of memory. He strove to make the understanding not only go along with every step of the teaching, but, if possible, precede it. Anything which could be found out by thinking I never was told, until I had exhausted my efforts to find it out for myself. As far as I can trust my remembrance, I acquitted myself very lamely in this department; my recollection of such matters is almost wholly of failures, hardly ever of success. It is true the failures were often in things in which success in so early a stage of my progress, was almost impossible. I remember at some time in my thirteenth year, on my happening to use the word idea, he asked me what an idea was; and expressed some displeasure at my ineffectual efforts to define the word: I recollect also his indignation at my using the common expression that something was true in theory but required correction in practice; and how, after making me vainly strive to define the word theory, he explained its meaning, and showed the fallacy of the vulgar form of speech which I had used; leaving me fully persuaded that in being unable to give a correct definition of Theory, and in speaking of it as something which might be at variance with practice, I had shown unparalleled ignorance. In this he seems, and perhaps was, very unreasonable; but I think, only in being angry at my failure. A pupil from whom nothing is ever demanded which he cannot do, never does all he can.

One of the evils most liable to attend on any sort of early proficiency, and which often fatally blights its promise, my father most anxiously guarded against. This was self-conceit. He kept me, with extreme vigilance, out of the way of hearing myself praised, or of being led to make self-flattering comparisons between myself and others. From his own intercourse with me I could derive none but a very humble opinion of myself; and the standard of comparison he always held up to me, was not what other people did, but what a man could and ought to do. He completely succeeded in preserving me from the sort of influences he so much dreaded. I was not at all aware that my attainments were anything unusual at my age. If I accidentally had my attention drawn to the fact that some other boy knew less than myself— which happened less often than might be imagined—I concluded, not that I knew much, but that he, for some reason or other, knew little, or that his knowledge was of a different kind from mine. My state of mind was not humility, but neither was it arrogance. I never thought of saying to myself, I am, or I can do, so and so. I neither estimated myself highly nor lowly: I did not estimate myself at all. If I thought anything about myself, it was that I was rather backward in my studies, since I always found myself so, in comparison with what my father expected from me. I assert this with confidence, though it was not the impression of various persons who saw me in my childhood. They, as I have since found, thought me greatly and disagreeably self-conceited; probably because I was disputatious, and did not scruple to give direct contradictions to things which I heard said.

[My father] was earnestly bent upon my escaping not only the corrupting influence which boys exercise over boys, but the contagion of vulgar modes of thought and feeling; and for this he was willing that I should pay the price of inferiority in the accomplishments which schoolboys in all countries chiefly cultivate. The deficiencies in my education were principally in the things which boys learn from being turned out to shift for themselves, and from being brought together in large numbers. From temperance and much walking, I grew up healthy and hardy, though not muscular; but I could do no feats of skill or physical strength, and knew none of the ordinary bodily exercises. It was not that play, or time for it, was refused me. Though no holidays were allowed, lest the habit of work should be broken, and a taste for idleness acquired, I had ample leisure in every day to amuse myself; but as I had no boy companions, and the animal need of physical activity was satisfied by walking, my amusements, which were mostly solitary, were in general, of a quiet, if not a bookish turn, and gave little stimulus to any other kind even of mental activity than that which was already called forth by my studies: I consequently remained long, and in a less degree have always remained, inexpert in anything requiring manual dexterity.

I was brought up from the first without any religious belief, in the ordinary acceptation of the term. My father, educated in the creed of Scotch Presbyterianism, had by his own studies and reflections been early led to reject not only the belief in Revelation, but the foundations of what is commonly called Natural Religion. . . .

As it was, his aversion to religion, in the sense usually attached to the term, was of the same kind with that of Lucretius: he regarded it with the feelings due not to a mere mental delusion, but to a great moral evil. He looked upon it as the greatest enemy of morality: first, by setting up fictitious excellences,—belief in creeds, devotional feelings, and ceremonies, not connected with the good of human-kind,—and causing these to be accepted as substitutes for genuine virtues: but above all, by radically vitiating the standard of morals; making it consist in doing the will of a being, on whom it lavishes indeed all the phrases of adulation, but whom in sober truth it depicts as eminently hateful. I have a hundred times heard him say, that all ages and nations have represented their gods as wicked, in a constantly increasing progression, that mankind have gone on adding trait after trait till they reached the most perfect conception of wickedness which the human mind can devise, and have called this God, and prostrated themselves before it. This ne plus ultra of wickedness he considered to be embodied in what is commonly presented to mankind as the creed of Christianity. Think (he used to say) of a being who would make a Hell—who would create the human race with the infallible foreknowledge, and therefore with the intention, that the great majority of them were to be consigned to horrible and everlasting torment. The time, I believe, is drawing near when this dreadful conception of an object of worship will be no longer identified with Christianity; and when all persons, with any sense of moral good and evil, will look upon it with the same indignation with which my father regarded it. . . .

I am thus one of the very few examples, in this country, of one who has, not thrown off religious belief, but never had it: I grew up in a negative state with regard to it. I looked upon the modern exactly as I did upon the ancient religion, as something which in no way concerned me. It did not seem to me more strange that English people should believe what I did not, than that the men I read of in Herodotus should have done so.

My father's moral convictions, wholly dissevered from religion, were very much of the character of those of the Greek philosophers; and were delivered with the force and decision which characterized all that came from him. . . . My father's moral inculcations were at all times mainly those of the "Socratici viri"; justice, temperance (to which he gave a very extended application), veracity, perseverance, readiness to encounter pain and especially labour; regard for the public good; estimation of persons according to their merits, and of things according to their intrinsic usefulness; a life of exertion in contradiction to one of self-indulgent ease and sloth. These and other moralities he conveyed in brief sentences, uttered as occasion arose, of grave exhortation, or stern reprobation and contempt. . . .

In his views of life he partook of the character of the Stoic, the Epicurean, and the Cynic, not in the modern but the ancient sense of the word. In his personal qualities the Stoic predominated. His standard of morals was Epicurean, inasmuch as it was utilitarian, taking as the exclusive test of right and wrong, the tendency of actions to produce pleasure or pain. But he had (and this was the Cynic element) scarcely any belief in pleasure; at least in his later years, of which alone, on this point, I can speak confidently. He was not insensible to pleasures; but he deemed very few of them worth the price which, at least in the present state of society, must be paid for them. The greater number of miscarriages in life, he considered to be attributable to the over-valuing of pleasures. Accordingly, temperance, in the large sense intended by the Greek philosophers—stopping short at the point of moderation in all indulgences—was with him, as with them, almost the central point of educational precept.

He thought human life a poor thing at best, after the freshness of youth and of unsatisfied curiosity had gone by. This was a topic on which he did not often speak, especially, it may be supposed, in the presence of young persons: but when he did, it was with an air of settled and profound conviction. He would sometimes say, that if life were made what it might be, by good government and good education, it would be worth having: but he never spoke with anything like enthusiasm even of that possibility. He never varied in rating intellectual enjoyments above all others, even in value as pleasures, independently of their ulterior benefits. The pleasures of the benevolent affections he placed high in the scale; and used to say, that he had never known a happy old man, except those who were able to live over again in the pleasures of the young. . . .

The element which was chiefly deficient in his moral relation to his children was that of tenderness. I do not believe that this deficiency lay in his own nature. I believe him to have had much more feeling than he habitually showed, and much greater capacities of feeling than were ever developed. He resembled most Englishmen in being ashamed of the signs of feeling, and by the absence of demonstration, starving the feelings themselves. If we consider further that he was in the trying position of sole teacher, and add to this that his temper was constitutionally irritable, it is impossible not to feel true pity for a father who did, and strove to do, so much for his children, who would have so valued their affection, yet who must have been constantly feeling that fear of him was drying it up at its source. This was no longer the case later in life, and with his younger children. They loved him tenderly: and if I cannot say so much of myself, I was always loyally devoted to him.

But the Spartan régime had not destroyed Mill's emotional nature. "The middle-age achitecture, the baronial hall, and the spacious and lofty rooms" *of Ford Abbey, Jeremy Bentham's summer home* "were to me a sort of poetic cultivation"; *and he felt the romantic appeal of the Abbey grounds,* "which were *riant* and secluded, umbrageous, and full of the sound of falling waters." *During a trip to the Pyrenees with Sir Samuel Bentham's family, the sublime and awful mountain scenery* "made the deepest impression" *on him.*

In 1821 his father introduced him to the philosophy of Bentham.

My previous education had been, in a certain sense, already a course of Benthamism. . . . Yet in the first pages of Bentham it burst upon me with all the force of novelty. What thus impressed me was the chapter in which Bentham passed judgment on the common modes of reasoning in morals and legislation, deduced from phrases like "law of nature," "right reason," "the moral sense," "natural rectitude," and the like, and characterized them as dogmatism in disguise, imposing its sentiments upon others under cover of sounding expressions which convey no reason for the sentiment, but set up the sentiment as its own reason. It had not struck me before, that Bentham's principle put an end to all this. The feeling rushed upon me, that all previous moralists were superseded, and that here indeed was the commencement of a new era in thought. . . . The "principle of utility" understood as Bentham understood it, and applied in the manner in which he applied it through these three volumes, fell exactly into its place as the keystone which held together the detached and fragmentary component parts of my knowledge and beliefs.

The rising liberalism of the times made them seem ripe for reform. The leadership of the Burdetts and Cobbetts rendered radicalism formidable, and the vigorous eloquence and mental resources of James Mill were powerful forces.

I conceive that the description so often given of a Benthamite, as a mere reasoning machine, though extremely inapplicable to most of those who have been designated by that title, was during two or three years of my life not altogether untrue of me. . . . Ambition and desire of distinction, I had in abundance; and zeal for what I thought the good of mankind was my strongest sentiment, mixing with and colouring all others. But my zeal was as yet little else, at that period of my life, than zeal for speculative opinions. . . . We found all the opinions to which we attached most importance, constantly attacked on the ground of feeling. Utility was denounced as cold calculation; political economy as hard-hearted; anti-population doctrines as repulsive to the natural feelings of mankind. We retorted by the word "sentimentality," which, along with "declamation" and "vague generalities," served us as common terms of opprobrium.

From the winter of 1821, when I first read Bentham, and especially from the commencement of the *Westminster Review,* I had what might truly be called an object in life; to be a reformer of the world. My conception of my own happiness was entirely identified with this object. The personal sympathies I wished for were those of fellow labourers in this enterprise. I endeavoured to pick up as many flowers as I could by the way; but as a serious and permanent personal satisfaction to rest upon, my whole reliance was placed on this; and I was accustomed to felicitate myself on the certainty of a happy life which I enjoyed, through placing my happiness in something durable and distant, in which some progress might be always making, while it could never be exhausted by complete attainment . . .

But the time came when I awakened from this as from a dream. It was in the autumn of 1826. I was in a dull state of nerves, such as everybody is occasionally liable to; unsusceptible to enjoyment or pleasurable excitement; one of those moods when what is pleasure at other times, becomes insipid or indifferent; the state, I should think, in which converts to Methodism usually are, when smitten by their first "conviction of sin." In this frame of mind it occurred to me to put the question directly to myself: "Suppose that all your objects in life were realized; that all the changes in institutions and opinions which you are looking forward to, could be completely effected at this very instant: would this be a great joy and happiness to you?" And an irrepressible self-consciousness distinctly answered, "No!" At this my heart sank within me: the whole foundation on which my life was constructed fell down . . .

At first I hoped that the cloud would pass away of itself; but it did not. A night's sleep, the sovereign remedy for the smaller vexations of life, had no effect on it. I awoke to a renewed consciousness of the woful fact. I carried it with me into all companies, into all occupations. Hardly anything had power to cause me even a few minutes' oblivion of it. For some months the cloud seemed to grow thicker and thicker. The lines in Coleridge's *Dejection*—I was not then acquainted with them—exactly describe my case:

> *"A grief without a pang, void, dark and drear,*
> *A drowsy, stifled, unimpassioned grief,*
> *Which finds no natural outlet or relief*
> *In word, or sigh, or tear."*

In vain I sought relief from my favourite books; those memorials of past nobleness and greatness from which I had always hitherto drawn strength and animation. I read them now without feeling, or with the accustomed feeling minus all its charm; and I became persuaded, that my love of mankind, and of excellence for its own sake, had worn itself out. I sought no comfort by speaking to others of what I felt. If I had loved any one sufficiently to make confiding my griefs a necessity, I should not have been in the condition I was . . .

My father, to whom it would have been natural to me to have recourse in any practical difficulties, was the last person to whom, in such a case as this, I looked for help. Everything convinced me that he had no knowledge of any such mental state as I was suffering from, and that even if he could be made to understand it, he was not the physician who could heal it. My education, which was wholly his work, had been conducted without any regard to the possibility of its ending in this result; and I saw no use in giving him the pain of thinking that his plans had failed, when the failure was probably irremediable, and, at all events, beyond the power of *his* remedies.

My course of study had led me to believe, that all mental and moral feelings and qualities, whether of a good or of a bad kind, were the results of association; that we love one thing, and hate another, take pleasure in one sort of action or contemplation, and pain in another sort, through the clinging of pleasurable or painful ideas to those things, from the effect of education or of experience. All those to whom I looked up, were of opinion that the pleasure of sympathy with human beings, and the feelings which made the good of others, and especially of mankind on a large scale, the object of existence, were the greatest and surest sources of happiness. Of the truth of this I was convinced, but to know that a feeling would make me happy if I had it, did not give me the feeling. My education, I thought, had failed to create these feelings in sufficient strength to resist the dissolving influence of analysis, while the whole course of my intellectual cultivation had made precocious and premature analysis the inveterate habit of my mind. I was thus, as I said to myself, left stranded at the commencement of my voyage, with a well-equipped ship and a rudder, but no sail; without any real desire for the ends which I had been so carefully fitted out to work for: no delight in virtue, or the general good, but also just as little in anything else. The fountains of vanity and ambition seemed to have dried up within me, as completely as those of benevolence. . . .

These were the thoughts which mingled with the dry heavy dejection of the melancholy winter of 1826–7. During this time I was not incapable of my usual occupations. I went on with them mechanically, by the mere force of habit. . . . Two lines of Coleridge, in whom alone of all writers I have found a true description of what I felt, were often in my thoughts, not at this time (for I had never read them), but in a later period of the same mental malady:

> *"Work without hope draws nectar in a sieve,*
> *And hope without an object cannot live."*

*From this state of congealed grief he was aroused by a burst of
tears over a pathetic passage in Marmontel's* Mémoires.

From this moment my burden grew lighter. The oppression of
the thought that all feeling was dead within me, was gone. I was
no longer hopeless: I was not a stock or a stone. . . . Thus the
cloud gradually drew off, and I again enjoyed life: and though
I had several relapses, some of which lasted many months, I never
again was as miserable as I had been.

The experiences of this period had two very marked effects
on my opinions and character. . . . Those only are happy (I
thought) who have their minds fixed on some object other than
their own happiness; on the happiness of others, on the improvement of mankind, even on some art or pursuit, followed not as
a means, but as itself an ideal end. Aiming thus at something
else, they find happiness by the way. . . . Ask yourself whether
you are happy, and you cease to be so. The only chance is to treat,
not happiness, but some end external to it, as the purpose of life.

The other important change which my opinions at this time un-
derwent, was that I, for the first time, gave its proper place, among
the prime necessities of human well-being, to the internal culture
of the individual. I ceased to attach almost exclusive importance
to the ordering of outward circumstances, and the training of the
human being for speculation and for action. . . .

The cultivation of the feelings became one of the cardinal
points in my ethical and philosophical creed. . . . I now began to
find meaning in the things which I had read or heard about the
importance of poetry and art as instruments of human culture. But
it was some time longer before I began to know this by personal
experience.

This state of my thoughts and feelings made the fact of my
reading Wordsworth for the first time (in the autumn of 1828),
an important event in my life. I took up the collection of his
poems from curiosity, with no expectation of mental relief from
it, though I had before resorted to poetry with that hope. . . .
What made Wordsworth's poems a medicine for my state of mind,
was that they expressed, not mere outward beauty, but states of

feeling, and of thought coloured by feeling, under the excitement of beauty. They seemed to be the very culture of the feelings, which I was in quest of. . . .

At the conclusion of the Poems came the famous Ode, falsely called Platonic, *Intimations of Immortality:* in which, along with more than his usual sweetness of melody and rhythm, and along with the two passages of grand imagery but bad philosophy so often quoted, I found that he too had had similar experience to mine; that he also had felt that the first freshness of youthful enjoyment of life was not lasting; but that he had sought for compensation, and found it, in the way in which he was now teaching me to find it. The result was that I gradually, but completely, emerged from my habitual depression, and was never again subject to it. . . . The intensest feeling of the beauty of a cloud lighted by the setting sun, is no hindrance to my knowing that the cloud is vapour of water, subject to all the laws of vapours in a state of suspension; and I am just as likely to allow for, and act on, these physical laws whenever there is occasion to do so, as if I had been incapable of perceiving any distinction between beauty and ugliness.

With this harmonious resolution of the conflict between his rational and emotional natures, he made rapid strides forward. His father regarded Carlyle's writing as "insane rhapsody"; *Mill came to see its* "wonderful power," "not as philosophy to instruct, but as poetry to animate." *In philosophy, Comte's doctrine* "of the natural succession of three stages in every department of human knowledge; first, the theological, next the metaphysical, and lastly, the positive." *

The scheme gradually unfolded by the St. Simonians, under which the labour and capital of society would be managed for the general account of the community, every individual being required to take a share of labour, either as thinker, teacher, artist, or producer, all being classed according to their capacity, and remunerated according to their work, appeared to me a far superior

---

* *Mill found himself in recoil, however, in after years, from Comte's later political philosophy as* "the completest system of spiritual and temporal despotism which ever yet emanated from a human brain."

description of Socialism to Owen's. . . . I honoured them most of all for what they have been most cried down for—the boldness and freedom from prejudice with which they treated the subject of family, the most important of any, and needing more fundamental alterations than remain to be made in any other great social institution, but on which scarcely any reformer has the courage to touch. In proclaiming the perfect equality of men and women, and an entirely new order of things in regard to their relations with one another, the St. Simonians, in common with Owen and Fourier, have entitled themselves to the grateful remembrance of future generations.

Again, in politics, though I no longer accepted the doctrine of the Essay on Government as a scientific theory; though I ceased to consider representative democracy as an absolute principle, and regarded it as a question of time, place, and circumstance; though I now looked upon the choice of political institutions as a moral and educational question more than one of material interests, thinking that it ought to be decided mainly by the consideration, what great improvement in life and culture stands next in order for the people concerned, as the condition of their further progress, and what institutions are most likely to promote that; nevertheless, this change in the premises of my political philosophy did not alter my practical political creed as to the requirements of my own time and country. I was as much as ever a Radical and Democrat for Europe, and especially for England.

I thought the predominance of the aristocratic classes, the noble and the rich, in the English constitution, an evil worth any struggle to get rid of; not on account of taxes, or any such comparatively small inconvenience, but as the great demoralizing agency in the country. Demoralizing, first, because it made the conduct of the Government an example of gross public immorality, through the predominance of private over public interests in the State, and the abuse of the powers of legislation for the advantage of classes. Secondly, and in a still greater degree, because the respect of the multitude always attaching itself principally to that which, in the existing state of society, is the chief passport to power; and under English institutions, riches, hereditary or acquired, being the almost exclusive source of political importance; riches, and the signs of riches, were almost the only things really respected, and the life of the people was mainly devoted to the pursuit of them. . . .

In this frame of mind the French Revolution of July found me. It roused my utmost enthusiasm, and gave me, as it were, a new existence. I went at once to Paris, was introduced to Lafayette, and laid the groundwork of the intercourse I afterwards kept up with several of the active chiefs of the extreme popular party.

My father's tone of thought and feeling, I now felt myself at a great distance from: greater, indeed, than a full and calm explanation and reconsideration on both sides, might have shown to exist in reality. But my father was not one with whom calm and full explanations on fundamental points of doctrine could be expected, at least with one whom he might consider as, in some sort, a deserter from his standard. Fortunately we were almost always in strong agreement on the political questions of the day, which engrossed a large part of his interest and of his conversation. On those matters of opinion on which we differed, we talked little. He knew that the habit of thinking for myself, which his mode of education had fostered, sometimes led me to opinions different from his, and he perceived from time to time that I did not always tell him how different. I expected no good, but only pain to both of us, from discussing our differences: and I never expressed them but when he gave utterance to some opinion or feeling repugnant to mine, in a manner which would have made it disingenuousness on my part to remain silent.

It was at the period of my mental progress which I have now reached that I formed the friendship which has been the honour and chief blessing of my existence, as well as the source of a great part of all that I have attempted to do, or hope to effect hereafter, for human improvement. My first introduction to the lady who, after a friendship of twenty years, consented to become my wife, was in 1830, when I was in my twenty-fifth and she in her twenty-third year. . . . It is not to be supposed that she was, or that any one, at the age at which I first saw her, could be, all that she afterwards became. Least of all could this be true of her, with whom self-improvement, progress in the highest and in all senses, was a law of her nature; a necessity equally from the ardour with which she sought it, and from the spontaneous tendency of faculties which could not receive an impression or an experience without making it the source or the occasion of an accession of wisdom.

To her outer circle she was a beauty and a wit, with an air of natural distinction, felt by all who approached her: to the inner, a woman of deep and strong feeling, of penetrating and intuitive intelligence, and of an eminently meditative and poetic nature. Married at an early age, to a most upright, brave, and honourable man, of liberal opinions and good education, but without the intellectual or artistic tastes which would have made him a companion for her, though a steady and affectionate friend, for whom she had true esteem and the strongest affection through life, and whom she most deeply lamented when dead; shut out by the social disabilities of women from any adequate exercise of her highest faculties in action on the world without; her life was one of inward meditation, varied by familiar intercourse with a small circle of friends, of whom one only (long since deceased) was a person of genius, or of capacities of feeling or intellect kindred with her own . . .

In her, complete emancipation from every kind of superstition (including that which attributes a pretended perfection to the order of nature and the universe), and an earnest protest against many things which are still part of the established constitution of society, resulted not from the hard intellect, but from strength of noble and elevated feeling, and co-existed with a highly reverential nature. In general spiritual characteristics, as well as in temperament and organization, I have often compared her, as she was at this time, to Shelley: but in thought and intellect, Shelley, so far as his powers were developed in his short life, was but a child compared with what she ultimately became. . . .

The same exactness and rapidity of operation, pervading as it did her sensitive as well as her mental faculties, would, with her gifts of feeling and imagination, have fitted her to be a consummate artist, as her fiery and tender soul and her vigorous eloquence would certainly have made her a great orator, and her profound knowledge of human nature and discernment and sagacity in practical life, would, in the times when such a *carrière* was open to women, have made her eminent among the rulers of mankind. Her intellectual gifts did but minister to a moral character at once the noblest and the best balanced which I have ever met with in life. . . . The passion of justice might have been thought to be her strongest feeling, but for her boundless generosity, and a lovingness ever ready to pour itself forth upon any or all human beings who were capable of giving the smallest feeling in return.

From this time, what is worth relating of my life will come into a very small compass; for I have no further mental changes to tell of, but only, as I hope, a continued mental progress; which does not admit of a consecutive history, and the results of which, if real, will be best found in my writings. I shall, therefore, greatly abridge the chronicle of my subsequent years.

Being now released from any active concern in temporary politics, and from any literary occupation involving personal communication with contributors and others, I was enabled to indulge the inclination, natural to thinking persons when the age of boyish vanity is once past, for limiting my own society to a very few persons. General society, as now carried on in England, is so insipid an affair, even to the persons who make it what it is, that it is kept up for any reason rather than the pleasure it affords. All serious discussion on matters on which opinions differ, being considered ill-bred, and the national deficiency in liveliness and sociability having prevented the cultivation of the art of talking agreeably on trifles, in which the French of the last century so much excelled, the sole attraction of what is called society to those who are not at the top of the tree, is the hope of being aided to climb a little higher in it; while to those who are already at the top, it is chiefly a compliance with custom, and with the supposed requirements of their station. . . . All these circumstances united, made the number very small of those whose society, and still more whose intimacy, I now voluntarily sought.

Among these, the principal was the incomparable friend of

whom I have already spoken. At this period she lived mostly with one young daughter, in a quiet part of the country, and only occasionally in town, with her first husband, Mr. Taylor. I visited her equally in both places: and was greatly indebted to the strength of character which enabled her to disregard the false interpretations liable to be put on the frequency of my visits to her while living generally apart from Mr. Taylor, and on our occasionally travelling together, though in all other respects our conduct during those years gave not the slightest ground for any other supposition than the true one, that our relation to each other at that time was one of strong affection and confidential intimacy only. For though we did not consider the ordinances of society binding on a subject so entirely personal, we did feel bound that our conduct should be such as in no degree to bring discredit on her husband, nor therefore on herself.

In this third period (as it may be termed) of my mental progress, which now went hand in hand with hers, my opinions gained equally in breadth and depth, I understood more things, and those which I had understood before, I now understood more thoroughly. . . .

The social problem of the future we considered to be, how to unite the greatest individual liberty of action, with a common ownership in the raw material of the globe, and an equal participation of all in the benefits of combined labour. . . . We saw clearly that to render any such social transformation either possible or desirable, an equivalent change of character must take place both in the uncultivated herd who now compose the labouring masses, and in the immense majority of their employers. Both these classes must learn by practice to labour and combine for generous, or at all events for public and social purposes, and not, as hitherto, solely for narrowly interested ones. But the capacity to do this has always existed in mankind, and is not, nor is ever likely to be, extinct. Education, habit, and the cultivation of the sentiments, will make a common man dig or weave for his country, as readily as fight for his country. . . . The deep-rooted selfishness which forms the general character of the existing state of society, is *so* deeply rooted, only because the whole course of existing institutions tends to

foster it; and modern institutions in some respects more than
ancient, since the occasion on which the individual is called on to
do anything for the public without receiving its pay, are far less
frequent in modern life, than in the smaller commonwealths of
antiquity.

Between the time of which I have now spoken, and the present,
took place the most important events of my private life. The first
of these was my marriage, in April, 1851, to the lady whose incomparable worth had made her friendship the greatest source to
me both of happiness and of improvement, during many years in
which we never expected to be in any closer relation to one another. Ardently as I should have aspired to this complete union
of our lives at any time in the course of my existence at which it
had been practicable, I, as much as my wife, would far rather have
foregone that privilege for ever, than have owed it to the premature
death of one for whom I had the sincerest respect, and she the
strongest affection.

That event, however, having taken place in July, 1849, it was
granted to me to derive from that evil my own greatest good, by
adding to the partnership of thought, feeling, and writing which
had long existed, a partnership of our entire existence. For seven
and a-half years that blessing was mine; for seven and a-half only!
I can say nothing which could describe, even in the faintest manner, what that loss was and is. But because I know that she would
have wished it, I endeavour to make the best of what life I have
left, and to work on for her purposes with such diminished strength
as can be derived from thoughts of her, and communion with her
memory.

Since then I have sought for such alleviation as my state admitted of, by the mode of life which most enabled me to feel her
still near me. I bought a cottage as close as possible to the place
where she is buried, and there her daughter (my fellow-sufferer
and now my chief comfort) and I, live constantly during a great
portion of the year. My objects in life are solely those which were
hers; my pursuits and occupations those in which she shared, or
sympathized, and which are indissolubly associated with her. Her

memory is to me a religion, and her approbation the standard by which, summing up as it does all worthiness, I endeavour to regulate my life.

Mill's "strongest feelings were engaged in" "the American civil war." *He knew that* "the slavery quarrel in America" "was in all its stages an aggressive enterprise of the slave-owners to extend the territory of slavery; under the combined influences of pecuniary interest, domineering temper, and the fanaticism of a class for its class privileges." *The armed rebellion of the South would, he hoped, make the people of the North* "join their banner with that of the noble body of Abolitionists, of whom Garrison was the courageous and single-minded apostle, Wendell Phillips the eloquent orator, and John Brown the voluntary martyr." *Brown's saying* "that he was worth more for hanging than for any other purpose" *reminded Mill,* "by its combination of wit, wisdom, and self-devotion, of Sir Thomas More."

"It may be imagined," *he concludes,* "with what feelings I contemplated the rush of nearly the whole upper and middle classes of my own country, even those who passed for Liberals, into a furious pro-Southern partisanship." "England is paying the penalty, in many uncomfortable ways, of the durable resentment which her ruling classes stirred up in the United States by their ostentatious wishes for the ruin of America as a nation."

In 1865 the electors of Westminster asked Mill to stand as their candidate for Parliament. He told them he would not do house-to-house canvassing nor incur any election expenses, forewarned them that he would give no time to purely local interests, and outlined his general political principles, including his belief in women's suffrage. They begged him to stand, and he was elected. At an election meeting an effort was made to discredit him with the working-class audience by asking him if he had written that they were generally liars. Mill bluntly said, " 'I did.' Scarcely were these two words out of my mouth, when vehement applause resounded through the whole meeting."

In Parliament he spoke for a broader basis of suffrage than was provided in Gladstone's Reform Bill, defeated a bill to prevent public meetings in parks, led the prosecution of Governor Eyre for the lawless violence with which he had suppressed an uprising in Jamaica, and helped defeat an Extradition Bill that would have led to the surrender of political refugees to the governments against which they had rebelled. His pamphlet on the Irish problem was called, as he knew it would be, extreme.

It is the character of the British people, or at least of the higher and middle classes who pass muster for the British people, that to induce them to approve of any change, it is necessary that they should look upon it as a middle course: they think every proposal extreme and violent unless they hear of some other proposal going still farther, upon which their antipathy to extreme views may discharge itself.

In the autumn of 1868 the Parliament which passed the Reform Act was dissolved, and at the new election for Westminster I was thrown out; not to my surprise.

He was now more obnoxious to the Tories than ever before, and the Conservative Liberals were by no means enthusiastic for him; his refusal to work for local interests also told against him. He was requested to become a candidate by several other constituencies, but made up his mind to return to private life. He retired to Avignon, where he spent his last five years.

SCOTCH PROPHET

IN HIS LATER YEARS CARLYLE HAD ASSUMED A STRANGE EMINENCE. He had become the Sage of Chelsea, something remote, prophetic, godlike, speaking words of gnomic wisdom. He dwelt in an august and blinding cloud. Froude's *Life,* which revealed him as a fallible being, destroyed an idol; the disciple who had presented his master in such an unlovely light was accused of vile taste, and hysterical screams of traitor, scavenger, and ghoul pierced the air.

But in truth Froude had loved and revered Carlyle "as he had loved and revered no other of the sons of men." And this very devotion demanded the unveiling for which he was execrated. Carlyle had poured torrents of scorn upon the decorous dressing-up of truth in conventional biography. Idealizing him, "to whom untruth of any kind was abominable"! Froude could not do it. Had he not consulted Carlyle on what to do about one of Mrs. Carlyle's letters in which an eminent living person was judged in terms "more just than flattering"? Carlyle had said, "It will do him no harm to know what a sensible woman thought of him." No, Froude's hero-worship was as unqualified as Boswell's; he lacked Boswell's passion for minute verification, but his devotion would not allow him to omit a single wart.

There were depths and reservations, though, strange half-thoughts stirring in the heart of Froude, of which he himself was perhaps not entirely aware. Sometimes they find their way to the surface in flashes of curious innuendo. He tells, for example, of Carlyle analyzing his own faults in his *Journal,* and discovering that he was intolerant, contemptuous of others, discourteous. Then Froude says quietly:

"One discovery came on him as a startling surprise.

" 'On the whole art thou not among the *vainest* of living men?
At bottom the very *vainest?* "

The something not hero worship behind that one sentence the
shrewd reader may gradually discover for himself. For against the
prickliness and acerbity of Carlyle there does stand out one figure
that is "white" and "stainless": the image of Mrs. Carlyle. Froude
revered the sage, but he was bewitched by the enchanting Jane.
He sees through her eyes the lonely years at Craigenputtock, with
Jane baking the bread, blacking the grate, scouring the floor,
"while Carlyle looked on encouragingly with his pipe"; he sees
her ill, lonely, and discontented while Carlyle writes in his silent
upper room or goes off by himself to a party at Lady Ashburton's.
It was not a pretty picture. And Carlyle himself deepened it by
torturing himself in his old age with lamentable exclamations for
his lost darling.

But if Froude was unjust he neither knew nor intended it. And
in all the larger outlines of Carlyle's character his judgment is
generous, his portrait sharply convincing. "When the Devil's
advocate has said his worst against Carlyle," Froude summarizes,
"he leaves a figure still of unblemished integrity, purity, loftiness
of purpose, and inflexible resolution to do right . . ." "In the
weightier matters of the law Carlyle's life had been without speck
or flaw."

Such is Froude's final estimate. It had been written not without inward struggle. There was loyalty to Carlyle; loyalty to con-
flicting affections; loyalty to truth. But the task was done. Bitten
deep in the lines, Carlyle lives before us: a figure of grotesque, self-
deluded comedy and of tragic woe. The lighting glares with lava-
flame and smoke and strange shadow as it were Carlyle's own fiery
apocalyptic utterance. It is a fantastic image. But it is no caricature, for Carlyle was his own caricature.

Thomas Carlyle

A History of the First Forty
Years of His Life

JAMES ANTHONY FROUDE

[Carlyle died in 1881. Froude's biography was published in 1882. *The First Forty Years* carries Carlyle's
life to 1835; *Life in London* takes the story into the
later years.]

CARLYLE WAS BORN AT ECCLEFECHAN, 4 DECEMBER, 1795, IN A STONE
*house which his father, a mason, had built with his own hands.
The boy ran barefoot in the single village street, down one side
of which flowed an open brook; he fed on oatmeal, milk, and
potatoes. At two, in a violent temper, he threw his little brown
stool at his brother, breaking one of its legs. It was a family trait:
Carlyle said of his father,* "In anger, he had no need of oaths; his
words were like sharp arrows that smote into the very heart."
"We all had to complain that we dared not freely love our father.
His heart seemed as if walled in."

But James Carlyle was also a man of mental power, with a
"bold, glowing style," "full of metaphor, though he knew not
what metaphor was, with all manner of potent words." *The son
inherited intellectaul abilities; he did well at school; it was decided
to send him* "to the university, with final outlook to the ministry."

To English ears university life suggests splendid buildings,
luxurious rooms, rich endowments as the reward of successful
industry; as students, young men between nineteen and twenty-

three with handsome allowances, spending each of them on an
average double the largest income which James Carlyle had
earned in any year of his life. Universities north of the Tweed
had in those days no money prizes to offer, no fellowships and
scholarships, nothing at all but an education, and a discipline
in poverty and self-denial. The lads who went to them were
the children, most of them, of parents as poor as Carlyle's father.
. . . They were sent to Edinburgh, Glasgow, or wherever it might
be, when they were mere boys of fourteen. They had no one to
look after them either on their journey or when they came to the
end. They walked from their homes, being unable to pay for coach-
hire. They entered their own names at the college. They found
their own humble lodgings, and were left entirely to their own
capacity for self-conduct. The carriers brought them oatmeal,
potatoes, and salt butter from the home farm, with a few eggs
occasionally as a luxury. With their thrifty habits they required
no other food. In the return cart their linen went back to their
mothers to be washed and mended.

*At Edinburgh, Carlyle claimed, he learned little. The profes-
sors were uninspired and perfunctory:* "The hungry young looked
up to their spiritual nurses, and . . . were bidden eat the east
wind." *Two things the University did: undermined his Calvinist
orthodoxy, and nourished ambitions that at the moment seemed
able to find no outlet but the unsatisfactory one of teaching in a
school at Kirkcaldy.*

"Grant me [Carlyle exclaimed] that, with a heart of inde-
pendence unyielding to thy favours and unbending to thy frowns,
I may attain to literary fame; and though starvation be my lot,
I will smile that I have not been born a king."

Carlyle had by this time abandoned the thought of the "ministry" as his possible future profession—not without a struggle,
for both his father's and his mother's hearts had been set upon
it; but the "grave prohibitive doubts" which had risen in him
of their own accord had been strengthened by Gibbon, whom he
had found in Irving's library and eagerly devoured. . . . The

"schoolmastering" too, after two years' experience of it, became intolerable. His disposition, at once shy and defiantly proud, had perplexed and displeased the Kirkcaldy burghers. . . .

The end was, that when December came Carlyle and Irving [Edward Irving, a friend] "kicked the schoolmaster functions over," removed to Edinburgh, and were adrift on the world. . . .

[Carlyle] was poor, unpopular, comparatively unknown, or, if known, known only to be feared and even shunned. In Edinburgh "from my fellow-creatures," he says, "little or nothing but vinegar was my reception when we happened to meet or pass near each other—my own blame mainly, so proud, shy, poor, at once so insignificant-looking and so grim and sorrowful. That in *Sartor* of the worm trodden on and proving a torpedo is not wholly a fable, but did actually befall once or twice, as I still with a kind of small, not ungenial, malice can remember." He had, however, as was said, nearly a hundred pounds, which he had saved out of his earnings; he had a consciousness of integrity worth more than gold to him. He had thrifty self-denying habits which made him content with the barest necessaries, and he resolutely faced his position. His family, though silently disapproving the step which he had taken and necessarily anxious about him, rendered what help they could. Once more the Ecclefechan carrier brought up the weekly or monthly supplies of oatmeal, cakes, butter, and, when needed, under-garments, returning with the dirty linen for the mother to wash and mend, and occasionally presents which were never forgotten; while Carlyle, after a thought of civil engineering, for which his mathematical training gave him a passing inclination, sate down seriously, if not very assiduously, to study law. . . .

He was beginning now, in addition to the problem of living which he had to solve, to learn what affliction meant. He was attacked with dyspepsia, which never wholly left him, and in these early years soon assumed its most torturing form, like "a rat gnawing at the pit of his stomach." . . .

Men who are out of humour with themselves often see their own condition reflected in the world outside them, and everything seems amiss because it is not well with themselves. But the state of Scotland and England also was well fitted to feed his discontent. The great war had been followed by a collapse. Wages were low, food at famine prices. Tens of thousands of artisans were out of work, their families were starving, and they themselves were growing mutinous.

[Carlyle] had not yet, as he expressed it, "taken the Devil by the horns." He did not mean to trouble the world with his doubts, and as yet he had not much else to trouble it with. But he was more and more restless. Reticence about his personal sufferings was at no time one of his virtues. Dyspepsia had him by the throat. Even the minor ailments to which our flesh is heir, and which most of us bear in silence, the eloquence of his imagination flung into forms like the temptations of a saint. His mother had early described him as "gey ill to live wi'," and while in great things he was the most considerate and generous of men, in trifles he was intolerably irritable.

Like Mill, he began to pass through a purgatory of doubt and despair.

"The men and women round me, even speaking with me, were but figures; I had practically forgotten that they were alive, that they were not merely automatic. In the midst of their crowded streets and assemblages, I walked solitary, and (except as it was my own heart, not another's, that I kept devouring), savage also as the tiger in his jungle. Some comfort it would have been could I, like Faust, have fancied myself tempted and tormented of the devil; for a hell as I imagine, without life, though only diabolic life, were more frightful: but in our age of downpulling and disbelief, the very devil has been pulled down, you cannot so much as believe in a devil. To me the universe was all void of life, of purpose, of volition, even of hostility: it was one huge, dead, immeasurable steam-engine, rolling on in its dead indifference, to grind me limb from limb. Oh, the vast, gloomy, solitary Golgotha and mill of death! . . .

"So had it lasted, as in bitter protracted death-agony through long years. The heart within me, unvisited by any heavenly dew-drop, was smouldering in sulphurous slow-consuming fire. . . .

Having no hope, neither had I any definite fear, were it of man or devil; nay, I often felt as if it might be solacing could the arch-devil himself, though in Tartarean terrors, but rise to me, that I might tell him a little of my mind. And yet, strangely enough, I lived in a continual indefinite pining fear; tremulous, pusillanimous apprehension of I knew not what. . . .

"Full of such humour was I one sultry dogday after much per-ambulation toiling along the dirty little Rue St. Thomas de l'Enfer in a close atmosphere and over pavements hot as Nebu-chadnezzar's furnace; whereby doubtless my spirits were little cheered; when all at once there rose a thought in me, and I asked myself: 'What art thou afraid of? wherefore, like a coward, dost thou for ever pip and whimper, and go cowering and trembling? Despicable biped! what is the sum total of the worst that lies before thee? Death? Well, death; and say the pangs of Tophet too, and all that the devil and man may, will, or can do against thee! Hast thou not a heart? canst thou not suffer whatsoever it be; and as a child of freedom, though outcast, trample Tophet itself under thy feet, while it consumes thee? Let it come, then, and I will meet it and defy it.' And as I so thought, there rushed like a stream of fire over my whole soul, and I shook base fear away from me for ever. I was strong; of unknown strength; a spirit; almost a god. Ever from that time, the temper of my misery was changed; not fear or whining sorrow was it, but in-dignation and grim fire-eyed defiance."

Miss Jane Welsh was a dark beauty, her eyes shining with mockery, her temper fiery. Her accomplishments were beyond those of the average young lady. She had wanted to "learn Latin like a boy"; and she teased and cajoled an indulgent father into allowing her. At school the master told her she was "a little deevil," but she made rapid strides in mathematics and in Vergil. A young lady so advanced, she was persuaded, should no longer play with dolls; she stabbed a favorite doll with a penknife, and, reciting the last sad words of Dido, immolated it upon a funeral pyre.

Such was the young lady whom Carlyle met through Edward

Irving, and with whom he established a correspondence that im-
perceptibly became more intimate.

Her relations with him were drifting gradually in the direction
in which friendships between young men and young women usually do drift. She had no thought of marrying him, but she was
flattered by his attachment. It amused her to see the most remarkable person that she had ever met with at her feet. His birth
and position seemed to secure her against the possibility of any
closer connection between them. Thus he had a trying time of
it. In serious moments she would tell him that their meeting
had made an epoch in her history, and had influenced her character and life. When the humour changed, she would ridicule
his Annandale accent, turned his passionate expressions to scorn,
and when she had toned him down again she would smile once
more, and enchant him back into illusions. She played with him,
frightened him away, drew him back, quarrelled with him, received him again into favour as the fancy took her, till at last
the poor man said, "My private idea is that you are a witch like
Sapphira in the New Testament, concerning whom Dr. Nimmo
once preached in my hearing: 'It seems probable, my friends, that
Ananias was tempted into this by some spirit more wicked than
his wife.'" At last, in the summer of 1823, just after he was settled
at Kinnaird, she was staying in some house which she particularly
disliked, and on this occasion, in a fit of impatience with her surroundings—for she dated a letter which she wrote to him thence,
very characteristically, as from "Hell"—she expressed a gratitude
for Carlyle's affection for her, more warm than she had ever expressed before. He believed her serious, and supposed that she had
promised to be his wife. . . .

"My friend (she said), I love you. I repeat it, though I find
the expression a rash one. All the best feelings of my nature are
concerned in loving you. But were you my brother I should love
you the same. No. Your friend I will be, your truest, most devoted
friend, while I breathe the breath of life. But your wife, never.
Never, not though you were as rich as Crœsus, as honoured and renowned as you yet shall be."

Carlyle took his rebuke manfully. "My heart," he said, "is too old by almost half a score of years, and is made of sterner stuff than to break in junctures of this kind. I have no idea of dying in the Arcadian shepherd's style for the disappointment of hopes which I never seriously entertained, or had no right to entertain seriously." Could they have left matters thus, it had been better for both of them. Two diamonds do not easily form cup and socket.

Carlyle's emotional disturbances were aggravated by his dyspepsia.

There can be no doubt that Carlyle suffered and perhaps suffered excessively. It is equally certain that his sufferings were immensely aggravated by the treatment to which he was submitted. "A long hairy-eared jackass," as he called some eminent Edinburgh physician, had ordered him to give up tobacco, but he had ordered him to take mercury, as well; and he told me that along with the mercury he must have swallowed whole hogsheads of castor oil. Much of his pain would be so accounted for; but of all the men whom I have ever seen, Carlyle was the least patient of the common woes of humanity. Nature had, in fact, given him a constitution of unusual strength. He saw his ailments through the lens of his imagination, so magnified by the metaphors in which he described them as to seem to him to be something supernatural; and if he was a torment to himself, he distracted every one with whom he came in contact. . . .

I have dwelt more fully on these aspects of Carlyle's character than in themselves they deserve, because the irritability which he could not or would not try to control followed him through the greater part of his life. It was no light matter to take charge of such a person, as Miss Welsh was beginning to contemplate the possibility of doing. Nor can we blame the anxiety with which her mother was now regarding the closeness of the correspondence between Carlyle and her daughter. Extreme as was the undesirableness of such a marriage in a worldly point of view, it is to Mrs. Welsh's credit that inequality of social position was not the cause of her alarm, so much as the violence of temper which Carlyle could not restrain even before her. The fault, however, was of the surface merely, and Miss Welsh was not the only person who could see the essential quality of the nature which lay below.

Meanwhile, in London, where he was tutoring a young man named Charles Buller, he was finding little to admire and a great deal to censure. Coleridge was "flat, flabby, incurvated, with a watery mouth, a snuffy nose, a pair of strange, brown, timid, yet earnest-looking eyes, a high tapering brow, and a great bush of grey hair . . . He has no resolution . . . in walking he does not tread, but shovel and slide. . . . He is also always busied to keep, by strong and frequent inhalations, the water of his mouth from overflowing." *His conversation was wandering, unprofitable, and tedious.* Macaulay was "a sophistical, rhetorical, ambitious young man" *who made* "flash speeches." *Charles Lamb was a* "pitiful, ricketty, gasping, staggering, stammering Tomfool" *who had become* "a confirmed, shameless drunkard; *asks* vehemently for gin and water in strangers' houses." *Rogers was* "an elegant, politely malignant old lady," *Moore* "a lascivious triviality of great name," *Bentham* "a driveller and garrulous old man."

Paris was worse:

"Of Paris I shall say nothing till we meet. It is the Vanity Fair of the Universe, and cannot be described in many letters. With few exceptions the streets are narrow and crowded and unclean, the kennel in the middle, and a lamp hanging over it here and there on a rope from side to side. There are no footpaths, but an everlasting press of carriages and carts and dirty people hastening to and fro among them, amidst a thousand gare-gares and sacrés and other oaths and admonitions; while by the side are men roasting chestnuts in their booths, fruitshops, wineshops, barbers; silk merchants selling à prix juste (without cheating), restaurateurs, cafés, traiteurs, magasins de bonbons, billiard-tables, estaminets (gin-shops), débits de tabac (where you buy a cigar for a half-penny and go out smoking it), and every species of dépôt and entrepôt and magasin for the comfort and refreshment of the physical part of the natural man, plying its vocation in the midst of noise and stink, both of which it augments by its produce and by its efforts to dispose of it. The Palais Royal is a spot unrivalled in the world, the chosen abode of vanity and vice, the true palace of the tigre-singes (tiger-apes), as Voltaire called his countrymen, a place which I rejoice to think is separated from me by the girdle of the ocean, and never likely to be copied in the British Isles."

He had reflected much on his engagement with Miss Welsh. He had felt that perhaps he had done wrong in allowing her to entangle herself with a person whose future was so uncertain, and whose present schemes, even if realised successfully, would throw her, if she married him, into a situation so unlike what she had anticipated, so unlike the surroundings to which she had been accustomed. In his vehement way he had offered to release her if she wished it; and she had unhesitatingly refused. As little, however, was her ambition gratified with the prospect of being mistress of a Scotch farm. She had mocked at his proposal. She had pointed out with serious truth his own utter unfitness for a farmer's occupation. She had jestingly told him that she had land of her own at Craigenputtock. The tenant was leaving. If he was bent on trying, let him try Craigenputtock. He took her jest in earnest. Why should he not farm Craigenputtock? Why should not she, as she was still willing to be his life companion, live with him there? . . .

"I little thought [Jane replied] that my joke about your farming Craigenputtock was to be made the basis of such a serious and extraordinary project. . . . You have sometimes asked me did I ever think? For once in my life at least I have thought myself into a vertigo, and without coming to any positive conclusion. However, my mind, such as it is, on the matter you have thus precipitately forced on my consideration I will explain to you frankly and explicitly, as the happiness of us both requires. I love you, and I should be the most ungrateful and injudicious of mortals if I did not. But I am not *in love* with you; that is to say, my love for you is not a passion which overclouds my judgment and absorbs all my regards for myself and others. It is a simple, honest, serene affection made up of admiration and sympathy, and better perhaps to found domestic enjoyment on than any other. In short, it is a love which *influences,* but does not *make* the destiny of a life.

"And now let me ask you, have you any *certain* livelihood to maintain me in the manner I have been used to live in? any *fixed* place in the rank of society I have been born and bred in? No. You have projects for attaining both, capabilities for attaining both, and much more. But as yet you have not attained them. . . . Devise then how you may gain yourself a moderate but *settled* income. Think of some more promising plan than farming the most barren spot in the county of Dumfriesshire. What a thing that would be to be sure! You and I keeping house at Craigenputtock! I would as soon think of building myself a nest on the Bass Rock. Nothing but your ignorance of the spot saves you from the imputation of insanity for admitting such a thought. Depend upon it you could not exist there a twelvemonth. For my part I could not spend a month at it with an angel. . . . At all events I will marry no one else. This is all the promise I can or will make."

"The maxims you proceed by [Carlyle answered] are those of common and acknowledged prudence; and I do not say that it is not wise in you to walk exclusively by them. But for me, my case is peculiar; and unless I adopt other than common maxims, I look upon my ruin as already sure. In fact I cannot but perceive that the stations from which we have looked at life, and formed our schemes of it, are in your case and mine essentially different. You have a right to anticipate excitement and enjoyment. The highest blessing I anticipate is peace. You are bound to pay deference to the criticisms of others, and expect their approbation; I, to pay comparatively little deference to their criticisms, and to overlook their contempt. This is not strange; but it accounts for the wide discrepancy in our principles and intentions and demands the serious study of us both.

"In your opinion about sacrifices, *felt to be such,* I entirely agree; but at the same time need I remind your warm and generous heart that the love which will not make sacrifices to its object is no proper love? Grounded in admiration and the feeling of enjoyment, it is a fit love for a picture or a statue or a poem; but for a living soul it is not fit. Alas! without deep sacrifices on both sides, the possibility of our union is an empty dream. It remains for us both to determine what extent of sacrifice it is worth. To me, I confess the union with such a spirit as yours might be, is worth all price but the sacrifice of those very principles which would enable me to deserve and enjoy it."

The functions of a biographer are, like the functions of a Greek chorus, occasionally at the important moments to throw in some moral remarks which seem to fit the situation. The chorus after such a letter would remark, perhaps, on the subtle forms of self-deception to which the human heart is liable, of the momentous nature of marriage, and how men and women plunge heedlessly into the net, thinking only of the satisfaction of their own immediate wishes. . . . Self-sacrifice it might say was a noble thing. But a sacrifice which one person might properly make, the other might have no reasonable right to ask or to allow. It would conclude, however, that the issues of human acts are in the hands of the gods, and would hope for the best in fear and trembling. Carlyle spoke of self-denial. The self-denial which he was prepared to make was the devotion of his whole life to the pursuit and setting forth of spiritual truth; throwing aside every meaner ambition. But apostles in St. Paul's opinion were better unwedded.

Carlyle, restless and feverish, was convinced that no real work could be got out of him till he was again in a home of his own, and till his affairs were settled on some permanent footing. His engagement, while it remained uncompleted, kept him anxious and irritated. Therefore he conceived that he must find some cottage suited to his circumstances, and that Miss Welsh ought to become immediately the mistress of it. He had money enough to begin housekeeping; he saw his way, he thought, to earning money enough to continue it on the scale on which he had himself been bred up—but it was on condition that the wife that he took to himself should do the work of a domestic servant as his own mother and sisters did; and he was never able to understand that a lady differently educated might herself, or her friends for her, find a difficulty in accepting such a situation. He was in love, so far as he understood what love meant. . . .

Mrs. Welsh being left a widow, and with no other child, the

pain of separation from her daughter was unusually great. Notwithstanding a certain number of caprices, there was a genuine and even passionate attachment between mother and daughter. It might have seemed that a separation was unnecessary, and that if Mrs. Welsh could endure to have Carlyle under her own roof, no difficulty on his side ought to have arisen. Mrs. Welsh indeed, romantically generous, desired to restore the property, and go back to live with her father at Templand; but her daughter decided peremptorily that she would rather live with Carlyle in poverty all the days of her life than encroach in the smallest degree on her mother's independence. She could expect no happiness, she said, if she failed in the first duty of her life. Her mother should keep the fortune, or else Miss Welsh refused to leave her.

All difficulties might be got over, the entire economic problem might be solved, if the family could be kept together. . . . Mrs. Welsh was as unhappy as ever at an alliance that she regarded as not imprudent only, but in the highest degree objectionable. . . . Yet for her daughter's sake she was willing to make an effort to like him, and, since the marriage was to be, either to live with him or to accept him as her son-in-law in her own house and in her own circle. . . .

Her consent to take Carlyle into her family removed Miss Welsh's remaining scruples, and made her perfectly happy. It never occurred to her that Carlyle himself would refuse, and the reasons which he alleged might have made a less resolute woman pause before she committed herself further. It would never answer, he said; "two households could not live as if they were one, and he would never have any right enjoyment of his wife's company till she was all his own." Mrs. Welsh had a large acquaintance. He liked none of them, and "her visitors would neither be diminished in numbers nor bettered in quality." No! he must have the small house in Edinburgh; and "the moment he was master of a house, the first use he would turn it to would be to slam the door against nauseous intruders." It never occurred to him, as proved too fatally to be the case, that he would care little for "the right companionship" when he had got it; that he would be absorbed in his work; that, after all, his wife would see but little of him, and that little too often under trying conditions of temper; that her mother's companionship, and the "intrusion" of her mother's old friends, might add more to her comfort than it could possibly detract from his own. . . .

Jane was hurt, deeply hurt, but her old imperiousness was dead now. In a tearful and frightened letter she wailed that they were "already married, married past redemption. God knows in that case what is to become of us. At times I am so disheartened that I could sit down and weep."

"Carlyle could just perceive that he had not been gracious," *but he was adamantine.*

"There is one thing that strikes me more and more the longer I think of it—this, the grand objection of all objections, the head and front of offence, the soul of all my counterpleading—an objection which is too likely to overset the whole project. It may be stated in a word: *'The man should bear rule in the house, and not the woman.'* This is an eternal axiom, the law of nature, which no mortal departs from unpunished. I have meditated on this many years, and every day it grows plainer to me. I must not, and I cannot, live in a house of which I am not head. I should be miserable myself, and make all about me miserable.". . .

Mrs. Welsh had resolved to leave Haddington and to give up her house there immediately. The associations of the place after her daughter was gone would necessarily be most painful. All her friends, the social circle of which she had been the centre, regarded the marriage with Carlyle as an extraordinary mésalliance. . . .

It occurred to Carlyle that since Mrs. Welsh was going away the house at Haddington would do well for himself. There it stood, ready provided with all that was necessary. He recollected that Edinburgh was noisy and disagreeable, Haddington quiet, and connected with his own most pleasant recollections. It might have occurred to him that under such altered circumstances, where she would be surrounded by a number of acquaintances, to every one of whom her choice appeared like madness, Miss Welsh might object to living there as much as her mother. She made her objections as delicately as she could; but he pushed them aside as if they were mere disordered fancies; and the fear of "nauseous intruders," which had before appeared so dreadful to him, he disposed of with the most summary serenity. "To me," he calmly wrote, "among the weightier evils and blessings of existence, the evil of impertinent visitors, and so forth, seems but a small drop of the bucket, and an exceedingly little thing. I have nerve in me to despatch that sort of deer for ever by dozens in the day."

But they did not go to Haddington. Ultimately a small house was found in Edinburgh, at Comely Bank. Neither had any prescience of the six long years, from 1828 to 1834, at Craigenputtock, where, Jane had said, she "would not spend a month with an Angel."

The wedding day drew on; not without (as was natural) more than the usual nervousness on both sides at the irrevocable step which was about to be ventured. Carlyle knew too well "that he was a perverse mortal to deal with," "that the best resolutions made shipwreck in practice," and that "it was a chance if any woman could be happy with him." . . .

Miss Welsh, too, as well as Carlyle, had a fiery temper. When provoked she was as hard as flint, with possibilities of dangerous sparks of fire. She knew her tendencies and made the best resolutions:—

"I am going really to be a very meek-tempered wife," she wrote.

Jest as she would, however, Miss Welsh was frightened and Carlyle was frightened. . . .

Carlyle, on his side, tried to allay his fears of what Miss Welsh called "the odious ceremony" by reading Kant, and had reached the hundred and fiftieth page of the *Kritik der reinen Vernunft,* when he found that it was too abstruse for his condition, and that Scott's novels would answer better.

The married life of Carlyle and Jane Welsh was not happy in the roseate sense of happiness. In the fret and chafe of daily life the sharp edges of the facets of two diamonds remain keen, and they never wear into surfaces which harmoniously correspond. A man and a woman of exceptional originality and genius are proper mates for one another only if they have some other object before them besides happiness, and are content to do without it. For the forty years which these two extraordinary persons lived together, their essential conduct to the world and to each other was sternly upright. They had to encounter poverty in its most threatening aspect—poverty which they might at any moment have escaped if Carlyle would have sacrificed his intellectual integrity, would have carried his talents to the market, and written down to the level of the multitude. If he ever flagged, it was his wife who spurred him on; nor would she ever allow him to do less than his very best. She never flattered anyone, least of all her husband; and when she saw cause for it the sarcasms flashed out from her as the sparks fly from lacerated steel. Carlyle, on his side, did not find in his marriage the miraculous transformation of nature which he had promised himself. He remained lonely and dyspeptic, possessed by thoughts and convictions which struggled in him for utterance, and which could be fused and cast into form only (as I have heard him say) when his whole mind was at white heat. . . .

The victory was won, but, as of old in Aulis, not without a victim. Miss Welsh had looked forward to being Carlyle's intellectual companion, to sharing his thoughts and helping him with his writings. She was not over-rating her natural powers when she felt equal to such a position and deserving it. The reality was not like the dream. . . .

The hardest part of all was that he did not see that there was occasion for any special acknowledgment. Poor men's wives had to work. She was a poor man's wife, and it was fit and natural that she should work. . . . When he was at work he could bear no one in the room; and, at least through middle life, he rode and walked alone, not choosing to have his thoughts interrupted. The slightest noise or movement at night shattered his nervous system; therefore he required a bedroom to himself; thus from the first she saw little of him, and as time went on less and less; and she, too, was human and irritable. Carlyle proved, as his mother had known him, "ill to live with."

Carlyle was essentially solitary. He went out in all weathers, indifferent to wet and, in spite of his imagined ill-health impervious to cold. But he preferred to be alone with his thoughts, and Mrs. Carlyle was left at home to keep the house in proper order. She by education, and he by temperament, liked everything to be kept well and trim. He was extremely dainty about his food. He did not care for delicacies, but cleanliness and perfect cookery of common things he always insisted on, and if the porridge was smoked, or the bread heavy, or the butter less than perfect, or a plate or a dish ill-washed, he was entirely intolerable. Thus the necessary imperfections of Scotch farm-servant girls had to be supplemented by Mrs. Carlyle herself. She baked the bread, she dressed the dinner or saw it dressed, she cleaned the rooms. Among her other accomplishments she had to learn to milk the cows, in case the byre-woman should be out of the way, for fresh milk was the most essential article of Carlyle's diet. Nay, it might happen that she had to black the grates to the proper polish, or even scour the floors while Carlyle looked on encouragingly with his pipe.

At last an escape to London offered: Mill and a number of Radicals were founding a new review that they wanted Carlyle to write for. "If they pay me rightly they shall have a paper or two; if not, not. The Radicals, I say always are barren as Sahara, but *not* poisonous." . . .

"Yes, we must try it! Life here is but a kind of life-in-death, or rather, one might say, a not-being-born: one sits as in the belly of some Trojan horse, weather screened, but pining, inactive, neck and heels crushed together. Let us burst it in the name of God!"

Thus the six years' imprisonment on the Dumfriesshire moors came to an end. To Carlyle himself they had been years of inestimable value. . . . He had been tried in the furnace. Poverty, mortification, and disappointment had done their work upon him, and he had risen above them elevated, purified, and strengthened. . . .

He had laid in, too, on the moors a stock of robust health.

Lamentations over indigestion and want of sleep are almost totally absent from the letters written from Craigenputtock. The simple, natural life, the wholesome air, the daily rides or drives, the simple food—milk, cream, eggs, oatmeal, the best of their kind— had restored completely the functions of a stomach never, perhaps, so far wrong as he had imagined. Carlyle had ceased to complain on this head, and in a person so extremely vocal when anything was amiss with him, silence is the best evidence that there was nothing to complain. . . .

To Mrs. Carlyle Craigenputtock had been a less salutary home. She might have borne the climate, and even benefited by it, if the other conditions had been less ungenial. But her life there, to begin with, had been a life of menial drudgery, unsolaced (for she could have endured and even enjoyed mere hardship) by more than an occasional word of encouragement or sympathy or compassion from her husband. . . . Mrs. Carlyle's bodily health never recovered from the strain of those six years. The trial to her mind and nervous system was still more severe. . . . When he was busy she rarely so much as saw him, save, as he himself pathetically tells, when she would steal into his dressing-room in the morning when he was shaving, to secure that little of his society. The loneliness of Craigenputtock was dreadful to her. Her hard work, perhaps, had so far something of a blessing in it, that it was a relief from the intolerable pressure.

CHILD SACRIFICE

JAMES AND MARGARET RUSKIN MORE UTTERLY DOMINATED THE ENTIRE life of their only child than James Mill would ever have aspired to do. And they were not two philosophical radicals trying to fashion a mind that should be a perfect instrument. They were merely a respectable and honest sherry-merchant and his very sober, evangelical, and sternly upright wife. Few things are stranger in autobiography than the almost detached objectivity with which, years later, their son analyzes them. Very clearly John Ruskin sees the oddness of that solitary family group, and he probes into its hidden relationships with an almost painful minuteness. For the tragedy of it was that these two intelligent and conscientious people maimed the life of their dearly beloved son.

He was not given any toys except a cart and a ball and two boxes of blocks. He was not allowed to eat the fruit in the garden at Herne Hill. He listened to long Sunday sermons from the bottom of the pew. He read and reread every line of the Bible. He was hardly allowed to see other children; at the seashore he was not allowed to row or sail or walk near the harbor alone. Everywhere the Ruskins were together and everywhere they were alone. When they went abroad in their big traveling carriage, they "no more partook of the life about them than do the curious who go under the sea in a diving bell." They were tourists, not travelers; they went for the picturesque, not as an eighteenth century gentleman did, to observe the arts, manufactures, and governments of other nations and mingle with their famous men.

But at the same time the Ruskins were utterly indulgent. Nothing was too good for their son; nothing that could be helpful or gratifying to him would they withhold; nothing that could be made easy would they allow to be hard. Virtually convent-bred, he was kept solitary, indulged, restrained, given no responsibility, fussed over, worshiped, and distrusted. All told, Ruskin's two devoted parents made a dreadful mess out of his life.

He took refuge in work. He wrote, he lectured eloquently in a beautiful voice that enchanted his listeners. He was famous, but more and more the world afflicted him with "great fits of vexation." He was "always howling and bawling the right road," he complained, "to a generation of drunken coachmen," his head up through the trapdoor and his face all over mud, "and no right road to be got gone upon after all." But people paid no attention, or they angrily cried out that what he wrote was insane raving. The loves of his life brought him only misery: Adèle-Clotilde, Charlotte Lockhart, Rose La Touche, for whom he had hoped since he was forty-five, and who had been estranged from him and died when he was fifty-six. His mother's apronstrings held him securely from them all. "He is the gentlest and most innocent of mankind," Benjamin Jowett said, "of great genius, but inconsecutive, and he has never rubbed his mind against others, so that he is ignorant of very obvious things."

Never rubbed his mind against others! It was, as Ruskin himself had come to know, the truth. That is what gives *Praeterita* its odd, bitter, sweet, and pathetic flavor. There are pages of eloquence and sarcasm and beauty. Mingled with the hurt are gentleness and understanding too. There are abounding passages of strange insight, a curious almost impersonal penetration in his dissection of old wounds. There are also long-winded wanderings from the point, eccentricities, fantastic intrusions that build up a mood of impatience in some readers' minds. But no other nineteenth century autobiographer so deeply and touchingly reveals the hidden springs of his life.

Praeterita

JOHN RUSKIN

[Ruskin was born in 1819 and lived until 1900. *Praeterita* was issued at irregular intervals between 1885 and 1889.]

MY FATHER BEGAN BUSINESS AS A WINE-MERCHANT, WITH NO CAPITAL, and a considerable amount of debts bequeathed him by my grandfather. He accepted the bequest, and paid them all before he began to lay by anything for himself, for which his best friends called him a fool, and I, without expressing any opinion as to his wisdom, which I knew in such matters to be at least equal to mine, have written on the granite slab over his grave that he was "an entirely honest merchant." As days went on he was able to take a house in Hunter Street, Brunswick Square, No. 54, (the windows of it, fortunately for me, commanded a view of a marvellous iron post, out of which the water-carts were filled through beautiful little trap-doors, by pipes like boa-constrictors; and I was never weary of contemplating that mystery, and the delicious dripping consequent) ; and as years went on, and I came to be four or five years old, he could command a postchaise and pair for two months in the summer, by help of which, with my mother and me, he went the round of his country customers (who liked to see the principal of the house his own traveller) ; so that, at a jog-trot pace, and through the panoramic opening of the four windows of a postchaise, made more panoramic still to me because my seat was a little bracket in front, (for we used to hire the chaise regularly for the two months out of Long Acre, and so could have it bracketed and pocketed as we liked,) I saw all the high-roads, and most of the cross ones, of England and Wales, and great part of lowland Scotland, as far as Perth, where every other year we spent the whole summer . . .

My mother's general principles of first treatment were, to guard me with steady watchfulness from all avoidable pain or danger; and, for the rest, to let me amuse myself as I liked, provided I was neither fretful nor troublesome. But the law was, that I should find my own amusement. No toys of any kind were at first allowed;—and the pity of my Croydon aunt for my monastic poverty in this respect was boundless. On one of my birthdays, thinking to overcome my mother's resolution by splendor of temptation, she bought the most radiant Punch and Judy she could find in all the Soho bazaar—as big as a real Punch and Judy, all dressed in scarlet and gold, and that would dance, tied to the leg of a chair. I must have been greatly impressed, for I remember well the look of the two figures, as my aunt herself exhibited their virtues. My mother was obliged to accept them; but afterward quietly told me it was not right that I should have them; and I never saw them again.

Nor did I painfully wish, what I was never permitted for an instant to hope, or even imagine, the possession of such things as one saw in toy-shops. I had a bunch of keys to play with, as long as I was capable only of pleasure in what glittered and jingled; as I grew older, I had a cart, and a ball; and when I was five or six years old, two boxes of well-cut wooden bricks. With these modest, but, I still think, entirely sufficient possessions, and being always summarily whipped if I cried, did not do as I was bid, or tumbled on the stairs, I soon attained serene and secure methods of life and motion; and could pass my days contentedly in tracing the squares and comparing the colors of my carpet;—examining the knots in the wood of the floor, or counting the bricks in the opposite houses; with rapturous intervals of excitement during the filling of the water-cart, through its leathern pipe, from the dripping iron post at the pavement edge; or the still more admirable proceedings of the turncock, when he turned and turned till a fountain sprang up in the middle of the street. But the carpet, and what patterns I could find in bed-covers, dresses, or wall-papers to be examined, were my chief resources, and my attention to the particulars in these was soon so accurate, that when at three and a half I was taken to have my portrait painted by Mr. North-cote, I had not been ten minutes alone with him before I asked him why there were holes in his carpet. The portrait in question represents a very pretty child with yellow hair, dressed in a white frock like a girl, with a broad light-blue sash and blue shoes to match; the feet of the child wholesomely large in proportion to its body; and the shoes still more wholesomely large in proportion to the feet.

These articles of my daily dress were all sent to the old painter for perfect realization; but they appear in the picture more re-markable than they were in my nursery, because I am represented as running in a field at the edge of a wood with the trunks of its trees striped across in the manner of Sir Joshua Reynolds; while two rounded hills, as blue as my shoes, appear in the distance, which were put in by the painter at my own request; for I had already been once, if not twice, taken to Scotland; and my Scottish nurse having always sung to me as we approached the Tweed or Esk,—

"For Scotland, my darling, lies full in my view,
With her barefooted lassies, and mountains so blue,"

the idea of distant hills was connected in my mind with approach to the extreme felicities of life, in my (Scottish) aunt's garden of gooseberry bushes, sloping to the Tay. But that, when old Mr. Northcote asked me (little thinking, I fancy, to get any answer so explicit) what I would like to have in the distance of my pic-ture, I should have said "blue hills" instead of "gooseberry bushes," appears to me—and I think without any morbid tendency to think overmuch of myself—a fact sufficiently curious, and not without promise, in a child of that age.

I think it should be related also that having, as aforesaid, been steadily whipped if I was troublesome, my formed habit of serenity was greatly pleasing to the old painter; for I sat contentedly motionless, counting the holes in his carpet, or watching him squeeze his paint out of its bladders,—a beautiful operation, indeed, to my thinking;—but I do not remember taking any interest in Mr. Northcote's application of the pigments to the canvas; my ideas of delightful art, in that respect, involving indispensably the possession of a large pot, filled with paint of the brightest green, and of a brush which would come out of it soppy. But my quietude was so pleasing to the old man that he begged my father and mother to let me sit to him for the face of a child which he was painting in a classical subject; where I was accordingly represented as reclining on a leopard skin, and having a thorn taken out of my foot by a wild man of the woods.

My mother had, as she afterward told me, solemnly "devoted me to God" before I was born; in imitation of Hannah.

Very good women are remarkably apt to make away with their children prematurely, in this manner. . . .

"Devoting me to God," meant, as far as my mother knew herself what she meant, that she would try to send me to college, and make a clergyman of me: and I was accordingly bred for "the Church." My father, who—rest be to his soul—had the exceedingly bad habit of yielding to my mother in large things and taking his own way in little ones, allowed me, without saying a word, to be thus withdrawn from the sherry trade as an unclean thing; not without some pardonable participation in my mother's ultimate views for me. For, many and many a year afterward, I remember, while he was speaking to one of our artist friends, who admired Raphael, and greatly regretted my endeavors to interfere with that popular taste,—while my father and he were condoling with each other on my having been impudent enough to think I could tell the public about Turner and Raphael,—instead of contenting myself, as I ought, with explaining the way of their souls' salvation to them—and what an amiable clergyman was lost in me,—"Yes," said my father, with tears in his eyes— (true and tender tears, as ever father shed,) "he would have been a Bishop."

Luckily for me, my mother, under these distinct impressions of her own duty, and with such latent hopes of my future eminence, took me very early to church;—where, in spite of my quiet habits, and my mother's golden vinaigrette, always indulged to me there, and there only, with its lid unclasped that I might see the wreathed open pattern above the sponge, I found the bottom of the pew so extremely dull a place to keep quiet in, (my best story-books being also taken away from me in the morning,) that, as I have somewhere said before, the horror of Sunday used even to cast its prescient gloom as far back in the week as Friday—and all the glory of Monday, with church seven days removed again, was no equivalent for it.

Notwithstanding, I arrived at some abstract in my own mind of the Rev. Mr. Howell's sermons; and occasionally, in imitation of him, preached a sermon at home over the red sofa cushions;—this performance being always called for by my mother's dearest friends, as the great accomplishment of my childhood. The sermon was, I believe, some eleven words long;—very exemplary, it seems to me, in that respect—and I still think must have been the purest gospel, for I know it began with, "People, be good."

When the child was four the family moved to Herne Hill.

It had front and back garden in sufficient proportion to its size; the front, richly set with old evergreens, and well-grown lilac and laburnum; the back, seventy yards long by twenty wide, renowned over all the hill for its pears and apples, which had been chosen with extreme care by our predecessor, (shame on me to forget the name of a man to whom I owe so much!) —and possessing also a strong old mulberry tree, a tall whiteheart cherry tree, a black Kentish one, and an almost unbroken hedge, all round, of alternate gooseberry and currant bush; decked, in due season, (for the ground was wholly beneficent,) with magical splendor of abundant fruit: fresh green, soft amber, and rough-bristled crimson bending the spinous branches; clustered pearl and pendant ruby joyfully discoverable under the large leaves that looked like vine.

The differences of primal importance which I observed between the nature of this garden, and that of Eden, as I had imagined it, were, that, in this one, *all* the fruit was forbidden; and there were no companionable beasts: in other respects the little domain

answered every purpose of Paradise to me; and the climate, in that
cycle of our years, allowed me to pass most of my life in it. My
mother never gave me more to learn than she knew I could easily
get learnt, if I set myself honestly to work, by twelve o'clock. She
never allowed anything to disturb me when my task was set; if it
was not said rightly by twelve o'clock, I was kept in till I knew it,
and in general, even when Latin Grammar came to supplement the
Psalms, I was my own master for at least an hour before half-past
one dinner, and for the rest of the afternoon.

My mother, herself finding her chief personal pleasure in her
flowers, was often planting or pruning beside me, at least if I
chose to stay beside her. I never thought of doing anything behind her back which I would not have done before her face;
and her presence was therefore no restraint to me; but, also, no
particular pleasure, for, from having always been left so much
alone, I had generally my own little affairs to see after; and, on
the whole, by the time I was seven years old, was already getting
too independent, mentally, even of my father and mother; and,
having nobody else to be dependent upon, began to lead a very
small, perky, contented, conceited, Cock-Robinson-Crusoe sort of
life, in the central point which it appeared to me, (as it must
naturally appear to geometrical animals,) that I occupied in the
universe.

This was partly the fault of my father's modesty; and partly of
his pride. He had so much more confidence in my mother's judgment as to such matters than in his own, that he never ventured
even to help, much less to cross her, in the conduct of my education; on the other hand, in the fixed purpose of making an
ecclesiastical gentleman of me, with the superfinest of manners,
and access to the highest circles of fleshly and spiritual society,
the visits to Croydon, where I entirely loved my aunt, and young
baker-cousins, became rarer and more rare: the society of our
neighbors on the hill could not be had without breaking up our
regular and sweetly selfish manner of living; and on the whole,
I had nothing animate to care for, in a childish way, but myself,
some nests of ants, which the gardener would never leave un-
disturbed for me, and a sociable bird or two; though I never had

the sense or perseverance to make one really tame. But that was partly because, if ever I managed to bring one to be the least trustful of me, the cats got it. . . .

In the afternoons, when my father returned (always punctually) from his business, he dined, at half-past four, in the front parlor, my mother sitting beside him to hear the events of the day, and give counsel and encouragement with respect to the same;— chiefly the last, for my father was apt to be vexed if orders for sherry fell the least short of their due standard, even for a day or two. I was never present at this time, however, and only avouch what I relate by hearsay and probable conjecture; for between four and six it would have been a grave misdemeanor in me if I so much as approached the parlor door. After that, in summer time, we were all in the garden as long as the day lasted; tea under the white-heart cherry tree; or in winter and rough weather, at six o'clock in the drawing-room,—I having my cup of milk, and slice of bread-and-butter, in a little recess, with a table in front of it, wholly sacred to me; and in which I remained in the evenings as an Idol in a niche, while my mother knitted, and my father read to her,—and to me, so far as I chose to listen.

The series of the Waverley novels, then drawing toward its close, was still the chief source of delight in all households caring for literature; and I can no more recollect the time when I did not know them than when I did not know the *Bible;* but I have still a vivid remembrance of my father's intense expression of sorrow mixed with scorn, as he threw down *Count Robert of Paris,* after reading three or four pages; and he knew that the life of Scott was ended: the scorn being a very complex and bitter feeling in him,— partly, indeed, of the book itself, but chiefly of the wretches who were tormenting and selling the wrecked intellect, and not a little, deep down, of the subtle dishonesty which had essentially caused the ruin. My father never could forgive Scott his concealment of the Ballantyne partnership.

Such being the salutary pleasures of Herne Hill, I have next with deeper gratitude to chronicle what I owed to my mother for the resolutely consistent lessons which so exercised me in the Scriptures as to make every word of them familiar to my ear in habitual music,—yet in that familiarity reverenced, as transcending all thought, and ordaining all conduct.

This she effected, not by her own sayings or personal authority; but simply by compelling me to read the book thoroughly, for myself. As soon as I was able to read with fluency, she began a course of Bible work with me, which never ceased till I went to Oxford. She read alternate verses with me, watching, at first, every intonation of my voice, and correcting the false ones, till she made me understand the verse, if within my reach, rightly, and energetically. It might be beyond me altogether; that she did not care about; but she made sure that as soon as I got hold of it at all, I should get hold of it by the right end.

In this way she began with the first verse of Genesis, and went straight through, to the last verse of the Apocalypse; hard names, numbers, Levitical law, and all; and began again at Genesis the next day. If a name was hard, the better the exercise in pronunciation,—if a chapter was tiresome, the better lesson in patience,— if loathsome, the better lesson in faith that there was some use in its being so outspoken. After our chapters, (from two to three a day, according to their length, the first thing after breakfast, and no interruption from servants allowed,—none from visitors, who either joined in the reading or had to stay upstairs,—and none from any visitings or excursions, except real travelling,) I had to learn a few verses by heart, or repeat, to make sure I had not lost, something of what was already known; and, with the chapters thus gradually possessed from the first word to the last, I had to learn the whole body of the fine old Scottish paraphrases, which are good, melodious, and forceful verse; and to which, together with the *Bible* itself, I owe the first cultivation of my ear in sound.

And it is perhaps already time to mark what advantages and mischief, by the chances of life up to seven years old, had been irrevocably determined for me.

I will first count my blessings (as a not unwise friend once recommended me to do, continually; whereas I have a bad trick of always numbering the thorns in my fingers and not the bones in them) .

And for best and truest beginning of all blessings, I had been taught the perfect meaning of Peace, in thought, act, and word.

I never had heard my father's or mother's voice once raised in any question with each other; nor seen an angry, or even slightly hurt or offended, glance in the eyes of either. I had never heard a servant scolded; nor even suddenly, passionately, or in any severe manner, blamed. I had never seen a moment's trouble or disorder in any household matter; nor anything whatever either done in a hurry, or undone in due time. I had no conception of such a feeling as anxiety; my father's occasional vexation in the afternoons, when he had only got an order for twelve butts, after expecting one for fifteen, as I have just stated, was never manifested to me; and itself related only to the question whether his name would be a step higher or lower in the year's list of sherry exporters; for he never spent more than half his income, and therefore found himself little incommoded by occasional variations in the total of it. I had never done any wrong that I knew of—beyond occasionally delaying the commitment to heart of some improving sentence, that I might watch a wasp on the window pane, or a bird in the cherry tree; and I had never seen any grief.

Next to this quite priceless gift of Peace, I had received the perfect understanding of the natures of Obedience and Faith. I obeyed word, or lifted finger, of father or mother, simply as a ship her helm; not only without idea of resistance, but receiving the direction as a part of my own life and force, a helpful law, as necessary to me in every moral action as the law of gravity in leaping. And my practice in Faith was soon complete: nothing was ever promised me that was not given; nothing ever threatened me that was not inflicted, and nothing ever told me that was not true.

Peace, obedience, faith; these three for chief good; next to these, the habit of fixed attention with both eyes and mind—on which I will not further enlarge at this moment, this being the main practical faculty of my life, causing Mazzini to say of me, in conversation authentically reported, a year or two before his death, that I had "the most analytic mind in Europe." An opinion in which, so far as I am acquainted with Europe, I am myself entirely disposed to concur. . . .

Such I esteem the main blessings of my childhood;—next, let me count the equally dominant calamities.

First, that I had nothing to love.

My parents were—in a sort—visible powers of nature to me, no more loved than the sun and the moon: only I should have been annoyed and puzzled if either of them had gone out; (how much, now, when both are darkened!) —still less did I love God; not that I had any quarrel with Him, or fear of Him; but simply found what people told me was His service, disagreeable; and what people told me was His book, not entertaining. I had no companions to quarrel with, neither; nobody to assist, and nobody to thank. Not a servant was ever allowed to do anything for me, but what it was their duty to do; and why should I have been grateful to the cook for cooking, or the gardener for gardening,— when the one dared not give me a baked potato without asking leave, and the other would not let my ants' nests alone, because they made the walks untidy? The evil consequence of all this was not, however, what might perhaps have been expected, that I grew up selfish or unaffectionate; but that, when affection did come, it came with violence utterly rampant and unmanageable, at least by me, who never before had anything to manage.

For (second of chief calamities) I had nothing to endure. Danger or pain of any kind I knew not: my strength was never exercised, my patience never tried, and my courage never fortified. Not that I was ever afraid of anything,—either ghosts, thunder, or beasts; and one of the nearest approaches to insubordination which I was ever tempted into as a child, was in passionate effort to get leave to play with the lion's cubs in Wombwell's menagerie.

Thirdly. I was taught no precision nor etiquette of manners; it was enough if, in the little society we saw, I remained unobtrusive, and replied to a question without shyness: but the shyness came later, and increased as I grew conscious of the rudeness arising from the want of social discipline, and found it impossible to acquire, in advanced life, dexterity in any bodily exercise, skill in any pleasing accomplishment, or ease and tact in ordinary behavior.

Lastly, and chief of evils. My judgment of right and wrong,

and powers of independent action, were left entirely undeveloped; because the bridle and blinkers were never taken off me. Children should have their times of being off duty, like soldiers; and when once the obedience, if required, is certain, the little creature should be very early put for periods of practice in complete command of itself; set on the barebacked horse of its own will, and left to break it by its own strength. But the ceaseless authority exercised over my youth left me, when cast out at last into the world, unable for some time to do more than drift with its vortices.

My present verdict, therefore, on the general tenor of my education at that time, must be, that it was at once too formal and too luxurious; leaving my character, at the most important moment for its construction, cramped indeed, but not disciplined; and only by protection innocent, instead of by practice virtuous. My mother saw this herself, and but too clearly, in later years; and whenever I did anything wrong, stupid, or hard-hearted,— (and I have done many things that were all three,) —always said, "It is because you were too much indulged."

At six punctually I joined my father and mother at tea, being, in the drawing-room, restricted to the inhabitation of the sacred niche above referred to, a recess beside the fireplace, well lighted from the lateral window in the summer evenings, and by the chimney-piece lamp in winter, and out of all inconvenient heat, or hurtful draught. A good writing-table before it shut me well in, and carried my plate and cup, or books in service. After tea, my father read to my mother what pleased themselves, I picking up what I could, or reading what I liked better instead. Thus I heard all the Shakespeare comedies and historical plays again and again,—all Scott, and all *Don Quixote,* a favorite book of my father's, and at which I could then laugh to ecstasy; now, it is one of the saddest, and, in some things, the most offensive of books to me.

My father was an absolutely beautiful reader of the best poetry and prose;—of Shakespeare, Pope, Spenser, Byron, and Scott; as of Goldsmith, Addison, and Johnson. Lighter ballad poetry he had not fineness of ear to do justice to: his sense of the strength and wisdom of true meaning, and of the force of rightly ordered syllables, made his delivery of *Hamlet, Lear, Cæsar,* or *Marmion,* melodiously grand and just; but he had no idea of modulating the refrain of a ballad, and had little patience with the tenor of its sentiment. He looked always, in the matter of what he read, for heroic will and consummate reason: never tolerated the morbid love of misery for its own sake, and never read, either for his own pleasure or my instruction, such ballads as *Burd Helen,* the *Twa Corbies,* or any other rhyme or story which sought its interest in vain love or fruitless death.

On the Sunday evening my father would sometimes read us a sermon of Blair's, or it might be, a clerk or a customer would dine with us, when the conversation, in mere necessary courtesy, would take generally the direction of sherry. Mary and I got through the evening how we could, over the *Pilgrim's Progress,* Bunyan's *Holy War,* Quarles's *Emblems,* Foxe's *Book of Martyrs,* Mrs. Sherwood's *Lady of the Manor,*—a very awful book to me, because of the stories in it of wicked girls who had gone to balls, dying immediately after of fever . . .

My father and mother, though due cheques for charities were of course sent to Dr. Andrews, and various civilities at Christmas, in the way of turkeys or boxes of raisins, intimated their satisfaction with the style of his sermons and purity of his doctrine,— had yet, with their usual shyness, never asked for his acquaintance.

The clergyman himself finally made overtures toward an acquaintance, and little John became so fond of him that Mr. Ruskin asked the Doctor if he would initiate the boy into Greek.

[But, presently], it having been perceived by my father and mother that Dr. Andrews could neither prepare me for the University, nor for the duties of a bishopric, I was sent as a day scholar to the private school kept by the Rev. Thomas Dale, in Grove Lane, within walking distance of Herne Hill. Walking down with my father after breakfast, carrying my blue bag of books, I came home to half-past one dinner, and prepared my lessons in the evening for next day.

Finding me in all respects what boys could only look upon as an innocent, they treated me as I suppose they would have treated a girl; they neither thrashed nor chaffed me,—finding, indeed, from the first that chaff had no effect on me. Generally I did not understand it, nor in the least mind it if I did, the fountain of pure conceit in my own heart sustaining me serenely against all deprecation, whether by master or companion. I was fairly intelligent of books, had a good quick and holding memory, learned whatever I was bid as fast as I could, and as well; and since all the other boys learned always as little as they could, though I was far in retard of them in real knowledge, I almost always knew the day's lesson best.

In her own son's education, [Mrs. Ruskin] had sacrificed her pride in his heroism to her anxiety for his safety; and never allowed me to go to the edge of a pond, or be in the same field with a pony. Instead, they took me back to London, and my father spared time from his business hours, once or twice a week, to take me to a four-square, sky-lighted, sawdust-floored prison of a riding-school in Moorfields, the smell of which, as we turned in at the gate of it, was a terror and horror and abomination to me: and there I was put on big horses that jumped, and reared, and circled, and sidled; and fell off them regularly whenever they did any of those things; and was a disgrace to my family, and a burning shame and misery to myself, till at last the riding-school was given up on my spraining my right-hand forefinger (it has never come straight again since),—and a well-broken Shetland pony bought for me, and the two of us led about the Norwood roads by a riding-master with a leading string. I used to do pretty well as long as we went straight, and then get thinking of something, and fall off when we turned a corner. I might have got some inkling of a seat in Heaven's good time, if no fuss had been made about me, nor inquiries instituted whether I had been off or on; but as my mother, the moment I got home, made searching scrutiny into the day's disgraces, I merely got more and more nervous and helpless after every tumble; and this branch of my education was at last abandoned, my parents consoling themselves, as best they might, in the conclusion that my not being able to learn to ride was the sign of my being a singular genius.

Margaret Ruskin was, her son summarizes her character, "a faultless and accomplished housekeeper, and a natural, essential, unassailable, yet inoffensive prude." But it should not be imagined "that she was in any wise like Esther's religious aunt in Bleak House."

Far on the contrary, there was a hearty, frank, and sometimes even irrepressible, laugh in my mother! Never sardonic, yet with a very definitely Smollettesque turn in it! so that between themselves, she and my father enjoyed their *Humphrey Clinker* extremely, long before I was able to understand either the jest or gist of it. Much more, she could exult in a harmless bit of Smollettesque reality. Years and years after this time, in one of our crossings of the Simplon, just at the top, where we had stopped to look about us, Nurse Anne sat down to rest herself on the railings at the roadside, just in front of the monastery;—the off roadside, from which the bank slopes steeply down outside the fence. Turning to observe the panoramic picturesque, Anne lost her balance, and went backward over the railings down the bank. My father could not help suggesting that she had done it expressly for the entertainment of the Holy Fathers; and neither he nor my mother could ever speak of the "performance" (as they called it) afterward, without laughing for a quarter of an hour.

If, however, there was the least bitterness or irony in a jest, my mother did not like it; but my father and I liked it all the more, if it were just; and, so far as I could understand it, I rejoiced in all the sarcasm of *Don Juan*.

On a visit to Paris, the Ruskins dined with M. Domecq, the Spanish partner of the wine firm, and the following year the four younger daughters of the Domecqs came to visit the Ruskins.

How we got them all into Herne Hill corners and cupboards would be inexplicable but with a plan of the three stories! The arrangements were half Noah's ark, half doll's house, but we got them all in: Clotilde, a graceful oval-faced blonde of fifteen;

Cécile, a dark, finely-browed, beautifully-featured girl of thirteen; Elise, again, fair, round-faced like an English girl, a treasure of good nature and good sense; Caroline, a delicately quaint little thing of eleven. They had all been born abroad, Clotilde at Cadiz, and of course convent-bred; but lately accustomed to be much in society during vacation at Paris. Deeper than any one dreamed, the sight of them in the Champs Élysées had sealed itself in me, for they were the first well-bred and well-dressed girls I had ever seen—or at least spoken to. I mean of course, by well-dressed, perfectly simply dressed, with Parisian cutting and fitting. They were all "bigoted"—as Protestants would say; quietly firm, as they ought to say—Roman Catholics; spoke Spanish and French with perfect grace, and English with broken precision; were all fairly sensible, Clotilde sternly and accurately so, Élise gayly and kindly, Cécile serenely, Caroline keenly. A most curious galaxy, or southern cross, of unconceived stars, floating on a sudden into my obscure firmament of London suburb.

How my parents could allow their young novice to be cast into the fiery furnace of the outer world in this helpless manner the reader may wonder, and only the Fates know; but there was this excuse for them, that they had never seen me the least interested or anxious about girls—never caring to stay in the promenades at Cheltenham or Bath, or on the parade at Dover; on the contrary, growling and mewing if I was ever kept there, and off to the sea or the fields the moment I got leave; and they had educated me in such extremely orthodox English Toryism and Evangelicalism that they could not conceive their scientific, religious, and George the Third revering youth, wavering in his constitutional balance toward French Catholics. And I had never said anything about the Champs Élysées! Virtually convent-bred more closely than the maids themselves, without a single sisterly or cousinly affection for refuge or lightning-rod, and having no athletic skill or pleasure to check my dreaming, I was thrown, bound hand and foot, in my unaccomplished simplicity, into the fiery furnace, or fiery cross, of these four girls,—who of course reduced me to a mere heap of white ashes in four days. Four days, at the most, it took to reduce me to ashes, but the Mercredi des cendres lasted four years.

Anything more comic in the externals of it, anything more tragic in the essence, could not have been invented by the skilfullest designer in either kind. In my social behavior and mind I was a curious combination of Mr. Traddles, Mr. Toots, and Mr. Winkle. I had the real fidelity and single-mindedness of Mr. Traddles, with the conversational abilities of Mr. Toots, and the heroic ambition of Mr. Winkle;—all these illuminated by imagination like Mr. Copperfield's, at his first Norwood dinner.

Clotilde (Adèle Clotilde in full, but her sisters called her Clotilde, after the queen-saint, and I Adèle, because it rhymed to shell, spell, and knell) was only made more resplendent by the circlet of her sisters' beauty; while my own shyness and unpresentableness were farther stiffened, or rather sanded, by a patriotic and Protestant conceit, which was tempered neither by politeness nor sympathy; so that, while in company I sate jealously miserable like a stockfish (in truth, I imagine, looking like nothing so much as a skate in an aquarium trying to get up the glass), on any blessed occasion of tête-à-tête I endeavored to entertain my Spanish-born, Paris-bred, and Catholic-hearted mistress with my own views upon the subjects of the Spanish Armada, the Battle of Waterloo, and the doctrine of Transubstantiation. . . .

The old people, meanwhile, saw little harm in all this. Mr. Domecq, who was extremely good-natured, and a good judge of character, rather liked me, because he saw that I was good-natured also, and had some seedling brains, which would come up in time: in the interests of the business he was perfectly ready to give me any of his daughters I liked, who could also be got to like me, but considered that the time was not come to talk of such things. My father was entirely of the same mind . . . My mother, who looked upon the idea of my marrying a Roman Catholic as too monstrous to be possible in the decrees of Heaven, and too preposterous to be even guarded against on earth, was rather annoyed at the whole business, as she would have been if one of her chimneys had begun smoking,—but had not the slightest notion her house was on fire. She saw more, however, than my father, into the depth of the feeling, but did not, in her motherly tenderness, like to grieve me by any serious check to it. She hoped, when the Domecqs went back to Paris, we might see no more of them, and that Adèle's influence and memory would pass away—with next winter's snow.

Under these indulgent circumstances,—bitterly ashamed of the figure I had made, but yet not a whit dashed back out of my daily swelling foam of furious conceit, supported as it was by real depth of feeling, and (note it well, good reader) by a true and glorious sense of the newly revealed miracle of human love, in its exaltation of the physical beauty of the world I had till then sought by its own light alone,—I set myself in that my seventeenth year, in a state of majestic imbecility, to write a tragedy on a Venetian subject, in which the sorrows of my soul were to be enshrined in immortal verse,—the fair heroine, Bianca, was to be endowed with the perfections of Desdemona and the brightness of Juliet,—and Venice and Love were to be described, as never had been thought of before. . . . The entirely inscrutable thing to me, looking back on myself, is my total want of all reason, will, or design in the business: I had neither the resolution to win Adèle, the courage to do without her, the sense to consider what was at last to come of it all, or the grace to think how disagreeable I was making myself at the time to everybody about me. There was really no more capacity nor intelligence in me than in a just fledged owlet, or just open-eyed puppy, disconsolate at the existence of the moon.

Out of my feebly melodious complaints to that luminary, however, I was startled by a letter to my father from Christ Church, advising him that there was room for my residence in the January term of 1837, and that I must come up to matriculate in October of the instant year, 1836.

Strangely enough, my father had never inquired into the nature and manner of matriculation, till he took me up to display in Oxford;—he, very nearly as much a boy as I, for anything we knew of what we were about. He never had any doubt about putting me at the most fashionable college, and of course my name had been down at Christ Church years before I was called up; but it had never dawned on my father's mind that there were two, fashionable and unfashionable, orders, or castes, of undergraduate at Christ Church, one of these being called Gentlemen-Commoners, the other Commoners; and that these last seemed to occupy an almost bisectional point between the Gentlemen-Commoners and the Servitors. . . .

My father did not like the word "commoner,"— all the less, because our relationships in general were not uncommon. Also, though himself satisfying his pride enough in being the head of the sherry trade, he felt and saw in his son powers which had not their full scope in the sherry trade. His ideal of my future,—now entirely formed in conviction of my genius,—was that I should enter at college into the best society, take all the prizes every year, and a double first to finish with; marry Lady Clara Vere de Vere; write poetry as good as Byron's, only pious; preach sermons as good as Bossuet's, only Protestant; be made, at forty, Bishop of Winchester, and at fifty, Primate of England.

I wonder mightily now what sort of a creature I should have turned out, if at this time Love had been with me instead of against me; and instead of the distracting and useless pain, I had had the joy of approved love, and the untellable, incalculable motive of its sympathy and praise.

It seems to me such things are not allowed in this world. The men capable of the highest imaginative passion are always tossed on fiery waves by it: the men who find it smooth water, and not scalding, are of another sort. . . .

Of course, when Adèle and her sisters came back at Christmas, and stayed with us four or five weeks, every feeling and folly that had been subdued or forgotten, returned in redoubled force. I don't know what would have happened if Adèle had been a perfectly beautiful and amiable girl, and had herself in the least liked me. I suppose then my mother would have been overcome. But though extremely lovely at fifteen, Adèle was not prettier than French girls in general at eighteen; she was firm, and fiery, and high principled; but, as the light traits already noticed of her enough show, not in the least amiable; and although she would have married me, had her father wished it, was always glad to have me out of her way. My love was much too high and fantastic to be diminished by her loss of beauty; but I perfectly well saw and admitted it, having never at any time been in the slightest degree blinded by love, as I perceive other men are, out of my critic nature. And day followed on day, and month to month, of complex absurdity, pain, error, wasted affection, and rewardless semi-virtue, which I am content to sweep out of the way of what better things I can recollect at this time, into the smallest possible size of dust heap, and wish the Dustman Oblivion good clearance of them.

One evening Ruskin felt a curious taste in his mouth, "which I presently perceived to be that of blood." *The doctors diagnosed it as consumption, and recommended spending the autumn and winter abroad.* "My father, to whom the business was nothing, but for me, left his desk, and all other cares of life, but that of nursing me." *His illness was almost as much misery and despair, however, as weakness of the lungs. Abroad, Ruskin was gloomily bent on enjoying nothing, but gradually his cough improved. In May, 1842, he went back to Oxford to take his degree. But he was left at a loose end.*

What should I be, or do? my utterly indulgent father ready to let me do anything; with my room always luxuriously furnished in his house,—my expenses paid if I chose to travel. I was not heartless enough, yet, to choose to do that, alone. Perhaps it may deserve some dim praise that I never seriously thought of leaving my father and mother to explore foreign countries; and certainly the fear of grieving them was intermingled more or less with all my thoughts; but then, I did not much want to explore foreign countries. I had not the least love of adventure, but liked to have comfortable rooms always ordered, and a three-course dinner ready by four o'clock. Although no coward under circumstances of accidental danger, I extremely objected to any vestige of danger as a continuous element in one's life. I would not go to India for fear of tigers, nor to Russia for fear of bears, nor to Peru for fear of earthquakes; and finally, though I had no rightly glowing or grateful affection for either father or mother, yet as they could not well do without me, so also I found I was not altogether comfortable without them.

The mold of a lifetime had been irretrievably set. His parents had enclosed him within an emotional tyranny which they used with a deadly devotion. Though he became a famous art critic and a radical critic of social institutions, he never learned to mingle with and adapt himself to the world. Enmeshed within the narrow Ruskin family circle, he was caught, conditioned, and held fast. He never escaped.

AN OLD MAN IN A DRY MONTH

THE DRYNESS IN HENRY ADAMS IS A DRYNESS OF THE SOUL. AMONG the most absorbing of all autobiographies, the education or rather the failure of education it outlines has the desert quality of the world as Adams found it, with hardly ever an oasis of green palms and sparkling water. For all its intellectual interest, *The Education of Henry Adams* is a long Odyssey of futility.

Possibly it reflects Adams' feeling that alone among his distinguished family he had been a failure. That feeling of personal failure in turn perhaps colors his feeling that modern civilization has been a failure. By any ordinary standard, certainly, his career as writer, teacher, historian, was not failure but brilliant success. But his great-grandfather and his grandfather had wielded the concrete power of the Presidency; even his father had moved the sacred levers at the very center of political power. In his childhood and youth it seemed likely that Charles Francis Adams too might be elected President and that the White House might become almost one of the Adams family mansions. Such power was the only thing Henry Adams really wanted. Anything but it was failure. Like that of John Stuart Mill, Adams's autobiography records a life-long education: but, embittered by personal frustration, unsustained by any mood of historical faith, baffled by the chaotic multiplicity of the universe, unlike that of Mill, it runs off into lost streams, broken threads, blind alleys, and cosmic despair.

The sense of failure darkens every page. The very prestige and position of his family he sees as a heavy handicap. The class to which he belonged, "an upper-class *bourgeoisie,*" was to prove itself incapable of adaptive change in a changing world. Harvard did not educate; it only stamped the mind with a water-mark. German student life was "the thinnest of beer." In Rome, "Gibbon might have gone on for the whole century, sitting among the ruins of the Capitol" and found no one "capable of telling him what it meant. Perhaps it meant nothing." England disconcertingly favored the South instead of keeping faithful to the antislavery principles it professed; the behavior of its political leaders was inexplicable.

By the conclusion of the Civil War he had worked his way to a dead end. The political machinery of 1789 had broken down, "but some narrow trait of the New England nature seemed to blight socialism," or indeed any course or faith whatsoever, and he was left staring at emptiness. "The world, after 1865, became a bankers' world," submitting to "the yoke of the coming capitalism": "The climax of empire could be seen approaching, year after year, as though Sulla were a President or McKinley a Consul." And increasingly the tendency of history itself seemed merely a race to chaos and breakdown.

The mood of tired emptiness, the vanitas vanitatum, that runs through all this is unmistakable. In Henry Adams the emotions generated by the industrial revolution have run through a great circle. The boundless a priori optimism of the romantic era became tempered to a tentative empiricism by the great Victorians. But it was sustained in them by an inner drive of energy and of confidence in the powers of the mind to solve the problems it uncovered. The enthusiasm of Shelley and his compeers gave way to the searchings of Mill and Darwin. But by the end of the century, to one of the most favored and gifted of its scions, modern culture appeared a meaningless disintegration and all it had to offer tasted of ashes.

Henry Adams is thus a key-personality to understanding our own times. The modern dwellers in "the waste land," the "lost generation" not confined to Hemingway's novels or T. S. Eliot's poems, are his spiritual heirs. Asking themselves agonizingly if Europe was a success, losing themselves in a tissue of self-spun hesitations, clinging to an irresolute and dubious affirmation of

half-hearted belief, they echo the mood if not the intelligence of
Adams's despair.

To escape that despair takes courage and generous hearts. But
men of good will are finding these things in the determination
that democracy shall not be a delusion or a mere political trick
or the possession of a small group. By a full spiral they return to
Shelley's mood of affirmation, of courage, and of hope.

The Education of Henry Adams

[Adams was born in 1838 and died in 1918. *The Education* was privately printed in 1907; the first published edition came out in 1918, about six months after his death.]

UNDER THE SHADOW OF BOSTON STATE HOUSE, TURNING ITS BACK ON the house of John Hancock, the little passage called Hancock Avenue runs, or ran, from Beacon Street, skirting the State House grounds, to Mount Vernon Street, on the summit of Beacon Hill; and there, in the third house below Mount Vernon Place, February 16, 1838, a child was born, and christened later by his uncle, the minister of the First Church after the tenets of Boston Unitarianism, as Henry Brooks Adams.

Had he been born in Jerusalem under the shadow of the Temple and circumcised in the Synagogue by his uncle the high priest, under the name of Israel Cohen, he would scarcely have been more distinctly branded, and not much more heavily handicapped in the races of the coming century, in running for such stakes as the century was to offer; but, on the other hand, the ordinary traveller, who does not enter the field of racing, finds advantage in being, so to speak, ticketed through life, with the safeguards of an old, established traffic. Safeguards are often irksome, but sometimes convenient, and if one needs them at all, one is apt to need them badly. A hundred years earlier, such safeguards as his would have secured any young man's success; and although in 1838 their value was not very great compared with what they would have had in 1738, yet the mere accident of starting a twentieth-century career from a nest of associations so colonial—so troglodytic—as the First Church, the Boston State House, Beacon Hill, John Hancock and John Adams, Mount Vernon Street and Quincy, all crowding on ten pounds of unconscious babyhood, was so queer as to offer a subject of curious speculation to the baby long after he had witnessed the solution. What could become of such a child of the seventeenth and eighteenth centuries, when he should wake up to find himself required to play the game of the twentieth? Had he been consulted, would he have cared to play the game at all, holding such cards as he held, and suspecting that the game was to be one of which neither he nor any one else back to the beginning of time knew the rules or the risks or the stakes? He was not consulted and was not responsible, but had he been taken into the confidence of his parents, he would certainly have told them to change nothing as far as concerned him. He would have been astounded by his own luck. Probably no child, born in the year, held better cards than he. Whether life was an honest game of chance, or whether the cards were marked and forced, he could not refuse to play his excellent hand. He could never make the usual plea of irresponsibility. He accepted the situation as though he had been a party to it, and under the same circumstances would do it again, the more readily for knowing the exact values. To his life as a whole he was a consenting, contracting party and partner from the moment he was born to the moment he died. Only with that understanding—as a consciously assenting member in full partnership with the society of his age—had his education an interest to himself or to others.

As it happened, he never got to the point of playing the game at all; he lost himself in the study of it, watching the errors of the players; but this is the only interest in the story, which otherwise has no moral and little incident. A story of education—seventy years of it—the practical value remains to the end in doubt, like other values about which men have disputed since the birth of Cain and Abel; but the practical value of the universe has never been stated in dollars. Although every one cannot be a Gargantua-Napoleon-Bismarck and walk off with the great bells of Notre Dame, every one must bear his own universe, and most persons are moderately interested in learning how their neighbors have managed to carry theirs . . .

Of all this that was being done to complicate his education, he knew only the color of yellow. He first found himself sitting on a yellow kitchen floor in strong sunlight. He was three years old when he took this earliest step in education; a lesson of color. The second followed soon; a lesson of taste. On December 3, 1841, he developed scarlet fever. For several days he was as good as dead, reviving only under the careful nursing of his family. When he began to recover strength, about January 1, 1842, his hunger must have been stronger than any other pleasure or pain, for while in after life he retained not the faintest recollection of his illness, he remembered quite clearly his aunt entering the sick-room bearing in her hand a saucer with a baked apple. . . .

As a means of variation from a normal type, sickness in childhood ought to have a certain value not to be classed under any fitness or unfitness of natural selection; and especially scarlet fever affected boys seriously, both physically and in character, though they might through life puzzle themselves to decide whether it had fitted or unfitted them for success; but this fever of Henry Adams took greater and greater importance in his eyes, from the point of view of education, the longer he lived. At first, the effect was physical. He fell behind his brothers two or three inches in height, and proportionally in bone and weight. His character and processes of mind seemed to share in this fining-down process of scale. He was not good in a fight, and his nerves were more delicate than boys' nerves ought to be. He exaggerated these weaknesses as he grew older. The habit of doubt; of distrusting his own judgment and of totally rejecting the judgment of the world; the tendency to regard every question as open; the hesitation to act except as a choice of evils; the shirking of responsibility; the love of line, form, quality; the horror of ennui; the passion for companionship and the antipathy to society—all these are well-known qualities of New England character in no way peculiar to individuals but in this instance they seemed to be stimulated by the fever, and Henry Adams could never make up his mind whether, on the whole, the change of character was morbid or healthy, good or bad for his purpose. His brothers were the type; he was the variation.

As far as the boy knew, the sickness did not affect him at all, and he grew up in excellent health, bodily and mental, taking life as it was given; accepting its local standards without a difficulty, and enjoying much of it as keenly as any other boy of his age. He seemed to himself quite normal, and his companions seemed always to think him so. Whatever was peculiar about him was education, not character, and came to him, directly and indirectly, as the result of that eighteenth-century inheritance which he took with his name.

The atmosphere of education in which he lived was colonial, revolutionary, almost Cromwellian, as though he were steeped, from his greatest grandmother's birth, in the odor of political crime. Resistance to something was the law of New England nature; the boy looked out on the world with the instinct of resistance; for numberless generations his predecessors had viewed the world chiefly as a thing to be reformed, filled with evil forces to be abolished, and they saw no reason to suppose that they had wholly succeeded in the abolition; the duty was unchanged. That duty implied not only resistance to evil, but hatred of it. Boys naturally look on all force as an enemy, and generally find it so, but the New Englander, whether boy or man, in his long struggle with a stingy or hostile universe, had learned also to love the pleasure of hating; his joys were few.

Politics, as a practice, whatever its professions, had always been the systematic organization of hatreds, and Massachusetts politics had been as harsh as the climate. The chief charm of New England was harshness of contrasts and extremes of sensibility—a cold that froze the blood, and a heat that boiled it—so that the pleasure of hating—one's self if no better victim offered —was not its rarest amusement; but the charm was a true and natural child of the soil, not a cultivated weed of the ancients. The violence of the contrast was real and made the strongest motive of education. The double exterior nature gave life its relative values.

Winter and summer, cold and heat, town and country, force and freedom, marked two modes of life and thought, balanced like lobes of the brain. Town was winter confinement, school, rule, discipline; straight, gloomy streets, piled with six feet of snow in the middle; frosts that made the snow sing under wheels or runners; thaws when the streets became dangerous to cross; society of uncles, aunts, and cousins who expected children to behave themselves, and who were not always gratified; above all else, winter represented the desire to escape and go free. Town was restraint, law, unity. Country, only seven miles away, was liberty, diversity, outlawry, the endless delight of mere sense impressions given by nature for nothing, and breathed by boys without knowing it.

Boys are wild animals, rich in the treasures of sense, but the New England boy had a wider range of emotions than boys of more equable climates. He felt his nature crudely, as it was meant. To the boy Henry Adams, summer was drunken. Among senses, smell was the strongest—smell of hot pine-woods and sweet-fern in the scorching summer noon; of new-mown hay; of ploughed earth; of box hedges; of peaches, lilacs, syringas; of stables, barns, cowyards; of salt water and low tide on the marshes; nothing came amiss. Next to smell came taste, and the children knew the taste of everything they saw or touched, from pennyroyal and flagroot to the shell of a pignut and the letters of a spelling-book—the taste of A–B, AB, suddenly revived on the boy's tongue sixty years afterwards. Light, line, and color as sensual pleasures, came later and were as crude as the rest. The New England light is glare, and the atmosphere harshens color. The boy was a full man before he ever knew what was meant by atmosphere; his idea of pleasure in light was the blaze of a New England sun. His idea of color was a peony, with the dew of early morning on its petals. The intense blue of the sea, as he saw it a mile or two away, from the Quincy hills; the cumuli in a June afternoon sky; the strong reds and greens and purples of colored prints and children's picture-books, as the American colors then ran; these were ideals. The opposites or antipathies, were the cold grays of November evenings, and the thick, muddy thaws of Boston winter. With such standards, the Bostonian could not but develop a double nature. Life was a double thing.

After a January blizzard, the boy who could look with pleasure

into the violent snow-glare of the cold white sunshine, with its
intense light and shade, scarcely knew what was meant by tone.
He could reach it only by education.

Winter and summer, then, were two hostile lives, and bred two
separate natures. Winter was always the effort to live; summer was
tropical license. Whether the children rolled in the grass, or
waded in the brook, or swam in the salt ocean, or sailed in the
bay, or fished for smelts in the creeks, or netted minnows in the
salt-marshes, or took to the pine-woods and the granite quarries,
or chased muskrats and hunted snapping-turtles in the swamps,
or mushrooms or nuts on the autumn hills, summer and country
were always sensual living, while winter was always compulsory
learning. Summer was the multiplicity of nature; winter was
school.

The bearing of the two seasons on the education of Henry
Adams was no fancy; it was the most decisive force he ever knew;
it ran through life, and made the division between its perplexing,
warring, irreconcilable problems, irreducible opposites, with growing emphasis to the last year of study. From earliest childhood the
boy was accustomed to feel that, for him, life was double. Winter
and summer, town and country, law and liberty, were hostile,
and the man who pretended they were not, was in his eyes a schoolmaster—that is, a man employed to tell lies to little boys. Though
Quincy was but two hours' walk from Beacon Hill, it belonged in
a different world. For two hundred years, every Adams, from
father to son, had lived within sight of State Street, and sometimes
had lived in it, yet none had ever taken kindly to the town, or
been taken kindly by it. The boy inherited his double nature.
He knew as yet nothing about his great-grandfather, who had died
a dozen years before his own birth: he took for granted that any
great-grandfather of his must have always been good, and his
enemies wicked; but he divined his great-grandfather's character
from his own. Never for a moment did he connect the two ideas
of Boston and John Adams; they were separate and antagonistic;
the idea of John Adams went with Quincy. He knew his grandfather John Quincy Adams only as an old man of seventy-five or
eighty who was friendly and gentle with him, but except that he

heard his grandfather always called "the President," and his grandmother "the Madam," he had no reason to suppose that his Adams
grandfather differed in character from his Brooks grandfather who
was equally kind and benevolent. He liked the Adams side best,
but for no other reason than that it reminded him of the country,
the summer, and the absence of restraint. Yet he felt also that
Quincy was in a way inferior to Boston, and that socially Boston
looked down on Quincy. The reason was clear enough even to a
five-year old child. Quincy had no Boston style. Little enough
style had either; a simpler manner of life and thought could hardly
exist, short of cave-dwelling. The flint-and-steel with which his
grandfather Adams used to light his own fires in the early morning
was still on the mantel-piece of his study. The idea of a livery or
even a dress for servants, or of an evening toilette, was next to
blasphemy. Bathrooms, water-supplies, lighting, heating, and the
whole array of domestic comforts, were unknown at Quincy. Boston had already a bathroom, a water-supply, a furnace, and gas.
The superiority of Boston was evident, but a child liked it no better for that.

The magnificence of his grandfather Brooks's house in Pearl
Street or South Street has long ago disappeared, but perhaps his
country house at Medford may still remain to show what impressed
the mind of a boy in 1845 with the idea of city splendor. The President's place at Quincy was the larger and older and far the more interesting of the two; but a boy felt at once its inferiority in fashion.
It showed plainly enough its want of wealth. It smacked of colonial
age, but not of Boston style or plush curtains. To the end of his life
he never quite overcame the prejudice thus drawn in with his
childish breath. He never could compel himself to care for nineteenth-century style. He was never able to adopt it, any more than
his father or grandfather or great-grandfather had done. Not that
he felt it as particularly hostile, for he reconciled himself to much
that was worse; but because, for some remote reason, he was born
an eighteenth-century child. The old house at Quincy was eighteenth century. What style it had was in its Queen Anne mahogany panels and its Louis Seize chairs and sofas. The panels
belonged to an old colonial Vassall who built the house; the furni-

ture had been brought back from Paris in 1789 or 1801 or 1817, along with porcelain and books and much else of old diplomatic remnants; and neither of the two eighteenth-century styles—neither English Queen Anne nor French Louis Seize—was comfortable for a boy, or for any one else. The dark mahogany had been painted white to suit daily life in winter gloom. Nothing seemed to favor, for a child's objects, the older forms. On the contrary, most boys, as well as grown-up people, preferred the new, with good reason, and the child felt himself distinctly at a disadvantage for the taste.

Nor had personal preference any share in his bias. The Brooks grandfather was as amiable and as sympathetic as the Adams grandfather. Both were born in 1767, and both died in 1848. Both were kind to children, and both belonged rather to the eighteenth than to the nineteenth centuries. The child knew no difference between them except that one was associated with winter and the other with summer; one with Boston, the other with Quincy. Even with Medford, the association was hardly easier. Once as a very young boy he was taken to pass a few days with his grandfather Brooks under charge of his aunt, but became so violently homesick that within twenty-four hours he was brought back in disgrace. Yet he could not remember ever being seriously homesick again.

The attachment to Quincy was not altogether sentimental or wholly sympathetic. Quincy was not a bed of thornless roses. Even there the curse of Cain set its mark. There as elsewhere a cruel universe combined to crush a child. As though three or four vigorous brothers and sisters, with the best will, were not enough to crush any child, every one else conspired towards an education which he hated. From cradle to grave this problem of running order through chaos, direction through space, discipline through freedom, unity through multiplicity, has always been, and must always be, the task of education, as it is the moral of religion, philosophy, science, art, politics, and economy; but a boy's will is his life, and he dies when it is broken, as the colt dies in harness, taking a new nature in becoming tame. Rarely has the boy felt kindly towards his tamers. Between him and his master has always been war. Henry Adams never knew a boy of his generation to like a master, and the task of remaining on friendly terms with one's own family, in such a relation, was never easy.

All the more singular it seemed afterwards to him that his first serious contact with the President should have been a struggle of will, in which the old man almost necessarily defeated the boy, but instead of leaving, as usual in such defeats, a lifelong sting, left rather an impression of as fair treatment as could be expected from a natural enemy. The boy met seldom with such restraint. He could not have been much more than six years old at the time—seven at the utmost—and his mother had taken him to Quincy for a long stay with the President during the summer. What became of the rest of the family he quite forgot; but he distinctly remembered standing at the house door one summer morning in a passionate outburst of rebellion against going to school. Naturally his mother was the immediate victim of his rage; that is what mothers are for, and boys also; but in this case the boy had his mother at unfair disadvantage, for she was a guest, and had no means of enforcing obedience. Henry showed a certain tactical ability by refusing to start, and he met all efforts at compulsion by successful, though too vehement protest. He was in fair way to win, and was holding his own, with sufficient energy, at the bottom of the long staircase which led up to the door of the President's library, when the door opened, and the old man slowly came down. Putting on his hat, he took the boy's hand without a word, and walked with him, paralyzed by awe, up the road to the town. After the first moments of consternation at this interference in a domestic dispute, the boy reflected that an old gentleman close on eighty would never trouble himself to walk near a mile on a hot summer morning over a shadeless road to take a boy to school, and that it would be strange if a lad imbued with the passion of freedom could not find a corner to dodge around, somewhere before reaching the school door. Then and always, the boy insisted that this reasoning justified his apparent submission; but the old man did not stop, and the boy saw all his strategical points turned, one after another, until he found

himself seated inside the school, and obviously the centre of curious if not malevolent criticism. Not till then did the President
release his hand and depart.

The point was that this act, contrary to the inalienable rights
of boys, and nullifying the social compact, ought to have made
him dislike his grandfather for life. He could not recall that it
had this effect even for a moment. With a certain maturity of
mind, the child must have recognized that the President, though
a tool of tyranny, had done his disreputable work with a certain
intelligence. He had shown no temper, no irritation, no personal
feeling, and had made no display of force. Above all, he had held
his tongue. During their long walk he had said nothing; he had
uttered no syllable of revolting cant about the duty of obedience
and the wickedness of resistance to law; he had shown no concern
in the matter; hardly even a consciousness of the boy's existence.
Probably his mind at that moment was actually troubling itself
little about his grandson's iniquities, and much about the iniquities of President Polk, but the boy could scarcely at that age
feel the whole satisfaction of thinking that President Polk was
to be the vicarious victim of his own sins, and he gave his grandfather credit for intelligent silence. For this forbearance he felt
instinctive respect. He admitted force as a form of right; he admitted even temper, under protest; but the seeds of a moral education would at that moment have fallen on the stoniest soil in
Quincy, which is, as every one knows, the stoniest glacial and tidal
drift known in any Puritan land.

Down to 1850, and even later, New England society was still
directed by the professions. Lawyers, physicians, professors, merchants were classes, and acted not as individuals, but as though
they were clergymen and each profession were a church. In politics the system required competent expression; it was the old
Ciceronian idea of government by the best that produced the long
line of New England statesmen. They chose men to represent
them because they wanted to be well represented, and they chose
the best they had. Thus Boston chose Daniel Webster, and Webster took, not as pay, but as honorarium, the cheques raised for

him by Peter Harvey from the Appletons, Perkinses, Amorys, Searses, Brookses, Lawrences, and so on, who begged him to represent them. Edward Everett held the rank in regular succession to Webster. Robert C. Winthrop claimed succession to Everett. Charles Sumner aspired to break the succession, but not the system. The Adamses had never been, for any length of time, a part of this State succession; they had preferred the national service, and had won all their distinction outside the State, but they too had required State support and had commonly received it. The little group of men in Mount Vernon Street were an offshoot of this system; they were statesmen, not politicians; they guided public opinion, but were little guided by it.

The boy naturally learned only one lesson from his saturation in such air. He took for granted that this sort of world, more or less the same that had always existed in Boston and Massachusetts Bay, was the world which he was to fit. Had he known Europe he would have learned no better. The Paris of Louis Philippe, Guizot, and de Tocqueville, as well as the London of Robert Peel, Macaulay, and John Stuart Mill, were but varieties of the same upper-class bourgeoisie that felt instinctive cousinship with the Boston of Ticknor, Prescott, and Motley. Even the typical grumbler Carlyle, who cast doubts on the real capacity of the middle class, and who at times thought himself eccentric, found friendship and alliances in Boston—still more in Concord. The system had proved so successful that even Germany wanted to try it, and Italy yearned for it. England's middle-class government was the ideal of human progress.

Even the violent reaction after 1848, and the return of all Europe to military practices, never for a moment shook the true faith. No one, except Karl Marx, foresaw radical change.

One day in June, 1854, young Adams walked for the last time down the steps of Mr. Dixwell's school in Boylston Place, and felt no sensation but one of unqualified joy that this experience was ended. . . . The next regular step was Harvard College. He was more than glad to go. For generation after generation, Adamses and Brookses and Boylstons and Gorhams had gone to

Harvard College, and although none of them, as far as known, had ever done any good there, or thought himself the better for it, custom, social ties, convenience, and, above all, economy, kept each generation in the track. Any other education would have required a serious effort, but no one took Harvard College seriously. All went there because their friends went there, and the College was their ideal of social self-respect. . . .

Harvard College, as far as it educated at all, was a mild and liberal school, which sent young men into the world with all they needed to make respectable citizens, and something of what they wanted to make useful ones. Leaders of men it never tried to make. Its ideals were altogether different. The Unitarian clergy had given to the College a character of moderation, balance, judgment, restraint, what the French called *mesure;* excellent traits, which the College attained with singular success, so that its graduates could commonly be recognized by the stamp, but such a type of character rarely lent itself to autobiography. In effect, the school created a type but not a will. Four years of Harvard College, if successful, resulted in an autobiographical blank, a mind on which only a water-mark had been stamped. . . .

Beyond two or three Greek plays, the student got nothing from the ancient languages. Beyond some incoherent theories of free-trade and protection, he got little from Political Economy. He could not afterwards remember to have heard the name of Karl Marx mentioned, or the title of *Capital.* He was equally ignorant of Auguste Comte. These were the two writers of his time who most influenced its thought. The bit of practical teaching he afterwards reviewed with most curiosity was the course in Chemistry, which taught him a number of theories that befogged his mind for a lifetime. The only teaching that appealed to his imagination was a course of lectures by Louis Agassiz on the Glacial Period and Palæontology, which had more influence on his curiosity than the rest of the college instruction altogether. The entire work of the four years could have been easily put into the work of any four months in after life. . . .

Lowell, on succeeding Longfellow as Professor of Belles-Lettres, had duly gone to Germany, and had brought back whatever he found to bring. The literary world then agreed that truth survived in Germany alone, and Carlyle, Matthew Arnold, Renan, Emerson, with scores of popular followers, taught the German faith. The literary world had revolted against the yoke of coming capitalism—its money-lenders, its bank directors, and its railway magnates. Thackeray and Dickens followed Balzac in scratching and biting the unfortunate middle class with savage ill-temper, much as the middle class had scratched and bitten the Church and Court for a hundred years before. The middle class had the power, and held its coal and iron well in hand, but the satirists and idealists seized the press, and as they were agreed that the Second Empire was a disgrace to France and a danger to England, they turned to Germany because at that moment Germany was neither economical nor military, and a hundred years behind western Europe in the simplicity of its standard. German thought, method, honesty, and even taste, became the standards of scholarship. Goethe was raised to the rank of Shakespeare—Kant ranked as a law-giver above Plato. All serious scholars were obliged to become German, for German thought was revolutionizing criticism.

Abroad, therefore, to Germany, to study the Civil Law young Adams sailed in November, 1858. He duly landed in Liverpool.

Then came the journey up to London through Birmingham and the Black District, another lesson, which needed much more to be rightly felt. The plunge into darkness lurid with flames; the sense of unknown horror in this weird gloom which then existed nowhere else, and never had existed before, except in volcanic craters; the violent contrast between this dense, smoky, impenetrable darkness, and the soft green charm that one glided into, as one emerged—the revelation of an unknown society of the pit—made a boy uncomfortable, though he had no idea that Karl Marx was standing there waiting for him, and that sooner or later the process of education would have to deal with Karl Marx much more than with Professor Bowen of Harvard College or his Satanic free-trade majesty John Stuart Mill. The Black District was a practical education, but it was infinitely far in the distance.

The boy ran away from it, as he ran away from everything he disliked.

Had he known enough to know where to begin he would have seen something to study, more vital than the Civil Law, in the long, muddy, dirty, sordid, gas-lit dreariness of Oxford Street as his dingy four-wheeler dragged its weary way to Charing Cross. He did notice one peculiarity about it worth remembering. London was still London. A certain style dignified its grime; heavy, clumsy, arrogant, purse-proud, but not cheap; insular but large; barely tolerant of an outside world, and absolutely self-confident. The boys in the streets made such free comments on the American clothes and figures, that the travellers hurried to put on tall hats and long overcoats to escape criticism. No stranger had rights even in the Strand. The eighteenth century held its own. History muttered down Fleet Street, like Dr. Johnson, in Adams's ear; Vanity Fair was alive on Piccadilly in yellow chariots with coachmen in wigs, on hammer-cloths; footmen with canes, on the footboard, and a shrivelled old woman inside; half the great houses, black with London smoke, bore large funereal hatchments; every one seemed insolent, and the most insolent structures in the world were the Royal Exchange and the Bank of England. In November, 1858, London was still vast, but it was the London of the eighteenth century that an American felt and hated.

Education went backward. Adams, still a boy, could not guess how intensely intimate this London grime was to become to him as a man, but he could still less conceive himself returning to it fifty years afterwards, noting at each turn how the great city grew smaller as it doubled in size; cheaper as it quadrupled its wealth; less imperial as its empire widened; less dignified as it tried to be civil. He liked it best when he hated it.

Germany was worse: "German student life was on the whole the thinnest of beer." "So he took a room in the household of the usual small government clerk with the usual plain daughters . . ." "Possibly one might learn something more by accident . . ."

Perhaps Henry learned something in Rome, though he never knew it, and never sought it. Rome dwarfs teachers. The great-

est men of the age scarcely bore the test of posing with Rome
for a background. Perhaps Garibaldi—possibly even Cavour—
could have sat "in the close of the evening, among the ruins of the
Capitol," but one hardly saw Napoleon III there, or Palmerston
or Tennyson or Longfellow. . . . Rome was a bewildering complex of ideas, experiments, ambitions, energies; without her, the
Western world was pointless and fragmentary; she gave heart and
unity to it all; yet Gibbon might have gone on for the whole century, sitting among the ruins of the Capitol, and no one would
have passed, capable of telling him what it meant. Perhaps it meant
nothing.

*The Civil War broke out. Adams accompanied his father
Charles Francis Adams as secretary when he was appointed Minister to England. They believed they were going to a friendly
Government,* "true to the anti-slavery principles which had been
their steadiest profession." "He had to learn . . . that his ideas
were the reverse of the truth." *No one* "doubted that Jefferson
Davis had made or would make a nation, and nearly all were glad
of it . . ."

*Minister Adams found himself in a labyrinth of chicanery, dis-
ingenuousness, hostility, and downright falsehood. Adams neither
understood at the time nor ever learned later the truth behind the
bewildering appearances of Palmerston, Russell, Gladstone. Education had met with another failure. But whether Minister Adams
understood what was going on behind the curtains or no, he knew
how to deal with affairs. He pushed the British Government
steadily into weaker positions, stripped Russell* "of every rag of
defense," *and* "ended by the famous sentence: 'It would be superfluous in me to point out to your lordship that this is war!' "
"After a long and desperate struggle, the American Minister had
trumped their best card, and won the game."

But the end of the Civil War left Adams without a profession.
"For the law, diplomacy had unfitted him; for diplomacy he already knew too much."

Politics, diplomacy, law, art, and history had opened no outlet for future energy or effort, but a man must do something, even

in Portland Place, when winter is dark and winter evenings are exceedingly long. At that moment Darwin was convulsing society. The geological champion of Darwin was Sir Charles Lyell, and the Lyells were intimate at the Legation. Sir Charles constantly said of Darwin, what Palgrave said of Tennyson, that the first time he came to town, Adams should be asked to meet him, but neither of them ever came to town, or ever cared to meet a young American, and one could not go to them because they were known to dislike intrusion. The only Americans who were not allowed to intrude were the half-dozen in the Legation. Adams was content to read Darwin, especially his *Origin of Species* and his *Voyage of the Beagle*. He was a Darwinist before the letter; a predestined follower of the tide; but he was hardly trained to follow Darwin's evidences. Fragmentary the British mind might be, but in those days it was doing a great deal of work in a very un-English way, building up so many and such vast theories on such narrow foundations as to shock the conservative, and delight the frivolous. The atomic theory; the correlation and conservation of energy; the mechanical theory of the universe; the kinetic theory of gases, and Darwin's Law of Natural Selection, were examples of what a young man had to take on trust. Neither he nor any one else knew enough to verify them; in his ignorance of mathematics, he was particularly helpless; but this never stood in his way. The ideas were new and seemed to lead somewhere—to some great generalization which would finish one's clamor to be educated. That a beginner should understand them all, or believe them all, no one could expect, still less exact. Henry Adams was Darwinist because it was easier than not, for his ignorance exceeded belief, and one must know something in order to contradict even such triflers as Tyndall and Huxley.

By rights, he should have been also a Marxist, but some narrow trait of the New England nature seemed to blight socialism, and he tried in vain to make himself a convert. He did the next best thing; he became a Comteist, within the limits of evolution. He was ready to become anything but quiet.

As though the world had not been enough upset in his time, he was eager to see it upset more. He had his wish, but he lost his hold on the results by trying to understand them.

He never tried to understand Darwin; but he still fancied he might get the best part of Darwinism from the easier study of geology; a science which suited idle minds as well as though it were history. Every curate in England dabbled in geology and hunted for vestiges of Creation. Darwin hunted only for vestiges of Natural Selection, and Adams followed him, although he cared nothing about Selection, unless perhaps for the indirect amusement of upsetting curates. He felt, like nine men in ten, an instinctive belief in Evolution, but he felt no more concern in Natural than in unnatural Selection, though he seized with greediness the new volume on the *Antiquity of Man* which Sir Charles Lyell published in 1863 in order to support Darwin by wrecking the Garden of Eden. Sir Charles next brought out, in 1866, a new edition of his *Principles,* then the highest text-book of geology, but here the Darwinian doctrine grew in stature. Natural Selection led back to Natural Evolution, and at last to Natural Uniformity. This was a vast stride. Unbroken Evolution under uniform conditions pleased every one—except curates and bishops; it was the very best substitute for religion; a safe, conservative, practical, thoroughly Common-Law deity. Such a working system for the universe suited a young man who had just helped to waste five or ten thousand million dollars and a million lives, more or less, to enforce unity and uniformity on people who objected to it; the idea was only too seductive in its perfection; it had the charm of art. Unity and Uniformity were the whole motive of philosophy, and if Darwin, like a true Englishman, preferred to back into it—to reach God a posteriori—rather than start from it, like Spinoza, the difference of method taught only the moral that the best way of reaching unity was to unite. Any road was good that arrived.

Life depended on it. One had been, from the first, dragged hither and thither like a French poodle on a string, following always the strongest pull, between one form of unity or centralization and another. The proof that one had acted wisely because of obeying the primordial habit of nature flattered one's self-esteem. Steady, uniform, unbroken evolution from lower to higher seemed easy. So, one day when Sir Charles came to the Legation to inquire about getting his *Principles* properly noticed in America, young Adams found nothing simpler than to suggest that he could do it himself if Sir Charles would tell him what to say. Youth risks such encounters with the universe before one succumbs to it, yet even he was surprised at Sir Charles's ready assent, and still more so at finding himself, after half an hour's conversation, sitting down to clear the minds of American geologists about the principles of their profession.

This was getting on fast; Arthur Pendennis had never gone so far.

The geologists were a hardy class, not likely to be much hurt by Adams's learning, nor did he throw away much concern on their account. He undertook the task chiefly to educate, not them, but himself, and if Sir Isaac Newton had, like Sir Charles Lyell, asked him to explain for Americans his last edition of the *Principia,* Adams would have jumped at the chance. Unfortunately the mere reading such works for amusement is quite a different matter from studying them for criticism. Ignorance must always begin at the beginning. Adams must inevitably have begun by asking Sir Isaac for an intelligible reason why the apple fell to the ground. He did not know enough to be satisfied with the fact. The Law of Gravitation was so-and-so, but what was Gravitation? and he would have been thrown quite off his base if Sir Isaac had answered that he did not know.

At the very outset Adams struck on Sir Charles's Glacial Theory or theories. He was ignorant enough to think that the glacial epoch looked like a chasm between him and a uniformitarian world. If the glacial period were uniformity, what was catastrophe? To him the two or three labored guesses that Sir Charles suggested or borrowed to explain glaciation were proof of nothing, and were quite unsolid as support for so immense a superstructure as geological uniformity. If one were at liberty to be as lax in science as in theology, and to assume unity from the start, one might better say so, as the Church did, and not invite attack by appearing weak in evidence. Naturally a young man, altogether ignorant, could not say this to Sir Charles Lyell or Sir Isaac Newton; but he was forced to state Sir Charles's views, which he thought weak as hypotheses and worthless as proofs. Sir Charles himself seemed shy of them. Adams hinted his heresies in vain. At last he resorted to what he thought the bold experiment of inserting a sentence in the text, intended to provoke correction. "The introduction [by Louis Agassiz] of this new geological agent seemed at first sight inconsistent with Sir Charles's argument, obliging him to allow that causes had in fact existed on the earth capable of producing more violent geological changes than would be possible in our own day." The hint produced no effect. Sir Charles said not a word; he let the paragraph stand; and Adams never knew whether the great Uniformitarian was strict or lax in his uniformitarian creed; but he doubted.

Objections fatal to one mind are futile to another, and as far as concerned the article, the matter ended there, although the glacial epoch remained a misty region in the young man's Darwinism. Had it been the only one, he would not have fretted about it; but uniformity often worked queerly and sometimes did not work as Natural Selection at all. Finding himself at a loss for some single figure to illustrate the Law of Natural Selection, Adams asked Sir Charles for the simplest case of uniformity on record. Much to his surprise Sir Charles told him that certain forms, like Terebratula, appeared to be identical from the beginning to the end of geological time. Since this was altogether too much uniformity and much too little selection, Adams gave up the attempt to begin at the beginning, and tried starting at the end—himself. Taking for granted that the vertebrates would serve his purpose, he asked Sir Charles to introduce him to the first vertebrate. Infinitely to his bewilderment, Sir Charles informed him that the first vertebrate was a very respectable fish, among the earliest of all fossils, which had lived, and whose bones were still reposing, under Adams's own favorite Abbey on Wenlock Edge. . . .

All this seemed trivial to the true Darwinian, and to Sir Charles it was mere defect in the geological record. Sir Charles labored only to heap up the evidences of evolution; to cumulate them till the mass became irresistible. With that purpose, Adams gladly studied and tried to help Sir Charles, but, behind the lesson of the day, he was conscious that, in geology as in theology, he could prove only Evolution that did not evolve; Uniformity that was not uniform; and Selection that did not select.

Even if politics could now have satisfied Adams, it was doubtful if he could have maintained a foothold among the venalities that followed the Civil War. "The world, after 1865, became a bankers' world, and no banker would ever trust one who had deserted State Street, and had gone to Washington with purposes of doubtful credit, or of no credit at all," *one, moreover, who* "tempered obedience by mockery."

Grant's administration outraged every rule of ordinary decency, but scores of promising men, whom the country could not well spare, were ruined in saying so. The world cared little for decency. What it wanted, it did not know; probably a system that would work, and men who could work it; but it found neither. Adams had tried his own little hands on it, and had failed. His friends had been driven out of Washington or had taken to fisticuffs. He himself sat down and stared helplessly into the future. . . .

The political dilemma was as clear in 1870 as it was likely to be in 1970. The system of 1789 had broken down, and with it the eighteenth-century fabric of a priori, or moral, principles. Politicians had tacitly given it up. Grant's administration marked the avowal. Nine-tenths of men's political energies must henceforth be wasted on expedients to piece out—to patch—or, in vulgar language, to tinker—the political machine as often as it broke down.

In the academic life to which, for want of a possible alternative, he retreated, things were, if possible, worse. "Several score of the best-educated, most agreeable, and personally the most sociable people in America united in Cambridge to make a social desert that would have startled a polar bear." *Adams knew* "both Congressmen and professors, and he preferred Congressmen." *But he energetically studied medieval history and watched the swarming factories of industrialism and the inevitable tread of capitalist im-*

perialism. "The climax of empire could be seen approaching, year after year, as if Sulla were a President or McKinley a Consul."

And constantly he tried to find a formula which would give intelligibility to the movement of history.

Ignorance required that these political and social and scientific values of the twelfth and twentieth centuries should be correlated in some relation of movement that could be expressed in mathematics, nor did one care in the least that all the world said it could not be done, or that one knew not enough mathematics even to figure a formula beyond the schoolboy $S = \frac{gt^2}{2}$. If Kepler and Newton could take liberties with the sun and moon, an obscure person in a remote wilderness like La Fayette Square could take liberties with Congress, and venture to multiply half its attraction into the square of its time. He had only to find a value, even infinitesimal, for its attraction at any given time. A historical formula that should satisfy the conditions of the stellar universe weighed heavily on his mind; but a trifling matter like this was one in which he could look for no help from anybody—he could look only for derision at best.

All his associates in history condemned such an attempt as futile and almost immoral—certainly hostile to sound historical system. Adams tried it only because of its hostility to all that he had taught for history, since he started afresh from the new point that, whatever was right, all he had ever taught was wrong. He had pursued ignorance thus far with success, and had swept his mind clear of knowledge. In beginning again, from the starting-point of Sir Isaac Newton, he looked about him in vain for a teacher. Few men in Washington cared to overstep the school conventions, and the most distinguished of them, Simon Newcomb, was too sound a mathematician to treat such a scheme seriously. The greatest of Americans, judged by his rank in science, Willard Gibbs, never came to Washington, and Adams never enjoyed a chance to meet him. After Gibbs, one of the most distinguished was Langley, of the Smithsonian, who was more accessible, to whom Adams had been much in the habit of turning whenever he wanted an outlet for his vast reservoirs of ignorance. Langley listened with outward patience to his disputatious questionings; but he too nourished a scientific passion for doubt, and sentimental attachment for its avowal. He had the physicist's heinous fault of professing to know nothing between flashes of intense perception. Like so many other great observers, Langley was not a mathematician, and like most physicists, he believed in physics. Rigidly denying himself the amusement of philosophy, which consists chiefly in suggesting unintelligible answers to insoluble problems, he still knew the problems, and liked to wander past them in a courteous temper, even bowing to them distantly as though recognizing their existence, while doubting their respectability. He generously let others doubt what he felt obliged to affirm; and early put into Adams's hands the *Concepts of Modern Science,* a volume by Judge Stallo, which had been treated for a dozen years by the schools with a conspiracy of silence such as inevitably meets every revolutionary work that upsets the stock and machinery of instruction. Adams read and failed to understand; then he asked questions and failed to get answers.

Probably this was education. Perhaps it was the only scientific education open to a student sixty-odd years old, who asked to be as ignorant as an astronomer. For him the details of science meant nothing: he wanted to know its mass. Solar heat was not enough, or was too much. Kinetic atoms led only to motion; never to direction or progress. History had no use for multiplicity; it needed unity; it could study only motion, direction, attraction, relation.

Like most of his generation, Adams had taken the word of science that the new unity was as good as found. It would not be an intelligence—probably not even a consciousness—but it would serve. He passed sixty years waiting for it, and at the end of that time, on reviewing the ground, he was led to think that the final synthesis of science and its ultimate triumph was the kinetic theory of gases; which seemed to cover all motion in space, and to furnish the measure of time. So far as he understood it, the theory asserted that any portion of space is occupied by molecules of gas, flying in right lines at velocities varying up to a mile in a second, and colliding with each other at intervals varying up to 17,750,000 times in a second. To this analysis—if one understood it right— all matter whatever was reducible, and the only difference of opinion in science regarded the doubt whether a still deeper analysis would reduce the atom of gas to pure motion.

Thus, unless one mistook the meaning of motion, which might well be, the scientific synthesis commonly called Unity was the scientific analysis commonly called Multiplicity. The two things were the same, all forms being shifting phases of motion. Granting this ocean of colliding atoms, the last hope of humanity, what happened if one dropped the sounder into the abyss—let it go— frankly gave up Unity altogether? What was Unity? Why was one to be forced to affirm it?

Here everybody flatly refused help. Science seemed content with its old phrase of "larger synthesis," which was well enough for science, but meant chaos for man. One would have been glad to stop and ask no more, but the anarchist bomb bade one go on, and the bomb is a powerful persuader. One could not stop, even to enjoy the charms of a perfect gas colliding seventeen million times in a second, much like an automobile in Paris. Science itself had been crowded so close to the edge of the abyss that its attempts to escape were as metaphysical as the leap, while an ignorant old man felt no motive for trying to escape, seeing that the only escape possible lay in the form of vis a tergo commonly called Death. He got out his Descartes again; dipped into his Hume and Berkeley; wrestled anew with his Kant; pondered solemnly over his Hegel and Schopenhauer and Hartmann; strayed gaily away with his Greeks—all merely to ask what Unity meant, and what happened when one denied it.

Apparently one never denied it. Every philosopher, whether sane or insane, naturally affirmed it. The utmost flight of anarchy seemed to have stopped with the assertion of two principles, and even these fitted into each other, like good and evil, light and darkness. Pessimism itself, black as it might be painted, had been content to turn the universe of contradictions into the human thought as one Will, and treat it as representation. Metaphysics insisted on treating the universe as one thought or treating thought as one universe; and philosophers agreed, like kinetic gas, that the universe could be known only as motion of mind, and therefore as unity. One could know it only as one's self; it was psychology. . . .

Any schoolboy could see that man as a force must be measured by motion, from a fixed point. Psychology helped here by suggesting a unit—the point of history when man held the highest idea of himself as a unit in a unified universe. Eight or ten years of study had led Adams to think he might use the century 1150–1250, expressed in Amiens Cathedral and the Works of Thomas Aquinas, as the unit from which he might measure motion down to his own time, without assuming anything as true or untrue, except relation. The movement might be studied at once in philosophy and mechanics. Setting himself to the task, he began a volume which he mentally knew as *Mont-Saint-Michel and Chartres: a Study of Thirteenth-Century Unity*. From that point he proposed to fix a position for himself, which he could label: *The Education of Henry Adams: a Study of Twentieth-Century Multiplicity*. With the help of these two points of relation, he hoped to project his lines forward and backward indefinitely, subject to correction from any one who should know better. . . .

No one could say that the social mind now failed to respond to new force, even when the new force annoyed it horribly. Every day Nature violently revolted, causing so-called accidents with enormous destruction of property and life, while plainly laughing at man, who helplesly groaned and shrieked and shuddered, but never for a single instant could stop. The railways alone approached the carnage of war; automobiles and fire-arms ravaged society, until an earthquake became almost a nervous relaxation. An immense volume of force had detached itself from the unknown universe of energy, while still vaster reservoirs, supposed to be infinite, steadily revealed themselves, attracting mankind with more compulsive course than all the Pontic Seas or Gods or Gold that ever existed, and feeling still less of retiring ebb.

In 1850, science would have smiled at such a romance as this, but, in 1900, as far as history could learn, few men of science thought it a laughing matter. If a perplexed but laborious follower could venture to guess their drift, it seemed in their minds a toss-up between anarchy and order. Unless they should be more honest with themselves in the future than ever they were in the past, they would be more astonished than their followers when they reached the end. If Karl Pearson's notions of the universe were sound, men like Galileo, Descartes, Leibnitz, and Newton should have stopped the progress of science before 1700, supposing them to have been honest in the religious convictions they expressed. In 1900 they were plainly forced back on faith in a unity unproved and an order they had themselves disproved. They had reduced their universe to a series of relations to themselves. They had reduced themselves to motion in a universe of motions, with an acceleration, in their own case, of vertiginous violence. With the correctness of their science, history had no right to meddle, since their science now lay in a plane where scarcely one or two hundred minds in the world could follow its mathematical processes; but bombs educate vigorously, and even wireless telegraphy or airships might require the reconstruction of society. If any analogy whatever existed between the human mind, on one side, and the laws of motion, on the other, the mind had already entered a field of attraction so violent that it must immediately pass beyond, into new equilibrium, like the Comet of Newton, to suffer dissipation altogether, like meteoroids in the earth's atmosphere. If it behaved like an explosive, it must rapidly recover equilibrium; if it behaved like a vegetable, it must reach its limits of growth; and even if it acted like the earlier creations of energy—the saurians and sharks—it must have nearly reached the limits of its expansion. If science were to go on doubling or quadrupling its complexities every ten years, even mathematics would soon succumb. An average mind had succumbed already in 1850; it could no longer understand the problem in 1900 . . .

Meanwhile he was getting education. With that, a teacher who had failed to educate even the generation of 1870, dared not interfere. The new forces would educate. History saw few lessons in the past that would be useful in the future; but one, at least, it did see. The attempt of the American of 1800 to educate the

American of 1900 had not often been surpassed for folly; and since
1800 the forces and their complications had increased a thousand
times or more. The attempt of the American of 1900 to educate
the American of 2000, must be even blinder than that of the
Congressman of 1800, except so far as he had learned his ignorance.
During a million or two of years, every generation in turn had
toiled with endless agony to attain and apply power, all the while
betraying the deepest alarm and horror at the power they created.
The most elementary books of science betrayed the inadequacy of
old implements of thought. Chapter after chapter closed with
phrases such as one never met in older literature: "The cause of
this phenomenon is not understood"; "science no longer ventures
to explain causes"; "the first step towards a causal explanation
still remains to be taken"; "opinions are very much divided"; "in
spite of the contradictions involved"; "science gets on only by
adopting different theories, sometimes contradictory." Evidently
the new American would need to think in contradictions, and instead of Kant's famous four antinomies, the new universe would
know no law that could not be proved by its anti-law.

There it ended! Shakespeare himself could use no more than
the commonplace to express what is incapable of expression. "The
rest is silence!" The few familiar words, among the simplest in
the language, conveying an idea trite beyond rivalry, served Shakespeare, and, as yet, no one has said more. . . .
Education had ended . . . and only beyond some remoter horizon could its values be fixed or renewed. Perhaps some day—say
1938, their centenary—they might be allowed to return together
for a holiday, to see the mistakes of their own lives made clear in
the light of the mistakes of their successors; and perhaps then, for
the first time since man began his education among the carnivores,
they would find a world that sensitive and timid natures could regard without a shudder.

A DYING PURITANISM

Sir Edmund Gosse has written other biographies, but he will be remembered preëminently for one single foray into the field. In that one, published anonymously in 1907, he revealed himself as a significant literary artist and a striking biographical innovator.

Few people can have realized, at the time, what a portent glowed before them. That *Father and Son* was a fascinating book anyone could see. Two people were revealed in it—a sober and desperately devoted man, and an instinctively rebellious little boy—in all the sharpness and shading of life; and they were surrounded by brightly sketched minor figures. There was a strange mixture of hilarity and bitterness, seen as in life, and yet suffused with understanding. There was the spectacle of a spirit being enslaved, reduced almost to unresisting dust, by the purest and most noble-hearted affection.

The revolutionary character of the book, however, lay in other qualities. It mingled biography and autobiography, the narrator being the little boy so nearly crushed by his father's love. It was not the story of the father's life, and still less of his son's, but the story of a relationship and a struggle. Its details were selected with unerring craftsmanship. With deepening atmosphere, touched with sparkling highlights, it marched through crucial scenes to the ultimate flare-up of defiance. In these ways the genius of Gosse was exploratory, opening new realms of tense psychological struggle, and transcending any of those who have followed him.

Gosse is not alone in regarding his experience as historically significant. (We have seen that Mill and Henry Adams so regarded theirs.) But he is unique in finding its precise significance in a conflict. "This book," he begins, "is the record of a struggle between two temperaments, two consciences, and almost two epochs." It marked the dividing line between the nonconformist, evangelical conscience—"a state of soul once not uncommon in Protestant Europe"—and the modern mind. It is "the diagnosis of a dying Puritanism" that Gosse presents us.

His parents were extreme Calvinists, to whom every word of the Bible was literally and absolutely true. There were no stories for their little son, worldly gaieties were frowned upon, but they were a cheerful household, resounding with merry laughter. Still, omniscient and omnipotent, God was everywhere. Parental domination and the power of God hemmed the child in, more and more as he grew older: "My soul was shut up, like Fatima, in a tower . . ." Desperately he clung, deep within, "to a hard nut of individuality," almost destroyed and shriveling away.

The wild caprice by which his father "opened a window" in that prison-tower, the insensible degrees by which some of the sternest prohibitions melted away, the infiltration into the boy's mind of serene Apollo, and Venus in her undulations—the worlds of art and literature—against which in vain the father's face blazed with white Puritan fury, the impact of scientific materialism, and that final scene in the orchid-scented conservatory, when the youth broke into whimpering revolt: all these Gosse must be allowed to tell, as he does incomparably, for himself.

The deepest significance of all in *Father and Son* is in its historical meaning. The iron Calvinism of Gosse's elders was joined in battle with the modern age. The interplay of pragmatism, paganism, and poetry in the son looked as innocent as the waves of the sea; but they sucked and tore at the stone foundations of faith, crumbled gradually and remorselessly the joints in the rock. In vain the elder tried to save the edifice by striking at individual symptoms: he might as well strike the waves on the shore. Freedom, science, skepticism, a more flexible morality, an emancipated art: these were the tendencies of the contemporary world against which Philip Gosse dashed himself in vain.

The struggle between two ages was going on as much in the Gosses' narrow little London lodgings and country cottages as in the worlds of politics and philosophy inhabited by Mill and Adams. *Father and Son,* no less than *The Education of Henry Adams,* reveals a world in transition, in struggle and defeat. Adams was borne further along in the flood than the elder Gosse, but he too at the end is left among the wreckage and flotsam. Gosse enables us to understand, even sympathize with, the sentiments he leaves behind; then he flings us forward to the threshold of a new life.

Father and Son

A Study of Two Temperaments

SIR EDMUND GOSSE

[Gosse was born in 1849 and died in 1928. His father, Philip Gosse, was born 1810 and died 1888. *Father and Son* was first published in 1907.]

THIS BOOK IS THE RECORD OF A STRUGGLE BETWEEN TWO TEMPERA-ments, two consciences and almost two epochs. It ended, as was inevitable, in disruption. Of the two human beings here described, one was born to fly backward, the other could not help being carried forward. There came a time when neither spoke the same language as the other, or encompassed the same hopes, or was fortified by the same desires. But, at least, it is some consolation to the survivor, that neither, to the very last hour, ceased to respect the other, or to regard him with a sad indulgence. The affection of these two persons was assailed by forces in comparison with which the changes that health or fortune or place introduce are as nothing. It is a mournful satisfaction, but yet a satisfaction, that they were both of them able to obey the law which says that ties of close family relationship must be honoured and sustained. Had it not been so, this story would never have been told. . . .

It was a curious coincidence that life had brought both my parents along similar paths to an almost identical position in respect to religious belief. She had started from the Anglican standpoint, he from the Wesleyan, and each, almost without counsel from others, and after varied theological experiments, had come to take up precisely the same attitude towards all divisions of the Protestant Church, that, namely, of detached and unbiassed contemplation. So far as the sects agreed with my Father and my Mother, the sects were walking in the light; wherever they differed from them, they had slipped more or less definitely into a penumbra of their own making, a darkness into which neither of my parents would follow them. Hence, by a process of selection, my Father and my Mother alike had gradually, without violence, found themselves shut outside all Protestant communions, and at last they met only with a few extreme Calvinists like themselves, on terms of what may almost be called negation —with no priest, no ritual, no festivals, no ornament of any kind, nothing but the Lord's Supper and the exposition of Holy Scripture drawing these austere spirits into any sort of cohesion. They called themselves "the Brethren," simply; a title enlarged by the world outside into "Plymouth Brethren."

For over three years after their marriage, neither of my parents left London for a single day, not being able to afford to travel. They received scarcely any visitors, never ate a meal away from home, never spent an evening in social intercourse abroad. At night they discussed theology, read aloud to one another, or translated scientific brochures from French or German. It sounds a terrible life of pressure and deprivation, and that it was physically unwholesome there can be no shadow of a doubt. But their contentment was complete and unfeigned.

Out of the darkness of my infancy there comes only one flash of memory. I am seated alone, in my baby-chair, at a dinner-table set for several people. Somebody brings in a leg of mutton, puts it down close to me, and goes out. I am again alone, gazing at two low windows, wide open upon a garden. Suddenly, noiselessly, a large, long animal (obviously a greyhound) appears at one window-sill, slips into the room, seizes the leg of mutton and slips out again. When this happened I could not yet talk. The accomplishment of speech came to me very late, doubtless because

I never heard young voices. Many years later, when I mentioned this recollection, there was a shout of laughter and surprise:—

"That, then, was what became of the mutton! It was not you, who, as your Uncle A. pretended, ate it up, in the twinkling of an eye, bone and all!"

Meanwhile, capable as I was of reading, I found my greatest pleasure in the pages of books. The range of these was limited, for story-books of every description were sternly excluded. No fiction of any kind, religious or secular, was admitted into the house. In this it was to my Mother, not to my Father, that the prohibition was due. She had a remarkable, I confess to me still somewhat unaccountable impression, that to "tell a story," that is, to compose fictitious narrative of any kind, was a sin. . . .

My own state, however, was, I should think, almost unique among the children of cultivated parents. In consequence of the stern ordinance which I have described, not a single fiction was read or told to me during my infancy. The rapture of the child who delays the process of going to bed by cajoling "a story" out of his mother or his nurse, as he sits upon her knee, well tucked up, at the corner of the nursery fire,—this was unknown to me. Never, in all my early childhood, did any one address to me the affecting preamble, "Once upon a time!" I was told about missionaries, but never about pirates; I was familiar with humming-birds, but I had never heard of fairies. Jack the Giant-Killer, Rumpelstiltskin and Robin Hood were not of my acquaintance, and though I understood about wolves, Little Red Ridinghood was a stranger even by name. . . .

It is so generally taken for granted that a life strictly dedicated to religion is stiff and dreary, that I may have some difficulty in persuading my readers that, as a matter of fact, in these early days of my childhood, before disease and death had penetrated to our slender society, we were always cheerful and often gay. My parents were playful with one another, and there were certain stock family jests which seldom failed to enliven the breakfast table. My Father and Mother lived so completely in the atmosphere of faith, and were so utterly convinced of their intercourse with God, that, so long as that intercourse was not clouded by sin, to which they were delicately sensitive, they could afford to take the passing hour very lightly. They would even, to a certain extent, treat the surroundings of their religion as a subject of jest, joking very mildly and gently about such things as an attitude at prayer or the nature of a supplication. They were absolutely indifferent to forms. They prayed, seated in their chairs, as willingly as, reversed, upon their knees; no ritual having any significance for them. My Mother was sometimes extremely gay, laughing with a soft, merry sound. What I have since been told of the guileless mirth of nuns in a convent has reminded me of the gaiety of my parents during my early childhood.

My Father and Mother, in their serene discipline of me, never argued with one another, never even differed; their wills seemed absolutely one. My Mother always deferred to my Father, and in his absence spoke of him to me, as if he were all-wise. I confused him in some sense with God; at all events I believed that my Father knew everything and saw everything. One morning in my sixth year, my Mother and I were alone in the morning-room, when my Father came in and announced some fact to us. I was standing on the rug, gazing at him, and when he made this statement, I remember turning quickly, in embarrassment, and looking into the fire. The shock to me was as that of a thunderbolt, for what my Father had said *was not true.* My Mother and I, who had been present at the trifling incident, were aware that it had not happened exactly as it had been reported to him. My Mother gently told him so, and he accepted the correction. Nothing could possibly have been more trifling to my parents, but to me it meant an epoch. Here was the appalling discovery, never suspected before, that my Father was not as God, and did not know everything. The shock was not caused by any suspicion that he was not telling the truth, as it appeared to him, but by the awful proof that he was not, as I had supposed, omniscient.

Several things tended at this time to alienate my conscience from the line which my Father had so rigidly traced for it. The question of the efficacy of prayer, which has puzzled wiser heads than mine was, began to trouble me. It was insisted on in our household that if anything was desired, you should not, as my Mother said, "lose any time in seeking for it, but ask God to guide you to it." In many junctures of life, this is precisely what, in sober fact, they did. I will not dwell here on their theories, which my Mother put forth, with unflinching directness, in her published writings. But I found that a difference was made between my privileges in this matter and theirs, and this led to many discussions. My parents said: "Whatever you need, tell Him and He will grant it, if it is His will." Very well; I had need of a large painted humming-top which I had seen in a shop-window in the Caledonian Road. Accordingly, I introduced a supplication for this object into my evening prayer, carefully adding the words: "If it is Thy will." This, I recollect, placed my Mother in a dilemma, and she consulted my Father. Taken, I suppose, at a disadvantage, my Father told me I must not pray for "things like that." To which I answered by another query, "Why?" And I added that he said we ought to pray for things we needed, and that I needed the humming-top a great deal more than I did the conversion of the heathen or the restitution of Jerusalem to the Jews, two objects of my nightly supplication which left me very cold.

I have reason to believe, looking back upon this scene, conducted by candle-light in the front parlour, that my Mother was much baffled by the logic of my argument. She had gone so far as to say publicly that no "things or circumstances are too insignificant to bring before the God of the whole earth." I persisted that this covered the case of the humming-top, which was extremely significant to me. I noticed that she held aloof from the discussion, which was carried on with some show of annoyance by my Father. He had never gone quite so far as she did in regard to this question of praying for material things. I am not sure that she was convinced that I ought to have been checked; but he could not help seeing that it reduced their favourite theory to an absurdity for a small child to exercise the privilege. He ceased to argue, and told me peremptorily that it was not right for me to pray for things like humming-tops, and that I must do it no more.

His authority, of course, was paramount, and I yielded; but my faith in the efficacy of prayer was a good deal shaken. The fatal suspicion had crossed my mind that the reason why I was not to pray for the top was because it was too expensive for my parents to buy, that being the usual excuse for not getting things I wished for. . . .

All these matters drew my thoughts to the subject of idolatry, which was severely censured at the missionary meeting. I cross-examined my Father very closely as to the nature of this sin, and pinned him down to the categorical statement that idolatry consisted in praying to any one or anything but God himself. Wood and stone, in the words of the hymn, were peculiarly liable to be bowed down to by the heathen in their blindness. I pressed my Father further on this subject, and he assured me that God would be very angry, and would signify His anger, if any one, in a Christian country, bowed down to wood and stone. I cannot recall why I was so pertinacious on this subject, but I remember that my Father became a little restive under my cross-examination. I determined, however, to test the matter for myself, and one morning, when both my parents were safely out of the house, I prepared for the great act of heresy. I was in the morning-room on the ground-floor, where, with much labour, I hoisted a small chair on to the table close to the window. My heart was now beating as if it would leap out of my side, but I pursued my experiment. I knelt down on the carpet in front of the table, and looking up I said my daily prayer in a loud voice, only substituting the address "O Chair!" for the habitual one.

Having carried this act of idolatry safely through, I waited to see what would happen. It was a fine day, and I gazed up at the slip of white sky above the houses opposite, and expected something to appear in it. God would certainly exhibit his anger in some terrible form, and would chastise my impious and wilful action. I was very much alarmed, but still more excited; I breathed the high, sharp air of defiance. But nothing happened; there was not a cloud in the sky, not an unusual sound in the street. Presently I was quite sure that nothing would happen. I had committed idolatry, flagrantly and deliberately, and God did not care. The result of this ridiculous act was not to make me question the existence and power of God; those were forces which I did not dream of ignoring. But what it did was to lessen still further my confidence in my Father's knowledge of the Divine mind. My Father had said, positively, that if I worshipped a thing made of wood, God would manifest his anger. I had then worshipped a chair, made (or partly made) of wood, and God had made no sign whatever. My Father, therefore, was not really acquainted with the Divine practice in cases of idolatry.

In the little boy's seventh year his Mother fell ill. When he asked the meaning of the word that told her cruel disease he saw his parents "gazing at each other with lamentable eyes." In terrible pain, she met her death serenely.

When the very end approached, and her mind was growing clouded, she gathered her strength together to say to my Father, "I shall walk with Him in white. Won't you take your lamb and walk with me?" Confused with sorrow and alarm, my Father failed to understand her meaning. She became agitated, and she repeated two or three times: "Take our lamb, and walk with me!" Then my Father comprehended, and pressed me forward; her hand fell softly upon mine and she seemed content. Thus was my dedication, that had begun in my cradle, sealed with the most solemn, the most poignant and irresistible insistence, at the death-bed of the holiest and purest of women. But what a weight, intolerable as the burden of Atlas, to lay on the shoulders of a little fragile child!

In the spirit of my Father were then running, with furious velocity, two hostile streams of influence. I was standing, just now, thinking of these things, where the Cascine ends in the wooded point which is carved out sharply by the lion-coloured swirl of the Arno on the one side and by the pure flow of the Mugnone on the other. The rivers meet, and run parallel, but there comes a moment when the one or the other must conquer, and it is the yellow vehemence that drowns the purer tide.

So, through my Father's brain, in that year of scientific crisis, 1857, there rushed two kinds of thought, each absorbing, each

convincing, yet totally irreconcilable. There is a peculiar agony
in the paradox that truth has two forms, each of them indisputable,
yet each antagonistic to the other. It was this discovery, that there
were two theories of physical life, each of which was true, but the
truth of each incompatible with the truth of the other, which shook
the spirit of my Father with perturbation. It was not, really, a
paradox, it was a fallacy, if he could only have known it, but he
allowed the turbid volume of superstition to drown the delicate
stream of reason. He took one step in the service of truth, and
then he drew back in an agony, and accepted the servitude of
error.

This was the great moment in the history of thought when the
theory of the mutability of species was preparing to throw a flood
of light upon all departments of human speculation and action.
It was becoming necessary to stand emphatically in one army or
the other. Lyell was surrounding himself with disciples, who
were making strides in the direction of discovery. Darwin had
long been collecting facts with regard to the variation of animals
and plants. Hooker and Wallace, Asa Gray and even Agassiz, each
in his own sphere, were coming closer and closer to a perception
of that secret which was first to reveal itself clearly to the patient
and humble genius of Darwin. In the year before, in 1856, Darwin,
under pressure from Lyell, had begun that modest statement of
the new revelation, that "abstract of an essay," which developed
so mightily into *The Origin of Species*. Wollaston's *Variation of
Species* had just appeared, and had been a nine days' wonder in the
wilderness.

On the other side, the reactionaries, although never dreaming
of the fate which hung over them, had not been idle. In 1857 the
astounding question had for the first time been propounded with
contumely, "What, then, did we come from an orang-outang?"
The famous *Vestiges of Creation* had been supplying a sugar-and-
water panacea for those who could not escape from the trend
of evidence, and who yet clung to revelation. Owen was encouraging reaction by resisting, with all the strength of his
prestige, the theory of the mutability of species.

In this period of intellectual ferment, as when a great political

revolution is being planned, many possible adherents were con-
fidentially tested with hints and encouraged to reveal their bias
in a whisper. It was the notion of Lyell, himself a great mover of
men, that before the doctrine of natural selection was given to a
world which would be sure to lift up at it a howl of execration,
a certain body-guard of sound and experienced naturalists, expert in the description of species, should be privately made aware
of its tenor. Among those who were thus initiated, or approached
with a view towards possible illumination, was my Father. He was
spoken to by Hooker, and later on by Darwin, after meetings of
the Royal Society in the summer of 1857.

My Father's attitude towards the theory of natural selection was
critical in his career, and, oddly enough, it exercised an immense
influence on my own experience as a child. Let it be admitted
at once, mournful as the admission is, that every instinct in his
intelligence went out at first to greet the new light. It had hardly
done so, when a recollection of the opening chapter of Genesis
checked it at the outset. He consulted with Carpenter, a great
investigator, but one who was fully as incapable as himself of re-
modelling his ideas with regard to the old, accepted hypotheses.
They both determined, on various grounds, to have nothing to do
with the terrible theory, but to hold steadily to the law of the
fixity of species. It was exactly at this juncture that we left London, and the slight and occasional, but always extremely salutary
personal intercourse with men of scientific leading which my
Father had enjoyed at the British Museum and at the Royal
Society came to an end. His next act was to burn his ships, down
to the last beam and log out of which a raft could have been made.
By a strange act of wilfulness, he closed the doors upon himself
for ever.

My Father had never admired Sir Charles Lyell. I think that
the famous "Lord Chancellor manner" of the geologist intimidated
him, and we undervalue the intelligence of those whose conversation puts us at a disadvantage. For Darwin and Hooker, on the
other hand, he had a profound esteem, and I know not whether
this had anything to do with the fact that he chose, for his impetuous experiment in reaction, the field of geology, rather than

that of zoölogy or botany. Lyell had been threatening to publish a book on the geological history of Man, which was to be a bombshell flung into the camp of the catastrophists. My Father, after long reflection, prepared a theory of his own, which, as he fondly hoped, would take the wind out of Lyell's sails, and justify geology to godly readers of "Genesis." It was, very briefly, that there had been no gradual modification of the surface of the earth, or slow development of organic forms, but that when the catastrophic act of creation took place, the world presented, instantly, the structural appearance of a planet on which life had long existed.

The theory, coarsely enough, and to my Father's great indignation, was defined by a hasty press as being this—that God hid the fossils in the rocks in order to tempt geologists into infidelity. In truth, it was the logical and inevitable conclusion of accepting, literally, the doctrine of a sudden act of creation; it emphasised the fact that any breach in the circular course of nature could be conceived only on the supposition that the object created bore false witness to past processes, which had never taken place. For instance, Adam would certainly possess hair and teeth and bones in a condition which it must have taken many years to accomplish, yet he was created full-grown yesterday. He would certainly—though Sir Thomas Browne denied it—display an omphalos, yet no umbilical cord had ever attached him to a mother.

Never was a book cast upon the waters with greater anticipations of success than was this curious, this obstinate, this fanatical volume. My Father lived in a fever of suspense, waiting for the tremendous issue. This *Omphalos* of his, he thought, was to bring all the turmoil of scientific speculation to a close, fling geology into the arms of Scripture, and make the lion eat grass with the lamb. It was not surprising, he admitted, that there had been experienced an ever-increasing discord between the facts which geology brings to light and the direct statements of the early chapters of "Genesis." Nobody was to blame for that. My Father, and my Father alone, possessed the secret of the enigma; he alone held the key which could smoothly open the lock of geological mystery. He offered it, with a glowing gesture, to atheists and Christians alike. This was to be the universal panacea; this the system of intellectual therapeutics which could not but heal all the maladies of the age. But, alas! atheists and Christians alike looked at it and laughed, and threw it away.

In the course of that dismal winter, as the post began to bring in private letters, few and chilly, and public reviews, many and scornful, my Father looked in vain for the approval of the churches, and in vain for the acquiescence of the scientific societies, and in vain for the gratitude of those "thousands of thinking persons," which he had rashly assured himself of receiving. As his reconciliation of Scripture statements and geological deductions was welcomed nowhere; as Darwin continued silent, and the youthful Huxley was scornful, and even Charles Kingsley, from whom my Father had expected the most instant appreciation, wrote that he could not "give up the painful and slow conclusion of five and twenty years' study of geology, and believe that God has written on the rocks one enormous and superfluous lie,"—as all this happened or failed to happen, a gloom, cold and dismal, descended upon our morning teacups.

In the small village where they now lived, the Father had, "uninvited but unresisted," *assumed the leadership of the little flock of humble people who quaintly called themselves "the Saints."*

It is extraordinary what trouble it often gave my Father to know whether he was justified in admitting to the communion people of very limited powers of expression. A harmless, humble labouring man would come with a request to be allowed to "break bread." It was only by the use of strong leading questions that he could be induced to mention Christ as the ground of his trust at all. I recollect an elderly agricultural labourer being closeted for a long time with my Father, who came out at last, in a sort of dazed condition, and replied to our inquiries,—with a shrug of his shoulders as he said it,—"I was obliged to put the Name and Blood and Work of Jesus into his very mouth. It is true that he assented cordially at last, but I confess I was grievously daunted by the poor intelligence!"

But there was, or there might be, another class of persons, whom early training, separation from the world, and the care of

godly parents had so early familiarised with the acceptable calling
of Christ that their conversion had occurred, unperceived and
therefore unrecorded, at an extraordinarily early age. It would be
in vain to look for a repetition of the phenomenon in those cases.
The heavenly fire must not be expected to descend a second
time; the lips are touched with the burning coal once, and once
only. If, accordingly, these precociously selected spirits are to be
excluded because no new birth is observed in them at a mature
age, they must continue outside in the cold, since the phenomenon
cannot be repeated. When, therefore, there is not possible any
further doubt of their being in possession of salvation, longer
delay is useless, and worse than useless. The fact of conversion,
though not recorded nor even recollected, must be accepted on
the evidence of confession of faith, and as soon as the intelligence
is evidently developed, the person not merely may, but should be
accepted into communion, although still immature in body, although in years still even a child. This my Father believed to be
my case, and in this rare class did he fondly persuade himself to
station me.

As I have said, the congregation,—although docile and timid,
and little able, as units, to hold their own aginst their minister,—
behind his back were faintly hostile to this plan. None of their
own children had ever been so much as suggested for member-
ship, and each of themselves, in ripe years, had been subjected
to severe cross-examination. I think it was rather a bitter pill for
some of them to swallow that a pert little boy of ten should be
admitted, as a grown-up person, to all the hard-won privileges
of their order. Mary Grace Burmington came back from her visits
to the cottagers, reporting disaffection here and there, grumblings
in the rank and file. But quite as many, especially of the women,
enthusiastically supported my Father's wish, gloried aloud in the
manifestations of my early piety, and professed to see in it something of miraculous promise. The expression "another Infant
Samuel" was widely used. I became quite a subject of contention.
A war of the sexes threatened to break out over me; I was a
disturbing element at cottage breakfasts. I was mentioned at public prayer-meetings, not indeed by name, but, in the extraordinary

allusive way customary in the devotions, as "one amongst us of tender years" or as "a sapling in the Lord's vineyard."

To all this my Father put a stop in his own high-handed fashion. After the morning meeting, one Sunday in the autumn of 1859, he desired the attention of the saints to a personal matter which was, perhaps, not unfamiliar to them by rumour. That was, he explained, the question of the admission of his beloved little son to the communion of saints in the breaking of bread. He allowed —and I sat there in evidence, palely smiling at the audience, my feet scarcely touching the ground—that I was not what is styled adult; I was not, he frankly admitted, a grown-up person. But I was adult in a knowledge of the Lord; I possessed an insight into the plan of salvation which many a hoary head might envy for its fullness, its clearness, its conformity with Scripture doctrine. This was a palpable hit at more than one stumbler and fumbler after the truth, and several hoary heads were bowed.

My Father then went on to explain very fully the position which I have already attempted to define. He admitted the absence in my case of a sudden, apparent act of conversion resulting upon conviction of sin. But he stated the grounds of his belief that I had, in still earlier infancy, been converted, and he declared that if so, I ought no longer to be excluded from the privileges of communion. He said, moreover, that he was willing on this occasion to waive his own privilege as a minister, and that he would rather call on Brother Fawkes and Brother Bere, the leading elders, to examine the candidate in his stead. This was a master-stroke, for Brothers Fawkes and Bere had been suspected of leading the disaffection, and this threw all the burden of responsibility on them. The meeting broke up in great amiability, and my Father and I went home together in the very highest of spirits. I, indeed, in my pride, touched the verge of indiscretion by saying: "When I have been admitted to fellowship, Papa, shall I be allowed to call you 'belovèd Brother'?" My Father was too well pleased with the morning's work to be critical. He laughed, and answered; "That, my love, though strictly correct, would hardly, I fear, be thought judicious!" . . .

Events showed that I had no need of fear. Fawkes and Bere were sometimes accused of a rivalry, which indeed broke out a few years later, and gave my Father much anxiety and pain. But on this occasion their unanimity was wonderful. Each strove to exceed the other in the tributes which they paid to my piety. My answers had been so full and clear, my humility (save the mark!) had been so sweet, my acquaintance with Scripture so amazing, my testimony to all the leading principles of salvation so distinct and exhaustive, that they could only say that they had felt confounded, and yet deeply cheered and led far along their own heavenly path, by hearing such accents fall from the lips of a babe and a suckling. I did not like being described as a suckling, but every lot has its crumpled rose-leaf, and in all other respects the report of the elders was a triumph. . . .

The entire congregation was now silent, so silent that the uncertain splashing of my feet as I descended seemed to deafen me. Mr. S., a little embarrassed by my short stature, succeeded at length in securing me with one palm on my chest and the other between my shoulders. He said, slowly, in a loud, sonorous voice that seemed to enter my brain and empty it, "I baptize thee, my Brother, in the name of the Father and of the Son and of the Holy Ghost!" Having intoned this formula, he then gently flung me backwards until I was wholly under the water, and then—as he brought me up again, and tenderly steadied my feet on the steps of the font, and delivered me, dripping and sputtering, into the anxious hands of the women, who hurried me to the tent—the whole assembly broke forth in a thunder of song, a pæan of praise to God for this manifestation of his marvellous goodness and mercy. So great was the enthusiasm, that it could hardly be restrained so as to allow the other candidates, the humdrum adults who followed in my wet and glorious footsteps, to undergo a ritual about which, in their case, no one in the congregation pretended to be able to take even the most languid interest.

My Father's happiness during the next few weeks it is now pathetic to me to look back upon. His sternness melted into a universal complaisance. He laughed and smiled, he paid to my opinions the tribute of the gravest consideration, he indulged,—utterly unlike his wont,—in shy and furtive caresses. I could express no wish that he did not attempt to fulfil, and the only warning which he cared to give me was one, very gently expressed, against spiritual pride.

Despite this external triumph, there was no real desire in the child to embrace a religious career. "I felt like a small and solitary bird, caught and hung out hopelessly and endlessly in a great glittering cage . . . I saw myself imprisoned forever in the religious system which had caught me and would whirl my helpless spirit as in the concentric wheels of my nightly vision."

I should do myself an injustice, however, if I described my attitude to faith at this time as wanting in candour. I did very earnestly desire to follow where my Father led. That passion for imitation, which I have already discussed, was strongly developed at this time, and it induced me to repeat the language of pious books in godly ejaculations which greatly edified my grown-up companions, and were, so far as I can judge, perfectly sincere. I wished extremely to be good and holy, and I had no doubt in my mind of the absolute infallibility of my Father as a guide in heavenly things. But I am perfectly sure that there never was a moment in which my heart truly responded, with native ardour, to the words which flowed so readily, in such a stream of unction, from my anointed lips. I cannot recall anything but an intellectual surrender; there was never joy in the act of resignation, never the mystic's rapture at feeling his phantom self, his own threadbare soul, suffused, thrilled through, robed again in glory by a fire which burns up everything personal and individual about him.

Through thick and thin I clung to a hard nut of individuality, deep down in my childish nature.

An indulgent caprice of his Father's, almost unaccountable, provided secret nourishment for this resistance. The child had become fascinated by the geography of the West Indies:

One day as I multiplied inquiries, he rose, as I did so, in his impetuous way, and climbing to the top of a bookcase, brought down a thick volume and presented it to me. "You'll find all about the Antilles there," he said, and left me with *Tom Cringle's Log* in my possession.

The embargo laid upon every species of fiction by my Mother's powerful scruple had never been raised, although she had been dead four years. As I have said in an earlier chapter, this was a point on which I believe that my Father had never entirely agreed with her. He had, however, yielded to her prejudice, and no work of romance, no fictitious story, had ever come in my way. It is remarkable that among our books, which amounted to many hundreds, I had never discovered a single work of fiction until my Father himself revealed the existence of Michael Scott's wild masterpiece. So little did I understand what was allowable in the way of literary invention, that I began the story without a doubt that it was true, and I think it was my Father himself who, in answer to an inquiry, explained to me that it was "all made up." He advised me to read the description of the sea, and of the mountains of Jamaica, and "skip" the pages which gave imaginary adventures and conversations. But I did not take his counsel; these latter were the flower of the book to me. I had never read, never dreamed of anything like them, and they filled my whole horizon with glory and with joy.

I suppose that when my Father was a younger man, and less pietistic, he had read *Tom Cringle's Log* with pleasure, because it recalled familiar scenes to him. Much was explained by the fact that the frontispiece of this edition was a delicate line-engraving of Blewfields, the great lonely house in a garden of Jamaican allspice where for eighteen months he had lived as a naturalist. He could not look at this print without recalling exquisite memories and airs that blew from a terrestrial paradise. But Michael Scott's noisy amorous novel of adventure was an extraordinary book to put in the hands of a child who had never been allowed to glance at the mildest and most febrifugal story-book.

It was like giving a glass of brandy neat to some one who had never been weaned from a milk diet. I have not read *Tom Cringle's Log* from that day to this, and I think that I should be unwilling now to break the charm of memory, which may be largely illusion. But I remember a great deal of the plot and not a little of the language, and, while I am sure it is enchantingly spirited, I am quite as sure that the persons it describes were far from being unspotted by the world. The scenes at night in the streets of Spanish Town surpassed not merely my experience, but, thank goodness, my imagination. The nautical personages used in their conversations what is called "a class of language," and there ran, if I am not mistaken, a glow and gust of life through the romance from beginning to end which was nothing if it was not resolutely pagan.

There were certain scenes and images in *Tom Cringle's Log* which made not merely a lasting impression upon my mind, but tinged my outlook upon life. The long adventures, fightings and escapes, sudden storms without, and mutinies within, drawn forth as they were, surely with great skill, upon the fiery blue of the boundless tropical ocean, produced on my inner mind a sort of glimmering hope, very vaguely felt at first, slowly developing, long stationary and faint, but always tending towards a belief that I should escape at last from the narrowness of the life we led at home, from this bondage to the Law and the Prophets.

I must not define too clearly, or endeavour too formally to insist on the blind movements of a childish mind. But of this I am quite sure, that the reading and re-reading of *Tom Cringle's Log* did more than anything else, in this critical eleventh year of my life, to give fortitude to my individuality, which was in great danger—as I now see—of succumbing to the pressure my Father brought to bear upon it from all sides. My soul was shut up, like Fatima, in a tower to which no external influences could come, and it might really have been starved to death, or have lost the power of recovery and rebound, if my captor, by some freak not yet perfectly accounted for, had not gratuitously opened a little window in it and added a powerful telescope. The daring chapters of Michael Scott's picaresque romance of the tropics were that telescope and that window.

His Father's second marriage aided the boy to a further excited plunge into beauty.

My step-mother brought with her a little library of such books as we had not previously seen, but which yet were known to all the world except us. Prominent among these was a set of the poems of Walter Scott, and in his unwonted geniality and provisional spirit of compromise, my Father must do no less than read these works aloud to my step-mother in the quiet spring evenings. This was a sort of aftermath of courtship, a tribute of song to his bride, very sentimental and pretty. She would sit, sedately, at her work-box, while he, facing her, poured forth the verses at her like a blackbird. I was not considered in this arrangement, which was wholly matrimonial, but I was present, and the exercise made more impression upon me than it did upon either of the principal agents.

My Father read the verse admirably, with a full,—some people (but not I) might say with too full—a perception of the metre as well as of the rhythm, rolling out the rhymes, and glorying in the proper names. He began, and it was a happy choice, with *The Lady of the Lake*. It gave me singular pleasure to hear his large voice do justice to "Duncrannon" and "Cambus-Kenneth," and wake the echoes with "Roderigh Vich Alphine dhu, ho! ieroe!" I almost gasped with excitement, while a shudder floated down my backbone, when we came to:

> "*A sharp and shrieking echo gave,*
> *Coir-Uriskin, thy goblin cave!*
> *And the grey pass where birches wave,*
> *On Beala-nam-bo.*"

Seeing me so much fascinated, thrown indeed into a temporary frenzy, by the epic poetry of Sir Walter Scott, my step-mother asked my Father whether I might not start reading the Waverley Novels. But he refused to permit this . . . But, stranger still, and amounting almost to a whim, was his sudden decision that, although I might not touch the novels of Scott, I was free to read those of Dickens. I recollect that my step-mother showed some surprise at this, and that my Father explained to her that Dickens "exposes the passion of love in a ridiculous light." She did not seem to follow this recommendation, which indeed tends to the ultra-subtle,

but she procured for me a copy of *Pickwick,* by which I was instantly and gloriously enslaved. My shouts of laughing at the
richer passages were almost scandalous, and led to my being reproved for disturbing my Father while engaged, in an upper room,
in the study of God's Word. I must have expended months on
the perusal of *Pickwick,* for I used to rush through a chapter, and
then read it over again very slowly, word for word, and then shut
my eyes to realise the figures and the action.

I suppose no child will ever again enjoy that rapture of unresisting humorous appreciation of *Pickwick.* I felt myself to be in
the company of a gentleman so extremely funny that I began to
laugh before he began to speak; no sooner did he remark "the sky
was dark and gloomy, the air was damp and raw," than I was in
fits of laughter.

I remember, on one occasion, when the Browns, a family of
Baptists who kept a large haberdashery shop in the neighboring
town, asked for the pleasure of my company "to tea and games,"
and carried complacency so far as to offer to send that local
vehicle, "the midge," to fetch me and bring me back, my Father's
conscience was so painfully perplexed, that he desired me to come
with him, that we might "lay the matter before the Lord." We
did so, kneeling side by side, with our backs to the window and
our foreheads pressed upon the horsehair cover of the small coffin-
like sofa. My Father prayed aloud, with great fervour, that it
might be revealed to me, by the voice of God, whether it was or
was not the Lord's will that I should attend the Browns' party.
My Father's attitude seemed to me to be hardly fair, since he did
not scruple to remind the Deity of various objections to a life of
pleasure and of the snakes that lie hidden in the grass of evening
parties.

It would have been more scrupulous, I thought, to give no hint
of the kind of answer he desired and expected.

It will be justly said that my life was made up of very trifling
things, since I have to confess that this incident of the Browns' invitation was one of its landmarks. As I knelt, feeling very small,
by the immense bulk of my Father, there gushed through my

veins like a wine the determination to rebel. Never before, in all these years of my vocation, had I felt my resistance take precisely this definite form. We rose presently from the sofa, my forehead and the backs of my hands still chafed by the texture of the horse-hair, and we faced one another in the dreary light. My Father, perfectly confident in the success of what had really been a sort of incantation, asked me in a loud wheedling voice, "Well, and what is the answer which our Lord vouchsafes?" I said nothing, and so my Father, more sharply, continued, "We have asked Him to direct you to a true knowledge of His will. We have desired Him to let you know whether it is, or is not, in accordance with His wishes that you should accept this invitation from the Browns." He positively beamed down at me; he had no doubt of the reply. He was already, I believe, planning some little treat to make up to me for the material deprivation. But my answer came, in the high-piping accents of despair: "The Lord says I may go to the Browns." My Father gazed at me in speechless horror. He was caught in his own trap, and though he was certain that the Lord had said nothing of the kind, there was no road open for him but just sheer retreat. Yet surely it was an error in tactics to slam the door. . . .

Although ours was perhaps the most cultivated household in the parish, I had never seen so much as a representation of a work of sculpture till I was thirteen. My mother then received from her earlier home certain volumes, among which was a gaudy gift-book of some kind, containing a few steel engravings of statues.

These attracted me violently, and here for the first time I gazed on Apollo with his proud gesture, Venus in her undulations, the kirtled shape of Diana, and Jupiter voluminously bearded. Very little information, and that to me not intelligible, was given in the text, but these were said to be figures of the old Greek gods. I asked my Father to tell me about these "old Greek gods." His answer was direct and disconcerting. He said—how I recollect the place and time, early in the morning, as I stood beside the window in our garish breakfast-room—he said that the so-called gods of the Greeks were the shadows cast by the vices of the heathen, and reflected their infamous lives; "it was for such things as these that God poured down brimstone and fire on the Cities of the Plain, and there is nothing in the legends of these gods, or rather devils, that it is not better for a Christian not to know." His face blazed white with Puritan fury as he said this—I see him now in my mind's eye, in his violent emotion. You might have thought that he had himself escaped with horror from some Hellenic hippodrome.

My Father's prestige was by this time considerably lessened in my mind, and though I loved and admired him, I had now long ceased to hold him infallible. I did not accept his condemnation of the Greeks, although I bowed to it. In private I returned to examine my steel engravings of the statues, and I reflected that they were too beautiful to be so wicked as my Father thought they were. The dangerous and pagan notion that beauty palliates evil budded in my mind, without any external suggestion, and by this reflection alone I was still further sundered from the faith in which I had been trained.

In London, whither he was now sent to school, it was not long before he was reveling in the sorcery of Shakespeare and the passion and music of Hero and Leander. *But even in London his Father's solicitude pursued him in daily letters.*

The letter, the only too-confidently expected letter, would lie on the table as I descended to breakfast. It would commonly be, of course, my only letter, unless tempered by a cosy and chatty note from my dear and comfortable step-mother, dealing with such perfectly tranquillising subjects as the harvest of roses in the garden or the state of health of various neighbours. But the other, the solitary letter, in its threatening whiteness, with its exquisitely penned address—there it would lie awaiting me, destroying the taste of the bacon, reducing the flavour of the tea to insipidity. I might fatuously dally with it, I might pretend not to observe it, but there it lay. Before the morning's exercise began, I knew that it had to be read, and what was worse, that it had to be answered. Useless the effort to conceal from myself what it contained. . . .

It little mattered what form of weakness I put forth by way of baffling my Father's direct, firm, unflinching strength. To an appeal against the bondage of a correspondence of such unbroken solemnity I would receive—with what a paralysing promptitude!—such a reply as this:—

"Let me say that the 'solemnity' you complain of has only been the expression of tender anxiousness of a father's heart, that his only child, just turned out upon the world, and very far out of his sight and hearing, should be walking in God's way. . . . But I will try henceforth to trust you, and lay aside my fears; for you are worthy of my confidence; and your own God and your father's God will hold you with His right hand."

Over such letters as these I am not ashamed to say that I sometimes wept; the old paper I have just been copying shows traces of tears shed upon it more than forty years ago, tears commingled of despair at my own feebleness, distraction at my want of will, pity for my Father's manifest and pathetic distress.

My growing distaste for the Holy Scriptures began to occupy my thoughts, and to surprise as much as it scandalised me. My desire was to continue to delight in those sacred pages, for which I still had an instinctive veneration. Yet I could not but observe the difference between the zeal with which I snatched at a volume of Carlyle or Ruskin—since these magicians were now first revealing themselves to me—and the increasing languor with which I took up Alford for my daily "passage." Of course, although I did not know it, and believed my reluctance to be sinful, the real reason why I now found the *Bible* so difficult to read was my familiarity with its contents.

Then came a moment when my self-sufficiency revolted against the police-inspection to which my "views" were incessantly subjected. There was a morning, in the hot-house at home, among the gorgeous waxen orchids which reminded my Father of the tropics in his youth, when my forbearance or my timidity gave way. The enervated air, soaked with the intoxicating perfumes of all those voluptuous flowers, may have been partly responsible for my outburst. My Father had once more put to me the customary interrogatory. Was I "walking closely with God?" Was my sense of the efficacy of the Atonement clear and sound? Had the Holy Scriptures still their full authority with me? My replies on this occasion were violent and hysterical. I have no clear recollection what it was that I said,—I desire not to recall the whimpering sentences in which I begged to be let alone, in which I demanded the right to think for myself, in which I repudiated the idea that my Father was responsible to God for my secret thoughts and my most intimate convictions.

It was the end. He hurried to London, whither he had hardly arrived when a letter, "furiously despatched in the track of the fugitive, buried itself like an arrow in my heart." *In it his Father reviewed with sorrow the stages of his breaking away from God. He prayed that his son might be restored to grace.* "If this grace were granted to you, oh! how joyfully should I bury all the past, and again have sweet and tender fellowship with my beloved Son, as of old." *It was an ultimatum that allowed no truce or compromise, and none was made. Then and there,* "as respectfully as he could," *the young man* "took a human being's privilege to fashion his inner life for himself."

BIRD OF PREY

THE MOOD OF HENRY ADAMS WAS THE MOOD IN WHICH MANY MEN
were left by the end of the World War in 1918. They had been
duped, they felt, by all their leaders. Civilization itself was a
failure. Its ideals—progress, liberalism, mechanical-industrial prosperity, international justice, humanitarianism—so painfully built
up, so solemnly adulated by the nineteenth century—were a hypocritical farce now irretrievably tarnished. Disillusion and horror
stung men to revulsion against the cultural heritage that had betrayed them to such defeat.

To this mood of distorted hatred Lytton Strachey powerfully appealed. He gave it a form of intellectual detachment and justice.
His air of scientific objectivity lent authority, made interpretation
seem no more than an analysis of unescapable fact. His irony was
an equivocal destroying-and-preserving fluid that transformed his
victims to mere specimens arranged by a disinterested classifying
zeal. By an adroit mingling of contempt and comedy he reduced
them to pigmy insignificance, but retained just a hint of the
monstrous with which to justify revulsion.

The truth was that Strachey himself reacted with violence
against Victorian culture. It was, he said, "like one of those queer
fishes that one sees behind glass at an aquarium, before whose
grotesque proportions and somber, menacing agilities one hardly
knows whether to laugh or shudder." Strachey became hawk to
that strange marine creature, swooping down, then soaring with
the fantastic object transfixed between glittering claws. Helpless,
indeed, but still horrible: faced by the somber, menacing agilities
he had called up from the deep, Strachey—as Clara Stillman ob-

serves—"both laughed and shuddered; perhaps he gave biography a new shudder, with laughter in it."

He was enabled to do so by two strands curiously mingled in his nature. The first was a feeling for the virtues of classicism: clarity, balance, concision. They shaped his structure, kept it to economy; sharpened his style, and gave it a wit of ice and acid. The second was a romantic feeling for the colorful, the exotic, the eccentric. It selected the most striking of his epithets—and, most important of all, it dictated his attitude toward his themes. Strachey's emotional range, to be sure, is much narrower than we usually find in a romantic writer. He seldom has grandeur or pathos; no lyricism, sublimity, or terror. But he is personal and idiosyncratic, even fantastic and melodramatic. There is a glare of theatrical contrast in his revelations of the difference between pretension and reality. His psychology is a psychology of humours, all of character types etched with deepening bite around a few strongly defined traits.

These qualities appear everywhere in Strachey's work: with romantic sympathy in his treatments of the Elizabethan age; with balanced understanding—predominantly—in his eighteenth century portraits; with a mingling of derision and unwilling self-surrender in *Queen Victoria;* with brilliant but hardly adulterated malice in *Eminent Victorians.* His "Thomas Arnold" is a hilarious distortion that achieves delectable extremes of absurdity and fatuousness. His "Florence Nightingale" destroys the syrupy legend of the Lady with the Lamp, ministering angelic comfort to anguished brows, and simultaneously bathes in acid the blundering inefficiencies of military bureaucracy. "General Gordon" insinuates a behind-the-scenes arraignment of nineteenth-century imperialism—one of those very forces that had brought about the catastrophe of the World War.

"Cardinal Manning" is perhaps the most characteristic and the most cruel of Strachey's biographical writings. It has all his adroitness, his wit, his compression, his sharpness of delineation. It is dramatic without a single development in character, for the character is known from the beginning, and the character never changes. It is ironic in its implications of the vulgarity of motive and the mediocrity that may lie hidden in the core of a great success. It is a laboratory dissection that seems midway to turn into a flaying.

These are the things that give Strachey's writing its tingling and astringent flavor. They are at the same time his greatest artistic failing. For, so persistently emphasized, they are not portrayal, but persecution. We realize that here is a very dexterous performer, and we realize that he is out to "get" Manning. The evidence seems convincing, to be sure, and yet—increasingly the suspicion refuses to down—and yet, may the facts perhaps be, we wonder, not fabricated, but—*manipulated?* Such doubts leave Strachey's writings no less delightful in their creative virtuosity; but they are fatal to our belief in that absolute veracity which should be the fundamental principle of the biographer.

The defects show all the more plainly if we take a hint from Strachey himself, and compare his portrait of Manning with Cavendish's rendering of Wolsey. Both ecclesiastics, as Strachey says, were "distinguished less for saintliness and learning than for practical ability." Both were politicians; Manning, Strachey remarks, "seemed almost to revive in his own person that long line of diplomatic and administrative clerics that, one would have thought, had come to an end with Cardinal Wolsey." Both were schemers. Both were ruthless and determined in their ambitions. Seen squarely, the Wolsey whom Cavendish reveals is almost indistinguishable from Strachey's hawklike old man.

But Cavendish, unlike Strachey, is clever enough to leave his own cleverness out of the picture. He hides and palliates nothing, but he wields no assassin's dagger. Sympathy and truth are joined, and together they produce more faith than Strachey's inquisitorial thumbscrews. Even had Strachey never deviated from fact by a fraction of an inch, the art which permits a suspicion of inaccuracy is inferior to the art of which such a question never arises.

Nevertheless, even with his faults, Strachey is not less than a brilliant writer and a memorable biographer. His very partisanship has a value. His strictures must be weighed, and weighed again, before we can reject his verdicts. And, indeed, in part his verdicts cannot be utterly rejected. He has added many permanent features to our portraits of a whole gallery of figures. His technique has sometimes been described as classical and sometimes as caricature. It is both. It is highly selective and stylized; it sometimes distorts. But at its best it uses these devices to reveal truth otherwise than by the way of documentary realism, but no less truth.

Above all, Strachey forced into the open the realization that no portrayal of character can be purely objective, because our conception of a personality is the intersection between it and ourselves. He made the author's point of view no longer a muzzy, unacknowledged projection of himself, but explicit. The fine balance of temper and perception that he achieved at his best, the selection and concision, are splendid and permanent contributions to biographical art.

Cardinal Manning

LYTTON STRACHEY

[Strachey was born in 1880 and died in 1932. *Eminent Victorians* was published in 1918.]

HENRY EDWARD MANNING WAS BORN IN 1807 AND DIED IN 1892. His life was extraordinary in many ways, but its interest for the modern inquirer depends mainly upon two considerations—the light which his career throws upon the spirit of his age, and the psychological problems suggested by his inner history. He belonged to that class of eminent ecclesiastics—and it is by no means a small class—who have been distinguished less for saintliness and learning than for practical ability. Had he lived in the Middle Ages he would certainly have been neither a Francis nor an Aquinas, but he might have been an Innocent. As it was, born in the England of the Nineteenth Century, growing up in the very seed-time of modern progress, coming to maturity with the first onrush of Liberalism, and living long enough to witness the victories of Science and Democracy, he yet, by a strange concatenation of circumstances, seemed almost to revive in his own person that long line of diplomatic and administrative clerics which, one would have thought, had come to an end with Cardinal Wolsey. In Manning, so it appeared, the Middle Ages lived again. The tall gaunt figure, with the face of smiling asceticism, the robes, and the biretta, as it passed in triumph from High Mass at the Oratory to philanthropic gatherings at Exeter Hall, from Strike Committees at the Docks to Mayfair drawing-rooms where fashionable ladies knelt to the Prince of the Church, certainly bore witness to

a singular condition of affairs. What had happened? Had a dominating character imposed itself upon a hostile environment? Or
was the Nineteenth Century, after all, not so hostile? Was there
something in it, scientific and progressive as it was, which went out
to welcome the representative of ancient tradition and uncompromising faith? Had it perhaps, a place in its heart for such as
Manning—a soft place, one might almost say? Or, on the other
hand, was it he who had been supple and yielding? he who had
won by art what he would never have won by force, and who
had managed, so to speak, to be one of the leaders of the procession
less through merit than through a superior faculty for gliding
adroitly to the front rank? And, in any case, by what odd chances,
what shifts and struggles, what combinations of circumstance and
character had this old man come to be where he was? Such questions are easier to ask than to answer; but it may be instructive,
and even amusing, to look a little more closely into the complexities of so curious a story.

Undoubtedly, what is most obviously striking in the history of
Manning's career is the persistent strength of his innate characteristics. Through all the changes of his fortunes the powerful
spirit of the man worked on undismayed. It was as if the Fates
had laid a wager that they would daunt him, and in the end they
lost their bet.

His father was a rich West India merchant, a governor of the
Bank of England, a Member of Parliament, who drove into town
every day from his country seat in a coach and four, and was
content with nothing short of a bishop for the christening of his
children. Little Henry, like the rest, had his bishop; but he was
obliged to wait for him—for as long as eighteen months. In those
days, and even a generation later, as Keble bears witness, there was
great laxity in regard to the early baptism of children. The delay
has been noted by Manning's biographer as the first stumbling-
block in the spiritual life of the future Cardinal: but he sur-
mounted it with success. . . .

At Harrow . . . on the whole he led the unspiritual life of an
ordinary school-boy. We have glimpses of him as a handsome lad,

playing cricket, or strutting about in tasselled Hessian top-boots. And on one occasion at least he gave proof of a certain dexterity of conduct which deserved to be remembered. He went out of bounds, and a master, riding by and seeing him on the other side of a field, tied his horse to a gate, and ran after him. The astute youth outran the master, fetched a circle, reached the gate, jumped on to the horse's back, and rode off. For this he was very properly chastised; but of what use was chastisement? No whipping, however severe, could have eradicated from little Henry's mind a quality at least as firmly planted in it as his fear of Hell . . .

It had been his father's wish that Manning should go into the Church; but the thought disgusted him; and when he reached Oxford, his tastes, his ambitions, his successes at the Union, all seemed to mark him out for a political career. . . .

But . . . on his leaving Oxford, the brimming cup was dashed from his lips. He was already beginning to dream of himself in the House of Commons, the solitary advocate of some great cause whose triumph was to be eventually brought about by his extraordinary efforts, when his father was declared a bankrupt, and all his hopes of a political career came to an end forever.

Yet . . . Manning still continued to indulge in secular hopes. He entered the Colonial Office as a supernumerary clerk, and it was only when the offer of a Merton Fellowship seemed to depend upon his taking orders that his heavenly ambitions began to assume a definite shape. Just then he fell in love with Miss Deffell, whose father would have nothing to say to a young man without prospects, and forbade him the house. It was only too true; what *were* the prospects of a supernumerary clerk in the Colonial Office? Manning went to Oxford and took orders. He was elected to the Merton Fellowship, and obtained through the influence of the Wilberforces a curacy in Sussex. At the last moment he almost drew back. "I think the whole step has been too precipitate," he wrote to his brother-in-law. "I have rather allowed the instance of my friends, and the allurements of an agreeable curacy in many respects, to get the better of my sober judgment." His vast ambitions, his dream of public service, of honours, and of power, was all this to end in a little country curacy "agreeable in many respects"? But there was nothing for it; the deed was done; and the Fates had apparently succeeded very effectively in getting rid of Manning. All he could do was to make the best of a bad business. Accordingly, in the first place, he decided that he had received a call from God "ad veritatem et ad seipsum"; and, in the second, forgetting Miss Deffell, he married his rector's daughter. . . .

In after years, the memory of his wife seemed to be blotted from his mind; he never spoke of her; every letter, every record, of his married life he destroyed; and when word was sent to him that her grave was falling into ruin: "It is best so," the Cardinal answered; "let it be. Time effaces all things."

When Froude succeeded in impregnating Newman with the ideas of Keble, the Oxford Movement began. The original and remarkable characteristic of these three men was that they took the Christian Religion au pied de la lettre. This had not been done in England for centuries. When they declared every Sunday that they believed in the Holy Catholic Church, they meant it. When they repeated the Athanasian Creed, they meant it. Even when they subscribed to the Thirty-nine Articles, they meant it— or at least they thought they did. Now such a state of mind was dangerous—more dangerous, indeed, than they at first realised. They had started with the innocent assumption that the Christian Religion was contained in the doctrines of the Church of England; but the more they examined into this matter, the more difficult and dubious it became.

Tracts for the Times *began appearing under Newman's editorship, and the Oxford Movement was launched upon the world.*

The Tracts were written "with the hope of rousing members of our Church to comprehend her alarming position . . . as a man might give notice of a fire or inundation, to startle all who heard him." They may be said to have succeeded in their object, for the sensation which they caused among clergymen throughout the country was extreme. They dealt with a great variety of questions, but the underlying intention of all of them was to attack the accepted doctrines and practices of the Church of England.

Dr. Pusey wrote learnedly on Baptismal Regeneration; he also wrote on Fasting. His treatment of the latter subject met with considerable disapproval, which surprised the Doctor. "I was not prepared," he said, "for people questioning, even in the abstract, the duty of fasting; I thought serious-minded persons at least supposed they practised fasting in some way or other. I assumed the duty to be acknowledged and thought it only undervalued." We live and learn, even though we have been to Germany. . . .

Writings of this kind could not fail of their effect. Pious youths in Oxford were carried away by them, and began to flock round the standard of Newman. Newman himself became a party chief, encouraging, organising, persuading. His long black figure, swiftly passing through the streets, was pointed at with awe; his sermons were crowded; his words repeated from mouth to mouth. "Credo in Newmannum" became a common catchword. Jokes were made about the Church of England, and practices, unknown for centuries, began to be revived. Young men fasted and did penance, recited the hours of the Roman Breviary, and confessed their sins to Dr. Pusey. Nor was the movement confined to Oxford; it spread in widening circles through the parishes of England; the dormant devotion of the country was suddenly aroused. The new strange notion of taking Christianity literally was delightful to earnest minds; but it was also alarming. Really to mean every word you said, when you repeated the Athanasian Creed! How wonderful! And what enticing and mysterious vistas burst upon the view! But then, those vistas, where were they leading to? Supposing—oh heavens!—supposing after all they were to lead to——!

In due course the Tracts made their appearance at the remote Rectory in Sussex. Manning was some years younger than Newman, and the two men had only met occasionally at the University; but now, through common friends, a closer relationship began to grow up between them. It was only to be expected that Newman should be anxious to enroll the rising young Rector among his followers; and on Manning's side there were many causes which impelled him to accept the overtures from Oxford.

He was a man of a serious and vigorous temperament, to whom it was inevitable that the bold, high principles of the Movement should strongly appeal. There was also an element in his mind —that element which had terrified him in his childhood with Apocalyptic visions, and urged him in his youth to Bible readings after breakfast—which now brought him under the spell of the Oxford theories of sacramental mysticism. And besides, the Movement offered another attraction; it imputed an extraordinary, a transcendent merit to the profession which Manning himself pursued. The cleric was not as his lay brethren; he was a creature apart, chosen by Divine will and sanctified by Divine mysteries. It was a relief to find, when one had supposed that one was nothing but a clergyman, that one might, after all, be something else—one might be a priest.

Accordingly, Manning shook off his early Evangelical convictions, started an active correspondence with Newman, and was soon working for the new cause. . . . But, as time went on, the situation became more complicated. Tractarianism began to arouse the hostility, not only of the Evangelical, but of the moderate churchmen, who could not help perceiving, in the ever deepening "catholicism" of the Oxford party, the dread approaches of Rome. The *Record* newspaper—an influential Evangelical journal—took up the matter, and sniffed Popery in every direction; it spoke of certain clergymen as "tainted"; and after that, Manning seemed to pass those clergymen by. The fact that Manning found it wise to conduct his confessional ministrations in secret was in itself highly significant. It was necessary to be careful, and Manning was very careful indeed.

Into this fermenting situation fell Tract No. 90, whose "object was to prove that there was nothing in the Thirty-nine Articles incompatible with the creed of the Roman Church." *Its effect was sensational:* "it seemed to be a deadly and treacherous blow aimed at the very heart of the Church of England."

Archdeacon Manning was in too conspicuous a position to be able to remain silent; he was obliged to declare himself, and he did not hesitate. In an archidiaconal charge, delivered within a few months of his appointment, he firmly repudiated the Tractarians. But the repudiation was not deemed sufficient, and a year later he repeated it with greater emphasis. Still, however, the horrid rumours were afloat. The *Record* began to investigate matters, and its vigilance was soon rewarded by an alarming discovery: the sacrament had been administered in Chichester Cathedral on a week-day, and "Archdeacon Manning, one of the most noted and determined of the Tractarians, had acted a conspicuous part on the occasion." It was clear that the only way of silencing these malevolent whispers was by some public demonstration whose import nobody could doubt. The annual sermon preached on Guy Fawkes Day before the University of Oxford seemed to offer the very opportunity that Manning required. He seized it; got himself appointed preacher; and delivered from the pulpit of St. Mary's a virulently Protestant harangue. This time there could indeed be no doubt about the matter: Manning had shouted "No Popery!" in the very citadel of the Movement, and everyone, including Newman, recognised that he had finally cut himself off from his old friends. Everyone, that is to say, except the Archdeacon himself. On the day after the sermon, Manning walked out to the neighbouring village of Littlemore, where Newman was now living in retirement with a few chosen disciples, in the hope of being able to give a satisfactory explanation of what he had done. But he was disappointed; for when, after an awkward interval, one of the disciples appeared at the door, he was informed that Mr. Newman was not at home.

Meanwhile the English Roman Catholics were growing impatient; was the great conversion never coming, for which they had prayed so fervently and so long? Dr. Wiseman, at the head of them, was watching and waiting with special eagerness. His hand was held out under the ripening fruit; the delicious morsel seemed to be trembling on its stalk; and yet it did not fall. At last, unable to bear the suspense any longer, he dispatched to Littlemore Father Smith, an old pupil of Newman's, who had lately joined the Roman communion, with instructions that he should do his best, under cover of a simple visit of friendship, to discover how the land lay. Father Smith was received somewhat coldly, and the conversation ran entirely on topics which had nothing to do with religion. When the company separated before dinner, he was beginning to think that his errand had been useless; but on their reassembling he suddenly noticed that Newman had changed his trousers and that the colour of the pair which he was now wearing was grey. At the earliest moment, the emissary rushed back post-haste to Dr. Wiseman. "All is well," he exclaimed; "Newman no longer considers that he is in Anglican orders." "Praise be to God!" answered Dr. Wiseman. "But how do you know?" Father Smith described what he had seen. "Oh, is that all? My dear father, how can you be so foolish?" But Father Smith was not to be shaken. "I know the man," he said, "and I know what it means. Newman will come, and he will come soon."

And Father Smith was right. A few weeks later, Newman suddenly slipped off to a priest, and all was over.

Manning was now thirty-eight, and it was clear that he was the rising man in the Church of England. He had many powerful connections: he was the brother-in-law of Samuel Wilberforce, who had lately been made a bishop; he was a close friend of Mr. Gladstone, who was a Cabinet Minister; and he was becoming well known in the influential circles of society in London. . . .

In his archdeaconry, Manning lived to the full the active life of a country clergyman. His slim, athletic figure was seen everywhere—in the streets of Chichester, or on the lawns of the neighbouring rectories, or galloping over the downs in breeches and gaiters, or cutting brilliant figures on the ice. He was an excellent judge of horseflesh, and the pair of greys which drew his hooded phaeton so swiftly through the lanes were the admiration of the country. His features were already beginning to assume their ascetic cast, but the spirit of youth had not yet fled from them, so that he seemed to combine the attractions of dignity and grace. He was a good talker, a sympathetic listener, a man who understood the difficult art of preserving all the vigour of a manly character and yet never giving offence. No wonder that his sermons were crowded, no wonder that his spiritual advice was sought for eagerly by an ever-growing crowd of penitents, no wonder that men would say, when his name was mentioned, "Oh, Manning! No power on earth can keep *him* from a bishopric!"

Such was the fair outward seeming of the Archdeacon's life; but the inward reality was different. The more active, the more fortunate, the more full of happy promise his existence became, the more persistently was his secret imagination haunted by a dreadful vision—the lake that burneth for ever with brimstone and fire. The temptations of the Evil One are many, Manning knew; and he knew also that, for him at least, the most subtle and terrible of all temptations was the temptation of worldly success. He tried to reassure himself, but it was in vain. He committed his thoughts to a diary, weighing scrupulously his every motive, examining with relentless searchings into the depths of his heart. Perhaps, after all, his longings for preferment were merely legitimate hopes for "an elevation into a sphere of higher usefulness." But no, there was something more than that. "I do feel pleasure," he noted, "in honour, precedence, elevation, the society of great people, and all this is very shameful and mean." After Newman's conversion, he almost convinced himself that his "visions of an ecclesiastical future" were justified by the rôle that he would play as a "healer of the breach in the Church of England." Mr. Gladstone agreed with him; but there was One higher than Mr. Gladstone, and did He agree?

Manning agonized, in elaborate tables with numbered heads and subheads. His ambition threw him into "an agony of self-examination." *Ultimately he fell ill.*

It was significant, but hardly surprising, that, after his illness, Manning should have chosen to recuperate in Rome. He spent several months there, and his Diary during the whole of that period is concerned entirely with detailed descriptions of churches, ceremonies, and relics, and with minute accounts of conversations with priests and nuns. There is not a single reference either to the objects of art or to the antiquities of the place; but another omission was still more remarkable. Manning had a long inter-

view with Pius IX., and his only record of it is contained in the
bald statement: "Audience to-day at the Vatican." . . .

On his return to England, he took up once more the work in
his Archdeaconry with what appetite he might. Ravaged by doubt,
distracted by speculation, he yet managed to maintain an outward
presence of unshaken calm. His only confidant was Robert Wilberforce, to whom, for the next two years, he poured forth in a series
of letters, headed "Under the Seal" to indicate that they contained
the secrets of the confessional, the whole history of his spiritual
perturbations. The irony of his position was singular; for during
the whole of this time Manning was himself holding back from
the Church of Rome a host of hesitating penitents by means of
arguments which he was at the very moment denouncing as fallacious to his own confessor.

When Manning joined the Church of Rome he acted under the
combined impulse of the two dominating forces in his nature.
His preoccupation with the supernatural might, alone, have been
satisfied within the fold of the Anglican communion; and so
might his preoccupation with himself: the one might have found
vent in the elaborations of High Church ritual, and the other
in the activities of a bishopric. But the two together could not be
quieted so easily. The Church of England is a commodious institution; she is very anxious to please; but, somehow or other,
she has never managed to supply a happy home to superstitious
egotists. "What an escape for my poor soul!" Manning is said to
have exclaimed when, shortly after his conversion, a mitre was
going a-begging. But, in truth, Manning's "poor soul" had scented
nobler quarry. To one of his temperament, how was it possible,
when once the choice was plainly put, to hesitate for a moment
between the respectable dignity of an English bishop, harnessed by
the secular power, with the Gorham judgment as a bit between his
teeth, and the illimitable pretensions of the humblest priest of
Rome?

For the moment, however, it seemed as if the Fates had at last
been successful in their little game of shunting Manning. The
splendid career which he had so laboriously built up from the

small beginnings of his Sussex curacy was shattered—and shattered
by the inevitable operation of his own essential needs. He was
over forty, and he had been put back once more to the very
bottom rung of the ladder—a middle-aged neophyte with, so far
as could be seen, no special claim to the attention of his new
superiors. The example of Newman, a far more illustrious convert, was hardly reassuring: he had been relegated to a complete
obscurity, in which he was to remain until extreme old age.
Why should there be anything better in store for Manning? Yet
it so happened that within fourteen years of his conversion Manning was Archbishop of Westminster and the supreme ruler of
the Roman Catholic community in England. This time the Fates
gave up their unequal struggle; they paid over their stakes in
despair, and retired from the game.

Nevertheless it is difficult to feel quite sure that Manning's
plunge was as hazardous as it appeared. Certainly he was not a
man who was likely to forget to look before he leaped, nor one
who, if he happened to know that there was a mattress spread to
receive him, would leap with less conviction. In the light of
after-events, one would be glad to know what precisely passed at
that mysterious interview of his with the Pope, three years before
his conversion. It is at least possible that the authorities in Rome
had their eye on Manning; they may well have felt that the Archdeacon of Chichester would be a great catch. What did Pio Nono
say? It is easy to imagine the persuasive innocence of his Italian
voice. "Ah, dear Signor Manning, why don't you come over to us?
Do you suppose that we should not look after you?"

*But his position in England was difficult. The Old Catholics,
under Dr. Errington, regarded him as an ambitious interloper;
Monsignor Searle, Cardinal Wiseman's confidant, made scenes
at which all the enormous bulk of the Cardinal shuddered. In the
midst of such* "explosions and recriminations" *the Cardinal*
"wished many times that he were already dead."

Yet he was not altogether without his consolations; Manning
took care to see to that. His piercing eye had detected the secret
way into the recesses of the Cardinal's heart—had discerned the

core of simple faith which underlay that jovial manner and that facile talk. Others were content to laugh and chatter and transact their business; Manning was more artistic. He watched his opportunity, and then, when the moment came, touched with a deft finger the chord of the Conversion of England. There was an immediate response, and he struck the same chord again, and yet again. He became the repository of the Cardinal's most intimate aspirations. He alone sympathised and understood.

The precise details of what followed are doubtful. It is only possible to discern with clearness, amid a vast cloud of official documents and unofficial correspondences in English, Italian, and Latin, of Papal decrees and voluminous scritture, of confidential reports of episcopal whispers and the secret agitations of Cardinals, the form of Manning, restless and indomitable, scouring like a stormy petrel the angry ocean of debate. Wiseman, dilatory, unbusinesslike, and infirm, was ready enough to leave the conduct of affairs in his hands. Nor was it long before Manning saw where the key of the whole position lay. As in the old days, at Chichester, he had secured the good will of Bishop Shuttleworth by cultivating the friendship of Archdeacon Hare, so now, on this vaster scale of operations, his sagacity led him swiftly and unerringly up the little winding staircase in the Vatican and through the humble door which opened into the Cabinet of Monsignor Talbot, the private secretary of the Pope. Monsignor Talbot was a priest who embodied in a singular manner, if not the highest, at least the most persistent traditions of the Roman Curia. He was a master of various arts which the practice of ages has brought to perfection under the friendly shadow of the triple tiara. He could mingle together astuteness and holiness without any difficulty; he could make innuendoes as naturally as an ordinary man makes statements of fact; he could apply flattery with so unsparing a hand that even Princes of the Church found it sufficient; and, on occasion, he could ring the changes of torture on a human soul with a tact which called forth universal approbation. With such accomplishments, it could hardly be expected that Monsignor Talbot should be remarkable either for a delicate sense of conscientiousness or for an extreme refinement of feeling, but then it was not for those qualities that Manning was in search when he went up the winding stair. He was looking for the man who had the ear of Pio Nono; and, on the other side of the low-arched door, he found him. Then he put forth all his efforts; his success was complete; and an alliance began which was destined to have the profoundest effect upon Manning's career, and was only dissolved when, many years later, Monsignor Talbot was unfortunately obliged to exchange his apartment in the Vatican for a private lunatic asylum at Passy.

"Wiseman died, and there ensued in Rome a crisis of extraordinary intensity." *Who was now to be named in his place?*

But the Holy Father himself was doubting. In his indecision, he ordered a month of prayers and masses. The suspense grew and grew. Everything seemed against Manning. The whole English episcopate was opposed to him; he had quarrelled with the Chapter; he was a convert of but few years' standing; even the congregated Cardinals did not venture to suggest the appointment of such a man. But suddenly the Holy Father's doubts came to an end. He heard a voice—a mysterious inward voice—whispering something in his ear. "Mettetelo lì!" "Mettetelo lì!" the voice repeated over and over again. "Mettetelo lì!" It was an inspiration; and Pius IX., brushing aside the recommendations of the Chapter and the deliberations of the Cardinals, made Manning, by a Pontifical act, Archbishop of Westminster.

Monsignor Talbot's felicity was complete; and he took occasion, in conveying his congratulations to his friend, to make some illuminating reflections upon the great event.

"My policy throughout," he wrote, "was never to propose you *directly* to the Pope, but to make others do so; so that both you and I can always say that it was not I who induced the Holy Father to name you, which would lessen the weight of your appointment. This I say, because many have said that your being named was all my doing. I do not say that the Pope did not know that I thought you the only man eligible; as I took care to tell him over and over again what was against all the other candidates;

and in consequence he was almost driven into naming you. After he had named you, the Holy Father said to me, What a diplomatist you are, to make what you wished come to pass!

"Nevertheless," concluded Monsignor Talbot, "I believe your appointment was specially directed by the Holy Ghost."

Manning's appointment filled his opponents with alarm. Wrath and vengeance seemed to be hanging over them; what might not be expected from the formidable enemy against whom they had struggled for so long, and who now stood among them armed with archiepiscopal powers and invested with the special confidence of Rome? Great was their amazement, great was their relief, when they found that their dreaded master breathed nothing but kindness, gentleness, and conciliation. The old scores, they found, were not to be paid off, but to be wiped out. The new archbishop poured forth upon every side all the tact, all the courtesy, all the dignified graces of a Christian magnanimity. It was impossible to withstand such treatment. Bishops who had spent years in thwarting him became his devoted adherents; even the Chapter of Westminster forgot its hatred. Monsignor Talbot was extremely surprised. "Your greatest enemies have entirely come round," he wrote. "I received the other day a panegyric of you from Searle. This change of feeling I cannot attribute to anything but the Holy Ghost." Monsignor Talbot was very fond of the Holy Ghost; but, so far at any rate as Searle was concerned, there was another explanation. Manning, instead of dismissing Searle from his position of "œconomus" in the episcopal household, had kept him on—at an increased salary; and the poor man, who had not scrupled in the days of his pride to call Manning a thief, was now duly grateful . . .

It might be supposed that Manning could now feel that his triumph was complete. His position was secure; his power was absolute; his prestige was daily growing. Yet there was something that irked him still. As he cast his eyes over the Roman Catholic community in England, he was aware of one figure which, by virtue of a peculiar eminence, seemed to challenge the supremacy of his own. That figure was Newman's.

Since his conversion Newman's life had been a long series of misfortunes and disappointments . . . His delicate mind, with its refinements, its hesitations, its complexities—his soft, spectacled, Oxford manner, with its half-effeminate diffidence—such things were ill calculated to impress a throng of busy Cardinals and Bishops . . . Was it possible that Dr. Newman did not understand that ideas in Rome were, to say the least of it, out of place?

Once he was considered for a bishopric, but some secret influence worked against him. He struggled on in obscurity and tribulation until he was an old man of sixty-three. Then "an unexpected event occurred which produced a profound effect upon his life."

Charles Kingsley attacked his good faith and the good faith of Catholics in general in a magazine article; Newman protested, and Kingsley rejoined in an irate pamphlet. Newman's reply was the *Apologia pro Vita Sua,* which he wrote in seven weeks, sometimes working twenty-two hours at a stretch, "constantly in tears, and constantly crying out with distress." The success of the book, with its transparent candour, its controversial brilliance, the sweep and passion of its rhetoric, the depth of its personal feeling, was immediate and overwhelming; it was recognised at once as a classic, not only by Catholics, but by the whole English world. From every side expressions of admiration, gratitude, and devotion poured in.

Proposals were made that an oratory be established at Oxford, with Newman at the head.

It so happened that it was at this very time that Manning was appointed to the See of Westminster. The destinies of the two men, which had run parallel to one another in so strange a fashion and for so many years, were now for a moment suddenly to converge. Newly clothed with all the attributes of ecclesiastical supremacy, Manning found himself face to face with Newman, upon whose brows were glittering the fresh laurels of spiritual victory—the crown of an apostolical life. It was the meeting of the eagle and the dove. What followed showed, more clearly perhaps than any other incident in his career, the stuff that Manning was made of. Power had come to him at last; and he seized it with all the avidity of a born autocrat, whose appetite for supreme dominion had been whetted by long years of enforced abstinence and the hated simulations of submission. He was the ruler of Roman Catholic England, and he would rule. The nature of Newman's influence it was impossible for him to understand, but he saw that it existed; for twenty years he had been unable to escape the unwelcome iterations of that singular, that alien, that rival renown; and now it stood in his path, alone and inexplicable, like a defiant ghost. "It is remarkably interesting," he observed coldly, when somebody asked him what he thought of the *Apologia;* "it is like listening to the voice of one from the dead." And such voices, with their sepulchral echoes, are apt to be more dangerous than living ones; they attract too much attention; they must be silenced at all costs. It was the meeting of the eagle and the dove; there was a hovering, a swoop, and then the quick beak and the relentless talons did their work.

Even before his accession to the Archbishopric, Manning had scented a peculiar peril in Newman's Oxford scheme, and so soon as he came into power he privately determined that the author of the *Apologia* should never be allowed to return to his old University. Nor was there any lack of excellent reasons for such a decision. Oxford was by this time a nest of liberalism; it was no fit place for Catholic youths, and they would inevitably be attracted there by the presence of Father Newman. And then, had not Father Newman's orthodoxy been impugned? Had he not been heard to express opinions of most doubtful propriety upon the question of the Temporal Power? Was it not known that he might almost be said to have an independent mind? An influence? Yes, he had an influence, no doubt; but what a fatal kind of influence to which to subject the rising generation of Catholic Englishmen!

Such were the reflections whch Manning was careful to pour into the receptive ear of Monsignor Talbot. That useful priest, at his post of vantage in the Vatican, was more than ever the devoted servant of the new Archbishop. A league, offensive and defensive, had been established between the two friends.

"I daresay I shall have many opportunities to serve you in Rome," wrote Monsignor Talbot modestly, "and I do not think my support will be useless to you, especially on account of the peculiar character of the Pope, and the spirit which pervades Propaganda; therefore I wish you to understand that a compact exists between us; if you help me, I shall help you." And a little later he added, "I am glad you accept the league. As I have already done for years, I shall support you, and I have a hundred ways of doing so. A word dropped at the proper occasion works wonders." Perhaps it was hardly necessary to remind his correspondent of that.

Monsignor Talbot added: "To be Roman is to an Englishman an effort. Dr. Newman is more English than the English. His spirit must be crushed." *When the Oratory was authorized at Rome, a proviso was attached to it.*

Propaganda had issued a secret instruction to the effect that Newman himself was by no means to reside there. If he showed signs of doing so, he was, blandly and suavely ("blande suaviterque" were the words of the Latin instrument) to be prevented. And now the secret instruction had come into operation: blande suaviterque Dr. Newman's spirit had been crushed. . . .

At about this time the Curate of Littlemore had a singular experience. As he was passing by the Church he noticed an old man, very poorly dressed in an old grey coat with the collar turned up, leaning over the lych gate, in floods of tears. He was apparently in great trouble, and his hat was pulled down over his eyes, as if he wished to hide his features. For a moment, however, he turned towards the Curate, who was suddenly struck by something familiar in the face. Could it be—? A photograph hung over the Curate's mantelpiece of the man who had made Littlemore famous by his sojourn there more than twenty years ago; he had never seen the original; but now, was it possible—? He looked again, and he could doubt no longer. It was Dr. Newman. He sprang forward, with proffers of assistance. Could he be of any use? "Oh no, no!" was the reply. "Oh no, no!" But the Curate felt that he could not turn away, and leave so eminent a character in such distress. "Was it not Dr. Newman he had the honour of addressing?" he asked, with all the respect and sympathy at his command. "Was there nothing that could be done?" But the old man hardly seemed to understand what was being said to him. "Oh no, no!" he repeated, with the tears streaming down his face. "Oh no, no!"

In 1875 Manning's labours received their final reward: he was made a Cardinal. His long and strange career, with its high hopes, its bitter disappointments, its struggles, its renunciations, had come at last to fruition in a Princedom of the Church.

"Ask in faith and in perfect confidence," he himself once wrote, "and God will give us what we ask. You may say, But do you mean that He will give us the very thing? That, God has not said. God has said that He will give you whatsoever you ask; but the form in which it will come, and the time in which He will give it, He keeps in His own power. Sometimes our prayers are answered in the very things which we put from us; sometimes it may be a chastisement, or a loss, or a visitation against which our hearts rise, and we seem to see that God has not only forgotten us, but has begun to deal with us in severity. Those very things are the answers to our prayers. He knows what we desire, and He gives us the things which we ask; but in the form which His own Divine Wisdom sees to be best."

There was one to whom Manning's elevation would no doubt have given a peculiar satisfaction—his old friend Monsignor Talbot. But this was not to be. That industrious worker in the cause of Rome had been removed some years previously to a sequestered Home at Passy, whose padded walls were impervious to the rumours of the outer world. Pius IX. had been much afflicted by this unfortunate event; he had not been able to resign himself to the loss of his secretary, and he had given orders that Monsignor Talbot's apartment in the Vatican should be preserved precisely as he had left it, in case of his return. But Monsignor Talbot never returned. Manning's feelings upon the subject appear to have been less tender than the Pope's. In all his letters, in all his papers, in all his biographical memoranda, not a word of allusion is to be found to the misfortune, nor to the death, of the most loyal of his adherents. Monsignor Talbot's name disappears suddenly and for ever—like a stone cast into the waters.

Manning was now an old man, and his outward form had assumed that appearance of austere asceticism which is, perhaps, the one thing immediately suggested by his name to the ordinary Englishman. The spare and stately form; the head, massive, emaciated, terrible, with the great nose, the glittering eyes, and the mouth drawn back and compressed into the grim rigidities of age, self-mortification, and authority—such is the vision that still lingers in the public mind—the vision which, actual and palpable like some embodied memory of the Middle Ages, used to pass and repass, less than a generation since, through the streets of London. For the activities of this extraordinary figure were great and varied. He ruled his diocese with the despotic zeal of a born administrator. He threw himself into social work of every kind; he organised charities, he lectured on temperance. He delivered innumerable sermons; he produced an unending series of devotional books. And he brooked no brother near the throne: Newman languished in Birmingham; and even the Jesuits trembled and obeyed.

The death of Pius IX. brought to Manning a last flattering testimony of the confidence with which he was regarded at the court of Rome. In one of the private consultations preceding the Conclave, a Cardinal suggested that Manning should succeed to the Papacy. He replied that he was unfitted for the position, because it was essential for the interests of the Holy See that the next Pope should be an Italian. The suggestion was pressed, but Manning held firm. Thus it happened that the Triple Tiara seemed to come, for a moment, within the grasp of the late Archdeacon of Chichester; and the cautious hand refrained.

Leo XIII. was elected, and there was a great change in the policy of the Vatican. Liberalism became the order of the day. And now at last the opportunity seemed ripe for an act which, in the opinion of the majority of English Catholics, had long been due—the bestowal of some mark of recognition from the Holy See upon the labours and the sanctity of Father Newman. It was felt that a Cardinal's Hat was the one fitting reward for such a life, and accordingly the Duke of Norfolk, representing the Catholic laity of England, visited Manning, and suggested that he should forward the proposal to the Vatican. Manning agreed, and then there followed a curious series of incidents—the last encounter in the jarring lives of those two men. A letter was drawn up by Manning for the eye of the Pope, embodying the Duke of Norfolk's proposal; but there was an unaccountable delay in the transmission of this letter; months passed, and it had not reached the Holy Father. The whole matter would, perhaps, have dropped out of sight and been forgotten, in a way which had become customary when honours for Newman were concerned, had not the Duke of Norfolk himself, when he was next in Rome, ventured to recommend to Leo XIII. that Dr. Newman should be made a Cardinal. His Holiness welcomed the proposal; but, he said, he could do nothing until he knew the views of Cardinal Manning. Thereupon the Duke of Norfolk wrote to Manning, explaining what had occurred; shortly afterwards Manning's letter of recommendation, after a delay of six months, reached the Pope, and the offer of a Cardinalate was immediately dispatched to Newman.

"Newman was now an infirm old man of seventy-eight"; *he could not make the obligatory trip to Rome, and he was too modest to request that it be excused. But the suggestion was made through Manning for him, with the understanding that Manning should transmit it to Rome.*

After [Manning] had left England, the following statement appeared in the *Times:*—

"Pope Leo XIII. has intimated his desire to raise Dr. Newman to the rank of Cardinal, but with expressions of deep respect for the Holy See, Dr. Newman has excused himself from accepting the Purple."

When Newman's eyes fell upon this announcement, he realized at once that a secret and powerful force was working against him. He trembled, as he had so often trembled before; and certainly the danger was not imaginary. In the ordinary course of things, how could such a paragraph have been inserted without his authority? . . .

The crushing indictment pointed straight at Manning. And it was true. Manning had done the impossible deed. Knowing what he did, with the Bishop of Birmingham's two letters in his pocket, he had put it about that Newman had refused the Hat. But a change had come over the spirit of the Holy See. Things were not as they had once been: Monsignor Talbot was at Passy, and Pio Nono was—where? The Duke of Norfolk intervened once again; Manning was profuse in his apologies for having misunderstood Newman's intentions, and hurried to the Pope to rectify the error. Without hesitation, the Sovereign Pontiff relaxed the rule of Roman residence, and Newman became a Cardinal.

He lived to enjoy his glory for more than ten years. Since he rarely left the Oratory, and since Manning never visited Birmingham, the two Cardinals met only once or twice. After one of these occasions, on returning to the Oratory, Cardinal Newman said, "What do you think Cardinal Manning did to me? He kissed me!"

On Newman's death, Manning delivered a funeral oration, which opened thus:

"We have lost our greatest witness for the Faith, and we are all poorer and lower by the loss.

"When these tidings came to me, my first thought was this. in what way can I, once more, show my love and veneration for my brother and friend of more than sixty years?"

In private, however, the surviving Cardinal's tone was apt to be more . . . direct. "Poor Newman!" he once exclaimed in a moment of genial expansion. "Poor Newman! He was a great hater!"

In that gaunt and gloomy building—more like a barracks than an Episcopal palace—Archbishop's House, Westminster, Manning's existence stretched itself out into an extreme old age. As his years increased, his activities, if that were possible, increased too. Meetings, missions, lectures, sermons, articles, inter-

views, letters—such things came upon him in redoubled multitudes, and were dispatched with an unrelenting zeal. But this was
not all; with age, he seemed to acquire what was almost a
new fervour, an unaccustomed, unexpected, freeing of the
spirit, filling him with preoccupations which he had hardly felt
before. "They say I am ambitious," he noted in his diary, "but
do I rest in my ambition?" No, assuredly he did not rest; but he
worked now with no arrière pensée for the greater glory of God.
A kind of frenzy fell upon him. Poverty, drunkenness, vice, all the
horrors and terrors of our civilisation, seized upon his mind, and
urged him forward to new fields of action and new fields of
thought. The temper of his soul assumed almost a revolutionary
cast. "I am a Mosaic Radical," he exclaimed; and, indeed, in the
exaltation of his energies, the incoherence of his conceptions, the
democratic urgency of his desires, combined with his awe-in-
spiring aspect and his venerable age, it was easy enough to trace
the mingled qualities of the patriarch, the prophet, and the
demagogue. As, in his soiled and shabby garments, the old man
harangued the crowds of Bermondsey or Peckham upon the virtues of Temperance, assuring them, with all the passion of conviction, as a final argument, that the majority of the Apostles were
total abstainers, this Prince of the Church might have passed as a
leader of the Salvation Army.

His popularity was immense, reaching its height during the
great Dock Strikes of 1889, when after the victory of the men
was assured, Manning was able, by his persuasive eloquence
and the weight of his character, to prevent its being carried to
excess. After other conciliators—among whom was the Bishop
of London—had given up the task in disgust, the octogenarian
Cardinal worked on with indefatigable resolution. At last, late
at night, in the schools in Kirby Street, Bermondsey, he rose to
address the strikers. An enthusiastic eye-witness has described the
scene.

"Unaccustomed tears glistened in the eyes of his rough and
work-stained hearers as the Cardinal raised his hand, and solemnly
urged them not to prolong one moment more than they could help
the perilous uncertainty and the sufferings of their wives and chil-

dren. Just above his uplifted hand was a figure of the Madonna
and Child; and some among the men tell how a sudden light
seemed to swim around it as the speaker pleaded for the women
and children. When he sat down all in the room knew that he
had won the day, and that, so far as the Strike Committee was
concerned, the matter was at an end."

In those days, there were strange visitors at Archbishop's House.
Careful priests and conscientious secretaries wondered what the
world was coming to when they saw labour leaders like Mr. John
Burns and Mr. Ben Tillett, and land-reformers like Mr. Henry
George, being ushered into the presence of his Eminence. Even
the notorious Mr. Stead appeared, and his scandalous paper with
its unspeakable revelations lay upon the Cardinal's table. This
proved too much for one of the faithful tonsured dependents of
the place, and he ventured to expostulate with his master. But
he never did so again.

When the guests were gone, and the great room was empty, the
old man would draw himself nearer to the enormous fire, and review once more, for the thousandth time, the long adventure of
his life. He would bring out his diaries and his memoranda, he
would rearrange his notes, he would turn over again the yellow
leaves of faded correspondences; seizing his pen, he would pour
out his comments and reflections, and fill, with an extraordinary
solicitude, page after page with elucidations, explanations, justi-
fications, of the vanished incidents of a remote past. He would
snip with scissors the pages of ancient journals, and with delicate
ecclesiastical fingers drop unknown mysteries into the flames.
Sometimes he would turn to the four red folio scrapbooks
with their collection of newspaper cuttings concerning himself
over a period of thirty years. Then the pale cheeks would flush
and the close-drawn lips grow more menacing even than before.
"Stupid, mulish malice," he would note. "Pure lying—conscious,
deliberate and designed." "Suggestive lying. Personal animosity is
at the bottom of this."
And then he would suddenly begin to doubt. After all, where
was he? What had he accomplished? Had any of it been worth

while? Had he not been out of the world all his life? Out of the world!

"Croker's 'Life and Letters,' and Hayward's 'Letters,' " he notes, "are so full of politics, literature, action, events, collision of mind with mind, and that with such a multitude of men in every state of life, that when I look back, it seems as if I had been simply useless."

And again, "the complete isolation and exclusion from the official life of England in which I have lived, makes me feel as if I had done nothing." He struggled to console himself with the reflexion that all this was only "the natural order." "If the natural order is moved by the supernatural order, then I may not have done nothing. Fifty years of witness for God and his Truth, I hope, has not been in vain." But the same thoughts recurred. "In reading Macaulay's life I had a haunting feeling that his had been a life of public utility and mine a vita umbratilis, a life in the shade." Ah! it was God's will. "Mine has been a life of fifty years out of the world as Gladstone's has been in it. The work of his life in this world is manifest. I hope mine may be in the next. I suppose our Lord called me out of the world because He saw that I should lose my soul in it." Clearly, that was the explanation. . . .

So though Death came slowly, struggling step by step with that bold and tenacious spirit, when he did come at last the Cardinal was ready. Robed, in his archiepiscopal vestments, his rochet, his girdle, and his mozeta, with the scarlet biretta on his head, and the pectoral cross upon his breast, he made his solemn Profession of Faith in the Holy Roman Church. A crowd of lesser dignitaries, each in the garments of his office, attended the ceremonial. The Bishop of Salford held up the Pontificale and the Bishop of Amycla bore the wax taper. The provost of Westminster, on his knees, read aloud the Profession of Faith, surrounded by the Canons of the Diocese. Towards those who gathered about him the dying man was still able to show some signs of recognition, and even, perhaps, of affection; yet it seemed that his chief preoccupation, up to the very end, was with his obedience to the rules prescribed by the Divine Authority. "I am glad to have been able to do everything in due order," were among his last words. "Si fort qu'on soit," says one of the profoundest of the observers of the human heart, "on peut éprouver le besoin de s'incliner devant quelqu'un ou quelque chose. S'incliner devant Dieu, c'est toujours le moins humiliant."

Manning died on January 14, 1892, in the eighty-fifth year of his age. A few days later Mr. Gladstone took occasion, in a letter to a friend, to refer to his relations with the late Cardinal. Manning's conversion was, he said,

"altogether the severest blow that ever befell me. In a late letter the Cardinal termed it a quarrel, but in my reply I told him it was not a quarrel, but a death; and that was the truth. Since then there have been vicissitudes. But I am quite certain that to the last his personal feelings never changed; and I believe also that he kept a promise made in 1851, to remember me before God at the most solemn moments; a promise which I greatly valued. The whole subject is to me at once of extreme interest and of considerable restraint."

"His reluctance to die," concluded Mr. Gladstone, "may be explained by an intense anxiety to complete unfulfilled service."

The funeral was the occasion of a popular demonstration such as has rarely been witnessed in the streets of London. The route of the procession was lined by vast crowds of working people, whose imaginations, in some instinctive manner, had been touched. Many who had hardly seen him declared that in Cardinal Manning they had lost their best friend. Was it the magnetic vigour of the dead man's spirit that moved them? Or was it his valiant disregard of common custom and those conventional reserves and poor punctilios which are wont to hem about the great? Or was it something untameable in his glances and in his gestures? Or was it, perhaps, the mysterious glamour lingering about him of the antique organisation of Rome? For whatever cause, the mind of the people had been impressed; and yet, after all, the impression was more acute than lasting. The Cardinal's memory is a dim thing to-day. And he who descends into the crypt of that Cathedral which Manning never lived to see, will observe, in the quiet niche with the sepulchral monument, that the dust lies thick on the strange, the incongruous, the almost impossible object which, with its elaboration of dependent tassels, hangs down from the dim vault like some forlorn and forgotten trophy—the Hat.

LIGHT

Lincoln Steffens was one of the great modern observers of life. Many people may not agree in regarding him as a student. Journalist, Wall-Street speculator, muckraker, friend and enemy and unveiler of machine-politicians, wanderer on the brink of political volcanoes, sympathetic watcher of revolutions, "red" and consorter with reds and anarchists—how was this seventy-yeared, smiling adventurer a student? Hadn't he been "showing up" institutions and people for years, as if he knew it all? and asking unanswerable questions, for all the world as if he had the answers?

Steffens knew he didn't have the answers. His career was a lifelong search for them. From the beginning he had a tremendous desire to know and understand. He observed, compared, analyzed, studied throughout his life. So doing, he found the answers to some of his questions. More than many a scholar in library or museum, more than most theorizers from statistics, he was a student of the modern world, living, asking his questions of life, proving his answers on his pulse.

And it was great fun to him. "Happier and happier," he calls his life, "right down to this, the last one: age, which, as it comes, comes a-laughing, the best of all." His world is like a clear sunshiny day, with spacious vistas opening round, air thin and cool. For him men and places and things are real in their own right, their identities hold the answers to the whole universe of what he wants to know. He grew, and his growth was toward a clear objectivity.

It would be an error, though, to think of Steffens as either unimaginative or unemotional. His boyhood imagination seethed with romantic color, transforming him from a boy on horseback to an explorer, a Crusader, a Napoleon. But as he grew his imagination turned to understanding men and their behavior, trying to see things as they are. And the boy who was filled with trembling pain and grief at the sale of the horse he loved appears again and again in the warmness and sympathy and courage of the mature man.

But most of all he wanted to understand. The endeavor taught him that the world is never done, discoveries are never completed, knowledge never final. "Everything in the world remains to be done or done over. 'The greatest picture is not yet painted, the greatest play isn't written (not even by Shakespeare), the greatest poem is unsung. There isn't in all the world a perfect railroad, nor a good government, nor a sound law.'" A breath-taking prospect for attainment! The realization turned him away from self-dramatization. He saw that "the world was more interesting than I am."

The endeavor also taught him that idealism hid the shape of reality from men's eyes. He mingled with the bad men, the crooked politicians, the bribers and bribe-takers, the policemen who protected criminals, the anarchists and dynamiters, the heads of railroads and electric-power companies and steel corporations who corrupted politics. He found out what they were really like, and how things really worked. The "idealism" of good citizens made them refuse to admit the facts staring them in the face. They wanted both to have the cake of idealism and to eat it for bread-and-butter. The reformers whom he studied as carefully as he studied the crooks and corrupters were never able, he shows, to deal with their problems realistically because a great deal of intensified emotion and lofty idealism prevented them from ever even grasping all the difficulties involved.

Steffens shows us how ideas and systems, deified into "the System," sacrifice good will, honesty, intelligence, ability, and even self-respect to machines—political machines, business machines, war-and-imperialism machines, until Machinery does almost seem to become, as Samuel Butler half feared, a modern Moloch. Steffens perceives that human emotions, human values, human welfare are the real touchstones, and that by them much of our world is condemned. But he also perceives that despite all the perversions to which they have been misused, machines may be made the instruments of emergent human good.

And with that perception we find the central value of Lincoln Steffens's *Autobiography*. We have been tracing in history a spiral course. Now, once more, we find ourselves breathing the air of optimism and hope for mankind. Steffens's confidence is animated by Shelley's enthusiasm, but it is no longer an iridescent dream. It seizes on the experimentalism of Mill, the patient fact-collecting of Darwin, to study the direction of modern society. It is pragmatic in the best and original sense. It believes that events make toward their own consummation—if—and only if—human beings concentrate their intelligence on seeing how things work and then direct their energies to the sound use of that knowledge.

Henry Adams thought the political machine was breaking down, because it was no longer operating in the way intended by the founders or congenial to his ideals. Its having been seized by a new group to him meant only collapse and failure. Steffens sees it as a going concern. It is doing what its users want it to do. Even their misuses are a scientific lesson in attaining your purpose. Study how they do it, says Steffens; nothing forbids applying that knowledge to humane ends.

Steffens died in 1935. Since his death the world has grown ever more darkly and hideously dominated by war and enslavement machines, by systems for which books must be burned, truth denied, all facts smothered unless they fit into the straitjacket of chauvinist dogmas, individual consciences garroted, men ground into mud by the Goliath of the State. Democracy today stands pitted against totalitarianism. "A people ruling," says a speaker in Herodotus, "first, the very name of it is beautiful." The entire life of Lincoln Steffens was devoted to the essence of democracy. It was a patient study of how democracy could be made to work. America, Steffens concluded, is one of the great experiments of the world. Its machine mass-production, he said, "is so tied to democracy that it cannot rise to its obviously potential heights without lifting and being lifted by the human race."

Autobiography of Lincoln Steffens

[Steffens died in 1935. The *Autobiography* was published in 1931.]

EARLY IN THE MORNING OF APRIL 6, 1866, IN A SMALL HOUSE "OVER in the Mission" of San Francisco, California, I was born—a remarkable child. This upon the authority of my mother, a remarkable woman, who used to prove her prophetic judgment to all listeners till I was old enough to make my own demonstration. Even then, even though I was there to frown her down, she was ever ready to bring forth her evidence, which opened with the earthquake of 1868. When that shock shook most San Franciscans out of their houses into the streets, she ran upstairs to me and found me pitched out of bed upon the floor but otherwise unmoved. As she said with swimming eyes, I was "not killed, not hurt, and, of course, not crying; I was smiling, as always, good as gold."

My own interpretation of this performance is that it was an exhibit less of goodness than of wisdom. I knew that my mother would not abandon me though the world rocked and the streets yawned. Nor is that remarkable. Every well-born baby is sure he can trust his mother. What strikes me as exceptional and promising in it is that I had already some sense of values; I could take such natural events as earthquakes all in my stride. That, I think, is why I smiled then; that is why I smile now; and that may be why my story is of a happy life—happier and happier. Looking back over it now for review, it seems to me that each chapter of my adventures is happier than the preceding chapters right down to this, the last one: age, which, as it comes, comes a-laughing, the best of all. I have a baby boy of my own now; my first—a remarkable child, who—when he tumbles out of bed—laughs; as good as gold.

I remember seeing the mule teams ringing into town, trains of four or five huge, high wagons, hauled by from twelve to twenty and more belled mules and horses driven by one man, who sometimes walked, sometimes rode the saddled near wheel-horse. Cowboys, mostly Mexicans and called vaqueros, used to come shouting on bucking bunches of bronchos into town to mix with the teamsters, miners, and steamboat men in the drinking, gambling, girling, fighting, of those days. My infant mind was snapping wide-eyed shots of these rough scenes and coloring and completing them with pictures painted on my memory by the conversations I overheard. I seem to have known of the gold strikes up in the mountains, of finding silver over the Range in Nevada, of men getting rich, or broke, or shot. I was kept away from this, of course, and I heard and saw it always darkly, under a shadow of disapproval. Other ideas and ideals were held up in the light for me. But secretly I was impatient to grow up and go out into that life, and meanwhile I played I was a teamster, a gun-playing, broncho-busting vaquero, or a hearty steamboat man, or a steamboat. I remember having a leaf from our dining-table on the floor, kneeling on it, and, taking hold of one end, jerking it backward over the carpet, tooting like a steamboat whistle. Three or four big chairs and all the small chairs in the house made me a mountain train of wagons and mules; a clothes line tied to the leader and strung through the other chairs was a rein which I could jerk just as the black-bearded teamsters did. And, of course, any chair is a horse for a boy who is a would-be vaquero.

Horses, real horses, played a leading part in my boyhood; I seem always to have wanted one. . . .

From the day my pony came to me I seem to have spent many, many hours, playing around in my imagination, which became the most active faculty of my mind. For, as I say, I was alone much of the time. I learned to like to be alone, and that pleasure I come back to always, even now. When I am tired of the crowd I go off somewhere by myself and have a good time inside my mind.

As a boy I would ride far, far away to some spot, give my pony a long rope to swing round on, and let him feed on the grass, while I sat and did nothing but muse. I read a great deal. Finding that books fed my fancies, I would take one along, and finding a quiet nook, I read. And my reading always gave me something to be. I liked to change the hero I was to the same thing on horseback, and once wholly in the part, I would remount my pony and be Napoleon, or Richard the Lion-hearted, or Byron, so completely that any actual happening would wake me up dazed as from a dreaming sleep. Dream people lived or lay in wait for me in the brush across the river, so that the empty spaces beyond my old horizon, the levee, became not only interesting but fascinating with dread or glory, and populated with Persons.

"Hey, kid! Don't swim the river there. The rapids'll sweep you clean to San Francisco."

I looked up. It was the bridge-tender, the man that walked the trestle over the American River after every train to put out fires started on the dry sleepers by live coals dropped from the locomotives. I respected a man that filled a responsible place like his, but I slid into the water, swam along shore, came out, and dressed. I could not tell him that Byron swam the Hellespont, which was harder to do than to cross the American at that point; and I did not like to confess that I had a trap set on the other side where the Chinamen had their peanut farm and represented the Saracens to me. When I was dressed, the trestle-walker bade me meet him at the end of the trestle. I did, and a friendship was well started. He didn't scold me, he praised my swimming, but he said that the current was strong at that place and that it wasn't brave, it was foolish, to go in there. "A boy oughtn't to do what a man wouldn't do." He asked me some questions, my name, age, where I lived, where my father's business was. He felt over and approved my pony. I asked him how he could walk so fast on the trestle, having no planks to go on, and stepping from one sleeper to the other.

"Oh," he said, "I can walk 'em fast now because I walked 'em slow at first."

I wanted to try. He took my hand and made me walk slowly,

one by one, until I was over my nervousness. When I could do it alone, he invited me to his watchman's cabin, about one-third of the way across. I went, he following. When we reached his little house we sat down, and we had, man to man, a nice, long talk, which became so confidential that I trusted him with the information that I was a trapper and had my traps set for beavers all up and down the river. And my faith was not misplaced. He didn't say that there were no beavers in that river; we both knew there weren't, and we both knew that that didn't matter. All he said was that he was a gold miner himself—and expected to strike it rich some day.

"I don't work at it much," he admitted. "Mostly I tend bridge. But in between trains, when I ain't got a thing to do, I think about it. I think how I came west to find a fat claim and work it and get rich, so I write home that that's what I'm doing, prospectin', and I am, too, and sometimes I play I have struck it and I go home and I spend my money."

After that I caught more beavers, and he and I spent my profits my way. Yes, and after that he struck it richer than ever, and him and me, we went back east and we just blew in his money his way. It was fun. I got a bad name from this. There were grown-ups who said I was a "fearful liar," and no doubt I was unconvincing sometimes.

The raw gravel of the river bottom, which he peopled "with Indians, Turks, beavers, and wild beasts," *an artist, Mr. Marple, painted in a sunset of burning gold, and said:* "Your Indians are where my gold is, where all beauty is, in our heads." *But through Mr. Marple's son, Charlie, who was a page in the California State Legislature, he learned another valuable lesson:*

The practices of debate, quite aside from the legislation under consideration, fascinated me. I wished it were real. It was beautiful enough to be true. But no, speeches were made on important subjects with hardly any one present but the Speaker, the clerks, and us boys. Where were the absent members? I did not ask that question often; not out loud. The pages laughed; everybody laughed. Charlie explained.

more profound. "I said that I had seen two highly trained, well-educated Masters of Arts and Doctors of Philosophy disagreeing upon every essential point of thought and knowledge. They had all there was of the sciences; and yet they could not find any knowledge on which they could base an acceptable conclusion." *He was stunned to realize* "that it is philosophically true that nothing is known; that it was precisely the foundation that is lacking for science; that all we call knowledge rested upon assumptions which the scientists did not all accept; and that likewise there is no scientific reason or saying, for example, that stealing is wrong."

He went abroad in 1889, to Berlin, then Heidelberg, Munich, Leipzig, Paris: perhaps the European universities could teach him more. But they turned out to be no more fruitful than Berkeley.

The best I had got out of all my scholastic wanderings was the belief, which was probably only a hope, that when there was a science of psychology, a science of sociology, and a science of biology, when we could know how man was born, bred, moved, and to what end, then we might lay out a program for the guidance of his conduct. For example, assuming that men are an evolving species, we might say that all acts, personal and social, that made for development were good, and that all conduct and conditions that hindered growth were bad. I did take that as a loose guide for myself, but to make it scientific, biology has to prove and describe evolution, psychology has to show us human possibilities, sociology has to be made a study of the effects of environment on human psychology; and even then, men have to know the possibilities of their growth and choose among them. . . .

The thing for me to do, I decided, was to leave the universities, go into business or politics, and see, not what thinkers thought, but what practical men did and why.

So he came back to the United States and became a reporter on the New York Evening Post. *Assigned to Wall Street, he set about forming a picture of what finance was like. James B. Dill taught him something of what legalized business piracy was.*

And to my amazement he opened up the criminal inside of the practices under the New Jersey legislation, a picture of such chicanery and fraud, of wild license and wrong-doing, that I could not, I dared not, take it all down; I was too confused. And Dill saw that, and he laughed; his eyes twinkled and his round little belly shook with the humor of the situation.

"You are astonished?" he said. "And well you may be. But you must write what I tell you. Don't quote me. I am the founder of this legislation, and as such you may name me, but don't say I gave you these facts; it would look odd; it might be suspicious, to make me the authority for an exposure of what I am the enabling founder of, but it is your duty to describe what is done under these laws, and if your editor shows any hesitation, you may tell him to call me up on the 'phone; I will stand back of whatever you print."

I did not write all that Dill told me; not then; I never have. I could not at the time, because, as I have said, I was too imbued with the Wall Street spirit and view of things to speak as this lawyer did of the holies of the holy. Upton Sinclair learned from him; he was a socialist. I was a Wall Street man myself, unconsciously, but literally. That's how I came finally to understand what corruption is and how it gets a man, not as the Reds and the writers think, but as the Whites and the Righteous are: rogues outside, but inside, honest men. However, that's for later. When James B. Dill told me first about Wall Street and his Jersey laws, and he saw that I would not, could not, take it in, he made merry with me, laughing and quizzing and telling me ever more and more.

Dill explained also why he had told Steffens these things.

"Why, Dr. Innocent," he said, "I was advertising my wares and the business of my State. When you and the other reporters and critics wrote as charges against us what financiers could and did actually do in Jersey, when you listed, with examples, what the trust-makers were doing under our laws, you were advertising our business—free. For financiers are dubs, as you know yourself now; don't you? They have to be told, and they have to be told plain so that they get it, and so, as I say, while I gave you the facts to roast us with, what you wrote as 'bad' struck business men all over the United States as good, and they poured in upon us to our profit to do business with us to their profit. The only drawback was that when Delaware and New York and other 'bad' political sovereigns saw what Jersey was doing and how we made money and friends out of our trust policy they copied us, and they went further than we did, or, to be exact, they tried to."

And so saying, Dill laughed and laughed and laughed; not cynically; not wickedly; but merrily, with his whole body and soul. James B. Dill was one of the "wisest," wisest and, yes, about the rightest man I ever met.

"Trusts are natural, inevitable growths out of our social and economic conditions," he said often. "You cannot stop them by force, with laws. They will sweep down like glaciers upon your police, courts, and States and wash them into flowing rivers. I am for clearing the way for them. Let them go, and if they cannot be brought into social use, why—then—then"—he would laugh— "then I would be for exploring their origin and dealing with—I mean closing up—their source."

Transferred to reporting police news when Dr. Parkhurst began denouncing the corruption of the force, he made further startling discoveries.

The police were protecting from the law and from public opinion the law-breakers they were appointed and paid to protect the public from. . . .

Why were these law-breakers so strong? And why was there such an opposition to the simple, superficial reforms of Dr. Parkhurst? I used to wonder at what I was seeing, and the reporters, policemen, politicians, who explained it all to me, wondered at my stupidity. I could understand the bribery and the contributions to political parties; that accounted for the police and Tammany Hall, and that satisfied the minds of my informants. But it did not explain to me the opposition to reform that was most bitter: that of good, prominent citizens who had no apparent connection with the underworld. As Dr. Parkhurst forced such results as the voluntary closing of some saloons, he was hated more and more openly by people whom one might expect to see approving his course: bankers, business men, and even other clergymen. There was something to find out about the organization of society, as it occurred in New York, something the "wise guys" of the underworld did not know or would not tell. I asked my friends in Wall Street to justify their indignation at Parkhurst, but all they would say was that his crusade "hurt business." That was the first time I heard that expression. "How can the closing of saloons hurt business in Wall Street?" I asked James B. Dill, who knew everything. He kicked my shin, hard, and when I exclaimed, he answered my question, "Why does your mouth cry out when only your shin is hurt?" That was the answer, but I could never be satisfied with a fact or a phrase; it was a picture I needed, a diagram of the connection between the saloon business and the banks, just as I had one of the nervous system that linked up my lower and upper extremities.

He joined the staff of McClure's Magazine *and began the muckraking series of exposures called* The Shame of the Cities. *Joseph Folk, the circuit attorney of the St. Louis district, gave him the "diagram" he wanted:* "It is good business men that are corrupting our bad politicians; it is good business that causes bad government." *Mayor Jones of Minneapolis confirmed the discovery.*

All through those muckraking days I was mistaken for an expert who knew all about graft and politics and government and could tell anybody just what to do about them. Thieves, politicians, business men, reformers, and our magazine readers, they all assumed that I had what I was trying to get: knowledge. In one way this was fortunate. The "wise guys" would tell me their secrets. Thinking I knew anyhow, they felt that they might as well talk, the big mitt men, for example; and I encouraged their self-deception. In another way my reputation for omniscience was embarrassing, as it was that morning when young Mayor Jones turned upon me for advice. He so needed it; he was so sure that I could give it—

This honest young mind that believed integrity and courage were all that a good mayor required, had taken office with the police problem pressing for solution. It looked simple. He would appoint as chief of police an honest man with no criminal or vice connections and let him organize a police force to drive out the law-breakers—all of them, of course. You don't traffic with crime. You simply enforce the law. His first discovery was that the police job is a specialty, calling for some technical experience. There were no men in his town with police experience enough to organize and direct a police force not tainted in some degree by the recent exposures and plottings. He finally chose for chief a church deacon and a personal friend, on the theory that he must have in that post a man whom he could trust. As policemen he and the deacon chose, cunningly, men whom the ex-mayor and his brother, the ex-chief, had discharged. There must have been something good in them, and so far as there was evil, it would be against the old gang and the old practices.

His next discovery was that he, the mayor, and his new police force could not enforce the law against prostitution. That vice had to be permitted to run. So the women were restricted to a certain patrol district and there allowed to do business free of blackmail and fines.

His third discovery was that good citizens, property owners, whose houses were cleaned of prostitution, rose up in wrath against this arrangement, which lost them their high rent. More astonishing to the good mayor, these landlords were able to set the clergy and other good citizens after him for compromising with sin and not only not enforcing but officially permitting the breaking of the law. He stood fast, Jones did. He might not have been able to if he had been a politician and sought reëlection. Mayor Jones could see that a "bad" man in his place would feel forced by the good people to be less honest with the bad. His strict, temporary, but well-intentioned regulation of other habits and vices brought up against him the power of the saloon-keepers, brewers, other property owners, and allied businesses.

Talking with Iz Durham, the political boss of Philadelphia, Steffens summarized his own conclusions:

"Political corruption," I went on, "is, then, a process. It is not a temporary evil, not an accidental wickedness, not a passing symptom of the youth of a people. It is a natural process by which a democracy is made gradually over into a plutocracy. Treason, in brief, is not a bad act; it is an inevitable, successful policy, and the cities differ one from another according to age. Philadelphia is worse than St. Louis because it is older—in experience."

I soon had the boss bewildered and as puzzled and serious and shocked as I had been.

"If this process goes on," I said, "then this American republic of ours will be a government that represents the organized evils of a privileged class." I had forgotten Durham; I wasn't accusing him of wrong-doing. But I remember the awed tone in which he broke into my soliloquy to ask how it could be stopped. I saw that he cared. I said I didn't know, and I rose to go to think over the ideas I had got into my head.

Tom Johnson, the fighting reform mayor of Cleveland, said the final word on the subject, and led Steffens to the answer of the problem:

"Oh, I could see," he said, "that you did not know what it was that corrupted politics. First you thought it was bad politicians, who turned out to be pretty good fellows. Then you blamed the bad business men who bribed the good fellows, till you discovered that not all business men bribed and that those who did were pretty good business men. The little business men didn't bribe; so you settled upon, you invented, the phrase 'big business,' and that's as far as you and your kind have got: that it is big business that does all the harm. Hell! Can't you see that it's privileged business that does it? Whether it's a big steam railroad that wants a franchise or a little gambling-house that wants not be to raided, a temperance society that wants a law passed, a poor little prostitute, or a big merchant occupying an alley for storage—it's those who seek privileges who corrupt, it's those who possess privileges that defend our corrupt politics. Can't you see that?"

This was more like a flash of light than a speech, and as I took it in and shed it around in my head, he added: "It is privilege that causes evil in the world, not wickedness; and not men."

And I remembered then something I heard him say one day

to a group of the business men he was fighting, something neither they nor I understood at the time. To a remonstrance of theirs that I do not recall, he blurted out: "It's fun, running the business of the city of Cleveland; it's the biggest, most complicated, most difficult, and most satisfying business in Cleveland. A street railway is child's play, compared with it; a coal mine is a snap; a bank?—Bah. There's something that blinds you fellows, and I know what it is. It's what fooled me so long when I was running public service corporations. And I'll tell you something you want to know: how to beat me.

"If I could take away from you the things you have, the franchises, the privileges, that make you enemies of your city, you would see what I see and run for my job yourselves, and you'd beat me for mayor and manage the city of Cleveland better than I do.". . .

If it was privilege that caused what we called evil, it was privilege that had to be dealt with, not men. Not big men, not bad men, not crooks, and not capitalists—not even the capitalist class! Punishment of individuals, the class struggle and strikes, wars— all hatred, vengeance, force, were unscientific. To put in prison a man who bought government to get a street railway franchise was wrong; we should put the franchise where men can't get it. To shift our votes from one to another of two political parties, both of which are organized to serve the privileged or the privilege-seekers, was folly. To throw out the rascals and put into office honest men without removing that which makes good men do bad things was as irrational as our experience had taught us it was "unpractical." The international wars of corrupted governments for trade routes, foreign markets, "empire" and the natural resources of backward countries, strikes and the class war for the conquest of economic power and advantages—these were as senseless as passing laws for reform and for peace. It's all upside down. What society does is to teach the ideal of success, set up the temptation of power and riches to men and nations—if they are brave enough to risk and able enough to escape the threats of penalties for getting caught. These warnings keep off all but the best men, biologically best. Then when these best men succeed we honor

them, and if they slip we hate and punish them. What we ought to
do is to let the losers of the race go, and take down the prizes we
offer to the winners.

After the McNamara dynamiting trial, Clarence Darrow, their
attorney, was tried on a charge of bribing jurors. Steffens was his
star witness; the state tried to "make a monkey" *of him.*

When Darrow bowed and waved to the prosecution to take the
witness, Fredericks rose, and to fix all eyes upon him, he stepped
back to the rail, raised his hand, and loudly began: "Mr. Steffens,"
and he walked slowly, forcefully toward me, with hand high in
the air, and step by step, word by word he threatened, "are—not—
you—" and he was now close up to me; he threw his pointing
finger into my face and finished—"an—avowed—anarchist?"

His play-acting really amused me. There was the typical lawyer,
the conceited, unfair prosecutor whom I had seen abusing his
power over weak witnesses all my life. I smiled, and slowly, very
quietly, I answered: "Oh, I am worse than that."

He staggered as if I had struck him. "Worse than that!" he
muttered.

"Yes, I believe in Christianity."

He stepped back, flustered, and it was minutes before he could
go on. He did not know what an anarchist was: a man that is
opposed to all force, including government. Fredericks thought an
anarchist was the opposite: a bomb-thrower. And as for Christianity, Fredericks was a churchman. By and by, when he recovered, he came at me again on that point. What did I mean by
calling myself a Christian? I hadn't, but I let that go. I swept my
hand around at the audience of labor men, socialists, anarchists,
and dumb morons, and said: "Well, you see, Captain Fredericks,
those people out there, they are anarchists, socialists, labor men,
and they believe, like you, in justice; but I'm a muckraker, and I
tell you that things are so bad in this world that justice won't fix
them. It's too late for that. I believe that nothing but love will
do the job. That's Christianity. That's the teaching that we must
love our neighbors."

"And that's worse than anarchy?" he was muttering.

"Yes." I smiled as affectionately as I could. "That means that, for example, you and I should love each other. And you will admit, won't you, that that is going some?"

The judge, who, I learned afterward, was a Christian Scientist, passed me his fan. I fanned myself cool, then handed it back to the judge. We kept that gentle fan going coolly all through that silly, blustering cross-examination—hours of it, while Fredericks consulted his assistants and tried to sock me. He couldn't. I had his goat, as he would say; he could not get mine, he and his advisers. They had their own ideas of the line of attack, and he tried some of theirs till I heard him say to one of them, "No, no. Every time I asked him one of your questions he socked me."

I enjoyed that day in court; so did the judge and the jurors. At a dinner they gave to Darrow afterward, they said they had the time of their lives. Picked for their anti-labor prejudice, these men, mostly small employers, said that they had got the philosophy of labor in that trial. And well they might have, for Darrow gave it and I gave it pretty fully in my testimony, which was made up of elaborate, philosophic addresses to the jury. Fredericks protested, but his questions were fine openings for all that I had to say. He really was a great help to us, and so, though he did not, the rest of us enjoyed that trial.

To Steffens, by now, revolution seemed the only solution. He began studying revolutions. The first one handy was Mexico, then came Russia. They taught him a number of mistakes about revolution.

The great leaders of the Russian revolutionary movement were not in Russia when the Russian Revolution began; they were in exile; and the lesser leaders who were there did not expect it to happen. Somebody did. On the roofs of buildings that commanded the main thoroughfares, the grand boulevards and squares, we found still standing the machine guns planted to deal with the revolution that the revolutionists did not know was going to happen. And we had a look at the plans drawn to put down mobs of people who did not know they were going to rise in revolt. Government blue prints. Government preparations. It was the government that anticipated, prepared for, started, the revolution in Russia, as in Mexico. . . .

The Czar's ministers, busy with the war, knew that the troops at the front were not warlike. They did not hate the Germans; they fraternized with them when they could; and meanwhile they suffered from lack of supplies, food, clothing, and ammunition. Evil reports of the evil conditions were leaking back to the people in the country, in the towns, in the cities; and the spies heard some exaggerated but not wholly untrue stories of catastrophes, corruption, and disloyalty. The people heard that ammunition for the guns on the right was sent to the left and that the ammunition to fit the guns on the left went to misfits on the right. They heard, and, true or false, they believed, that by force of bribery high up, the Russian high command had let the German high command actually direct the movements of Russian armies. In one battle the Russians had been deliberately marched into a swamp and there drowned and slaughtered. One can recognize there one of Hindenburg's victories. There were many such stories, some of them blaming Rasputin, some blaming individual generals. Call them the usual wild rumors of war, as you will; the ministers of the Czar in prison told us they were believed by the people, who meanwhile were as hungry as they were afraid.

The ministers felt they must do something; a revolution was due; and they must deal with it in advance. They decided to handle the menace as they had handled the threatening discontent in other crises, notably in 1905. They would get the people out into the streets of St. Petersburg and shoot the fear of God into them, as we do in strikes.

Starting with the bread lines, they held back the bread. The women, children, and old men assembled and formed in queues leading up to the police stations for bread. One day there was no bread. A lie: the bread was found rotting afterward in the cellars of the stations. . . .

On the afternoon of the third day of the bread riot—which was no riot—out in the great square in front of the Moscow railroad station an infantry officer was trying to command and

incite his men to shoot across the open into the quiet mob. They
would not. A student standing by jeered at the officer, who, in
a rage, thrust the student through. A Cossack in line on the
opposite side of the square saw this; he put spurs to his horse,
charged from the ranks, and drawing his sword as he rode, he
cut that officer down. There was a cry: "The soldiers are with
us!" and then there was another cry: "The revolution! The revolution is on!"

*From Russia he passed on to the Peace Conference, where two
French journalists narrated a perhaps apocryphal but probably
"inspired" anecdote to sound out the American newspaper men.*

Then one of them told how, when the president and the
premiers sat down at the table that morning and were about to
proceed to business, M. Clemenceau, who was fiddling with his
gray silk gloves, said, "One moment, gentlemen. I desire before
we go any further to be made clear on one very essential point."
The French reporter was entering into his story; he mimicked
Clemenceau, drawing tight and smooth his little silk gloves, and
bowing sweetly and smiling sardonically. And the reporter acted
the parts he quoted.

The president and the premiers halted and looked up ex-
pectantly at M. Clemenceau, who said: "I have heard something
about a permanent peace. There has been a great deal of talk
about a peace to end war forever, and I am interested in that.
All Frenchmen would like to make permanent peace. But I would
like to know—all the French would like to know—whether you
mean it, the permanent peace."

He looked at his colleagues and they nodded.

"So," Clemenceau said, "you really mean it! Well, it is possible. We can do it; we can make the permanent peace. And
we French need, we very much need, the permanent peace. Every
time you, our neighbors, get into a fight, France is the battlefield,
and our population, our armies, do not increase. If there is not
an end of wars we French may be all wiped out some day. So,
you see, it is we French more than you remote Americans, Mr.
President, more than you safe islanders, Mr. Lloyd George, who

require the security of the real peace. But we French cannot quite believe that you, our friends, neighbors, allies—that you really mean what you say. Do you, Mr. President?"

Mr. Wilson did.

"And you, Mr. Premier?"

Mr. Lloyd George did.

And the Italians did, of a certainty, yes.

"Very important," Mr. Clemenceau muttered, as if convinced, as if the whole prospect were changing, and his whole policy. "Very important. We can make this a permanent peace; we can remove all the causes of war and set up no new causes of war. It is very, very important what you say, what you have been so long saying, Mr. President. We here now have the opportunity to make a peace that shall last forever, and the French people, diminishing, will be safe. And you are sure you propose to seize this opportunity?"

They did, they emphatically did.

Clemenceau clucked in his throat; he pressed tight down the finger of his gloves. "And—you have counted the cost of such a peace?" he asked.

There was some hesitation at that. "What costs?"

"Well," said the French intelligence, "if we give up all future wars—if we are to prevent war, we must give up our empires and all hope of empire. You, Mr. Lloyd George, you English will have to come out of India, for example; we French shall have to come out of North Africa; and you Americans, Mr. President, you must get out of the Philippines and Porto Rico and leave Cuba alone and—Mexico. Oh, we can all go to these and other countries, but as tourists, traders, travelers; we cannot any more govern them or exploit or have the inside track in them. We cannot possess the keys to trade routes and spheres of influence. And, yes, we shall have to tear down our tariff walls and open the whole world to free trade and traffic. Those are some of the costs of permanent peace; there are other sacrifices we, the dominant powers, would have to make. It is very expensive, peace. We French are willing, but are you willing, to pay the price, all those costs of no more war in the world?"

The French correspondents became personal; they smiled. They said that the president and the premiers protested that they did not mean all that, that that was not necessary, not all at once. "No, no, they did not mean that, exactly."

"Then," said Clemenceau, sitting up straight and fisting the table sharply once, "then you don't mean peace. You mean war. And the time for us French to make war is now, when we have got one of our neighbors down; we shall finish him and get ready for—the next war."

Back in his own country, though, a new impression and a queer idea struck him.

I felt afresh the power, the momentum, of America as a going concern. The force of us had increased. There could be no stopping or turning us now. We were on the way; we might not know where we were going, but, for better or for worse, we were going, going. Whither? It would be worth trying to find out where we were bound, just as I had learned to see what foreign countries were tending to do. And I began to sense a direction here, a direction new to me. My wife's pointing finger, my old friends' cynical or sad hopelessness, and the contrast between the fixity of old Europe and the vigor and ever-changing movement of the United States braced me to see and to acknowledge that my country was not going my way, not the liberal, not the red radical, but also not exactly the English, French, or German way. It was going its own way. What way was that? I asked, but I could not credit the answer that occurred to me.

The American way was not the Russian way, no; ours was in the opposite direction, but—but, yes, Bolshevik Russia and the mass machine-making United States were more alike, essentially and politically, than any other two countries that I had seen. Wasn't it this, that these two young peoples, the Russians and the Americans, are driving, the one consciously, the other unwittingly, toward the same end?

My wife's observation about experimenting was the point. Mr. Owen D. Young told me one day something about the General Electric Company's big experimental plant where chemists, physicists—all sorts of scientific researchers—were gathered to carry on, partly for the company, but partly for science and themselves, their intensive specialized work. All that he said went to show that big business was absorbing science, the scientific attitude and the scientific method. Cocksureness, unconscious ignorance, were giving way to experiment, and alert patience was waiting "to see." About that time E. A. Filene came along, reporting that he had heard a vice president of General Motors, whose largest single plant was an experimental-research plant, say: "We don't think any more in business. Oh, we may have our opinions; we may think up how we can do or make something we need. We may think up a theory, but we don't act on our theories any more. We send our theory or our need into the laboratory and so have it tried out. If it doesn't work, we change the theory, scrap it. But if a theory, modified, works, we may make it into an engine or a car and put it out for trial on the market, but— even then, it's only a sort of working hypothesis. We go on monkeying with that and other theories and hunches to improve the car on trial."

This is revolutionary. If this spirit had got out of the science laboratories into business in a business country, it would seal the doom of our old Greek-Christian culture. It would spill over into politics, economics, life. No more thinking; no more right thinking; no more believing or logical reasoning from premises to conclusions. We would not have one city after another trying a commission form or some other fool idea of government and, whether it succeeded or failed, going right on believing in it. Wondering would supplant convictions, insight inspiration; experiment would blow up argument; and as for our conclusions, they would not be uplifted into principles and creeds but tried out as working cars or working hypotheses. No wonder my old liberal friends were sore and obstinate. A new, the new, culture was sweeping down over us, and big business, and the old root of all evil!

Seeing is one motion; believing is another. As I see my own country last, after seeing the rest of the world, I think I believe